AWAKENED

Memories of the Soul

24 Past Life Memories with
JESUS

BY KAREN WILLIS

First Edition

ISBN: 978-1-7374756-0-6

Published by LifeJourneys

Cover illustration created by Dianne Annestella

Design by Margaret Cogswell
www.margaretcogswell.com

TABLE of CONTENTS

I   Introduction........................7

II   My Personal Journey...................15
      The Journey Begins....................17

III   The Process Explained 36

IV   A Brief Historical Perspective........45

V   Client's Sessions –
      Chapter 1 through 24....................54

VI   Similarities in Clients Statements
      in Lifetimes with Jesus/Yeshua...583

VI   Conclusion...................624

VIII   Bibliography............................632

Acknowledgements

THIS BOOK IS DEDICATED TO THE MEMORY OF HENRY LEO BOLDUC, my first past life teacher and mentor. Henry Bolduc was the most egoless, compassionate person I have ever had the great pleasure of knowing. He used all his knowledge and work to help others continue in his path. He readily gave all his materials and works to everyone without monetary gain. He dedicated his life to this work and was a great teacher and mentor to many. I was truly blessed to have known him and learn from him on many levels, both professionally and spiritually.

THIS BOOK IS DEDICATED TO THE MEMORY OF DOLORES CANNON for the wonderful gift of her technique of helping others access their subconscious through the Quantum Healing Hypnosis. Her insight into accessing this part of our soul only enhances my work and I am truly grateful for her contribution.

THIS BOOK IS ALSO LOVINGLY DEDICATED TO MY AMAZING CLIENTS who so generously have given me permission to include their experiences with Jesus in their sessions to share with others. I have changed their names and other identifying qualities for purposes of their privacy.

Introduction

"And the savior answered, saying, "Blessed is the wise man who sought after the truth, and when he found it, he rested upon it forever and was unafraid of those who wanted to disturb him."
THE BOOK OF THOMAS

When I first began my work with clients, I would never have imagined writing a book. My sister was to be the writer in our family. She was the brilliant one, the talented one, and the one who was to write books. That was my belief and perception, because that is what I had heard my whole life. Little did I know that, I was the one that would be writing a book.

Many spiritual teachers have spoken about the importance of changing our beliefs about our limitations, thinking we are not good enough or capable enough. It was time to change my false beliefs about my ability to write a book, and believe in myself. While in a deep state of hypnosis, I was given instructions by many clients' subconscious on why and how the book should be written. After receiving these messages, I began to understand that this book was called to be written. An important message was delivered to me by a client who began to speak in an ancient language while in the Collective. I then asked the Collective to interpret the message in English, and it was conveyed to me that this book needed to be written. In the Collective, the client said, "The book needs to tell the truth of who Jesus was, what his purpose is, and to destroy the façade." After the session she explained, "I saw a bright golden shining light that looks like a star … moving like whoosh." ... "When you asked the question, you were directly connecting to him. It was waiting for you and shot directly to you." It was this powerful message that convinced me to pay attention to all the other messages that I ignored. In addition, synchronistic events were constantly happening. I was instructed to tell the truth, and that is what I hope to accomplish by relaying exactly what was conveyed in each session. It is time to open the door that had been closed so long ago, in telling my clients' truths of Jesus' amazing journey on Earth. These are the stories where ordinary people were drawn to the extraordinary in the presence of this great master teacher. I felt led by Jesus to tell their stories of his life and work, and of those he had touched. By sharing their stories, many others hopefully can be touched by his great unconditional love, wisdom and compassion.

At first I began to notice many clients coming to me who had lifetimes with Jesus. It began slowly at first with two clients in 2008, then one client in 2010 and 2011. In 2012 there were five, and two in 2013. Then it began to increase with five clients coming each year from 2014 to 2016. Around 2014 I began to see that indeed I would write this book. After that, there were three more clients in 2017 and two in 2018 and 2019. The sessions are not in chronological order other than the first and last client. There were a few other clients that are not included, due to the fact I had to be aware of the length of book. This book only includes the clients' session pertaining to their lifetime with Jesus/Yeshua.

In this book, the reader can experience each client's very personal experiences and observations of the true essence of the man we call Jesus or Yeshua. He came to have the experience on Earth as a man, as well as one of the greatest spiritual teachers showing us our human possibilities. Jesus allowed us to see who we truly are, as beautiful, powerful souls of light. We must remember that light within and show others, so they can also remember who they are. The more light that is shown, the greater the light will shine in the world as we remember we are all One. Jesus is a beautiful demonstration of how we should live our lives as human beings living on this planet earth.

As the Bible can be interpreted differently by each reader based on their perspective, people who had past life experiences with Jesus/Yeshua can also have their own interpretation. They can bring their own beliefs and interpretations to their experience based on their perspective at that time in history. The majority of the people in this time period were uneducated. As told here by David in his past life, many were unable to have complete understanding of Jesus' words on their level of awareness. However, what remains consistent in each client's experience with Jesus, is the feelings of unconditional love, acceptance emanating from him, and the awareness of their true essence and their feelings of Oneness. They each had a sense that he was so different from anyone they had ever met, feeling his energy of love and light. They felt forever changed. Provided at the end of this book are the numerous similarities spoken by my clients about their experiences with Jesus/Yeshua. The similarities far outweigh the differences.

Clients had also been changed in many way since they had met Jesus on their life journey. Most wanted to follow him from the beginning, after feeling drawn to his energy of total unconditional love. There was this magnetism which drew people in to his loving presence. One of his greatest lessons was to treat others with the same unconditional love he and God had for all. He came to show them their potential, as they reached that understanding within themselves. There was a clear message from the clients to remember that the Kingdom is within us, and we need look no further than within ourselves. It is important to remember that we are always loved by the Source, God, and that we are all One. It is difficult to give any name for the entity whom most of us call God. It is difficult to describe this unconditional loving energy with a name, but in our Earthly experience, we need to have a name to communicate with each other. God has been called by many names, Source, Creator, Yahweh, All That Is, I Am that I Am, Mother- Father God, Father and many more. In this book, I will use the names God and Source.

There was a sense of peace around the clients when they spoke of him, often becoming extremely emotional. They felt changed and loved unconditionally after their session, or as Jesus said to a client, "They were not changed, they became aware." It is difficult to explain the connection made between the therapist and the client, other than, I am with them on an energetic level. As I am always with a client in their experience, I can actually feel their emotions as they are describing their experiences. When clients were describing the love they felt in Jesus' presence, we both felt an overwhelming feeling of his unconditional love. I always feel so blessed to be in the presence of such glorious souls. When experiencing lifetimes with Jesus, there was a sense of peace; this cannot be captured in writing, only experienced. I will do my best, to give a voice to their experiences.

After many prayers and meditations, I have decided to include my own past life experience with Yeshua. This prompted me to use my real name to convey my experience. It is always important to listen to our inner voice. So often it is an easier path to remain silent, but when speaking your truth, one can finally feel free to be who they truly are without regrets. By his example, Jesus taught us to go within seeking the truth when he said, "And you will know the truth and the truth will set you free." *(John 8:32)*

I felt it was important to tell my story in understanding the spiritual and energetic connection I had with my clients who have been in his presence. Many clients explained that they were guided to me. I was told this is why these clients were sent to tell their stories, to tell their truth; and I was just the vessel to deliver their messages. There has been a common misconception that people go to lives in which they were famous or rich. As past life therapists we find most people lead ordinary, mostly poor and many times dreary lives, when accessing their past lives. It is uncommon for a past life therapist to have so many clients experience past lives with Jesus during the time he lived. It is also unusual to have so many clients experience the same time frame in history as other clients. I feel those who are drawn to me resonated with my energy and a knowing on a soul level, that I too have walked with Jesus in a past life. It is my belief, that if we need understandings or healing of any kind, we will be guided to that person we most resonate with on an energetic level.

I understand that there will be those who will doubt this information, and to some it may be controversial and sometimes challenging. After years of experience, it is my personal belief that the lifetimes presented in the book are genuine experiences of those who were in the presence of Jesus/Yeshua. But the truth of Jesus' powerful teachings will resonate with those who wish to hear and those who wish to remember. It is not my intention to change anyone's beliefs, but merely to present my own personal journey along with my client's experiences; allowing you to decide what resonates with you, the reader.

It is my hope that this book will empower others to ask questions about their spiritual beliefs as well as explore and discover their own answers. It is my hope that the book will create an open dialogue of the man we call Jesus or Yeshua, his teachings and his life experience. Hopefully it will touch those who have been touched by his words, and awaken the truth within themselves. I am reminded of words of Jesus in *Matthew 7:7* that have always resonated to me, "Ask, and it will be given you: seek, and you will find; knock and it will be opened to you. For everyone who asks, receives and he who seeks finds, and to him who knocks it will be opened." These beautiful souls decided on a soul level, that it was indeed time to open that door.

Not only are there stories of lifetimes with Jesus, but also included are accounts of powerful healings that occurred because of a client's awakening. The power of spiritual regression, is once you have the knowledge, you can remove the blockages and become who you are truly meant to be. By looking into our past we are able to release and be free of our past and move forward in our current life. If we are able to make a shift from identifying with our ego, insecurities and fears, then we open up to the gifts of our soul, our True Self, our Eternal Self. One is given the opportunity to heal any physical, emotional and personal difficulties, and therefore be free to continue their journey with greater spiritual wisdom and insight.

One can also benefit from looking at their past, bringing forth wonderful gifts and knowledge which has lain dormant and hidden for so long, and now can be awakened. Every significant event in our lives once understood, becomes an opportunity to learn, to experience and to heal. This is an important time in history when people need to recognize their true essence...not their ego...not their personality...not their job... and not their title, but find their True Self once again. And with that discovery, find their true magnificence.

Many clients spoke of Jesus' healing abilities. It was explained that all healing is about one's ability to remember who you are, as a child of God *(Jesus used children of God as a reference to help with understanding of God like a father figure at that time in history)*. He spoke of having the remembrance of pure intention of Oneness on the part of the healer and the person being healed. Many of clients come bringing doubt about their abilities to heal. When doubt enters the conscious mind, it can interfere with the healing process. Jesus spoke many times of one's doubt in their abilities to heal and manifest. As spoken in the *Bible, John 14:12*, "Very truly I tell you, whoever believes me will do the works I have been doing, and they will do even greater things than these." In *A Course in Miracles*, these words are so beautifully spoken as well; "The abilities you now possess are only shadows of your real strength."

This book not only contains stories about my client's personal journeys with Jesus, but also includes channeled material. As the work of this book unfolded, one of my clients asked if she could channel Jesus. As I am always open to new avenues of discovery, I agreed with the client's request. These channeled messages of Jesus, can provide new information and understandings, which I felt important to bring forth. Henry Bolduc describes channeling with this statement, "Channeling is a process wherein a person seeks high levels of awareness while seeking inner truth. A vessel is thus a messenger of soul guidance, opening to innermost light and sharing these eternal truths with those who ask." If you have the belief that we are all One, than you can understand the possibility of this channeled information. When Ruth asked if channeling was possible, Yeshua's response was "Why not? Because we are all connected." Ruth was the first of my clients to ask her subconscious if she could channel Yeshua. (*See Ruth's channeled session.*) Then Ellie and I were directed by subconscious to channel Jesus a number of times. (*See Ellie's channeled session.*) During the channeled information, the clients' voice changed, sometimes drastically, and the information flowed effortlessly. It was explained that when channeling, the person is given the information in such a form that is understandable in their own words or frame of mind at the time. The subconscious explained, "We have to use the language of the person who is in front of us. So sometimes the language is different from one person to another, but the intent of the information is the same."

The clients in these sessions come from all walks of life. They come from different backgrounds, various occupations, different ethnic affiliations, both male and female, and are from various religious and spiritual affiliations. I would like to thank my clients who have graciously given their permission to share their personal past life experiences allowing us to be a part of their amazing journey. I have changed their names and other identifying qualities so they can remain anonymous.

It is apparent that many people came in contact with Jesus during his lifetime, so there are many more stories of others to be told. I have listened to these client's stories numerous times in the editing process, and every time I learn something new from their powerful experiences with Jesus. It is my understanding, that this will be the first book to include so many personal past life regressions with Jesus. These are our stories and experiences with the Master Teacher Jesus, and hopefully you will also be touched by their amazing experiences!

My Personal Journey

*"The more and more each is impelled by that which is
intuitive, or the relying upon the soul force within, the greater,
the farther, the deeper, the broader, the more constructive
may be the result."*
EDGAR CAYCE; READING 792-2

As early as I can remember, I always felt a strong connection with Jesus' teachings concerning unconditional love and forgiveness. I always felt my path was to have a life of service and believed this was the understanding of all people. I felt a strong desire to pursue an occupation that would entail helping others. I also had an intense curiosity and a need to research spiritual concepts. As I grew older, I realized not everyone had these same feelings. Jesus is telling us to seek and learn and as we do so, all will be revealed, and not just listen to others perceptions of the truth. As I began to read the *New Testament*, I felt a strong connection to his words of love and compassion. There was a sense of love and comfort in reading the passages spoken by Jesus. I also felt that some of his words were misinterpreted, as they didn't resonate with his teachings of love and non-judgment.

As I have come to understand, much can be misinterpreted and lost in translating one language to another. The *Bible* as we know it has been translated into many different languages from its original text. The church also decided what should be included and excluded in the *Bible*. Edgar Cayce addressed this in *Reading 262-60*, "For much might be given respecting that ye have that ye call the *Bible*. This has passed through many hands. Many that would turn that which was written into the meanings that would suit their own purposes, as ye yourselves often do."

In reading the *Old Testament*, God was depicted as a God to fear and a God of vengeance. This was far from the God I knew. If you ask many people who is God, you will probably be given very different responses to that question. It is my personal belief God, Source, is an energy of total love, an energy of only love ... a love without any conditions. Whenever we express unconditional love, Oneness, hope, compassion, kindness, truth, forgiveness, faith, and joy; that is where God abides in us; that is God. God does not acknowledge what we call darkness or evil; this being man's creation. It is my belief that it is simply man's disconnection with God. Evil and the devil are created by man's ego and is perpetuated by the church's teachings. Fear was a way to control the people. When fear is present, love cannot come forth. We create our own heaven or hell. Similarly, Cayce states, "For, the heaven and hell is built by the soul! (*Reading 5357-1*)

The Journey Begins

It has been apparent to me that the universe will send you what you need and the people you need, when you are ready to be awakened. It is important to then pay attention to the signs given to us. It is like the old saying, "The teacher will come when the student is ready." In the early 1980's I reserved a book at my local library. When I went to pick up the book I had reserved, I was given another book called *Many Mansions*, by Gina Cervinia. I politely explained to the librarian that this was not the book I had reserved. Upon her opening the book, there in front of my eyes, was my full name written on the reserve marker in the book! I remember saying, "I guess this is the book I am supposed to read," not knowing at that time how my spiritual journey would forever change. I often talk about this experience in helping others to become aware of listening to the voice within. I believe we are given signs to help us move in the direction of knowingness. To my surprise, the book spoke of reincarnation, which was not a belief that I had held previously. I was overwhelmed with a deep sense of excitement and curiosity. As I continued to emerge myself in reading the book, it was if my soul awakened to a truth that was always there but hidden!

It finally answered all my questions that my church could not explain. I attended a Christian church called, The Church of Brethren for most of my early life. My mother felt it was necessary for all of us to attend church every Sunday. Based on her fear, she believed God kept a record of our sins and that we would ultimately be punished for those "sins." It is interesting now to look back and realize I never really felt I belonged in church, as much of what was taught did not resonate to me even then. I always had the feeling something was missing, but couldn't understand exactly what that was. At times I challenged my ministers and Sunday school teachers to some of the inconsistencies in the *Bible* about God and Jesus. They really couldn't explain to me why God would choose one soul to have a "wonderful life," and another one a life filled with difficulties and loss. I felt it was dismissed by them saying, "It is God's will or "It's not for us to understand." But if God is love ... there is the inconsistency! If you say God is love, why would God decide the fate of a person as to whether they would be rich or poor, happy or depressed, sick or healthy, handicapped or physically fit, feeling loved or unloved. It is interesting that in my work, clients constantly explain the reasons for this disparity when choosing their lifetimes. Although there was talk of Jesus and God's love for us in the sermons, there was also talk of our sins. There didn't seem to be any discussion of the Kingdom is within.

People in the church didn't seem to ask questions about what was being taught, it seemed as though there was acceptance of whatever was spoken by the minister and in the *Bible*. As children in Sunday school we were taught that God loved us, but we were also taught that we were sinners. Therefore there was a sense of being fearful of God. It was so refreshing to hear from a friend that Quakers never were taught to fear God. When I looked at people in church, I would see most of the time they were either sleeping, bored or just repeating what they were told without even understanding what they were saying. There was never any discussion of other Gospels or early Christian writings. There was no discussion of the history of how the church began and the early Christian leaders, other than what was written in the *Bible*. And of course there was no mention of the early Church and its connection to the belief of reincarnation. Most of my clients had never heard about Origen and his beliefs of reincarnation during the time of the early Church. Searching deeper spiritually was not encouraged. Everything was explained and taught on the premise that the *Bible* is the word of God; and therefore there was no further discussion.

People often use their religion to justify their own agenda. In religions around the world, the beliefs of their followers are based on religious dogma and rules. Many times they would quote from the *Bible* without reading the entire *Bible* to justify their beliefs. Some would say the *Bible* was the word of God without the deeper understanding of its history and how it came to be known as the *Bible* we have presently. Naomi explained the Jewish faith during the time of Jesus with this statement, "Many of the Jewish faith are tied to rules. They are more worried about the letter of the law rather than the spirit of the law." Religion has not encouraged people to search and discover their own spiritual knowledge and awareness, it is based on rules and ideology of their belief system of that religion. Religion does not speak of the power of the human experience, and that we are so much more than this physical body that we inhabit on the Earth plane. We are spiritual beings of light having a human experience in a physical body on this Earth plane. I felt that there was so much more to the story! Later to discover that there was much more that hadn't been taught or discussed. And there is so much more that I have yet to discover on this amazing journey.

After reading the book from the library, I began feverously emerging myself reading anything related to reincarnation and past lives. Interestingly, I was introduced to Edgar Cayce, and his readings continues to be a constant source of spiritual knowledge and understandings for study and learning. I have found that I was not alone in my spiritual understandings with the discovery that many people throughout history came to similar conclusions. I discovered I was in great company, as there are countless great writers, poets, philosophers, scientists and religious teachers throughout history who have expressed a belief in reincarnation. Just to name a few, they include, Benjamin Franklin, Plato, Shakespeare, Socrates,

Emerson, Wordsworth, Michelangelo, Henry Ford, Mark Twain, Edgar Allen Poe, Robert Frost, Louisa May Alcott, Leonard Da Vinci, Sir Water Scott, Kahlil Gibran, Arthur Conan Doyle, Julius Caesar, and Edgar Cayce. It is like we speak the same language spiritually.

I explained to my husband that even though I have read numerous books on reincarnation, I needed to have my own experience to understand if this was real. I felt this great desire to understand if I truly had past lives. In speaking with the past life therapist, I explained why I wanted to experience my past lives by saying, "I need to know." I later understood what I really needed to know, as those words would come to have entirely different meaning after the session. Many clients speak of just being curious, however there is always a different reason why they came. I feel they are drawn to heal their past in order to experience a greater awareness of their journey as a soul. They are ready to be awakened to who they truly are, their True Self.

I was drawn to my first past life therapist after hearing him speak about past life regression on a radio program in Baltimore. Upon entering his office, I remember my feelings of nervousness and anticipation as to what was going to happen. Questions began circling around in my mind as to what was going to occur. To my amazement, I had a transformative past life experience. I can best describe it as seeing my own personal movie, where I was the main character in that lifetime, while still aware of my current self. Even as I tried, I could not change what was happening in my movie. I felt all of the emotions connected to those experiences. After the session, I asked myself, did I make this up? But if I was going to make up a story would this be the story; of course not! I would want to have a wonderful life, rather than experience many difficult lifetimes and tragic deaths. The sessions explained the reason why I had an intense fear of water and public speaking in my current life. But most importantly it allowed me to see the strength within me that needed to be remembered. The experience also showed me that I was eternal! There is no death only a transition to another state of being, our true essence. Jesus was the demonstration that death is an illusion. It opened the door which allowed me to understand greater spiritual truths which fed my soul. This was just the beginning of my spiritual awakening.

Then came an unexpected surprise, enabling me to release the doubt. When talking with a woman at work about my experience, the manager asked what we were discussing. At the time I felt he wouldn't understand, so I ignored his request. He continued to press forward with his demand concerning our discussion. Finally, I explained our discussion was about my past life experience. He responded by stating that he probably lived in the Middle Ages, and had raped and pillaged. At that point, I felt the hair on my arm stand up, and I had to leave the room with an overwhelming feeling of hearing the truth. I felt that this was the person I knew in my past life in the Middle Ages that had been my rapist and jailer. After reflecting on what occurred, I understood why I felt so uncomfortable in his presence and had such difficulty looking into his eyes. This was an important confirmation of my past life memories that I could no longer deny. What are the chances of him choosing the time frame in the Middle Ages, and raping and pillage? (*Using the word pillage is unusual in of itself*). Years later, I believe his subconscious came through to deliver the message for me as a confirmation. Sometimes another person's subconscious will come through with messages for us, without their conscious mind being aware of what they are speaking. We need to listen to these messages as they are gifts from Spirit.

This was a turning point in my life. I finally understood who I was, a multi-dimensional spiritual light being coming to the Earth existence for the experience and learning. But most importantly, to come to the awareness of my True Self. The session took me out of the box that so many of us are in. I became so excited to share my experiences with others. However, at that time most people were not ready to hear that we have lived other lives in other bodies. This did not in any way deter me from finding my truth. Thus, began my spiritual quest, which would forever change my understanding of what I knew about the soul and its amazing journey. In my work, I continue to learn from my clients that there is so much more to our soul's experience than we could ever imagine. I doubt that I will know everything in this lifetime as we are not here to understand everything on this plane of existence. I feel truly blessed to witness and learn even more powerful and enlightening spiritual truths through my client's words and experiences. As my client Adam so truly stated, "Sometimes when you teach, you don't know who the teacher is and who the student is." My spiritual quest for knowledge will never cease. It is important for us to remember that we need to implement the spiritual knowledge in our daily lives, and be the example of what it looks like to be a spiritual person.

That experience helped me recognize and remember the strength within me as the creator of my own play. I was the actor, director, producer and stage manager in the role of my life. It was ultimately up to me to either grow from my experiences or create my own drama play. In Shakespeare's *As You Like It*, he wrote, "All the world's a stage, and all the men and women merely players. They have their exits and their entrances, and one man in his time plays many parts." I could no longer blame others in my life, but take responsibility for all of my actions and reactions. I began to understand that we choose everyone in our life for lessons and the experience. And it is ultimately how we react to our experiences that makes all the difference. As Edgar Cayce states, "For, no soul or entity enters without opportunities. And the choice is within self and the power, the ability to do things, be things, to accept things, is with the entity."(*Reading 3226-1*) This journey has given me a sense of peace and understanding that continues to guide me through my life.

I could no longer blame my circumstances on anyone, as I have chosen the experiences and lessons I am to learn. My soul was calling forth that it was time to take responsibility for my life and my choices. I could no longer play the role of victim or the blame game for the circumstances of my life. It was time for me to grow up as a soul. My past could no longer define who I was or who others thought I should be. It set me free to be who I needed to be in this life and to move forward. It gave me a sense of being fearless and taking chances in my life that at one time felt impossible. It is possible to be the main character in our own movie. It is all about our perceptions of who we are and what we are capable of accomplishing. After the session, I began to understand that I was in control of what I wanted my life to look like. This understanding has remained with me throughout my life. As Shakespeare wrote so beautifully in *Romeo and Juliet*, "It is not in the stars to hold our destiny but in ourselves."

In choosing my parents, I came to the realization, they were my greatest teachers. They taught me many lessons such as unconditional love, independence, acceptance, forgiveness, patience, and strength. They also prepared me for the art of listening in my current work, as I was very shy and not able to speak my truth at that time in my life. As I was not heard, I learned that everyone wants to be heard. Everyone has a story that needs to be told, so each person can be seen and heard. And in being heard whether in this life or another, one has the possibility of being free from their story and the illusion. If one looks at life from this belief, we can better cope with this earthly existence.

In looking at my family's life choices, they taught me that I wanted to be more than just someone going through life without any real purpose or meaning. My mother was an excellent teacher of how not to be a mother. My family taught me to love unconditionally. I began to learn acceptance of their journeys and their choices for learning. No matter what we may want for others, they may not want it for themselves, even if it is a difficult journey for them to travel. It is not our job to interfere or place judgment on another soul's journey. I also chose these family members to overcome patterns and to be free of the many triggers that ego is constantly showing us. Perhaps my greatest lesson was to teach me that the strength and light within me was always there. And to never allow anyone to dim my light. More importantly, everything I needed was always there, I just had to awaken to that knowledge.

I will often explain to clients, you cannot expect someone in kindergarten to understand college material. Some souls are just not ready in this life to gain awareness of their true essence and their power. Although difficult at times, we need to move into acceptance of where they are on their journey in this lifetime. Sometimes we need to back away rather than stay in a situation that will dim our light, and send love to them on their journey. We need to have compassion and forgiveness for others, as we most likely have also been in a state of forgetfulness in our past lives. In *The Gospel of Truth*, it illustrates the feelings of those around Yeshua so beautifully, "Through him he enlightened those who were in darkness because of forgetfulness. He enlightened them and gave them a path. And that path is the truth which he taught them."

We are in our own classrooms of life to learn various lessons. We can also decide to come for the experience in order to have greater understanding and compassion for others. As we continue along our journey there are many teachers; some helpful and some more challenging. Some show us to be our best selves, while others show us it is time to let go and release our old patterns. I often explain to others, your greatest adversary can be one of your greatest teachers. What better way to learn lessons of unconditional love, forgiveness, acceptance and compassion than to have someone that has harmed us in some way. Otherwise, it makes no sense why someone would have great difficulties in their lives. Our greatest challenges in life, can sometimes be our greatest opportunity to learn.

Years before my session, I received my degree in Sociology with a minor in Psychology. I initially wanted to be a social worker, but things took a turn that I will be forever grateful. After graduation, unable to find work in social work, my best friend suggested working at the Maryland School for the Blind in Baltimore, Maryland. She explained that it was similar to being a social worker. I still remember my first day at the school very vividly, and immediately being drawn to working with these special children who had multiple challenges. These special children are a perfect demonstration of unconditional love. I call many of them teacher souls, who came to teach us some of the greatest lessons of compassion, empathy, patience, unconditional love and the simple joy in just being.

Listening to my inner voice, I felt called to be a special educator after working as a teacher assistant for four years with these children with multiple challenges. (*After a few synchronicity events.*) I made the decision to go to night and summer school to receive my Masters in Special Education. At that time, I had two small children, worked part time and had an hour commute to Loyola College in Baltimore, Maryland for evening classes. As I look back I asked myself, "How did I do this!" But I realized I had this strong feeling or calling seeing myself able to accomplish anything I created, only later understanding the meaning of manifestation. I loved working with these special children; having such wonderful memories of them and their courage. However years later, many things began to change within the educational environment, and it no longer created a positive working environment. At this time I felt I needed to make a change in my life.

After working as a special educator for fifteen years at various schools, there was this strong sense of moving in a new direction. However at first there was some resistance, as I felt that this was my purpose. But once again I was drawn to the teacher who was to guide me to the understanding that our life path and purpose can change. In listening to that inner voice within, there was a sense of clarity telling me this journey needed to end for another journey to begin. I also had a strong feeling that if I didn't change this path, I would get cancer. Even though my husband didn't quite understand my leaving a steady job and steady income with all my education, he was somewhat supportive of my decision. I felt an intense pull to move away from this path, and instead being guided to a new journey. And what an amazing journey it has been!

I listened to that inner voice, not understanding where it would lead me. I first was led to become a professional stained glass artist working with clients to hopefully provide beauty and joy into their lives. After a two year period, I felt called to return to my passion connected to my past life experience, by becoming a past life therapist. It can only be explained as a very strong sense of knowing and a feeling that will not leave you. As demonstrated before, sometimes there are people, situations, and signs that guide us to the decision. Once acknowledged, we must act on this knowing with faith, while actually having to do the work involved to reach our goal. Many of us doubt this knowing, but once realized wondrous things begin to appear in our life. In reaching any goal, an integral part is working to achieve that goal no matter what obstacles may confront you on that path. It takes courage to step out of what we know and follow a different path. I realize that I previously wasn't ready to find the courage to move in a different direction. William Faulkner's quote speaks so beautifully about courage, "You cannot swim for new horizons until you have courage to lose sight of the shore."

At that time, I was part of a spiritual group and I spoke to the group about this feeling of being called to change my path. They all excitedly responded with a definite "yes." They understood my how past life regression had helped me on my spiritual journey, and clearly encouraged me to pursue this work. There were many other signs that ultimately led me to the understanding that this was to be my path. There are always signs for us to show our true path. It is that clear knowing, something we are so drawn to that cannot be explained or understood, nudging us to move forward no matter what the obstacles. Although difficult at times, I took several steps toward achieving my goal, with the understanding that anything is possible.

When searching for past life training, I initially called a past life therapist who was conducting a training. I was given instruction to leave a message for them to return my call. I called a second number and a man named Henry Bolduc answered with his kind, reassuring voice. I immediately felt that he was to be my teacher. I feel I was led to this special human being, Henry Leo Bolduc, for my training as past life therapist. Henry had forty five years of experience with past life regression and past life research. These words demonstrate his true essence, "Your inner knowledge of accomplishment far exceeds the applause of the public." From the very beginning, he said we could use anything in his training to use in our work. When I first met Henry, I knew I was in the presence of an enlightened special soul. I felt honored and blessed to be in the presence of his wisdom and teaching. The training took place in the small town of Wytheville, Virginia, around a seven hour drive from my home. However, I was determined to pursue my goal of becoming a past life therapist no matter the distance I needed to travel. When I arrived, I felt truly blessed for the experience of meeting such wonderful souls in my training. For the first time I felt we all had this powerful connection with this understanding of who we truly are as beings of light having a human experience. It was as though we all spoke the same spiritual language.

My husband was supportive, but a little bewildered as to what would happen when I returned home. He later told me he wasn't sure if I would come back differently or what to expect upon my return. Many times loved ones become fearful when the other one begins their spiritual quest, as to whether they will come back somehow changed. I did feel changed and no longer alone in my spiritual awareness.

This is where my story begins of my own personal experience with a lifetime with Jesus! While in training to become past life therapist in 2006, another trainee took the role of the therapist and I was her client. Nothing could have prepared me or the others in the room for what was to come ... a lifetime with Jesus! My previous past life experiences years earlier were so far removed from a lifetime with him. I didn't even know why I called him Yeshua in the session and not Jesus. It had been explained earlier that I needed to go with my feelings and impressions without judgment. The name Yeshua felt right to me, so I continued to call Jesus by that name throughout my entire session.

In conducting research on Jesus' name, it has been explained that Yeshua was an earlier Hebrew translation of the man we call Jesus. The name we use "Jesus," comes from the Latin translation of the Greek name "Iesous." According to many sources, Yeshua would be closer to the original translation. The name Jesus was said to be a much later English translation. Yehoshuah is the closest to how his name sounded. I will use the name Yeshua in referring Jesus, unless the client referred to him as Jesus.

Everyone in the room was unprepared with what was to come! It was extremely emotional for everyone in the room. Everyone was either stunned or crying at one point. The trained therapist Frank, took over at times by giving the trainee questions to ask me, as this was her first past life session as a therapist. I had often ask myself why this past life came through at this time while in training. I was later to discover; it was just time to know. And maybe it was time for others in the room to know as well.

My conscious mind tried to change the scenes, but I was unable to change what I felt and experienced. My soul said it is time to remember and know the truth. Doubtful thoughts brought on by feelings of disbelief as I told myself, "Who am I to have a lifetime with Jesus! Did I make this up, was this the real truth?" All of these thoughts of disbelief went swirling through my mind.

Before the session, I didn't have a clue of what lifetime I was going to experience. I remained open to whatever lifetime was for my highest good. Many of my clients had no prior knowledge of their connection to Jesus. It is difficult to explain the intense and powerful emotions while in the session. This was such an intense spiritual experience. The love I experienced was absolute, awe inspiring and difficult to put into words. The sadness was overwhelming and intense. I also found it fascinating that I called Jesus, Yeshua not knowing that was closer to his Jewish name. Whenever explaining my feelings associated with Jesus teachings, I became extremely emotional when raising my hands in the air describing his actions and words. This was a remembrance of when Jesus/Yeshua gently held his hands up in the air to quiet the crowd to speak. Initially there is a level of doubt with the clients as well. I explain that there will be signs that will tell them otherwise in the future. This I would later understand all too well.

After my first past life training, I felt drawn to attend Henry Bolduc's Advanced Past Life Training. The kind instructor Frank, who was present at my first past life session with Yeshua, was also present at this training. I asked him if he would take me back to that lifetime with Yeshua once again, as I felt there was more to the story. Deep down inside I also wanted more confirmation that this was indeed true. He explained it was possible to experience that lifetime once more if it was needed for my highest good. The past life therapist is merely the guide, and the subconscious will choose the lifetime that is needed at that time in a person's life. Frank readily agreed to guide me again in accessing my lifetime with Yeshua.

Some interesting events occurred before and during my session. Even before the session began, as I was walking down the hallway to begin the session, I almost literally ran into another trainee. After explaining that I would like to revisit my lifetime with Yeshua, she became excited and asked to join the session. There are no accidents as we found out later.

What was to be a unique experience, when nearing the end of the session, Frank's stomach made an extremely loud noise. Thereupon, a different voice came out of me, that I knew not from whence it came, loudly stating, "YOUR STOMACH IS RESPONDING TO THE TRUTH." I was overwhelmed and astonished, not understanding what just happened in the room or where this voice was coming from within me. It was as though I had no control of what was being spoken.

Frank was also surprised at these words coming out of me. I now understand that this was my subconscious speaking through me for confirmation that this indeed was true. But at that time, I really didn't understand the voice's origin. I felt that this voice came through giving me the affirmation to validate that this was indeed real. And years later I would be working with clients who were also able to tap into this higher level of awareness.

Interestingly, the session did not record on his tape recorder. Frank explained this had never happened in his 30 years of experience. Although it is rare, he was aware of this happening to others. As I have so often learned, there are no coincidences, everything is in divine order. The trainee who was present in the room also took notes of the session. (*Transcripts of both of their notes are in the book as well.*) Little did she know, that her notes would be so helpful in providing confirmation of what had occurred in the session, and later helpful in the book.There were so many synchronicities and unusual events involved with these sessions that cannot be denied.

Many years later, I was drawn to read Dolores Cannon's books about past lives with Jesus, *They Walked With Jesus and Jesus and the Essenes*. I found it fascinating that before I went for her training, I didn't realize she was the same person who wrote the books on Jesus. Upon reading these books years later, I found many validations and similar feelings associated with my own past life experience with Jesus. (*As described later in book*). Since this experience, I was guided back to additional experiences in that lifetime with Jesus. I received even more information concerning the lifetime with Yeshua, when accessing my subconscious (SC) utilizing Dolores Cannon's Quantum Healing Hypnosis method.

I also received training as a hypnotherapist with the National Guild of Hypnotists. In one of my hypnosis workshop training, a well-known hypnotist at the time stated to never put past life regression on your business card. He acted as though it was the kiss of death to do so. I just had to chuckle a bit, as I knew that would not stop me from putting past life therapist on my card. There are more and more hypnotherapists beginning to utilize past life regression in their practice, as they have begun to see it as a powerful tool for healing.

It is interesting to note that in the beginning of my work I had many hypnosis sessions related to client's current lifetime, but my passion has always been spiritual hypnosis. I found more and more clients came searching for spiritual hypnosis sessions, and eventually those clients were the only ones coming for sessions. I believe we are guided on our journey to stay on the path for the highest good, and it became clear to me that this spiritual hypnosis work should be my focus.

There arose many other opportunities to enhance my work. I was privileged to receive training in Life between Life Spiritual Exploration (*LBL*), where clients are guided to the spirit world in between lives. Years later, I was invited to be a trainer at a (LBL) workshop to help mentor others to become Life between Life certified therapists which was sponsored by the National Association of Transpersonal Hypnotherapists (NATH). At the training session, I met a kind man and his wife while assisting them in their LBL training. He spoke of having this amazing training accessing the subconscious with a teacher named Dolores Cannon. Speaking highly of her method, he encouraged me to go to her training. Once again the teacher guided me to the right teacher. Due to synchronistic events, two years later I attended her training. This training would eventually help many clients to be awakened to even greater spiritual knowledge and wisdom. It would take my past life work to an even higher level of spiritual healing, knowledge and wisdom. It awakens that part of us which possess higher spiritual knowledge and wisdom, that is always present but not always acknowledged. It is our true essence; our connection to God, that we don't always listen to or act upon. It is the part of us where our ego and personality are no longer present.

There are no accidents in life; all is in perfect alignment. It was no accident that many years later I would be a student of Dolores Cannon's method of Quantum Healing Hypnosis and taught the method of reaching the subconscious. When speaking with Dolores Cannon, I asked her if she knew Henry Bolduc. Cannon spoke of Henry Bolduc with great admiration, and said he encouraged her to teach workshops on reaching the subconscious. The subconscious can be described when client's reach a higher state of spiritual knowledge and inner truths. Edgar Cayce refers to what comes through, as the subconscious and the superconscious. In Cayce's teachings our soul must progress through all the planes in order to be one with God. While in Amanda's subconscious state we were given this wonderful description as to how the subconscious worked, "We bring in the expanded awareness into alignment with human consciousness."

In my work, I have come to the same realization that there are many levels of awareness within the subconscious mind. As Jesus so beautifully described these levels of awareness with this statement, "In my Father's house are many mansions; if it were not so, I would not have told you." (*John 14:2*) It has been my experience, that each soul will be guided to the level of awareness that they are ready for, and the information that they will most benefit from at this time in their life. This method of speaking with a clients' subconscious has only enhanced the past life work that I offer clients. Many of the clients in the book, gathered information about their lives with Jesus/Yeshua accessing their subconscious and superconscious. When a client uses Yeshua as Jesus' name, then I will continue to use the name the client prefers. I feel both names are describing the man many know as Jesus.

I took a leap of faith when asked to teach classes about past life regression at a local community college. It was in these classes that I gently guided students to their own past life experience in a group setting. Even in a group regression, there has been many times where people were able to release past life issues and patterns. Many years before, I never would have thought that I could speak in front of so many people, as I previously I had the fear of public speaking. I was able to release a past life experience of being judged in a courtroom which manifested in the current life as a fear of speaking in large groups.

For me personally, my work has led me on an amazing spiritual journey of discovery. I feel blessed every day to have this opportunity to help others as it has helped me become who I am today. I have continued to realize there is so much more to the story than we know or understand. I will continue to seek, read, discover and learn as long as I am on the plane of existence. I now listen to the inner knowing, the voice within. I try to meditate daily and see it more of a necessity for even greater connection with God, and Yeshua. I now have a greater sense of who I truly am ... a shining light and part of the Oneness of all. I also come to understand, each one of us has the spark of God within us ready to be awakened and shine brighter.

The sessions that are included in this book, were recorded and transcribed by myself. I have included the sessions of my clients' lifetimes with Jesus/Yeshua. I felt it important to include how many clients first came to discover their lifetimes with Jesus. This will enable the reader to understand that they begin talking about the places they lived, who they were, and then later how Jesus became part of their life experience. Reading the sessions in the book is a completely different experience than actually being with the client in a session. There are sometimes body movements, uncontrollable crying, feelings of great happiness and sadness, wringing of their hands and other bodily movements that cannot be expressed in a book. To the best of my ability, I have tried to convey the client's feelings and impressions at that time. I am not trying to convince anyone or change anyone's belief system. I am simply telling their stories as they experienced them in a deep altered state while in hypnosis.

With each of these clients, I felt a beautiful change in their being and a sense of peace around them. They all said they felt lighter. All of them were in awe of what they were experiencing during and after the session. Some had doubts, but later most came to realize their own truth. Some remembered parts of the session while some remembered very little. It is always the client's choice as to whether they learn from the information given to them, and whether they incorporate that knowledge into their life. As a past life therapist, I provide a safe space for healing. Each session is recorded for the client to process and review as many times as needed for even greater understandings and healing. At one point I believed the book was complete, however to my surprise three more clients came forward with their experiences with Jesus while I was writing.

There were a few differences in perceptions related to the crucifixion, his death, and his marriage, but for me that is not what is really important. I believe that the true importance of his legacy are his teachings of Oneness and unconditional love. That is what we must remember, who we are as beautiful souls of light finding our way back home. For in the end there is only the love that matters, all else eventually fades away. Jesus was the great Master Teacher who came in a human body to show us the way to our True Selves and the truth of who we truly are; spiritual beings of the light having a human experience in a human body.

Some people want to understand why we can't remember who we are. It can be explained in this way; when the student is ready the information will be revealed. As explained by Plato in the Republic, "The experience the souls had chosen their lives. They all travelled into the plain of forgetfulness, each as he drinks, forgets everything." I believe that this is the time of remembering who we are, to me this is the beginnings of the great awakening. I believe this is why I was called to write this book at this time in our history, to awaken those who are ready to remember, through the words of the great Spiritual Master Teacher, Jesus.

This book was guided by the presence of loving Spiritual Masters and Jesus. I feel Jesus has guided me in this process with his loving words of encouragement. I feel that his teachings are as important today as it was in his life on Earth. Unconditional love and Oneness permeates throughout his teachings and his life through the words of my clients. There are many paths in becoming an awakened soul. This is just another powerful path to reach that understanding of who you truly are as a spiritual being of light and we are all One, and everyone is always loved by God.

The Process Explained

"Each soul or entity will and does return, or cycle, as does
nature in its manifestations about man; thus leaving, making
or presenting-as it were-those infallible,
indelible truths that it — Life is continuous."
EDGAR CAYCE

"The key to growth is the introduction of higher dimensions of
consciousness into our awareness."
LAO TZU

In order to have a clearer understanding of the transcripts of twenty-five past life regressions in this book, it is important to explain the terminology and process involved in past life regression and Quantum Healing Hypnosis. It is always made clear to a client before a session begins, that they are in control and I am merely a guide who provides a safe space for spiritual understanding, clarity and healing. As therapists we are not controlling the minds of our clients, but building on a sense trust and non-judgment for them to access the information. It is not necessary for people to have a belief in reincarnation in order for healing to occur.

Initially, the client is asked to set their intention to review a lifetime to gain greater knowledge and understanding that can help them in their current life. I believe their subconscious or Higher Self will choose the lifetimes that you are ready to experience, and which have the greatest benefit at that time in your life.

The subconscious always protects you, only giving you information that you are equipped to understand and process at this particular time in your life.

Utilizing the techniques in the induction of progressive relaxation and guided imagery, the client is gently guided into a deep state of hypnosis in order to access their past lives. Protection being an important aspect in a session, they are asked to place themselves in a pyramid of white light for protection. Clients are asked to imagine floating on a safe cloud to an important past life for their highest good. After what is called the induction, the client is asked when coming back down from a cloud, "What is the first thing you become aware of? What are you seeing, feeling or sensing?" They will begin to tell me what is happening around them and where they are. They are asked what type of clothing they are wearing, what is their sex, race, age, and health. As our memories are not always sequential and their story can be disjointed, clients are guided to have a clearer picture of that lifetime. It's like putting the pieces of a puzzle together delving deeper into their experience so it becomes understood on a deeper level.

It is important to allow the client to experience what they are seeing, sensing or feeling in a session. Most people perceive information visually, however many experience their past lives with only a knowing or sensing. There are a few clients who experience a sense of smell or taste, but most have a combination of some or all of these. There is no right or wrong way to process the information, it is up to the individual as to how they process the information. It is unique to each person. Those clients who are not visual, can receive just as much information as clients that visualize their experience like a movie or with pictures.

After much conversation concerning the details of who they were in that lifetime, I ask them to then move to important events they felt that were significant in that lifetime. Just as we have events in our current life that affect us, we also have important events to remember in our past lives. This allows the client to access vital information about their past life, helping the client to go directly to the source of what they need to understand for healing.

When the lifetime is completed, they are then asked to describe their death scene in that life, while feeling no discomfort in their body. Clients are asked, "What were the circumstances of your death? What is happening as they left their body?" Clients are usually greeted by loved ones or by loving spiritual beings. They initially feel a sense of lifting and freedom from their body. As they move further away from their body, there is a sense of great peace. They are then gently guided to go to a place to review that lifetime where they have greater wisdom and knowledge available to them than while in that lifetime. There is always a life review after each lifetime, where the soul can assess that lifetime from a higher level of understanding. This is a very important part of the session, as it explains how that lifetime affects the current lifetime and what needs to be understood, released and healed. The client is asked various questions while in their life review. The most important questions are, "What did you learn in that life that can help you in your current life? Do you need to release anything you brought from that lifetime into your present life? Is there a need to release any feelings of unforgiveness of self or others?"

Our memories of past lives are connected with our current life in many ways. These past life memories are typically connected to people, places, event, fears, phobias, triggers and emotions. Feelings connected with these past life memories can include fear, worry, sadness, unforgiveness, loss, unworthiness, guilt, sadness and grief. You can either create the same pattern or choose to release the pattern and triggers that plagued you in the past. When in a past life, difficulties in your current life can be resolved when understood, freeing yourself and living the life you want. Some therapists only have their clients look at their current life, however many times the real beginnings of their difficulties and issues originated in their past lives. As you have the ability to release negative patterns connected to the past, you also have the ability to bring forth any gifts or talents from the past.

It is also important to explain Delores Cannon's method of Quantum Healing Hypnosis. Before coming for a session, clients are asked to prepare any questions they would like to ask their subconscious for greater clarity and healing. The questions may include any issues or concerns, any difficulties both physical and emotionally, any spiritual questions, or any other questions that have had an impact on their current life. In this session, clients are guided to a much higher level of awareness, when accessing their subconscious.

After clients are guided to two past lives, I ask permission to speak to their subconscious. Once given permission to ask questions, I then begin to ask the subconscious the client's prepared questions. If I feel there is a need for greater clarity within their questions, I will ask additional questions. In the book, I only included those questions that were relevant to their lifetime with Yeshua. Once I understood that I would be writing this book, I was given permission to ask additional questions pertaining to their lifetime with Yeshua. It is important to explain to clients that this is a very intensive session which can last up to three to five hours, depending upon the needs of the client. When clients come out of the session, they are usually surprised how long they have been in hypnosis, as time seems to stand still.

The subconscious knows everything about you without the emotional component of the ego and personality. In this state ego and personality are no longer present. As my client Ellie so beautifully explained, "In human terminology there's levels in the spiritual realm. It is just an expanded awareness." The subconscious is the part within us that contains great spiritual knowledge and wisdom. We don't always listen to this wisest part of ourselves. The conscious mind will try to interfere whereupon doubt enters in, and sometimes we don't follow through with the advice and knowledge. Dolores Cannon said, "The subconscious not only records everything that has ever happened to the person in this lifetime, but everything that has happened to them in their past lives, and existences in the spirit state. An all knowing part of something that has access to all information."

The subconscious is also referred to as the superconscious, Higher Self, or the Collective, depending upon the level of awareness. It was explained by the subconscious that the terminology is really not that important. In the subconscious' explanation they are just words describing the same thing, and that it doesn't matter what we call it, it is already known. The subconscious is that highly evolved part of us where our true essence is stored. It is similar to a computer where all our memories are stored and preserved, which can be retrieved at any time. That part of us can sometimes present itself as the part of us that is wise beyond our human understanding. In Ellie's session, Jesus said that we need to understand that it really is our Inner Self. Whatever name it is called, it is the truest part of us that has all the spiritual wisdom and knowledge on our journey as a soul. When the subconscious is speaking, its language and manner of answering the questions are very similar.

Our subconscious is our remembrance of who we truly are. It is that part of us that is always with us, even though at times we are unaware of its presence. It is a letting go of the physical world, letting go of your body, your identity, your environment, your conditioning, and allowing yourself to be free allowing something greater than yourself to be your new reality. Unlike the conscious mind, the subconscious remains with us long after the body dies. It has been explained by many clients that all subconscious minds are One.

At times we may not even be aware that we are accessing our subconscious when given valuable information and direction. Our ego is our immature self, focusing on ourselves. It is that part of us that has fears and doubt. The ego wants to remain in control, while the subconscious focuses on the expansion of spiritual truths such as love, truth, Oneness and spiritual awakenings.

In a session, I always ask for the highest level of awareness that the client can reach at this time. Edgar Cayce spoke about these levels of consciousness. I have also found that there are different levels within those levels of awareness. He called the superconscious the highest level the subconscious. The superconscious level of awareness is where clients can access universal truths and universal wisdom. The subconscious always takes care of a client and will only allow them to gather information from the level of awareness that they are ready for at that time. This was made clear to me when my subconscious explained that I was not yet ready to understand in my first session that I was a healer in my lifetime with Yeshua.

The subconscious has explained that all physical healing is available to the client. Again there is a need to understand why, where, and when the physical difficulty or disease entered the body of the client. It is so beautifully stated in Angela's session when she spoke of Jesus, "He knows the ailment and the cause of your ailment, so when you go to him, you have changed your belief and faith; so that your love of God is expanding and growing. He knows that and then you are healed!"

Sometimes the voices of clients change drastically while in the subconscious, especially in the subconscious' higher levels. When listening to the recording of their session, many clients tell me, "That is not my voice." The subconscious mainly refers to the client in the third person as "he," or "she." It will sometimes say "we," as if it is a group responding to the questions, which I believe to be the collective. The language spoken may take on a different accent, or even be a different language from their normal everyday voice. I have had client's voices become very loud, some robotic like, some with completely different tones, some become very powerful. While in the subconscious, my voice became robotic, unlike my normal voice and tone. It was explained by the subconscious that it is not important if the voice does not alter. When in the subconscious, you have no control of what is being spoken.

Oftentimes the words spoken can be disjointed and not in perfect grammatical context. Clients speak differently in the subconscious mind, and oftentimes their words are both profound and beautiful. Many times in Quantum Healing Hypnosis sessions, the subconscious explains that it has difficulty translating words into our human understanding. The subconscious many times explains that the higher dimensions cannot be easily expressed in three dimensional terms. The subconscious delivers its messages in terms that would be understood by the client. While sometimes, the subconscious cannot find the words to convey their message in human terms.

In Life between Life sessions, clients are guided to the spirit world in the life between their current life. They are once again guided to two past lives before going to the spirit world. There are various experiences while in the spirit world. One of those experiences, is when they are guided to their Council, Council of Elders or the Enlightened Ones. The client goes before the Council of six to twelve members, where their questions are answered. The Council consists of very wise, highly spiritual beings who give the clients advice about their past and current life. The Council members offer only encouragement and advice, and there is no sense of judgment. In the book *The Boy Who Saw True*, the boy is told in 1887, "Remember that we Elder Brothers never command or impel, we merely suggest; and whether our suggestions are acted upon or disregarded may often have much to do with our future decisions." (*He later described them as the Council.*) I also found it interesting that there is mention of a council when speaking of judgment in the afterlife in *Matthew 5;22*, "But I say to you that everyone who is angry with his brother shall be liable to judgment; whoever insults his brother without cause shall be liable to the council." From my experience, the only judgment comes from ourselves, not from the council.

Clients who have released various issues, feel that the weights of the past have been lifted from them. Most say they feel different and lighter than when they first entered the room. Sometimes I will become aware of a beautiful light around their head and a certain glow about them when awakened from their session. This is especially true with those in sessions with Jesus. I also feel the presence of Jesus, my guides and the angels in many of the sessions. It is difficult to describe in words, how clients come out of the session different than when they first started the session. There is usually a feeling of peace and lightness after their session. With some clients doubt can enter, and they will ask, "Did I make this up or did I just imagine this to be true." I ask them if they would choose a lifetime, would this be the lifetime chosen, and they always answer in the negative. I also explain that there will always be a sign to show them the truth of their experience if they remain open. In my own experience there were many signs given to me verifying my past lives.

Sessions also include what is referred to as channeled information. In a deep hypnotic state, clients open the door to a different reality to an altered state of consciousness which is also referred to as the Collective or the superconscious. Profound spiritual information can come through the person who is channeling. Henry Bolduc explains "Channeling is the process by which a person becomes a vessel or channel for his or her Higher Self to come through or for the spirit and voice of an entity or entities from another dimension. The voice represents a superconscious, a collective unconscious, or a universal mind. Channeling is a process wherein a person seeks high levels of awareness while seeking inner truth." In this book, I have included Yeshua's channeled sessions by several clients.

In the years I have been blessed to do this work, I have come to believe that if we are able to look at the source of our behaviors, phobias, patterns, physical difficulties, then we are able to release them and move forward in our current life with a greater sense of our spiritual connection. We can begin to know ourselves with a much deeper spiritual understanding and knowledge. Also clients no longer have a fear of death, as they come to the realization there is no death, it is only a transition. The body may die, but their true essence is eternal. They often continue on their spiritual journey feeling a sense of peace and comfort. By looking at ones past lives, difficulties in their current life can be resolved when understood and healed, and we can be free to live the life we were destined to have.

I have transcribed what was happening in each session to the best of my ability. I did not include various personal details or real names of the clients in order for them to remain anonymous. In the transcripts, I have used three periods (...) to indicate the client's pauses between the words. I have also used [brackets] to add a word or phrase to help the reader better understand the meaning of the sentence. Since there were so many pauses in the sessions, I did not include all of them for easier reading.

In speaking with my clients after their sessions, they all agree that it is very difficult to explain the feelings and emotions that they experienced. Clients are encouraged to listen to their recordings of the session. By listening to their session again, it serves to assist in greater healing. It is also important as they may not remember the entire session, or not remember anything. There may be messages missed, or they may hear something different in their session. Once the session has ended, over time the client's recollections fade from the conscious mind and it becomes a distant memory. It is always up to clients to follow through with the information and knowledge given in the session. Clients are given valuable information and avenues for healing.

A Brief Historical Perspective

"Issa (Jesus) said, I came to show human possibilities. What has been created by me, all men can create. And that which I am, all men will be. These gifts belong to all nations and all lands— for this is the bread and the water of life."
NICOLAS ROERCH

One of the earliest references to reincarnation was around 2,600 years ago in the *Upanishads* which is the sacred text of Hinduism. Reincarnation is a basic tenet of the major Indian religions of Buddhism, Hinduism, Sikhism, and Jainism. Orthodox Islam does not accept reincarnation, however a few of the Muslim sects accept the belief of reincarnation specifically the Shia sect Ghulat, and other sects in the Muslim world such as Druzes. The Ghulat Shia Muslim sect believed its founders had divine incarnations. Some Sufis called mystical Muslims, also accept the belief. The Tibetan text *Bardo Thodol*, known in the west as *The Tibetan Book of the Dead* refers to "bardo" as the period between death and the next rebirth. The concept of reincarnation was also held by the Greeks and such philosophers as Pythagoras, Socrates and Plato. The Pythagorean doctrine teaches that Souls are immortal and enter a new body after many years.

In *The Republic*, Plato says that before our birth, "The souls who are to be reborn are brought to a place where they are able to see "the working of Universal Law." He also stated, "Heaven is guiltless. It was a truly wonderful sight ... to watch how each soul selected its life. The experience of their former life generally guided the choice." Now when all the souls had chosen their lives ... they all traveled into the plane of forgetfulness ... each as he drinks, forgets everything."

Various scholars feel that the Gnostics may have been the earliest Christians possessing the genuine esoteric teachings of Jesus. According to G.R.S Mead, a leading Gnostic researcher, "The whole of [*Gnosticism*] revolved round the conception of cyclic law for both universal and individual soul. Thus we find the Gnostics invariably teaching the doctrine not only of the pre-existence but of the rebirth of the human soul." Additionally, the Gnostics believed that Jesus represented their "Teacher," while they believed Christ is the Divine Spirit in everyone.

As indicated by many scholars, the *Bible* has been altered and changed many times. In recent times, it has come to light that various ancient documents have been excluded from the *Bible*. Many biblical scholars have concluded that there can be difficulty in translating the ancient Aramaic, Hebrew and the Greek *Bible* manuscripts into English from its original text, which has ultimately led to various versions of the *Bible*. According to many sources there were over five thousand Greek manuscripts of the New Testament having various interpretations in each manuscript. Scholars have also found that the *Bible* of today is not error-free, as there are many contradictions. It has also been challenged by various scholars, that some of the monks added their own interpretations in the *Bible* to suit their own agenda or the church's wishes. Perhaps they may have also lacked the knowledge of the true translations of various words. When translating another language the meaning of a word can be totally different. An example of a different interpretation is the Hebrew word "sin," which is interpreted as, "missing the mark." Many times people can have a different perspective of the same event. This can be understood even in current times, when two people give different accounts of the same event. In Ellie's session Jesus says, "There is a great amount of myth that has been interwoven into the historical accounts of my lifetime on earth in the life of Jesus. The message has been changed in some ways to suit certain intentions that aren't necessarily what my intentions were." Additionally, the consensus of scholars today is that some of the Gospel writings were written forty to sixty years after the crucifixion and were not eye witness accounts of the events in Jesus' life. And there is no actual proof that the texts in the Bible were actually written by the disciples themselves.

A substantial number of scholars accept that reincarnation was prevalent among many in the early church. According to church scholars, the first century Jewish teacher Philo (*20 BC – 50 AD*), taught reincarnation, which could be proof that reincarnation was a part of early Judaism, and may have had influence on Christianity. It also may have influenced the teachings of Jesus. Josephus, a famous Jewish historian from the time of Jesus wrote, "All pure and holy spirits live on in heavenly places, and in course of time they are again sent down to inhabit righteous bodies. The virtuous shall have the power to revive and live again."

As the Orthodox Church in Rome gained more political power, the Church theologian and Biblical scholar known as Origen, (*183-253 A.D.*) made an attempt to revive the secret teachings of Jesus within the orthodox teachings. His theology included "orthodox" and "gnostic" teachings which were considered to be the closest to the "Lost Christianity" of the original sects. He was considered by many as one of the most respected theologian of the early church. Origen is said to have believed and taught the preexistence of the soul and reincarnation into this world and other worlds. He also spoke of a constant upward progress of the soul through many lives. Although Origen was considered a leader in the early church, Emperor Decius and the church declared his writings to be heretical and had his works burned and destroyed. Like so many with differences from the church's views, he was subsequently tortured and killed along with those who had similar beliefs in the preexistence of the soul.

Saint Jerome in 402 A.D. wrote this statement against Origen words, "Now I find among many bad things written by Origen the following most distinctly heretical ... that, "there are innumerable worlds, succeeding one another in eternal ages; that angels have been turned into human souls; the soul of the Savior existed before it was born of Mary, so that we may have to fear that we who are now men may afterwards be born women and one who is now a virgin may chance then be a prostitute." According to this statement, it appears that Origen had taught the belief in the preexistence of the soul.

Many of the earlier writings found in various early texts, are not found in the current *Bible*. In tracing the origins of the *Bible*, it is important to understand the history of how the Bible was created and changed. In the year AD 325, when Constantine the Great called the First Council of Nicaea, this council was given the task of separating divinely inspired writings from those considered to be of questionable origins. Constantine mandated that anyone who believed in the concept of pre-existence should be anathema, excommunicated. There were other mandates concerning Jesus as the Son of God and a mandate condemning the belief that Jesus was reincarnation of Adam. There was actually historical evidence that the early Christians spoke of Jesus being the reincarnation of Adam, meaning "the first." Origen also spoke of this belief. In the *Bible* Jesus states in *John 8:58*, "Before Abraham, I was." Also there is this statement in *Corinthians 15; 45-47*, "The first man Adam became a living soul, so the last Adam became a life-giving Spirit. The first Man is made of dust out of the Earth. The Second Man is the Lord out of Heaven."

When Constantine came into power he used his views of Christianity to gain control of the masses. This was a concerted effort to control others by not allowing them to understand that they were in control of their destiny. Once again it is all about politics and who is in power; just as the Romans during the time of Jesus. The church would ultimately once again declare Origen's writings as heretical. This was also the time when there was a question of the divinity of Jesus. A group of men decided what should be included in the Bible as we know it today, and what should be excluded. We may not even be aware of some of the writings that have been excluded. The church is extremely protective of its interpretations of the *Bible*, and does not accept any other ancient manuscripts or writings. Some of the early writings have since been discovered, but discounted by the Church. These writings include the *Dead Sea Scrolls*, the *Gnostic Gospels* and many more scrolls that have been discovered more recently.

In the *Bible*, there are several references to the belief in reincarnation. One of the most suggestive passages concerning this belief was when Jesus asked of his disciples is in *Matthew 16:13, 14*, "Who do men say that I am the Son of Man?" They replied, "Some say John the Baptist; others say Elijah; and still others, Jeremiah or one of the prophets." This clearly suggests that there was a belief in reincarnation if the disciples and the people of that time believed that Jesus was the reincarnation of one of the prophets.

The Zohar in the Kabala discusses reincarnation as part of their belief, "The souls must re-enter the absolute substance whence they have emerged. But to accomplish this end they must develop all the perfections, and if they have not fulfilled this condition during one life, they must commence another, a third, and so forth, until they have acquired the condition which fits them for reunion with God."

Helena Blavatsky (*1831-1891*) was the founder of the Theological Society in 1875 gaining international attention, advancing the belief in reincarnation and karma. She published *The Secret Doctrine* and many believe her work was instrumental in the spiritualism movement of the nineteenth century. She was also considered very controversial and ridiculed as a charlatan by many critics at that time.

Even before Blavatsky, a French teacher, translator and author named Hypolyte Leon Rivail (*1804 – 1869*) was also instrumental in advancing many of the spiritual beliefs of today including reincarnation. Although originally a skeptic, he began his own investigation of psychic phenomena and mediumship. Under the pen name of Allan Kardec he published the book *The Spirits' Book* in 1857, which was comprised of a series of questions answered by those in the spirit world. He asked various spiritual questions to ten famous mediums whom were unknown to each other, and documented their responses which he found to be very consistent. This was quite controversial at that time, and he had to overcome many obstacles and ridicule. This is just one of the many statements in Kardec's book explaining reincarnation, "Yes, we all had many lives. Those who preach we live only once lack real awareness and, in this respect, misinform you with their conjectures." ... "With each new life, a spirit takes a step forward on the path of progress. When it has stripped itself of all impurities it has no longer needs of the trials of incarnate life." Kardec opened the door for acceptance of mediumship, past lives, automatic writing and many other spiritual concepts which are widely accepted today. Although not as well-known as Blavatsky and Cayce, he is still regarded as one of the early pioneers of the belief in past lives and was instrumental in the spiritual movement of the nineteenth century called "Spiritism."

Edgar Cayce was one of the first to have the greatest influence with regard to the understanding of reincarnation in the Western World in modern history. Cayce known as "The Sleeping Prophet," gave fifteen thousand metaphysical readings throughout his life. He began by giving physical readings while in a deep state of hypnosis to facilitate healing people of their illnesses. While in a deep self-induced hypnotic state, Cayce was actually accessing the superconscious when giving readings. In a reading on October 1924, for the first time Cayce spoke of a past life, something that was totally contrary to his belief system. As a devout Christian who read the *Bible* every day of his life, and born in Kentucky, Cayce initially didn't believe in reincarnation or understand its principles. Only having a ninth grade education, it is amazing how the language in his readings are expressed so eloquently. In this deep trance state, Cayce was able to access information that was far removed from his personal beliefs and understandings. In a reading of his friend in 1923, he indicated that Arthur Lammers' last incarnation on Earth was when he had been a monk. Later he explained to Cayce that he would be the catalyst for others in changing the belief of reincarnation and eternal life. Lammers felt that Cayce was chosen to bring hope of eternal life to many. I believe that Cayce's readings continues to be instrumental in bringing forth greater awareness, spiritual knowledge and wisdom.

In 1956 *The Search for Bridey Murphy* by Morey Bernstein spoke of a housewife' past life in Ireland. Under hypnosis, Virginia Tighe went into her past life as a woman named Bridey Murphy, born on December 20, 1798, in the town of Cork, Ireland. When this book was first published, it caused quite a sensation, however many newspapers and skeptics became critical of her experience. I have found that many of the skeptics of Bridey Murphy had their own agendas, and therefore I am not convinced of their findings. Many times clients can have difficulties with dates and names, but the details are more specific to their memory.

Much like Cayce and their predecessors, more recent pioneers of past life regression did not always have a prior belief in reincarnation. The majority were professional psychiatrists or psychologists, with scientific backgrounds discovering past lives of clients quite by accident. Most of them did not consider themselves as Christians or religious, but some were either agnostics or atheists. Therefore, nearly all were extremely skeptical of the results of past life regression, but gradually became convinced as their work progressed that it could be used as a powerful tool for healing their clients. Spending years in traditional therapy, many of their clients had shown little or no improvement and were unable to move forward with their healing. They eventually found that their clients had greater success when experiencing their past lives, than when they were in a traditional therapy session.

Brian Weiss was a well-respected psychiatrist as the Head of Psychiatry at a Miami Hospital and initially a skeptic of past life regression. He is best known for his inspirational book, *Many Lives, Many Masters*. While working with his client Catherine for many therapeutic sessions, he decided to use hypnosis to help her in remembering her childhood to address various struggles in her current life. When he asked her to go the first time she had experienced the issue, Weiss was quite surprised when she began to describe another lifetime thousands of years ago. According to Weiss, she had therapy for many years with no success. However, when she had the past life experience, he noted that there was an immediate release of her issues. Since that session in working with thousands of clients, Weiss has found greater understanding and healing has occurred when experiencing their past lives. Other pioneers of past life regression include, Ian Stevenson, Jess Stearn, Edith Fiore, Henry Bolduc, Ruth Montgomery, Gina Cerminara, Dolores Cannon, Ian Lawton, Michael Newton, and Carol Bowman; just to name of few, all of whom came to similar conclusions. All eventually would write books of their experiences with their clients and the spiritual truths that came from those sessions.

With regards to the history of reincarnation, I would have to write another book entirely just on that subject. This is just a brief synopsis of a much larger body of historical information. If anyone is interested in a more intensive historical perspective, there are numerous books on this subject.

HENRY FORD (1863-1947) – Inventor, Founder of the Ford Company, industrialist
"Genius is experience. Some seem to think that it is a gift or talent, but it is the fruit of long experience in many lives."

LOUISA MAY ALCOTT (1832-1881)-Author of the novel, LITTLE WOMEN
"I think immortality is the passing of a Soul through many lives or experiences, and such as are truly lived, used, and learned, help on to the next each growing richer, happier and higher, carrying with it only the real memories of what has gone before...I seem to remember former states and feel that in them I have learned some of the lessons that have never since been mine here and in my net step I hope to leave behind many of the trials. They have done well in many phases of this great school and bring into our class the virtue or the gifts that make them great or good. We don't remember the lesser things. They slip away as childish trifles, and we carry on only the real experiences."

HENRY DAVID THOREAU (1817- 1862) - American author, philosopher
"As far back as I can remember I have unconsciously referred to the experiences of previous existences. I have lived in Judea eighteen hundred years ago, but I never knew that there was such a one as Christ among my contemporaries. As the stars looked to me when I was a shepherd in Assyria, they look to me now as a New-Englander."

BENJAMIN FRANKLIN – Inventor, scientist, politician, philosopher, diplomat
"I believe I shall in some shape or other always exist; and, with all the inconveniences human life is liable to, I shall not object to a new edition of mine, hoping, however, that the errata of the last may be corrected"

Chapter One

"...and you will know the truth
and the truth will set you free." *JOHN 8:32*

"The key to growth is the introduction of higher dimensions
of consciousness into our awareness." *LAO TZU*

Karen's First
Lifetime Experience with Yeshua

I was attending my first past life regression training with Henry Bolduc in 2006. In the training, the trainees were taking turns as therapists and clients. I was the client with another trainee as the therapist. Also present was an experienced past life therapist to help guide the therapist being trained, if assistance was required. I was guided to a past life and was quite stunned when I found myself in a lifetime with Jesus during this training. I never had any idea that I would be going to a lifetime with Jesus/Yeshua at that time in my life.

I described myself as a young shepherd boy having sandals on my feet, and wearing sheep skin with around my waist. I had dark brown hair and dark skin. My father was ill and bedridden. My mother was well loved and respected by me (*Josephus*). **My comments after each conversation appear in italics throughout the book.**

The Past Life Session

K (Karen) I've seen this before in a group regression.

I had a very brief view of a scene where I was in an area wearing the same clothes with my sheep in a group regression, but it wasn't very clear to me. Nor did I understand that it was a life with Jesus at the time.

T (Therapist) Do you want to go to another lifetime?

K No. But I need to look at it.

I did not understand why I needed to review this lifetime, but it would be clarified later in the session.

T Where are you now?

K I'm looking and I have a hook with a staff. My sheep are around me. It's beautiful ... open.

T What is your name?

K Joseph ... us ... Josephus.

> *I had difficulty pronouncing the name Josephus, and I did not know this was an actual name at that time. Later when I researched the name, I found that this was a common Jewish name at the time of Yeshua.*

T What do you hear around you?

K BA ... BA! I hear the sheep whine.

> *This indicates that clients' interpretations are taken literally while in hypnosis, as I literally told the therapist what I was hearing at that time.*

T What happens next?

K I'm asking my mom if I can go to hear a man speak, and my mom says "no." I keep arguing ... I am very persistent. I say he is very special. She finally gives in, but says I need to complete all my chores and then I can go.

T Can you describe what you need to pursue?

K I couldn't help him!

T Tell me about that?

K He's carrying his cross. (*Becoming extremely emotional and crying.*) And I couldn't help him. I couldn't help him! (*I continued crying.*)

> *At that point I literally couldn't stop crying. I became extremely emotional, as it felt heart wrenching. I later learned that everyone in the room became emotional as well. Clients cannot control their emotions when in a difficult or emotionally charged situation while in the hypnotic state. I have had sessions where many clients begin crying and demonstrating extreme*

emotional upset about various circumstances that were difficult in their past lives. Even though there are strong emotions connected to an event, clients are able to release and heal their connection to that event when in their life review.

T Could you describe what type of trouble he is in?

K (*Extremely emotional*) They treated him so badly and he was so weak. People are yelling and screaming and people are crying!

T What is causing the chaos?

K Some are saying "Crucify him!"... And others are crying. No ... No ... No!
(*Crying uncontrollably in a very different tone, almost like a whaling.*)
They don't know who he is!

T They are crucifying someone? Who?

K Yeshua!

At the time I had no prior knowledge that Yeshua was the Hebrew name for Jesus. I did not understand why I called Jesus by the name Yeshua, but all I knew was that Yeshua seem like the right name. I remember being somewhat annoyed when the therapist, Frank wasn't pronouncing Yeshua's name correctly. His pronunciation sounded like Jeshua, but I continued say Yeshua with a "Y"sound. On my tape you can clearly hear me saying, Yeshua with a "Y" sound rather than the "J" sound. I also noted he wrote Jeshua in his notes. This was an interesting twist of fate, as I would eventually use the Hebrew word of Yeshua in the title of this book. Jesus is the English word used, and Joshua or Jeshua was used in the Greek interpretation. All of my clients who used the name to be Yeshua, spoke with the "Y" sounding pronunciation. Later I discovered in the book by Dolores Cannon, JESUS AND THE ESSENES, a client referred to him as Yeshua. And even later, many of my clients also called him Yeshua.

T And you can't help him?

K He is special. (*Breathing heavily and crying at this point*)

T What is happening now?

K We are following him but they won't let us go further. They stop us!

T Is Yeshua a friend or relative?

K He is a teacher ... a great teacher! I've listened to him many times.

T Could you tell me about his teachings?

K Love, peace and loving one another. But they don't understand.

T Who are the people that don't understand?

K They're jealous. I'm not really sure. Each person has their own agenda.

> *Many clients mentioned jealousy as a reason why Yeshua was killed in their sessions as well.*

T Were you aware of Yeshua before?

K Before?

> *I became confused with the question. Client can be confused with a question while in the hypnotic state if the therapist is not specific in conveying their meaning.*

T Another time, before the crucifixion?

K Yes. I used to go and listen.

T What did he say? Did you hear him speak?

K OH! ... Yes! (*Becoming very emotional.*)

T Would like to tell us about that?

K He said, "The Kingdom is within. The truth will set you free ... and love!"

T Are there lots of followers there?

K Yes, but we aren't as many as the angry people. We are few compared to the many.

T What was your name?

K Josephus.

The therapist was verifying if my name was the same as spoken earlier in the session.

T Lets go on further in that life and you are a little older.

K We are meeting in a room. We are a group and we are discussing his teachings, and talking about him and enjoying each other company.

T Were you involved in hiding him?

K Hiding who?

Once again I was confused with whom he was speaking of with that question.

T Were you involved in hiding them?

K No … just listening to teachings.

T You're getting older now. Are you still having these meetings?

K The Romans come and take us. They don't like what we're doing. [The Romans said,] "You can't do this!"

T Can you tell me more about the situations with the Romans?

K They are very cruel … they don't understand. We kind of knew this would happen eventually, so we were prepared.

T What happens when they take you?

K I am in prison with others. It is dirty and smelling, and dark. I am hungry and cold. There is a bunch of us. I worry about my family. I decided to leave early before it was too much. So I died in prison.

In reflecting after the session, this was interesting in the fact that we can decide to leave this Earth when we no longer wish to remain. I remember feeling that it was okay to die rather than spending years in prison or worse.

T How did you decide?

K My body just dies. Yeshua spoke of this. We can leave if we choose. Some leave
and some don't.

T What happens after you die?

K Angels are lifting me ... I'm floating, lighter ... beautiful lights.

**After the death experience, I was guided to a place to review that
lifetime with greater wisdom and knowledge from a higher spiritual
level of awareness. Each soul has a life review after each lifetime.
This is a place of self-reflection.**

Review of that Lifetime
from a Higher Level of Awareness

T Knowing Yeshua, has that changed your life?

K Oh yes!

*When I made that statement, I cannot describe the emotion I felt when
speaking those words. I felt such joy and love at that moment.*

T How did it do that?

K It just gave me a light I never had. It's like we always knew but it's
indescribable. It's just the light! He was wonderful!

T What lessons were learned from that light and how did you gain spiritually?

K How could you not grow! Oh, such light, such energy ... yes!

*When I made that statement, I cannot describe in word show much joy and
peace I felt in that moment.*

T What brought you the greatest fulfillment?

K Being there when he was there!

I felt it was such an honor to be in his presence. I felt truly blessed.

T What did you learn or accomplish?

K Everything!

T You said there was something for you to finish, what was that?

K The guilt! Not stopping it. I realize I couldn't. A part of me realizes that, but a part of me just couldn't accept it because it was so hard.

It was extremely difficult for me to talk at this point as I became extremely emotional.

T Are you carrying that guilt now with you?

K Oh yes!

At this point I was crying with such overwhelming pain and guilt that I felt helpless to save him. Then the trained therapist, Frank, took charge of the session and began to ask what Yeshua would say.

T If Yeshua was in front of you now, what would he say?"

Immediately I envisioned Yeshua, and the guilt was completely released when he came through. It was as if all the weights of the past lifted off me.

K You are forgiven. There was nothing you could have done. It was to be.

Once I was able to release the guilt and forgiveness of self, I felt a sense of complete freedom. All the weights of the past were lifted from me and forgiveness was complete. For clients who have difficulty with forgiveness, I sometimes use this image of Yeshua forgiving them and releasing the guilt. This helps them remember the power of forgiveness, as Yeshua was the perfect role model for unconditional love and forgiveness.

It has been my experience, that the forgiveness of self or others is one of powerful aspects of freeing oneself and lifting of the weights of our past. I believe we carry these weights, and they weigh us down literally if they are not resolved in this life or our past lives. Yeshua was very clear that forgiveness was extremely important for us to embrace, as he understood how destructive it was for the soul.

Karen Second's Past Life with Yeshua and Second Experience with Therapist Frank

"Know that the purpose for which each soul enters a material
experience is that it may be as a light unto others."
EDGAR CAYCE READING 641-6

I felt I needed to have another session to understand if what I was seeing and feeling was real. I asked myself "Was this real," and "Who am I to have a lifetime with Jesus?" I decided I wanted to learn more about this life to see if it was real. I then asked Frank, who assisted us in our training, if we could go back to the lifetime with Yeshua. And he kindly agreed. It became evident that the sessions felt the same and had many of same details. And when my subconscious came through, I did not need any more confirmations, as I now knew it was real.

The Past Life Session

I began to describe what I was seeing, "I am a Shepherd boy around 15 or 16 in skins, sheep skin, a type of cloak and wearing sandals. I have dark hair, dark skin. I have a staff and there are sheep all around me. It's beautiful with great happiness. I enter house and no one else there." The food that he ate at time were described as being leafy, some meat, not much. I affirmed that my name was Josephus. I was hearing the wind and sheep sounds once again.

K (Karen) I asked my mother if I can go and listen to someone speak, someone special. Others wanted to hear him speak. It felt mesmerizing ... pure energy. He is speaking now. There were baskets of food. I brought some bread. Yeshua spoke about ... blessed are the poor ... the Kingdom is not a place ... it's here! He talked about forgiveness. I do not feel worthy.

> *When asked to describe his face I felt there is a peace about him. In the Bible Luke 17:21 there is a similar statement spoken by Yeshua, "Neither shall they say, Lo here! Or, lo there! For, behold, the kingdom of God is within you."*

T (Therapist) What else did he say about forgiveness?

K We need to learn to forgive. It may be difficult, but necessary. It is necessary for that person, but also us. Also for our enemies. Don't be concerned about heaven, it is within you. ... Everyone matters.

T What did he say about God?

K God is all loving. Man judges, God doesn't. We must spread Love ... that is what is most important.

T What does Yeshua say?

K "I'm a teacher. I'm here to teach for those who want to listen. They can follow me. Be not afraid." We are not afraid. Before we were afraid that others would come and take him away.

T Moving to an important day.

K I couldn't help him. He's carrying his cross and I couldn't help him. Some others not there are afraid. They don't understand him.

T Who?

K The priests.

T What did your parents think about you going to see him?

K My mother knows I'm here, she didn't tell my father.

T Why not?

K He wouldn't understand. He wouldn't want me to go. I have responsibilities to help care for the sheep and help in the house. I have to go back to where Yeshua was.

T What is Yeshua doing when he is talking with the crowd?

K He is holding out his hand and we can feel his love. Everyone feels his love.

T How many people?

K Many … many.

T What happened next?

K Next he brought his hands together and he said, "Take this love and express it." He was so wonderful. We felt blessed. He made us all feel special.

    He brought his hands together and then in a downward motion, which is similar to that used in Buddhist meditation.

T What happened next?

K He was walking, I wished to follow him, but I have responsibilities at home. My father is sick. I would rather hear Yeshua than watch the sheep.

    I felt torn between my family responsibilities and following Yeshua.

T What happens next?

K I am sad that I have to leave. I went to hear Yeshua speak. It's like the Sermon on the Mount.

    I have always been drawn to words spoken by Yeshua in the Sermon on the Mount, even as a young girl. If we are drawn to a particular event or time frame in history, we were probably there in our past life. I am not certain if this was actually the Sermon on the Mount or it was similar to another time when he spoke to the crowds. Sometimes clients will choose their current knowledge of a place or a person that is a symbol or representative of that place or person. As an example of this, I had a client who said he was Robin Hood. After realizing that he was not Robin Hood, he began to understand that Robin Hood represented his symbol for someone that reminded him of helping the poor.

T What do you share with your mother?

K I tell her about love. She says he is a dreamer and I am a dreamer. She says maybe I should come back to the real world. I will go and hear him again! My friend will tell me. Yeshua will come again and they will tell me. Sometimes I can't go, and others can, and they tell me about what happens. Others say he is not speaking the Truth and he is tricking you.

> *There was probably a perception held by many, that Yeshua was a dreamer or a trickster, like my mother expressed in that lifetime. In David's session he says others speak of Yeshua teachings as, "gibberish and magic."*

T Does he heal others?

K He healed the blind, lame, leprosy.

T Moving forward.

K I'm at the temple. They don't like him there. He upset the tables. *(I wave my hands in an upward motion.)* People get mad. We try to protect him so he won't get hurt.

> *This scene was very vivid to me. My conscious mind came in and started to judge what was happening. But I could not change this movie, and then I moved into acceptance of what was happening. I saw that our group was surrounding Yeshua and leading him away as he seemed to be in some kind of danger. There were many people who were extremely angry. I had a strong feeling that he was in great danger at that time.*

T Moving forward.

K He has left to an area nearby, and he is speaking at the temple. It was more about love and forgiveness. Some walk away, some are closed. A blind man comes and he is healed. More come to be healed. One man with legs that couldn't walk, and Yeshua healed him. I helped the blind man. Yeshua put his hand on his head and said "You are healed." He was asked, "Can everyone be healed." He said, "No, in time.

T Do you have helpers?

K Yes, many men and women. They are wonderful people.

T How do the people react?

K Some act strange. Not everyone understands. I fear for him, but he doesn't seem to be afraid.

T Does anyone ask questions?

K (*Yeshua*) He says, "I'm a teacher." A man asks "A teacher of what?" Yeshua says, "You know who I am," and the man walks away.

> *It felt as if Yeshua was very gently allowing him to see the truth within that he had already understood. There was no feeling of judgment, only a sense of disappointment in the way he spoke.*

T Can you hear him speak?

K He speaks softly, but everyone can hear him. He talks about how wonderful animals are. My sheep are like people, some stubborn, some loving. He says to not treat him as a God! (*This was a very clear message.*) "What I can do you can also do!" Love is the ultimate. We are all One ... love all ... forgive all. He starts to say, "Blessed are the poor for they shall become rich in spirit."

T Did you ever ask Yeshua to heal your father?

K Yes. He says he is not to be healed.

T You spoke about your sheep. What happens to the sheep when you go away?

K I asked the sheep to behave and they did. I am responsible for them. There are twenty. Sometimes they wonder but everyone watches out for them. Our sheep are marked with a die on their leg.

At the time, I had no prior knowledge of sheep having color markings on them to provide information as to who owns the sheep. Years later while in Ireland, it was explained to me that the sheep had the color markings indicating their owners.

T Moving forward in that life.

K I'm walking behind him up a hill ... everyone is happy. I follow Yeshua to Jerusalem.

T What happens there?

K A celebration. He is asked to leave. The Elders ask him to leave. The Elders are very harsh. We leave and sit by an olive tree. He said, "I'll be leaving you soon ... but not to care." He is talking about life everlasting ... life is eternal. That we have met many times before. He then draws a circle in the ground with his stick. He uses his finger to write the word love in the middle and says, "That is our greatest gift to each other." "My circle is complete!"

When he was speaking of his circle we all felt that we knew he was explaining that this was his time to leave us, and that he had completed all he needed to complete in this lifetime. We also understood he was speaking of his last days on this Earth and his ultimate death. As you can imagine, this was very difficult for us to hear at the time. We were all very sad hearing this.

Note: A few clients speak of Yeshua writing in the ground using a circle to explain his completion of journey on Earth plane. A few years later after my sessions with Yeshua, I found the book by Dolores Cannon called JESUS AND THE ESSENES. In the book, the client stated that Yeshua used circles many times to help them understand the circle of life. After reading Dolores Cannon's book JESUS AND THE ESSENES and THEY WALKED WITH JESUS, I was amazed at how much the feelings and words of Yeshua expressed by these clients, profoundly resonated to my own experience.

Some people may say that I took some of these experiences and made it my own. However, I read Cannon's book many years after my session. I will ask my clients; "Why did this book or movie resonate to you and not to me?" I answer them by saying, because they were memories of your past lives, and these memories were once again brought forth for you to remember. Everything is always there, it is just when we become aware and listen to our knowing that all is revealed that was once hidden.

T Moving ahead.

K I hear they have taken him away. My friend is crying. We feel that deep inside we knew ... when he said to not be afraid when they take him away. We heard the soldiers took him away.

T Where?

K Jerusalem ... I have to go and I tell my mother. I feel I am destined to go. It takes a while to get there. ... He is on trial. They are not good to him. He looks up and seems so strong. He is wonderful to behold! It looks like he is saying it is okay. I guess he knew.

> *At this time, I could actually feel his strength and a peace about him, even though it was rather chaotic. I found it interesting that I really felt his strength and calmness in the session at that time.*

T What happens next?

K He is carrying the cross. (*I began to experience great sadness.*)

T Does the crowd follow him?

K Yes. It is chaos! He is gone! He died on the cross! The soldiers prevented me from going.

> *I felt great sadness, but there was less emotion attached to the event than*

first session, because the guilt and pain was released from first session with Yeshua. Once the past life experience is released and healed, the emotions attached to the event no longer affects the person in the same way.

T What are you feeling?

K He can handle it. He went through it before. I knew it would unfold, and I loved him. He ascended and we can do the same.

T Does he say that to you?

K No. He told us that before. He prepared us in a lot of ways.

K ... "Your stomach is responding to the truth."

At this time Frank's stomach is making an extremely loud noise. And then out of nowhere, came a voice unlike my voice. This voice began to speak through me confirming that this experience was the truth. I had no control of what was coming out of my mouth. At the time I did not recognize that this was my subconscious speaking through me. After this event, I continued on with the session as usual.

T Did you have another life with Yeshua?

K Yes another time another place. In Persia his name was Melendenk ... something like that.

Although I have not had an actual past life experience, this may have been the man called Melchizedek. It was interesting to find, that In Hebrews 7:2, there are a number of analogies between Melchizedek and Jesus. Like Jesus he was called the "King of Righteousness" and also the "King of Peace." Additionally, in Hebrews 7:3 there is another analogy of Melchizedek and Jesus in this verse, "but resembling the Son of God, he remains a priest forever." Jesus was also considered to be Zoroaster in Persia by Edgar Cayce. Zoroaster spoke of one Universal Creator God and is considered to be one of the world's oldest monotheistic religions. At this time, it is not clear as to what lifetime I previously had with Jesus.

Impressions after the Past Life Session

In the notes of the therapist and the trainee, "Near the end of the session, suddenly Karen still in the altered state, became aware and she told me about the loud noise my stomach was making. She stated, "Your stomach is responding to the truth." After her remark she resumed with her past life experience."

At the time I didn't have any control what was coming out of my mouth, as it didn't feel like they were my own words. It was a very strange sensation, as the words just came out without thinking of what I was saying. In working with my subconscious, I now know my subconscious was speaking through me. After saying this, my conscious mind at first it thought it was funny, but then the subconscious indicated that this is real. I felt that it was a message should not be ignored. This was probably one of most powerful moments in my life!

Karen's Lifetime with Yeshua Revisited — Session with Mary

"The Kingdom of God is not coming with signs to be observed; nor will they say, 'Lo here it is! There! For behold, the Kingdom of God is in the midst of you."
LUKE 17:21

After my training with Dolores Cannon, I decided to access my subconscious with the assistance of another trained therapist. Before clients access the subconscious, one is guided to a past life. I was very surprised the lifetime with

Yeshua came up once again. There was something else I needed to learn about that lifetime. Much of what was said in the previous session was expressed once again in the beginning of the session.

The Past Life Session

K (Karen) My friend is coming over to tell me about this wonderful man. He's all excited. My friend takes me outside. He is telling me about this man who is special and I need to go to see him.

T (Therapist) What is special about him?

K He talks of good things, wonderful things that are not of this world. He says he talks of peace, love, joy and happiness.

T What happens when you go to see him?

K I go alone the first time as he can't come. I go quite a ways to see him. People on a huge hill. Some are camping out … waiting for him to come. I inch my way up the large hill.

T What are your first impressions?

K I'm in awe!

T What are you in awe of?

K Him!

T Can you describe?

K He is standing there with his hands high in the air and he quiets the crowd. He says, "The Kingdom is within!"

Once again I speak of the Kingdom being within. I found it interesting that there are twenty-one references in Cayce's readings when he specifically states, "The Kingdom is within." There are also thirteen references to the

"Kingdom is within" in these sessions. (Refer to the similarities in the back of the book.)

T This is new information isn't it?

K Yes. He speaks differently. He touches our hearts. He touches our truth ... who we truly are. (*I felt in awe of Yeshua.*)

T What does he look like?

K He radiates light. I don't know if everyone can see it.

T What color?

K Bright, white ... golden sparkles.

T Is he young?

K Not as young as me.

T What color of hair?

K Brownish red hair

T And his face is kind?

K Oh Yes! There is such a peace about him.

T Can you tell me more about what he speaks about?

K Oh yes! He speaks of forgiveness. We must forgive, as it affects the body as well. We must let go of all bad thinking ... bad thinking hurts us. Let your light shine. We feel our light shining brighter because of him. Even the children are quiet ... it is very interesting. There are many people.

There was just silence and a calmness when he spoke, confirming my prior experiences with him and later by many clients.

T Does he spend time with the people?

K We gather around him and he blesses us by holding his hands up in the air. We feel his energy.

T How does he hold his hands?

K Like this!

At this time I demonstrated what I was experiencing by raising my hands high in the air palms facing toward the crowd. This again remained such a powerful feeling, that I always become emotional when expressing my experience by raising my hands like he did that day. I feel this was such a powerful memory from the past, and it continues to remain with me to this day.

T Maybe then you didn't know what a blessing it was?

K Oh yes! I knew … everyone knew!

T Do you stay?

K I have to return to the family.

T Do you see him again?

K I have to!

T *Moving to an important day, a day that you felt was important.*

K I'm with him again.

T How much time has passed since you saw him last?

K A few years older

T What is your relationship with him?

K I follow him when I can … just like the others. They have responsibilities but they come and go, but not all the time. I have to help my family.

> *Once again I speak of my responsibilities at home. This has been verified by many clients that people would come and go because of other responsibilities in their lives.*

T Do you help Yeshua?

K Yes … healing!

T Can you explain further?

K Intention… you have to have the intention to heal. You have to have the knowing. It doesn't matter how … just so you can access the knowing.

T So seeing that person healed that is your intention?

K If that is to be!

T And do you see him heal?

K Oh, yes!

T And can you heal people?

K He says I can.

T So how did you learn to heal?

K You have to get the intention clear. Be clear and to become pure in thought.

T Does he teach you to become pure in thought?

K Correct. And he teaches you to release bad thinking, and intention becomes clear.

T Is there anyone you want to heal?

K My father, but it's not possible. It's in his contract.

T Are there others that are healers?

K Yes.

T Moving ahead to important day.

K I'm in the orchard. He is drawing a circle. He teaches us about circle of life, but there is sadness because he says his circle is complete ... by drawing the circle in the sand. We all have circles to complete and his circle is almost complete ... so we all know what that means. But he is not sad.

   Again this is confirmation of my first session where there is mention of circle and its importance.

T Does Yeshua tell you he is not sad?

K Yes.

T Are there women that are with Yeshua?

K Oh yes. They heal too. They go to different places.

   I found this to be another confirmation, as this was before many of the clients came and spoke of women being healers as well.

T Any one that he is close to?

K I see one woman. She has a rope on her head and a long white robe. She is a follower. He seems to talk with her a lot.

T What do they call her?

K Mary.

T Does he talk with others?

K My understanding is that he talks in smaller groups so we can understand at our level of understanding. But there is always danger. People hiding and spying. But is doesn't seem to bother him.

T Moving to another important day in that lifetime.

K I'm going in the cave like place. We are meeting together about how we can spread the word of the truth. We still have to be careful and some will go far away and some decide to stay in the area even though there is danger … I stay.

Karen in the Subconscious (SC)

T   Why was this lifetime brought forth? The lifetime with Yeshua once again?

SC A reminder of who she is. We want her to remember she is of the light.

T   How can she access that knowledge?

SC Remember Yeshua. Think of him [with his] hands high like this. (*I began demonstrating by the raising of my hands.*) Energy is from the hands … the energy of the light.

T   She spoke of intention.

SC Yes intention is most important!

Impressions after the Past Life Session

I was very surprised that the lifetime with Yeshua came through once more. It was about a decade later when I experienced another lifetime with Yeshua. However, my subconscious felt I needed more information about my healing in that lifetime, and a reminder of who I am. It has been my experience that information will only be revealed when one is ready to receive and understand its meaning.

Second Session with Mary with a Lifetime with Yeshua

The Past Life Session

T Why did Josephus decide to come in again?

At that point, I was trying to change the scene since I had been there before, but I was unable to do so. I have found that if someone has reviewed a lifetime previously they will no longer want to review it again if everything was completed in the first session.

K He is in the village now. Father is still alive.

T Go back to the house now.

K My father is in a room on his back lying in bed. He can't move. This was one of the times I was home.

T Moving to an important day, a day that you consider to be important.

K I'm with Yeshua. All those days are important!

T What words do you hear Yeshua speak?

K He teaches again about healing. He's showing his hands.

T What is he showing you?

K His hands are high above his head to the sides with his palms out.

> *Once again this scene remained clear to me and thus creating strong emotions.*

T Is he healing?

K Yes.

T Can you tell us about what he says to you? Can you find the words?

K All intention. He's indicating by raising vibrations within you ... connecting with the intention of healing.

T What does he teach you about healing?

K It's all intention.

T So he stands with his hands in the air with the intention to heal?

K Yes. If they are ready. He states not everybody is ready for healing and that makes him sad sometimes. But he is ready.

T Are there words spoken or images when you are healing?

K "I am the way, I am the light ... I am all!" Send intention from there.

> *When he said "I am all," I felt like it meant all being as One.*

T Is he teaching you all to do this?

K He is showing us the way. But we accept his way because he is the Master Teacher.

T When you look at him, what do you see?

K He is a beautiful human being inside and outside. What else could he be!

T Do you see light around him?

K Yes. It's brilliant!

T Where is he speaking?

K He likes to speak in small groups. He likes to touch many, but feels where he can reach their hearts.

T Is your friend there?

K No. We take turns. We take care of each other's families.

T So do you eventually go with him more often?

K I feel I have to!

T Does he teach you the way to heal?

K Well, he says there are all kinds of ways. He is just showing us his way. It's still intention.

T Did you see him heal others?

K Oh Yes! Energy comes out of his hands ... white. I don't know if they can see it but we can see it. He states his mantra.

T Do you know what his mantra is?

K He speaks it quietly. I cannot hear it. He has his own way. I feel his energy as he sent it into the room.

T Moving to an important day a day that was important.

K This was important! That we just witnessed healing in this room!

T What did you learn in that lifetime?

K I can do many things ... like healing. I didn't understand until now why when I raised my hands ... there was such energy in my hands. I learned to bring that sense of love and peace.

T What was the purpose of that lifetime?

K Compassion, healing and the knowledge that the Kingdom is Within. We all can ascend.

T Did Yeshua ascend?

K Yes! His circle was complete!

Impressions after my Session

Each of these sessions were years apart from another. My first two past life sessions with Yeshua was in 2006. It wasn't until a decade later that I had additional sessions. These sessions were with two other past life therapists whom I trusted in guiding me to the subconscious. I was so surprised that my lifetime with Yeshua kept coming through. All of these sessions had a very profound effect on my life and spiritual understandings. I cannot describe the feelings that were so profound that it is difficult to describe in the book. I tried my best to give you a glimpse of what I felt at that time.

A number of years later, having more personal questions, I had another session accessing my subconscious. The therapist, was a close friend who also received training with Dolores Cannon. In that session, my subconscious conveyed to me the following, "She will write the book. There will be others that will come to help." I feel that this was yet another confirmation that the book needed to be written.

Chapter Two

"Rather, the Kingdom is inside of you, and it is outside of you.
When you come to know yourselves, then you will become
known, and you will realize that it is you who are the sons of
the living father. But if you will not know yourselves, you dwell
in poverty and it is you who are that poverty."
GOSPEL OF THOMAS, 3

FAITH

I first met Faith at a spiritual place of business where I worked as a past life therapist. She was a teacher at the time. She later decided to come for a past life session to address some issues that affected her in this life. Faith was the first client that regressed back to a lifetime with Yeshua in 2008. I was using a tape recorder at that time and did not possess the recording. The thought of writing a book was far from my reality. I also had no idea that I was to write a book about the life of Yeshua. She was kind enough to lend me the tape of her session for this book. Many years later she decided to come back for the Quantum Healing session to learn more about her lifetime with Jesus, whom she also called Yeshua.

Faith's Past Life Sessions in 2008

Faith described herself as female wearing a robe and a blue shawl on her head, and sandals. She described an event with dancing in circles. She called the celebration "Horah," which is a traditional Jewish wedding celebration dance.

C (Client) I hear clapping. I think it is a wedding. There's lots of food.

K (Karen) Why are you at the celebration?

C Came with a friend, Elizabeth.

K Who is Elizabeth and how do you know her?

C She's related to me.

K How is she related to you?

C She is a cousin.

Faith as Mary, indicated that she did not know anyone at this celebration except Elizabeth. She also said Elizabeth was helping her to find a husband.

K What was your mother's name?

C Mariam.

K What name would your mother call you?

C Mary.

When asked about her father, whom she called "papa," she said he was in another town. The name of the town was unknown to her because she could not read; this being another indication that she was actually experiencing this lifetime. Later she spoke of crying when her papa died. A soldier had killed her father for speaking out about the taxes being too high.

K Moving to another significant event in that lifetime, what is happening?

C I'm with the teacher.

She spoke in a whisper, like it was a secret. She expressed that many thought Yeshua was a blasphemer, therefore she may have been hesitant to tell me. When listening to clients, one has to remember they are having their own personal experiences in that time frame. It is literally like stepping back in time.

K Who is this teacher?

C Yeshua. It's Yeshua! (*Expressing great happiness.*) I'm on the road with Peter and Andrew.

This was the also first time I had a client who had a past life with Yeshua, and actually called Jesus by the name Yeshua. This was a confirmation of my feelings that Jesus was called Yeshua. In later sessions, there were more clients who said that Yeshua was his name.

K Is Yeshua saying anything?

C No. Yeshua is singing. He's just making up songs. They always turn out differently. (*Laughing*) He doesn't sing very well, but he sings with such joy!

K How did you first meet Yeshua?

C He is in the village. He talking with Simon Peter … and I'm listening. Peter is just an oaf.

> *Faith often refers to her brother as Simon and Peter.*

K Can you explain what you mean that Peter is an oaf?

C He doesn't believe him. He thinks he's crazy. But I like Yeshua. I told Peter to come, but Peter said, "no" … he wasn't going. I told Peter he should go. I told him I was going. He told me I shouldn't go.

K Did you know Peter before this?

C Peter is my brother. He told me I was too young and I couldn't go, and that I was too young. I couldn't find a husband if I came with him.

K Was Peter married at that time?

C Yes.

K How did your parents feel about you going with Yeshua?

C I was young and I never could find a husband if I came with Yeshua. … I went with Yeshua. Yeshua is touching my chin. He told me I could come with him. (*She became very emotional.*) Peter got very angry. Peter said I can't go by myself. (*She was becoming upset with Peter.*)

K So does Peter still not believe?

C Peter is coming, so I don't get into trouble.

K Can you describe Yeshua's appearance?

C Yeshua is so tall. His robe is beige and missing a fastener, I can fix it for him. He has big hands and his hair is curly … but his overcoat needs fixing.

K Can you describe Peter?

C Bigger than my papa. Peter is a fisherman. He's got a round face, light brown hair. Yeshua is carrying a branch and is leaning on it. He has light brown skin, like the others in the village.

K Does he carry anything with him?

C Oh yes, he carries a branch.

K What does he do with this branch?

C Just leaning on it ... but he walks fine.

K Do you tell your mother that you are leaving?

C No. My mother is gone.

K How old are you at this time?

C I'm 15.

K Move to a significant event in that lifetime. What are you sensing, seeing, and feeling?

C Just watching him. I'm watching him playing ball with the children. He goes from place to place. He talks to the people.

K Can you tell me what he talks to the people about? What is his message as he goes from village to village?

C He says the same thing over and over.

K What does he say over and over?

C Give to the poor. Take care of your brother. Don't worry, you will be provided for. Sometimes they will ask if he will save them.

K What is his response?

C He says not to pick up the sword, but do what they tell you. And some people are disappointed. They wanted to kill the Romans. They were looking for someone to kill the Romans

K And they were disappointed in what he said?

C Yes. He says you shouldn't kill anyone.

K Are there more people following him?

C Yes. There are too many of them.

K Do they travel with him at different times? Are there people who come and go?

C They come and go.

Many years later this was confirmed by many clients that people would come and go.

K Move ahead in time when Yeshua speaks to a large number of people.

C He is speaking to a large group ... on the seashore. There are so many of them and it's hard to find a spot to sit because there is so many of them.

K How did people find out about Yeshua?

C We went the night before and told them where he would be. People are noisy. Priests are there. They came from the big shul ... with big steps. I smell fire. I sat down because I wanted hear what they would say. They were here to watch him.

The word "shul" in Hebrew means, a place of worship. When she spoke of "shul with big steps," this may refer to Jerusalem and the temple, and the southern wall of the Temple Mount, where an enormous flight of steps leads to the southern wall from the south. Even though Faith is not Jewish in her current life, she used the Hebrew word for a place of worship.

K What was their intention?

C They don't like him.

K Did they tell you that?

C No. I am just another woman in the crowd.

K Are there any other women there?

C There are other women there and he is talking to them.

K What is happening and how do you feel?

C He is quiet. I feel joy, love. People feel joy and love and the babies are still. Sometimes he is quiet ... and just holds his hand up to the crowds. He doesn't say anything.

There have been many similar descriptions of the crowd being quiet when Yeshua spoke to a large group of people. Similar to my experience, she also describes having difficulty finding a spot to sit.

K When he does speak, what does he say?

C Every day is different, but some things are the same. He tells the command. There is only One.

It was interesting that she said command instead of commandments. This may have been how the original word has been changed over time. Perhaps there was another commandment about Oneness.

K What is the command?

C To love.

K What are the other words he is saying?

C He says, "Love your God with all your heart, soul, mind and strength. And everything else will fall into place."

(*In a whisper, she began speaking in a different language.*) He talks about God and the universe and that the Kingdom of Heaven is within. (*Speaking again in the other language.*) "God of universe we thank you and gracious unto you." He prays for all the people.

It found it interesting that she began speaking in different language when Yeshua came through with a whisper. By her speaking in a different language, it is my feeling the Yeshua is giving her confirmation of this lifetime. Clients are usually unaware of speaking a different language while in the session. I had the impression that she was speaking in a language similar to Hebrew.

C The priests left.

K What was your sense of what they felt?

C They don't like him.

K Moving in time to another significant event in that lifetime as Mary. What is happening?

C He is in my house.

K What is he doing in your house?

C He is coming for dinner! (*She becomes very excited.*) We didn't know he was coming.

K And who is we?

C My older sister, Martha. She is very old. This is really her house but I live here too. But we came back. Peter and I have come and we are having a party. She is fussing at me. She had to bring in some more blankets to [put] the food on. We eat on the ground. Yeshua is talking about sewing of seeds ... planting. I don't want to know about the sewing of seeds! (*She seemed annoyed at this point.*) I want to know about the Kingdom of Heaven!

K What did Yeshua say when you said that?

C He told me to listen and be patient. He said I need patience. Martha is very angry at me. (*Laughing*) She wants me to bring in the water and wine. Again I told her to wait and I wanted to listen. I don't want to miss anything.

K So did he finish his story about the seeds?

C Yes, but it was for the other people. I already knew what he meant.

K What was your understanding of what he meant?

C There is always going to be some people that listen ... put God in their heart and other people just don't get it. Some people get tired of remembering who they are. (*Spoken in a sad voice.*)

K What did he mean by saying, some people get tired of remembering who they are?

C Don't forget the Kingdom of God is within. He tells me things he doesn't tell the others. He knows I understand. You see God is a presence and has pieces of Him in all of us. And I believe in Him. Andrew says it can't be [because he] doesn't believe.

> *There have been many instances where clients, as well as myself, have stated that Jesus/Yeshua said, "The Kingdom is within."*

K If Andrew doesn't believe, then why is he still following him?

C I don't know. He saw him heal people. The blind man was there once. We were on the road talking and he puts his hand on top of the boy's head, just in passing. And the man says, "I can see, I can see." He (*Yeshua*) just keeps walking. It's like … he will tell everyone and it will be fine. Yeshua says it's no big deal.

> *She is giving us a more personal depiction of what the disciples were like, especially her brother Simon Peter.*

K Does he say anything about healing?

C He says we all have the power.

K Do you sense or know anyone else there named Mary?

C Yes … but she's new and I don't know her very well.

K How did she come to be in the group?

C I wasn't there. She came from the other village. She just started being with us. She is very nice. She has gold trim on her prayer shawl and she wears earrings. She is very beautiful.

K How do the others feel about her and women in general?

C They feel fine. Well, they are okay about the little things like feeding them.

K And what does Jesus say about women?

C Jesus loves me. (*She became very emotional at this point.*)

K Tell me what is happening?

C Judas is trying to pick a fight and telling Jesus to stop giving money to the poor. He carries the money. And Jesus said it is fine, we can get more. Judas doesn't understand where. He doesn't trust.

K What are your feelings about Judas?

C He is all about business. Don't know why he is here. He tries ... he just doesn't get it. He is more my age. I'm 15 or 16, he is not much older than me. Sometimes he gets a little too close.

K Does he get to close to you?

C Yes.

K How does that make you feel?

C It makes me feel pretty. (*Laughing*) But Peter doesn't like it.

> *In many of her statements you can understand that these are the statements and feelings of a teenage girl.*

K How does Peter feel about Yeshua now?

C He adores him.

K What turned him around?

C Who knows what's in Peter's head. It's kind of like it wore him down, like old rock. It's a matter of trust. They are so close.

K Who are close?

C Peter and Yeshua.

K Does Yeshua tell him things he doesn't tell the others also?

C No.

K Because you said he tells you things that the others don't understand. Is it just you or others that he tells other things that are not understood by most?

C No it's just me. I like the way his voice sounds. I stay up late and he tells me things.

K What kind of things does he tell you about?

C He tells me about heaven.

K What does he tell you about heaven?

C He tells me about big rooms ... big places to live. (*Long pause*) I was crying because my dog got sick and died.

> *I believe Faith is explaining about the various levels that are in what we call Heaven. As Jesus said, "My Father's house has many mansions."*

K Did he tell you that your dog is in Heaven?

C Yes. And he lets me see him again ... then he took him back up.

> *In this beautiful statement it appears that he allows her to actually see her dog and then takes him back to Heaven. Yeshua spoke of his love of animals in my session.*

K What are his other views which are not accepted, that you accept?

C I tried to tell them that they'll come back through many lives ... so we can teach others, so they can teach other people. And that they have to go by themselves into other towns and heal. And they don't believe him.

K When you also talked about them coming back in other lifetimes, and how did they feel about that?

C They told him it's blasphemy.

K Why did they consider it to be blasphemy?

C Because ... they say we only have one life and they go to the garden [when they die].

K And are you going to the garden now?

C No. That's where they think they are going.

Evidently, they believed they would go to a garden when they died.

K And does Yeshua convince them?

C No. He stops telling them that and he says they are not ready.

K What is happening now?

C In a rich lady's house. She said we could spend the night, and there is a knock on the door. A lady had a baby and she is crying.

K What did the lady say?

C She says the baby won't wake up. Peter said to take the baby to Yeshua.

K He is sleeping, I didn't want to wake him up. I told Peter we can do this. He told me "not to be a fool," as I wanted to heal the baby myself. Peter said no and to go get Yeshua. The baby wouldn't wake up. So I kissed the baby on the head and held him tight as I could. I prayed I could heal the baby. And I put my hand on his head like I saw Yeshua do to the blind boy and held it there. And the baby started to cry and he woke up. (*She became very happy*) And Peter was very surprised. The lady cried and thanked me. And I told her should stay until Yeshua woke up so he should be blessed by Yeshua and he would be fine.

> *In many of the sessions, clients also said that there were others who were healers as well as Jesus.*

K Did she stay?

C Yes.

K And what did Yeshua say when heard what you did for the baby?

C He told me he knew I could heal.

K Does he say anything to Peter?

C He didn't say anything, he just looked at Peter, and Peter just huffed away. I got to hold the baby longer, and Yeshua talked to the lady a little longer.

K What was the name of the lady that brought you the boy?

C I didn't ask her name. There are so many people that need healing.

K What did Yeshua say about people who need healing?

C He said there will always be people who need healing and that are poor.

K Why did he say that?

C He was talking to Judas. Judas was fussing. I was anointing him with oil and

Judas said I shouldn't have spent the money on oils as they are very expensive. There is always some that will listen and some people forget remembering who they are. The kingdom is within. God is a presence ... pieces of him in all of us. I believe in him and Andrew doesn't believe.

K What was your sense of what they felt?

C They don't like him.

K Were there groups that healed?

C Yes ... many

K So many people were in your group of healers?

C Probably twenty of us followers.

K Now move to a significant event in that lifetime. Moving to a significant event in that lifetime. What is happening?

C Its Passover ... dinner. Peter told me to clean up the mess. It's getting really late. Peter is upset. I didn't see Yeshua. He made me go with him. They took Yeshua. They arrested him.

K And what did he do?

C He didn't do anything. I couldn't find Andrew or Judas. James is talking to people.

K Moving to a significant event. What is happening?

C People too many people. [They are] pushing me ... shouting ... blasphemy ... betrayer. A boy picked up a rock. I pushed the boy and he just laughed.

> *After listening to her description of what was happening, it brought me back to that memory of people shouting and pushing.*

K Let's move to another significant event in that lifetime, moving to significant event. What is happening?

C Peter came to get me. I didn't go.

K Moving ahead to another significant event. What is happening?

C I am sitting in the corner. Yeshua is gone. Feeling he is dead. Mary says, he's not there. He went to heaven ... part of him. Someone stole him.

K Moving to another significant event, what is happening?

C Jesus came back. I can't move. I was so excited. He is holding his hands out, [saying] we'll be there too. He will always come to me. Thomas had to touch him. He disappeared in the white Light. I miss him. (*She became very emotional and crying.*)

After the death experience, Faith is guided to a place to review that lifetime with greater wisdom and knowledge from a higher spiritual level of awareness. Each soul has a life review after each lifetime. This is a place of self- reflection.

Review of that Lifetime
from a Higher Level of Awareness

K It is time to review that lifetime now that you have more wisdom and knowledge then while you were in that lifetime.

K What were the lessons learned in that lifetime with Yeshua?

C The connection with Yeshua ... [is a] direct route to God Himself.

K Did you gain spiritually?

C So quickly. Just trust ... just be open. All things are possible. Do what Yeshua says.

K What was your greatest fulfillment in that lifetime?

C Greatest fulfillment was ... Yeshua holding my chin in his hands.

K How can this help you in your current life?

C Patience. Spirit of God is within you ... be open! Don't be afraid of anything you want.

K Are there any messages from Yeshua?

C He is hugging me! Hug the children. I love children!

Second Session with Faith in 2015

"In my Father's house are many mansions:
if it were not so, I would have told you."
JOHN 14:2

When I realized that I was to write a book about my client's experiences with Yeshua, I contacted Faith and asked if she would like to review her lifetime with Yeshua. She was very excited to have another opportunity to go to that lifetime once again. She was also excited to access her subconscious for answers to many of her questions concerning her current lifetime.

K What is happening?

C I haven't caught up to them yet.

K Who is this man?

C This man travels with Yeshua. I asked him where he was.

K You were with Yeshua?

C I can't find him.

K You seem very upset. Are you upset?

C Yes.

K Did you ever find him?

C Not today. I have to find Yeshua.

> *She is very upset that she is unable to find Yeshua.*

K Why do you have to find Yeshua?

C I have to take him to see my son. He needs to see him. Because he is too sad.

K How did you know to go to Yeshua?

C I have been with him before.

K Going back to the first time when you met Yeshua. How did you first meet him?

C My brother took me. He was with the fisherman and he was sitting on the edge of the boat on the beach. And all of the fisherman came to hear him and sat to listen to him and I did too. And they were asking him questions.

> *She spoke of Peter being her brother in her first session. In this session she called him Simon and later referred him to Simon Peter. This may have been that he was called by different names at different times. In the Bible, he is called Simon Peter. This is explained In John 1:41, "So you are Simon the son of John? You shall be called Cephas," (Cephas means Peter.)*

K What kinds of questions were they asking him?

C They asked him why it was okay to not be in church that day.

K And what did Yeshua say about that?

C "Church is where you are!"

K What did that mean to you?

C That you don't have to go to a temple.

K What other questions did they ask?

C The little boy sat on him in the boat. He lifted him over the boat and the boy wanted to know where his mother was. He said that she had died and he couldn't find her. And they tried to make the boy be quiet. And then Yeshua said, "No" and not to tell him to be quiet. And he explained to that boy that his mother isn't in that body and it doesn't matter that she's inside of that cave, as she is not really there. And the boy got confused and he told him to stand on his shoulder and lifted him up. He stood up and said to the boy, "Do you see how high you are?" And the boy said "Yes I am very high." And Yeshua said, "Heaven is not very high. Heaven is all around you, and there are different places where you can be. And your mother is in a place waiting for you." And he said, "When can I see her?" And Yeshua said, "When the time is right." And he picked him up and took him out of the boat. And then a man said, "Tell us more." And Yeshua said that, "Heaven is big and there is room for everyone. Everyone that believes that there is a place for them, they will have a place."

I can just see Yeshua saying these beautiful words to the man and the boy. It was so moving to hear these words.

K What about those that don't believe there is a place for them?

C They will learn. That is just what the man asked, and he said they will believe and then they will come.

K What happens to those that don't believe, will they eventually believe?

C He says, he will know the ones that belong. He knows his people … and they are all his people. Even though they are separate … they're still him. Like they are sheep, but he says it's different, because we have free will!

K Did Yeshua speak of free will?

C No. They didn't understand. I think I got it though!

K What did you get?

C That it's our choice … either to believe if we belong or not. Until the time comes and if he claims you and knows you and you are his … and he says they are all his. It's kind of confusing.

K Yes I understand, it is our choice.

K Now move to a significant event in that lifetime, a day that you consider to be important. What is happening? What are sensing, feeling?

C He's got both hands on my son's face and he kissed his forehead ... and I cried. And he said, "You will no longer be sad. You are one of mine!" And my son grabbed his two hands and kissed his hands and Yeshua embraced him. And he was filled with joy. And then Yeshua hugged me. I asked them to wait. They were just walking on the road and I asked Yeshua to stop and he stopped. I said this is my son and his name is Andrew. And he put his hands on Andrew and it was very beautiful. I don't have to tell him what was wrong ... he already knew.

K Can you describe what Yeshua looks like?

C He is very tall. He is very handsome. He has long arms and long fingers. I will never forget his hands. Tan skin like mine. He smells of Jasmine. It is very expensive.

K Were you a follower?

C Yes, but I couldn't always go. I don't always follow him.

K Did you go with him a lot?

C No. Not very much. I heard he was very popular.

K What was the most important thing he said to you?

C I think the day on the boat was the best one and when he talked about Heaven. He said I could see Mariam again. If he says it may be true.

K Did he say anything else important for you to remember?

C Just said we're all one family ... all one family.

K Did that make sense to you at the time?

C Kind of ... all about loving one another.

K What did you understand?

C Understanding is a key to love. People only are enemies out of fear. It's not good or bad. It's taking part in understanding. There can be no enemies if you love everyone. But not everyone is going to understand.

K So you are saying not everyone understands?

C Romans were very angry and mean.

K What did Yeshua say?

C He told them to listen to their laws. The law is the law, but try to understand their laws ... not in those exact words, but that is what I got.

K Were there others that did not believe?

C There were some people who thought he was a blasphemer.

K Why was he called a blasphemer?

C Some called him the Messiah?

K What did the Messiah mean to the people?

C We expected someone to smash the Romans. He was a different Messiah than they were looking for. There were some who wanted to be free of the Roman tyranny. So they thought he would free them.

K So was there something else he was to free them from?

C Fear! He told us not to worry so much. If we were in the field, and we couldn't wash our hands before we eat ... that is the Jewish law forever. But he said it was okay, you need to feed the body when it's hungry. But it's more important to feed the soul.

K What did he tell you about the soul?

C We are not what your body is, but who your soul is.

K Did you understand this?

C No! Sometimes we just don't get it.

   She is very honest that she doesn't understand everything Yeshua tells her which is understandable due to the time in which she lived.

K What did you have trouble getting that he told you?

C A lot of it doesn't make sense ... that we have something inside us ... not our bodies. I grew up in a body. We all have a body. We go to temple and we go to the shul. We make sure our prayer shawls are on and are heads are covered.

In this statement, she seemed very torn and confused about Yeshua's response concerning the soul. This may have been a difficult concept for many to understand at that time.

K Did you understand what happens after you die?

C We get to a heaven place he said, and God lives there. It's a big mystery! But he says the truth because I know it.

K Did you feel his energy?

C Yes. I don't have a better word than love. He is calm and assures, and [speaks] the truth.

K Does he speak of God?

C He is the Son of God - He is the word of God.

K In saying he is the Son of God, does he say that he is special?

C He says we are all Children of God. He says we are all Sons of God.

Once again there is a different interpretation between what is said in the Bible and what Yeshua said. This is a more inclusive statement, by saying we are all Sons of God and not just Yeshua.

K What was your concept of God?

C God is who brings the sun and the rain and the blessings on families.

K Does Yeshua address this?

C God's ways are on Earth … like they are in heaven. He said this prayer. He told us to call God our Father. And his name is Holy … and that we should do what He wants and he'll give us what we need. Those aren't those exact words. And to forgive anybody of whatever they do … and then says "Amen", which means, so be it. (*Speaking in Jewish language again.*)

K Were you aware of others healing?

C Yes. He taught his men to do healing and Mary was very good. The women that went with him.

> *Many years later, Grace in her session she said that Mary "was an incredible healer."*

K Were Mary and Yeshua married?

C I don't know … it is hard to say. One of them went ahead to make arrangements for the next day at different houses. And it was an honor to have him come to your house.

K When he went to these houses, did he talk to the people?

C Yes.

K Did your brother heal others as well?

C He came back to our village and he healed the blind man there.

> *It is so interesting that back in 2008, she was saying that there were many others that were healing the blind, sick and diseased. Many years later, this was also confirmed by many clients.*

K What did the village think about his healing the man?

C Some didn't like it. They thought he was not obeying God's law and his power came from somewhere else … somewhere evil, and they shunned him. But he was moving on anyway. I was sad to see him go. Jesus was already gone at this time.

K Did you hear what happened to Jesus?

C I didn't go. I didn't want to see it. I should have gone.

K Did you hear what happened?

C They made him walk through the streets carrying his cross. He only carried the top part of the cross. They beat him severely and he finally couldn't walk any more. And there was blood on the street. And they had a man help him carry it. And his feet were dangling and they put him on the cross but they didn't put him on the right way.

K Can you explain what you mean?

C There're supposed to put nails in the hands and put in the feet, but they pushed his knees up so he could breathe. You can't breathe if they put the legs down. This made him last longer. Simon told me this.

K Simon was there?

C He was there, but he was hiding … but he saw it.

K Why was he hiding?

C He was afraid they would arrest him.

K Who else was there at the cross?

C He didn't tell me.

K After Yeshua died what happened?

C That's the day they had the earthquake. First the sky went black … and the ground opened. And only the ground opened up at Pontius Pilate's place.

K What happened?

C They all screamed. Simon saw it. He was trying to find a place to hide and he couldn't go back to the place they were eating. Yeshua lasted longer than he should have. I only heard what he told me.

K After Yeshua died what else did the others do?

C Simon said they were hiding outside the city in one of the houses.

K Did you hear anything else about what happened after Yeshua's death?

C He came to them. He told them, he is here and he wanted something to eat. He was hungry and we gave him some fish. Simon told me Thomas felt his side.

K Did he tell them why he came to them?

C Just to spread the word of what he told them.

K Did Simon speak about Yeshua's work after he left?

C I never heard from him again. He told me he wouldn't probably come back for a while as he had work to do. But I always wondered what happened to him.

K So you never knew?

C No. (*She became very sad.*) It's so sad. I miss my brother, and I miss Yeshua, even though I didn't get to see him.

K What did you miss most about Yeshua?

C I just miss being around him. I miss his stories.

K What story did you like the best?

C He told us about a sheep that was lost and how if he is a good shepherd, he will leave the other sheep even if there are 99. Isn't that a funny number 99 to find the lost sheep? But he said he really wasn't talking about sheep, it was about us!

> *This story is very similar to the parable of good shepherd with the 99 sheep and the lost sheep in Matthew 18:12-14 and Luke 15:3-7.*

K So he spoke in parables or stories?

C Stories.

K Did he explain why he spoke in stories?

C No, but sometimes when he talked about Heaven ... I didn't get it.

K What didn't you get?

C He spoke of rooms in Heaven. There must be a lot of room up there! I didn't get it.

K What else did he say about these rooms?

C He said they're mansions ... big rooms.

> *In her first session, she mentioned rooms, but now she begins calling them mansions in Heaven. Jesus said, "My father's house has many mansions."*

K What is in the mansions?

C I don't know, but they belong to God.

K Did Simon ever tell you what was the most important thing Yeshua taught him?

C He made the blind man see … that was pretty important!

K What did Simon say about healing? How he was able to heal?

C He said he didn't do it. He just called on Yeshua and God, and they did it through him because he believed.

K Why did Simon follow Yeshua? Why was he drawn to him?

C Well he didn't want to go because his wife didn't want him to go. But he took her to hear Yeshua and she understood. But she had to be talked into it.

K By whom?

C By Yeshua. He told her he needed him and that was all it took! Yeshua said he was like a rock. Simon Peter is like a rock. He was very strong.

K So is he the same Simon Peter as in the Bible?

C Yes.

K Did he deny Yeshua as it was portrayed in the Bible?

C Yes. He cried when he told me. And he felt guilty for this for so long.

K Did Yeshua go to other places?

C He went away. His father let him go with some merchants. I wouldn't let my son go away like that! He went after his Bar Mitzvah. He wanted to go. He was gone for a long time. And the merchants came by and they were from Orient, and he went there with the merchants. That's just scary!

> *A Bar Mitzvah is a traditional Jewish ceremony held for a boy coming of age at thirteen.*

K Did you ever meet Yeshua's parents?

C I met them in the carpentry shop. I needed to buy a chair. I met his father there. His father was very old. This was long before Yeshua started talking to people. He was young. There were lots of other people working there.

K What was the most important thing you kept with you that Yeshua told you?

C Not to judge your brother.

K Did you judge others?

C Yes.

K Did you judge Yeshua?

C No. He was different. He was everything you were supposed to be!

K Did your son speak about what he felt when he was healed?

C He felt … just joy. He didn't have time to be sad. He understood who he was.

K Moving to an important day, a day you consider to be important.

C I'm lying on my cot. My son is back and holding my hand. I tell him not to cry. It's my time. And I'm tired.

After the death experience, Faith is guided to a place to review that lifetime with greater wisdom and knowledge from a higher spiritual level of awareness. Every soul has a life review after each lifetime. This is a place of self-reflection.

Review of that Lifetime from a Higher Level of Awareness

K Now that you have more wisdom and knowledge than while in that lifetime, what gave you the greatest happiness?

C When I was with Yeshua … feeling it was always good …it was always right. You can't do anything bad.

K Do you recognize this type of happiness?

C Yes.

K Was there a difficult aspect in that lifetime?

C Loosing loved ones … my brother, Yeshua, (her mother).

K What did you learn from that difficulty?

C Its temporary … just temporary.

K What did you learn or accomplish in that lifetimes that can help you in the current life?

C Not to judge … no judgment.

K Do you need to release this?

C Yes!

K Whenever we are unable to forgive ourselves and others we imprison ourselves and others in a type of corral or prison. So look inside the corral and see who is in there. It is time to accept forgiveness and release all unforgiveness of self and others. That was in the past and we will leave it in the past. It is time to let go of all judgment. It is no longer needed. It is time to lift all of the heavy weights of the past and be free. So send universal love and compassion to yourself and the others, and forgive them and let them go. And when everyone is forgiven, the gates of the corral will open and everyone will walk out free and forgiven. Let me know when everyone is out of the corral and free.

She was able to release judgment of self and others through forgiveness. She felt the weights of the past lifting off her and said she felt free.

K Were there lessons learned in that lifetime?

C Patience.

After experiencing another lifetime, I asked Faith's subconscious to come through for even a higher level of understanding. I only used those questions pertaining to Yeshua in her sessions.

Faith in the Subconscious

K   Why was that lifetime shown to her?

SC It was a gift ... a remembrance. Reminders of how close she was with him.

K   Why was that lifetime chosen to review?

SC Remind her who she is and the power she has.

K   Did Yeshua tell her about her power?

SC No! ... LOVE IS POWER!

K   What power is the subconscious speaking of?

SC Draw from Source whatever she needs.

K   She worked on forgiveness, was she able to completely release this?

SC We shall see!

K   Why?

> *I always ask the subconscious if healing was completed in the previous session before continuing to ask further questions. Sometimes there is a need to heal the issue in a more intensive way through the subconscious.*

SC She knows in her head, but her heart forgets.

K   So can the subconscious help her so she knows with her heart?

SC Yes. (*The subconscious worked on the healing.*) Done!

> *The subconscious will let me know when the healing is complete by saying, "Done" or saying "It is complete."*

K   How was the subconscious able to work with her to heal? How was this accomplished?

SC A deep knowing!

K   Is everything released?

SC Yes.

K   Is there anything else she needs to be aware of?

SC Speaking the Truth.

K   What is the Truth?

SC ALL IS TRUTH ... ALL IS GOOD! Share, don't hold back! (*Loudly spoken*)

Faith's Impressions after the Session

Throughout Faith's past life session she spoke about seeing her angels. She also saw a swirling green color and felt a tingling sensation in her head and toes. When I asked how the she felt about the session, Faith said it was very helpful and enlightening. When looking back at her session in 2008, I found it fascinating that much of what Faith experienced has been felt by other clients many years later. Even though she seemed to know certain details of the Jewish traditions, she was not Jewish in her current life. She also did not speak Hebrew. She explained," I can in no way claim that I know the language let alone recite it." Sometimes clients will speak in the language spoken during the time they lived in their past life.

Chapter Three

"Jesus said to him,
"I am the way, and the truth,
and the light."
JOHN 14:6

JOY

The first time I met Joy, I was immediately drawn to her loving energy. Little did I know, when I first felt drawn to her, that Joy's story was to reveal another connection with Yeshua. There was a deep connection between Joy and myself that I really can't explain. When Joy asked about having a session with me, she spoke of feeling a deep connection with Yeshua. She explained she also felt his presence in her spiritual work. After listening to her story, I understood our strong connection. Joy has the gift of psychic abilities and has worked as spiritual psychic and channel.

The Past Life Session

K Coming off the cloud down to the surface, very gently coming back down on the surface. Tell me the first thing you become aware of as you come back to the surface, your first impressions. What are you experiencing, sensing or feeling?

When Joy came off the cloud to the surface, she described herself as an attractive young man with curly hair, wearing sandals. Joy described his clothing as a beige robe held together with a rope around his waist.

C There is a tall wall in front of me.

K What is happening?

C I'm alone.

K Can you tell me more about the wall you were speaking of before?

C Its way over my head. I'm looking for a door.

K Is there a reason why you are looking for a door.

C Feeling ... like I can't see well. I'm touching the wall.

K Why are you touching the wall? Is it dark?

C No.

K Do you have vision problems in that life?

C Yes.

> *If clients say they cannot see anything, I need to make certain that they are not experiencing a life in which they are blind or visually impaired. Although it is uncommon, I have had several clients that were blind in their past life.*

K Are you blind?

C I can see shadows.

K Has this difficulty with your vision occurred since birth or more recently?

C Since birth.

K So what is happening? What are you sensing?

C I am supposed to meet someone ... my friend.

K When you meet your friend, what happens?

C My friends ... we play, talk and just tell stories. We're rough.

K Is there anyone you really feel connected to in this group of friends?

C Yes.

K And who is that?

C (*Long pause*) Yeshua.

> *Once again a client has used the name of Yeshua in connection with Jesus.*

K And have you been with him a long time?

C Yes.

K And how did you first meet?

C We lived in the same village.

K Does the village have a name?

C Capernaum.

> *The* Bible *says Yeshua was born in Bethlehem and brought up in Nazareth and preached in Jerusalem. However, the* Bible *mentions that much of his ministry years were spent in Capernaum. This is where he performed many of his miracles according to the* Bible. *The* Bible *says that Capernaum became his home.*

K So how are your connected to Yeshua?

C There are a lot of children. We are all friends.

K What types of games do you play?

C I see a stick. I can't see well.

> *In Grace's session she also speaks of a game with sticks when Yeshua was playing with other children, "Just having fun with sticks and balls."*

K It's okay. You are doing great! Does Yeshua say anything important to you at that age?

C He says you're my brother. He takes care of me.

K Is that because you can't see very well?

C Yes.

K If Yeshua was to call you by name, what would he call you?

C John. (*Sigh*)

K Do you play with Yeshua often?

C Every day.

K Now I want you to go the place where you lived in that life as John, what are you sensing, feeling?

C It's got a gate and there's a courtyard inside and a place for water [with a] circle like a well. There are rooms off that. It's a square, it is smooth like the wall. It's like mud, but smooth.

K Now go inside and describe what is inside the house.

C I have to bend to go through the doorway.

K Do you feel the house is big or small?

C Big.

K What types of foods do you eat?

C Berries, kind of a fruit, bread, and something pastry looking for bread.

K Do you have a family?

C I have a mother, father and younger brother. There is someone there that helps cook.

K Who in your family do you feel connected to?

C My father.

K Why do you feel close to him?

C He takes a lot of time with me. Helping me get around. I can't work. He teaches me.

K What does he teach you?

C He has his arm around my shoulder and teaches me to feel ... to be able to get around town and the house. He's kind.

K Is you mother kind?

C She is busy!

He seemed to be a little bothered by his mother being busy from his tone of voice.

K And your younger brother?

C He is busy too.

There was this similar feeling of being bothered by his brother.

K Do you ever go to Yeshua's house?

C Yes!

K Can you describe his house?

C It's similar to our house, but smaller. It has courtyard with well in middle. [There are] animals around ... chickens, donkey, dogs.

K Have you ever met Yeshua's parents?

C Yes.

K What are your impressions of them?

C I love them. I love them a lot.

K Why do you love them a lot?

C They are good to me.

K And how are they do good to you?

C They make me feel like I'm okay ... like I'm like the others.

K So they don't separate you from the others.

C Right.

K Do you ever feel the others are not accepting of you?

C Yes!

K Are they your friends or others that make you feel this way?

C Mostly my friends.

K What kind of things do they say?

C They don't mean any harm. They just say that I can't follow them as fast.

K I want you to move to an important day, a day that you feel is important in that life. What is happening? What are you sensing, feeling, experiencing?

C There a lot of people, and I'm on a hill with Yeshua.

K Are there others there?

C Many, many others are sitting all around ... gathering.

K And why are they gathering?

C People are coming to hear Yeshua talk.

K Are you much older now?

C Yes.

K What do you think of your friend Yeshua now?

C I love him! He's my best friend.

K Do you feel there is something special about him?

C Yes.

K And what is special about him?

C He's a teacher.

K When do you find out he was a teacher, or did you always know it?

C In the village ... people talked about him.

K Did they accept him?

C No.

K Why not?

C He was too young. But I listened to him.

K And what was important that he told you?

C He told me that I was perfect. (*Crying*) I was always perfect to him.

K That was very beautiful he made you feel that way.

C Yes!

K Let's go back to what happens when he gets ready to speak to the crowd.

C He waves his arms and there are many people on the hill and I'm sitting next to him. And I carry water. And he is like a priest, a teacher. He says, "I bring you words of the Father."

K What does he say about the Father?

C He says your Father loves you and blesses you. And all are a part of the Father. He touches everyone ... he touches everybody. (*Crying*)

K How does he touch everyone?

C He hold their hands and he hugs everyone. (*Crying*)

K So he holds each and everyone in the crowd?

C He does. (*Crying*) He speaks on top of the hill.

K And how does he quiet the crowd?

C They are quiet … they listen.

> *This is very similar to my experience when the crowd was very quiet.*
> *During the discussion afterward, Joy said it was so quiet you could hear*
> *a pin drop.*

K Do you think they understand what he is saying?

C Yes.

K What are the most important words that you can recall?

C He tells them that they are special. And that they do not sin. He says they are misled.

> *It is interesting that Yeshua says they were misled to think there is sin.*
> *Some clients also spoke of there being no sin.*

K And who misled them?

C That the priests have mislead them. He is tired.

K He is tired?

C Yes.

K So what happens next?

C We leave the hill and everyone follows us. There are lots of people. We are going somewhere.

K Where are you going?

C To the home of friends. I see Yeshua and Mark and Simon and the crowd begins to fall away. And we are a small group.

K So you go into someone's house is that correct?

C Yes.

K And whose house do you stay?

C Joshua's house. (*His name spoken with a "J" sound.*)

K Is Yeshua related to Joshua?

C No … just a friend.

K Once inside Joshua's house, what happens?

C We eat and drink. And Yeshua is tired, but he sits and talks with everyone. There is a woman and she has children and jokes … There is laughter and love, hugging. And I stay close to Yeshua.

K Do they ask questions of Yeshua?

C They say, "Master can we speak?" He says, "Yes, please speak freely, always speak freely to me never hold your thoughts. I am here for you and you are here for me."

K That is beautiful!

C Yes. (*Becoming very emotional*)

K What do they ask him?

C (*Crying*) "Tell us more," they say, "Tell us of the Father. Tell us who we are. Tell us how we can help you. How can we be of help and give assistance? What is it that you need? We are here for you. We will take you into the city and guide you."

K How does Yeshua respond?

C He thanks them and says he is not ready to enter the city as of yet, because there are more things to be done first. More gatherings before entering the city.

K Does he answer the question of who they are?

C He always says that you are the divine love of the Father, and that there is only one Father. He says that there is only One.

K Anything else that he says to them?

C He says, "You are my brother. I accept you as my brother, and together we will share the Father's love of others. We will journey together, and that there are many that need to hear the message ... I am the Light ... the Way ... I am the Path. I am doing the work of the Father. I am the Light .... and the Way ... I am the Path." And there is tears in everyone's eyes. (*Crying*) He is excited and he is tired.

K Does he get tired?

C Yes ... very tired.

K Why and does he explain why he get so tired?

C He gives so much. Everyone wants to talk with him and questions him, and people want to touch him and pull on his robe. He always stops everyone and talks to them, and I worry about him.

K Why do you worry about him?

C I am there to remind him to sleep.

K Does he ever tell you when he felt "the calling?"

C When we were just boys he told me I was to come to him because the Father had called him, and would I go with him. And I said, "Of course." I would never leave him, and we left our town and our families. We were just boys. He said he would take care of me. I depend upon him because I can't see things well . . . only shapes.

K Does he ever explain to you why you were born with this difficulty seeing and does he ever help you with it?

C Later.

K What happens later?

C (*Long pause*) Oh! (*Crying*) ... Oh ... Oh ...No ... Oh ... No!

K What is happening?

C After he dies ... I can see! Oh my God! I can see clearly now!

At this point Joy was crying with great emotion.

K What a wonderful gift he gave you. How did that manifest?

C I just stood up. I was there when he dies. (*Crying*) Oh my God!

   She once again became extremely emotional at this point.

K Everything is fine now. Going back to earlier times with Yeshua.

C We are all together and all our friends ... all with Yeshua.

K Does he have lots of people following him?

C Yes ... lots of people.

K Do people come and go or do some stay?

C Always people are coming and going.

K And do people have different jobs that they help Yeshua with?

C Yes. I am his personal servant, and there are other men that join and each has a purpose. Everyone's different and see Yeshua different. All are present to hear him speak, preach, and protect him from people who don't believe.

   Even in our current time, people have different perspectives of Yeshua. It is really about our own perspectives of others, and the events in our lives and how they can be seen with very different eyes.

K Why did he feel he needed protection?

C Because there are those that don't believe him. I am afraid for him.

   There are many accounts of his followers being afraid for him.

K Are the others afraid too?

C Not as much as I am.

K Does he ever speak of you about what might happen in the future?

C Yes. He tells me I need to be strong. He will always be with me ... if not in body, in spirit. But I don't want to hear that because he is my brother and he needs me and I need him.

K What we call the disciples, were they present all the time or were they like the others that came and went?

C They were present ... not all the time. They were his support. And many were sent out before his speaking and the others stayed closer to his side.

K Was there anyone that he was particularly close to?

C The other John.

K And what did the other John help him with?

C He was strong and loud. He was the mean one. We thought he was the mean one. He was the bold one.

K Are you speaking of John the Baptist or another John?

C There were many Johns ... three plus me. There is John the one and John the Baptist.

K And did Yeshua know John the Baptist?

C He was older, but they met. He was the loud one, and then there was John what you call a follower ... helper, and myself. I was only present to care for Yeshua and he took care of me too.

K Why did you feel John was mean?

C He spoke to the rest. ... He was preaching. He was loud and he corrected the Master.

K What did he say to the Master?

C He was pushing the Master. Pushing him and Yeshua said, "No." "All would happen in the right time."

> *I found this to be a very interesting observation about John the Baptist from his perspective. It is apparent that John was very protective of Yeshua at the time.*

K So he would want Yeshua to speak up more?

C Yes! (*Spoken very adamantly*)

K And did Yeshua agree to this?

C Not often. (*Sarcastically spoken*)

K So John the Baptist was very outspoken?

C Very uncomfortable.

K So you felt uncomfortable around him?

C Yes ... very!

K Did Yeshua feel very close to him?

C He put up with him!

K Did their relationship ever change?

C No!

K In the *Bible*, there was a friendly relationship, is that correct?

C I don't know ... I have no recollection of your *Bible*.

> *Since the* Bible *was not written at that time, it would not be known to him. This is also an indication that Joy is very deep in hypnosis, not possessing knowledge of the Bible of today.*

K You spoke of Yeshua speaking many times, did he also heal others?

C Yes!

K What types of healings occurred?

C The first time I saw this happen I was with a small child. A girl with a very bad broken leg ... she was tiny. There were very few people around and he touched the mother and said, "I will help you." (*Joy became very emotional and crying at this point.*) And he bent over and touched this little baby and baby cried out and then stood up! And the mother fell to her knees and cried. We all cried (*Very emotional and crying*). And she touched Yeshua, and touched his robe and wouldn't let go. She was grateful!

K I'm sure she was very grateful. Thank you, it's so beautiful!

C I saw many after that.

K Did you ever wonder why he didn't heal your eyes?

C I didn't ask.

K Did you ever wonder why? Did he ever mention anything to you?

C No. I was his faithful servant and he always guided me. I was always close to him. I could see a little bit, and could see shadows and walk by my own, but I couldn't see details.

K Did he ever explain why you had visual difficulties?

C I was born and that was a gift. That I could feel better, because I could not see well.

K So you could feel things more than others?

C Yes ... right.

K So that was a gift?

Yeshua was explaining to him that he had the gift of feeling things that the others did not possess. And because his sense of sight is not present, the other senses become enhanced.

C Yes.

K And did that give you comfort?

C Yes.

K Because of this, did you have spiritual gift such as psychic abilities? Could you feel things that others could not?

C I knew people were good or bad.

He seems to be sensing people's energies which is similar to Joy's gift in her current life.

K Did you sense this about John the Baptist?

C Yes ... yes! He was jealous. He wanted to be in charge. He made me angry.

K What did Yeshua say about him?

C He said just leave him alone. He was kind to him ... kind and loving to all.

K Did he ever tell you why he decided to come into that life as Yeshua?

C He said he was sent by the Father to open the hearts of woman and man. That is the heart ... he was there for the heart.

K Now moving to an important day, a day that you consider to be important in the life of Yeshua. What is happening? What are you sensing, feeling?

C I see them taking the body. Soldiers are taking him!

K What body?

C Yeshua's body.

K So he has died?

C Yes.

K Did you see him die?

C Yes, I was present.

K And who else was present?

C Just me.

> *There could possibly be more people present than he was aware of due to his visual impairment.*

K Was his mother present?

C Just for a short time. But people were afraid.

K So they were afraid to be associated with him?

C Yes. (*Becoming very emotional.*)

K Were you there when he was on the cross?

C Yes.

K As he was on the cross, did he say anything to you?

C No!

K Now going back when you said the soldiers were taking the body. Where were they taking the body?

C They took it to a place and left him.

K What kind of place?

C Like a grassy area with rocks nearby that they left it there and allowed others to take it. The people took it … but people were scared.

K I'm sure they were. So where did they take the body?

C There was a tomb and a rock ... not a big rock.

K What happens next?

C I was trying to manage the whole things. I wasn't in charge. I was quiet and praying. **And I could see!** I was overwhelmed!

> *When asked when his vision returned, again he said, when Yeshua died on the cross.*

K That is wonderful! Did any other miracles happen the time he died?

C I don't know.

> *Clients always tell the truth of not having any knowledge of the question when asked.*

K What is happening after he is placed in the tomb?

C I stayed there. I couldn't leave.

K Did others stay?

C Yes. Many people gathered there. I didn't know what I was going to do. I didn't know. He was my life!

K I'm sure you had difficulty when he died.

C He was my best friend ... I couldn't leave.

K So how long did you stay?

C I stayed a few days and I left with some others. I went back to the water with a friend.

K To the Sea of Galilee?

C Yes to the Sea.

K Why did you like the sea?

C I like the smell. I feel comfortable.

> *When visiting Israel in my current life, I also felt drawn to the Sea of Galilee. I felt it was a very special place that gave me a sense of peace*

and joy. Whenever we feel a deep connection to a certain place or time in history, it may trigger a memory of that previous lifetime experience.

K Did Yeshua like to go to the sea?

C Yes.

K What happens after you spent time at the sea?

C They said he looked like himself.

K Did he say anything?

C He said he was with the Father. I felt his presence … but never saw him as the others did.

K Who saw Yeshua?

C Mary saw him. (*Speaking of Mary Magdalene*) They were very close. I loved her too. She was beautiful. I saw her after my sight returned. She was close to us, as was the others. And Jesus loved her very much.

K Were they married?

C Not that I knew.

K Were you away when he went away to learn more?

C Yes, but not for too long. I returned to my family, but not for a long time. He was older and I was a young man.

K Where did he tell you he went?

C I did not ask. He was always wise. I always saw him the same!

K Did he have healing groups he worked with?

C People always talked about his healings, but he made the choice. It was always his choice. It's not that he wouldn't heal because it was requested of him, and there were many, many that asked, but he did not always heal … he made that decision himself.

In my session, I also understood that Yeshua believed healing would not always occur for various reasons. This would be easily understood, since he possessed a heightened awareness of those souls and their journeys. Only the subconscious knows the highest good of the individual, and that must always take priority over the physical act of healing.

K So did this make many people angry?

C Yes.

K Did he raise anyone from the dead as I have heard?

C He raised someone from a great illness, but they weren't dead. There was one that looked dead.

> *This could be another explanation of Yeshua raising Lazarus from the dead. Perhaps he may not have been actually died, but gravely ill and may have appeared to be dead.*

K What was the greatest gift he gave to you?

C (*She began crying*) His love and companionship. He was like a part of myself. It was his person for me that was important to me. I knew he did great things, but he was always just my best friend. (*Joy was crying and very emotional.*)

K What happens next?

C I returned home and I spent time with my brother.

K How did your parents feel about your time with Yeshua?

C They understood … and they loved him too.

K So did you ever speak to others of Yeshua?

C Yes. I spoke to many.

K What was the message you gave to others?

C I told others he was a great man. He taught us all about the greater things, important things and the love we have for each other. That we are children of the Father. That we were given the responsibility to help each other whenever possible, and that we were never alone. And he would always be there for us.

K Did he talk of prayer?

C Yes. He prayed many times.

K Can you tell us his prayer that he taught you?

C "Our Father, who art in me

And everyone I see

Glory is your name

For Thine Kingdom forever and ever"

K Beautiful! Thank you.

K What were the circumstances of your death in that life?

C I died in my sleep.

After the death experience, Joy is guided to a place to review that lifetime with greater wisdom and knowledge from a higher spiritual level of awareness. Each soul has a life review after each lifetime. This is a place of self-reflection.

Review of that Lifetime
from a Higher Level of Awareness

K It is time to review that lifetime now that you have more wisdom and knowledge available then while you were in that lifetime. What gave you the greatest happiness in that lifetime?

C Yeshua! It was not an easy life there was struggles, physical thing, and a hard life. I felt worn out.

K What did you learn or accomplish in that lifetime that can help you in your current life?

C I learned so much. I learned that even though I couldn't see, the body wasn't that important. I learned the soul, the spirit is what is important.

K What did Yeshua say about the soul?

C We have a light inside us and that light reached up to the highest power that there could be, and I learned that. I also learned to love all my brothers without reservation.

K Wonderful!

C I lived with heartache and learned to overcome the loss of Yeshua. I learned to forgive others.

K So you forgave the ones that killed Yeshua?

C Late in that lifetime.

After experiencing another lifetime, I asked Joy's subconscious to come through at the highest level of understanding and wisdom.

Joy in the Subconscious

K Do I have permission to speak to Joy's subconscious?

SC Yes.

K Do I have permission to ask questions?

SC Yes.

K Why was that lifetime shown to her?

SC Because she must be empowered to do the work she has been called to do. She must trust ... totally trust.

K How did the disciples respond to him in that lifetime?

SC They were jealous because I was so physically connected with him and I relied on him, and he told me everything. He told me his personal feelings, those things he wouldn't share with the others. When he was scared. He confided those things in me.

K   What was the high point with Yeshua?

SC The high point ... was to see, and the low point was to lose him. So the high point and the low point were the same.

What a touching statement!

K   Was the explanation of Yeshua correct?

SC Yes.

K   What is her ultimate lesson?

SC   To carry the love, the message. To carry all the wisdom forward with great confidence and worthiness knowing that she is fully capable of remembering, and feeling the connection now. There can be no doubt that this is true.

Many of the clients including myself, have experienced some level of doubt when experiencing a lifetime with Yeshua. They will ask, "Why did I have a lifetime with him, and who am I to have been with Yeshua?" And I respond to them, "Why not you!" We need to come to the realization that we are worthy to have been with him, and move into acceptance of this experience regardless of what others may think or say.

K   Why was there doubt?

SC She is so humble.

K   What can the subconscious tell her about being humble?

SC Soul's knowledge to those who need it so badly. Humbleness is good, if it does not restrain the message!

What a great explanation of being humble. It is okay to be humble,   but not giving up speaking ones' truth.

K Can the subconscious explain why there are so many variations of the life of

Yeshua?

SC There are many variations throughout history and many men and women have made a change to the story ... that one can only imagine that anything could be written.

K Was Yeshua married to Mary?

SC Yeshua ... he was married to her in love, but not in formality.

K Why did they not get married?

SC There was not time.

K Who was John close to?

SC John was close to Peter and Simon.

K What is important to know about that lifetime?

SC You were chosen to walk the path at that time due to previous experiences assisting others. And it was a decision that was made by yourself and your Council, to take this body at this point in history.

> *It has been my experience that our Council gives us guidance for our next incarnation. The decision is based on what we need to accomplish in the next lifetime.*

K Why did she desire to come to that lifetime with Yeshua?

SC Because she loved Yeshua!

K Did she have another lifetime with Yeshua?

SC Yes.

K Can the subconscious show her that lifetime?

SC Yes.

SC It was a place that no longer exists.

K Does that place have a name?

SC Atlantis.

K Can the subconscious tell us about that lifetime?

SC They were female friends.

K And in that lifetime did she have the same essence of Yeshua? Was she a great teacher?

SC Very privately ... not in big groups.

K And what did she speak about?

SC She spoke about the energy of the material world ... the natural world and the reverence for everything.

K Are you speaking of nature?

SC Yes.

K So what was important for Joy to take away from this lifetime?

SC It was a rest.

K I have heard of rest lifetimes. Was that a rest lifetime?

Many times, I have heard clients speak of "rest lifetimes." This is a lifetime with little drama or difficulties. Sometimes a "rest lifetime" is chosen after a difficult previous lifetime or just for the experience.

SC Yes.

K Why did she go to rest in that lifetime?

SC She needed a rest.

K Did she have had a lifetime before the rest lifetime that she needs to review. Can the subconscious guide her to that lifetime?

SC NO! Not Yet! ... NOT YET, because of the way the lifetime ended.

Joy's subconscious very forcibly stated that it was not the right time review another lifetime. The subconscious will not reveal information that a client is not ready for, and it will only be revealed when the time is right for them to understand.

Joy's Impressions after Her Session

Joy described her session as, "Awesome, amazing." She felt it would have a profound effect on her work. She said it felt wonderful to be out of the body and felt that it was the closest way to get to Spirit in the body. Joy indicated being unable to remember all of her session. When she first spoke of that lifetime with Yeshua she felt disoriented due to her blindness. She was so excited to have touched him and realized, "I was touching him because of the blindness." Joy understood that because her blindness enhanced the senses, it gave her the unique opportunity to touch him.

Joy explained that the emotion connected to the lifetime with Yeshua was profound; "Something about the emotional experience that is so powerful." I often explain to clients that by actually feeling the emotions and experiences in a past life, it is more powerful than someone telling you about your lifetimes. It is also allows you to heal the wounds of your past when you can access the lifetime that first created an issue. Once an issue is understood, it then can be released and healed.

Joy's Impressions Much Later after Her Session

Joy described her session as, "Awesome, amazing." She felt it would have a profound effect on her work. She said it felt wonderful to be out of the body and felt that it was the closest way to get to Spirit in the body. Joy indicated being unable to remember all of her session. When she first spoke of that lifetime with Yeshua she felt disoriented due to her blindness. She was so excited to have touched him and realized, "I was touching him because of the blindness." Joy understood that because her blindness enhanced the senses, it gave her the unique opportunity to touch him.

Joy explained that the emotion connect to the lifetime with Yeshua was profound; "Something about the emotional experience that is so powerful." I often explain to clients that by actually feeling the emotions and experiences in a past life, it is more powerful than someone telling you about your lifetimes. It is also allows you to heal the wounds of your past when you can access the lifetime that first created an issue. Once an issue is understood, it then can be released and healed.

Chapter Four

"I came into this world, that those who do not see may see,
and that those who see may become blind."
JOHN 9:39

DAVID

David indicated he came for spiritual growth and a sense of connection. At the time of the session, he was in the medical field. Prior to his session, there was no indication that he had a previous lifetime with Jesus. David's began his session assisting those who were wounded and killed in Gettysburg. In David's next past life experience, he described himself around forty years old and being very poor and hungry. Unlike the other sessions, this spoke of the impact on a man who wasn't a follower, but had a brief encounter with Jesus. During his short stay with Jesus he was able to come to greater awareness, but seemed unable to make use of the wisdom he was given. However at the end of that life, Saul said he had gained greater clarity in the words of the Prophet which has contributed to his spiritual awareness in his current life.

The Past Life Session

K Coming off the cloud down to the surface, very gently coming back down on the surface. Tell me the first thing you become aware of as you come back to the surface? What is happening?

C I'm in a house that has a dirt floor.

He said that his house was "not much," and that he was very poor.

K Looking down at your feet, what type of footwear are you wearing, or are you barefoot?

C Sandals.

K What are you type of clothing are you wearing?

C Some type of toga ... like burlap. It's not very nice.

K What are you experiencing?

C There is a lot of commotion outside.

K What is happening?

C The Prophet is coming. I don't believe in the Prophet, but I am curious.

K Why don't you believe in the Prophet?

C He speaks gibberish!

K What kind of gibberish does he speak of?

C The Kingdom is in the sky.

> *At this point, I felt that he is referring to Jesus. However, I can never assume anything in a session, as it will eventually be made clear.*

K What do you believe in?

C You work hard for what you get. This guy is a freeloader!

K Why do you say that he is a freeloader?

C He is a smart ass freeloader. But he's handsome ... he looks better than me, but poorer than me. Basically [he is] half dressed in rags, but he is handsome. He's charismatic, so you want to listen to him. He got something for nothing.

> *His resentment can be understandable, as he was very poor and no one ever seemed to help him in that life. He also saw the Prophet as handsome and charismatic with people giving him what he needed.*

K So did you listen to him speak?

C A little bit.

K So what did you think of him?

C I sort of got caught up in him ... there's something about him.

K What is there about him?

C He makes you want to walk behind him. Oh, all the women love him! He's getting a lot of free food.

K What do people call this Prophet?

C Some say he is the Promised One. But he's a magician.

K Why do you call him a magician?

C He's fooling everyone.

> *My mother in the past lifetime described her impressions of Yeshua with the following statement, "Others say he is not speaking the truth and he is tricking you."*

K Why do you say that he's fooling everyone?

C Because he can't deliver something you can't see.

K Was there a time when you were with him?

C I'm in a room with him drinking wine. He's saying a lot of nutty stuff. (*David became extremely emotional and began crying.*)

K You are getting emotional now, so what is he saying that makes you so emotional?

C He has an answer for everything. He is upsetting some of the men and they are leaving.

K Why are they leaving?

C What he says is nutty.

K What is he saying that is nutty?

C We are all special, but we are all dirt poor and he is lying ... he is lying again! (*Becoming emotional*)

K You don't feel special?

C I FEEL POOR! (*Spoken loudly.*)

> *This feeling of not being special is understandable since he was very poor, and it appears that his lack of self-confidence was due to his life experience.*

K Do you ask him about being poor?

C He said I'm seeing with the wrong eyes. He always has an answer. So I leave and as I walk out. I think my eyes are blind.

K Why do you say that your eyes are blind?

C My eyes are blind to what is being said.

In making this beautiful statement, he demonstrates amazing insight despite his understanding at the time.

K What happens next?

C I go back. We drink a lot of wine and we're laughing a lot. I like this guy!

K What do like about him?

C He knows me. He is like an old friend.

K Did you know him before?

C No.

K So you just felt a connection?

C Yes.

K What did he say that changed your opinion about him?

C He called me a blind man. I didn't know what he was talking about ... I could see just fine. I called him a smart ass.

K What did he do when you called him that?

C He said, "You are right. ... Your eyes are opening." That didn't make sense to me.

In John 9:39 Jesus said, "I came into this world, that those who do not see may see, and those who see may become blind."

K Are there a lot of people there with you?

C We are all out urinating ... maybe five or six men. We drank all the wine. It's time to sleep.

When he first spoke about Jesus and everyone urinating and drinking I found it to be quite humorous, but then I understood it on a deeper level. I

feel Jesus was able to deliver his message by connecting with the group of
men on a personal level.

K What happens when you wake up?

C I had to go to the market and sell something handmade. Nobody wants it ... it's not worth much.

K Was that to make money?

C Yes.

K Now move to important day in that lifetime, a day that you consider important. Moving to that day. What is happening, what are sensing, feeling?

C There are Roman soldiers are parading through the streets. I'm afraid ... you're helpless around them. They speak a funny language.

K Are you with anyone?

C No. I'm alone.

> *He indicated that there was someone who died, but there was no love*
> *with that person.*

K Is there anyone that you are connected with?

C No. I'm a grouchy old man. Even my neighbors don't like me.

K Why don't they like you?

C They're younger. I'm older ... I'm grouchy.

K What caused you to become grouchy?

C Certain emptiness.

K Was there a time when you didn't feel empty?

C I'm too old to remember that. My life is very boring here.

K Why?

C I'm not successful. I don't know how to be successful. I'm jealous.

> *Interestingly, he actually speaks of being jealous of others.*

K Who are you jealous?

C Everyone that is successful. I'm not charismatic. It's hard for me to barter.

K So you feel you need to be charismatic to be successful?

C The rich ones do.

K Do you have any friends in that lifetime?

C No, just competition.

K Did you ever meet the Prophet again?

C No.

K So what did you take away from that time you were with him?

C In the end I reflect back on what he had said many years earlier.

K What did you reflect back on?

C That ... I put too much stock in the physical. He was showing me how to see with the other eyes. As I die, my fondest memory is urinating with the prophet and there was lots of farting, and we were all laughing.

> *In the* Bible *Jesus spoke of those of us who are blind to the truth. And this message was clearly emphasized in the lifetime with Saul. It was very interesting, when he spoke of his fondest memory of urinating and farting with Jesus. It would it make sense that Jesus would join in with this group in any way he could so he could be heard. He was able to touch Saul, and I believe he probably touched the others as well that day. He met with people who were considered by many as bad, poor or "sinful", so why not join in with them in order to get his message across to those who otherwise may have not heard his message.*

K So it was a happy time?

C I felt lighter being with him.

K In what way did you feel lighter?

C Hopeful!

K Did he make the others feel hopeful?

C I didn't like the neighbors. They were all assholes and they never cared about me. They never cared about me. But that night we all had that one moment. He was staying at one of their houses as a guest.

K Was there anyone else with him?

C There was a woman with him.

K Can you recall her name?

C Mary ... she was his attendant. She was not seen much. She was pretty though.

K So could you sense that they were connected?

C Like a couple.

K Were they married?

C I don't know and I didn't care.

> *As Saul in that life, he is relating to his experience at that time. This is an example of the client being truthful in the session by saying that he didn't really know or care if Jesus was married.*

K What was the most important thing that this Prophet told you?

C To open my eyes and see the Truth.

K Did he talk about this Truth?

C He did ... that it is very deep within us.

K Did that make sense to you at that time or later?

C No. At my death it made sense.

K Did you find out what happened to the Prophet?

C He was killed.

K Why was he killed?

C For being a Prophet. I had heard about it.

K How did you hear about it?

C I knew it was coming.

K Why did you know it was coming?

C Because he was so cocky. He talked too much, we don't do that around the soldiers.

K What did he say to upset the soldiers?

C I think he became popular. That was not a good thing to be popular.

K Did he say anything that made them upset?

C He made his own people upset.

K Why did he upset them?

C They were jealous of him. He was just different. He was like a rock star. And there was a lot of jealousy.

> *Clients will give a name or word which represents their symbol in their current life. He said Jesus was like a "rock star," which is word that represents Jesus' status in that lifetime. Like many clients, he was using terminology that he recognized from the current life.*

K What was your name in that lifetime, if you heard you name called?

C Saul.

K Did you ever tell anyone else about your experience with the Prophet?

C In the market we passed the time talking about him.

K What did they say about him?

C There was no in between.

K Did you know his name?

C (*A long pause and becoming emotional.*) He was the One. He was just the Prophet.

K Can you describe the Prophet?

C [He had] all dark features. He had all his teeth and I didn't.

> *The Prophet having all of his teeth would be something he would notice, since he was very poor in that life and didn't have any teeth. And perhaps many of the poor at that time did not have teeth as well.*

C He had a round head and he walked briskly. His pace was brisk. He was young for his years. He didn't miss a thing.

K Why did you say he didn't miss a thing?

C He spoke to people when he walked by. And he spoke to all the wrong people.

K What do you mean by the wrong people?

C There were people poorer than me, and he took the time to talk to them.

K So he spoke to everyone, whether rich or poor?

C There were no rich that I saw.

K Did he have any others that were with him?

C No. I only saw him for that one evening.

K So did you hear any stories from others about him?

C Gibberish ... magic.

K What kind of magic?

C Dead people.

K What about dead people?

C Raising them ... It's all gibberish.

> *It was likely that many people thought Jesus was using some kind of magic when he healed people. Just imagine during that time what people were thinking about someone being raised from the dead. Even in the present, it would be something that people would have difficulty believing.*

K Any other magic that you heard about?

C Not that I heard. He was nice ... but a freeloader.

K I would like you to move to the last day of that lifetime, feeling no discomfort in the body. Going to the death scene, what is happening?

C I'm in the street on my way to work, was on my way to work. Clinching my chest, like a heart attack. I died

As he described himself clinching his chest, he began to hold his chest demonstrating physically what was happening in the session. Clients will demonstrate physically what is occurring in the body. An example of this is when someone is shot, their body movements replicate what is happening to them physically when in the session.

K As you were having the heart attack, is that when you became aware of he was?

C They were my last thoughts!

K What were your last thoughts?

C Seeing that he offered hope and I never had hope. I was full of despair, but the hope though was always in my mind … it not that it ever left me. But I was full of despair. Just that I couldn't come to grips with it because of my circumstances.

K What was happening as you died?

C I am looking down at and floating away from it. People gathering around me when I die. No one helping me. They're rolling me over. I was gone. I'm happy to be out of the body.

After the death experience, David is guided to a place to review that lifetime with greater wisdom and knowledge from a higher spiritual level of awareness. Every soul has a life review after each lifetime. This is a place of self-reflection.

Review of that Lifetime
from a Higher Level of Awareness

K It is time to review that lifetime now that you have more wisdom and knowledge then while you were in that lifetime. What gave you the greatest happiness in that lifetime?

C The Prophet.

K So he did give you happiness?

C Peace ... I felt safe. He talked about love ... it's so comfortable. I felt loved. His eyes looked through me when he looked at me.

K And you didn't feel much love in that lifetime? So how did it feel?

C It was wonderful ... it felt warm.

K So you felt different in his presence?

C I felt loved!

K What was difficult in that life?

C Eating ... I didn't eat much. I was very poor.

K Did you carry the feelings of lack of food in your current life?

C No.

K Is there a need for forgiveness of yourself or others in that lifetime?

C I was grumpy a lot.

K Do you need to release and forgive yourself for being grumpy in that lifetime?

C Yes.

> *He was able to release and forgive himself for his feelings of being "grumpy" in that lifetime. He was reminded that the Prophet would forgive him, and it was time to forgive himself and be free.*

K What did you learn or accomplish in that life?

C Letting go. Seeing with my ears. Listen to what is inside of me. Let go of ego … not to fear. There was no fear in him. The Master knows … to see the truth that is deep within. At my death it made sense! It made me hungry to know more. I was jealous of him.

K So you liked drinking with him?

C I liked it more when we were drinking. I didn't have much wine … my neighbors had wine. They were successful in the market place.

K So you had no fear when you were with him?

C Let the Master take over. The Master knows.

> *At this time he began to say Master instead of the Prophet, so it is apparent that Jesus is the Prophet. He confirmed the Prophet was Jesus, and that he only knew him as the Prophet at that time.*

K Why were you jealous of him?

C He knew more than what I knew. That's why he was so special. I liked it better when we were drinking.

K From a higher perspective what were the lessons learned?

C To believe in something. It was an empty life. But it is like a can that had one pea in it and even though I saw the pea, but I never reached in to take it. And I don't know why. Maybe I didn't feel I deserved the last pea.

> *What an insightful observation of that lifetime.*

K Why didn't you think you deserved it?

C Low self-esteem.

K Was the feelings of low esteem carried over into present lifetime?

C Somewhat.

K So it is time to release that feeling of low self-esteem. That was in the past and it is time to release it to move forward in your life. Remember what the

Prophet said that you are special, so bring forth what he said, and remember those words. So it is time to let it go. You did the best you could at that time under the circumstances. It is time to let it go, because that was in the past and no longer needed. Let go of the feeling of low self-esteem, however you feel will release those feelings of low self-esteem. Let me know when it is complete.

C It is complete. It's floating off to the sea.

> *David was able to release the feeling of low self-esteem from that lifetime. He saw it floating off to sea. Clients can have different ways of releasing issues from their past.*

K That is wonderful!

C It's gone.

K What gave you the greatest fulfillment?

C The Prophet's eyes! He knew who I was.

K Did you gain spiritually in that lifetime?

C It made me hungry to know more. I was jealous of him. Because he knew what I did not know. Why was he special? I liked it better when we were drinking. I didn't have much wine, my neighbors had the wine. They were successful in the marketplace. It was a beginning of a new direction. It was a necessary life.

K What would your past life self want to say to you?

C Understanding of God. (*Long pause*) There was something I had to release. Anger of not knowing. Why did I have to go through all this for a tidbit of knowledge?

K What would you like to say to that past life self?

C It was a beginning of a new direction. It was a necessary life.

> *I found this to be an insightful statement with David feeling it still was a necessary life, contributing to the beginning of his spiritual awakening.*

K So there is no need to hold onto that anger of not knowing. Because now you have that knowledge. So it is time to release the anger from that lifetime. At that lifetime you weren't ready, but now you are getting your answers. Can you let that go?

C I can let that go. It's gone.

David's Impressions After his Session

David spoke of some of his feelings and impressions after his session. When asked about his impressions after the session, he felt the session was vivid and very powerful. He spoke of having a vivid image of them farting and urinating, and having a good time. He spoke of the Prophet having such penetrating eyes. David spoke of the Prophet having a magnetism about him, as things and people were just drawn to him. In his explanation of the Prophet's death, he felt it took him a long time to receive the information. He said the Prophet was Jesus, but he only knew him as the Prophet at that time.

When he first entered the spirit world, he became aware of the presence of the disciples as well as the Prophet. He had a sense of such love. He said, "It's unlike energy I have felt before." In the part of the session he felt this life was a preparation for him to be spiritual guide in his next incarnation. After a period of four years David said that his experience "opened the door" for his spiritual awakening. He expressed that it was a "wonderful thing." He has since continued his spiritual quest with many new and exciting spiritual experiences.

Chapter Five

"Later, Joseph of Arimathea asked Pilate
for the body of Jesus. With Pilate's permission, he came
and took the body away."
JOHN 19:38

EMMA

Emma contacted me to conduct a Quantum Healing session as she was dealing with various health and emotional issues in her life, and she wanted some answers to those questions. At the time she was an aroma therapist. Before coming for her session, Emma had no prior knowledge that she was Joseph of Arimathea in a previous lifetime.

Emma begins her session without any mention of her being Joseph of Arimathea in the life of Jesus. As the session continued it became clear that she was Joseph, the Uncle of Jesus. In the Bible Joseph is mentioned, but there is no explanation of his relationship to Jesus, however Emma clearly states he is Jesus' uncle. In later sessions, several clients have also verified that Joseph was his uncle. While in the session, Emma's voice was very different from her normal speaking voice. It is important to recognize that not everyone's true relationships to Jesus was mentioned in the Bible, whether due to the deletions either purposely, or considered not relevant at the time. As Joseph appears to have had a close relationship with Jesus, it would make even more sense that a relative of Jesus would be allowed to retrieve Jesus body.

The Past Life Session

K When you come down to the surface tell me your first impressions. What is the very first thing you become aware of?

C I'm on a sandy beach. I'm male with animal skins ... very strong. I see a tent pitched in the sand. It is my quiet time and my get away place. I am a seaman of sorts. I'm on boats. The water is my life, my joy and it's heaven on Earth.

K Move to the time when you were on the boat. What does the boat look like?

C It's a cargo boat. I think we are moving stuff around. I make sure everybody else does what they are supposed to do.

K Are you like a captain?

C Yes. I can see myself. It's not the way I dressed on the boat, and I was [dressed] differently on the beach.

> *Joseph stated that normally he didn't wear the same clothes when he was on his boat.*

K What is happening on the boat?

C I see this again and I am talking. It's a working cargo boat and I am with Jesus. And we're talking. He is standing there, we are not really talking with our mouths. We are communicating with our thoughts. We are just comforting each other.

K Why are you comforting each other?

C We just find comforting in each other. We find comfort in each other's presence. Everyone is busy working and I'm standing. Everything is working out.

K Can the others communicate with Jesus?

C They are busy doing their work. We are merchants ... ship cargo.

K What type of cargo?

C We have wine barrels. I think there is cloth. [I am] involved in many things.

K How did you get to know Jesus?

C I say he is my son. Well, I see him as my son.

K Why did you see him as your son?

C I take care of him. He's not truly my son. He's the one and I have to guard to protect him.

K Why do you feel you have to guard and protect him?

C It's my duty. I love him. I enjoy his company.

K Are there others on this trip?

C No. It's just him and I. He comes with me. But there are the workers there.

K Why does he come with you?

C He's my son ... he helps. He has time away. He learns about many things.

K How does he do that?

C He travels with me. I take him to different parts.

K What areas do you take him to?

C Everywhere ... I would say China, but that's not what it is called. I would say Greece, France, Spain, and England. I also see a snowy areas where it is cold.

K Did Jesus ask you to take him to these places?

C I always did. No, I took him with me as a child.

K What do his parents think about you taking him as a child?

C It is good. He has to learn.

K What types of things is he learning?

C Many things ... of all nature and life. Everything there is to know about nature and he needs to know about the world.

K Does he study all the different religions?

C Yes ... of course! It is as it should be.

K You said you talk with Jesus in your mind. What kinds of things do you talk about?

C We don't really have conversations. We just have a connection.

K What kind of connection?

C A Love connection. It's as if we are men of few words, but much knowing that needs not be explained.

K How long does Jesus go with you?

C Sometimes months … years. We return home and we spend time with the family and enjoy the time with family. The family is growing, too many children. His mother is happy to see him.

> *This appears to be a logical explanation of Jesus' lost years that were not explained in the Bible. There were three other clients speak of Joseph taking Jesus with him to various places on his travels.*

K Does he have any brothers or sisters?

C Oh yes! It is a big family.

K Are you related to the family?

C I take care of them.

K What is your name?

C I am Joseph.

K How are you connected with the family?

C I am the protector! (*Spoken in a very loud voice.*) I am the Uncle. These are my brothers. (*Spoken with great conviction.*)

K Do you have a strong connection with your brother?

C My brother is gone … he died.

K So are you taking over for your brother?

C Oh yes! It is my duty! I am the guardian. (*Again spoken with conviction.*)

K How long ago did your brother die?

C Many years.

K When Jesus goes into town what does he do?

C He talks with everyone. He loves all people.

K What does he talk to everyone about?

C I will not say. I cannot say.

K Why can't you say?

C I don't know.

K It's okay, you can say, you are safe to tell.

C It is time to be quiet. These are times of silence.

>*During that lifetime Joseph felt he may put Jesus in danger, therefore he resisted telling me what Jesus talks about when he speaking.*

K So what does Jesus talk to you about? You are safe now, it is safe.

C He is a teacher. He is a Master. He is my beloved son.

K Why is he called the Master?

C Because he is!

K In what respect?

C He's wise. He knows many things. He is the true teacher.

K Are there false teachers?

C He is a Teacher of Truth.

K What does Jesus say the truth is?

C (*Very long pause*) I am getting angry! There is no need to talk of this.

>*Sometimes clients will resist telling me things they do not want to be discussed. In this case, Joseph appeared to be very agitated with me. He seemed to be very hesitant of speaking about Jesus, which would validate his feelings of being a protector of Jesus.*

K Why not? I am sure Emma would like to know.

C She knows and you know.

K She would like confirmation.

>*I will try to gather the information from the client in different ways. And sometimes they are willing to discuss it further, and sometimes they just refuse to answer. Joseph continues to be resistant to various questions presented to him.*

C She has been given it. She need not doubt. She simply must accept the truth.

K Now move to another important day, a day you consider to be important in that lifetime as Joseph. What is happening?

C He is gone now. He is dead ... he is on the cross. (*Crying*)

K Were you there?

C Yes!

K What were his final words?

C He gave charge and asked his brother to take of his mother.

K Was Jesus aware this was to happen?

C Yes. We all knew.

K Did he have many followers?

C Those who loved him followed him.

K Did he ever explain why this had to happen?

C He didn't need to, he knew and we all knew. Yes of course, this was his path. We all have our chosen path ... he knew his path. We all knew it, he knew it and his mother knew it. He loved people where ever he went, he was happy to speak to them. Wherever he went we was happy to speak to them. So there were big crowds and small. There were many [people].

K You said many loved him, but did they all follow him?

C There many who loved him ... who wanted to learn from him.

K Did you learn from him?

C I learned a great many things ... everything. I learned the Way. We were all taught in the same way.

K And what is the Way?

C The Way, the only Way ... the Way of the Father ... the Way of Truth.

K And you said he knew about his death?

C This was his destiny.

K Did he say anything else about his death?

C It is accepted.

K Did Jesus speak to you about where he was going after his death?

C He spoke of many things and many things we do. You cannot change your destiny.

K But don't we have free will?

C Yes of course you do! His love was so great. And his love of Yahweh, and his love for all of us. How could he change his destiny? His love would not allow him. That was his choice.

> *I found it interesting that she would say Yahweh instead of God in this statement. YHWH is the name of God in Judaism, as vowels were not used in ancient Hebrew. There are still some* Bible *versions such as the Jerusalem* Bible, *which use the name Yahweh.*

K What is your path as Joseph after Jesus died?

C Well … there is great hysteria. I must take and protect his mother. I must protect those who loved him.

K Why is there hysteria?

C There is great fear that many who have learned to love him, and there were many who walked the way he taught and spoke. They were fearful of us. They wanted to kill everyone.

K And who wanted to kill everyone?

C The Romans. Everyone … even I … they wanted to kill me too. I had to take them away to be safe. I had to protect them and bring them to safety!

K And where did you take them to be safe?

C Yes, many places, many lands. I have many merchant ships.

K Are you wealthy?

C Yes.

K Was Mary taken to safety and where?

C Yes, she was taken like everyone else. She was taken to safety.

K What country?

C It matters not.

K Emma would like to know.

C She knows. I don't want to talk about this anymore.

> *Once again he became very agitated and very adamant in his speech.*
> *I have had clients who would not reveal secrets from their past lives*
> *because they felt obligated to keep that secret. This was the second time*
> *that a client was so insistent, and at times annoyed with me when trying*
> *to acquire information about the secrets. He felt very strongly that he*
> *was the protector and he was always going to protect them.*

K What were the circumstances of Joseph's death?

C I died an old man. It's just a natural releasing and letting go.

K Moving away from the body. How are feeling? What is happening?

C It is complete.

K What is happening as you move away from your body?

C I was joined with my family. I am with my source. I will prepare for my next journey... but first I will rest.

After the death experience, Emma is guided to a place to review that lifetime with greater wisdom and knowledge from a higher spiritual level of awareness. Each soul has a life review after each lifetime. This is a place of self-reflection.

Review of that Lifetime
from a Higher Level of Awareness

K Now that you have more wisdom and knowledge in that lifetime, what gave you the greatest happiness in that lifetime as Joseph?

C To take and provide and share a life with him, and take care of him. And share a life and take care of my brother's wife, and his children. I was most fortunate ... a very blessed very blessed life. Many secrets to keep.

K Why were there so many secrets to keep?

C Because there were those who would kill all of us. We believed in the true God. Those who did not, feared us and they wanted to kill us all. They were threatened by the power of God within each and every one of us.

> *In this statement he explains why he felt he needed to keep his secrets which was related to the fear of those being killed for their beliefs.*

K Did Jesus teach you this?

C We were all taught this and we all knew this before his birth. We were taught as children in our community. It was a devoted community to the Truth and the Way.

> *This is a fascinating statement about their community knowing these things even before Jesus' birth, which might explain his connection of being taught by Essene teachers. In the community devoted to the Truth and Way being taught, this demonstrates another connection to Jesus' words of "I am the Way and the Truth" in John 14:6. And in Naomi lifetime as an Essene teacher, she said, "Jesus is the embodiment ... he is the Way."*

K Does it have a name, this community?

C We do not speak of its name.

K It's okay for you to speak now. It is safe.

C You are familiar with it? They were called the Essenes.

> *This is an interesting detail not spoken of in the* Bible, *in which Jesus and Mary were in the Essene community. Several clients also mention this connection to the Essene community. Due to the secrecy of the Essene community; this may be the reason why some clients weren't aware of their connection. It was made clear by Emma that it was to be kept secret the name of the Essenes. It also may have been a secret that Joseph of Aramethia was actually the brother of Jesus' father Joseph, because of safety concerns.*

K What was the most difficult aspect of that lifetime?

C There is no difficulty when you know the way and when you follow the way … but there are pressures. There are concerns for those you love. Sometimes they play heavy on your mind, but there is no real worry. How can there be when you just do what you have to do to bring forward your destiny.

K Is there a need for forgiveness of self or others?

C There is a holding on sorrow. There is holding on of sadness. Of course, he was the greatest that ever lived. We knew what his destiny was, and yet who wanted that, yet how could we not have not wanted to change and alter that. It was not to be. And yet is still saddens the human heart.

K It now time to release all that sorrow and sadness. That was in the past and we will leave it in the past. If Jesus was in front of you, what would he say to you? Wouldn't he want this for you?

C Yes. Of course. There is a rejoicing in my heart!

> *At this time she was breathing heavily during her healing. Many times a client will begin to exhibit heavy breathing when healing is occurring.*

I always wait until the client indicated that the healing is complete. Sometimes healing will take minutes and sometimes it can take longer. The time frame for healing is always dependent upon the client. Additionally, the degree of healing accomplished in a session is also dependent upon the belief of the client.

K What did you learn or accomplish in that life that can help you in the current life?

C Emma must know that her destiny must be fulfilled no matter what fear she may have around this life. She is safe and protected as I was as she was and as we all were.

After experiencing another lifetime, I asked Emma's subconscious to come through for even a higher level of awareness.

Emma in the Subconscious

K Do I have permission to speak to Emma's subconscious?

SC We agree.

K Why did the subconscious choose that lifetime with Jesus to show Emma?

SC It is of great significant that she realize her commitment, her devotion, and her love to the ultimate Supreme Christ.

K How will that help her in the current life?

SC She will accept that her love in that life for him ... has guaranteed her. She must recognize, she must accept that he will love her and protects her. For he remembers the great love and protection that he gave as Joseph in that life. She must accept this. She must have no doubt. Gratitude and his love for her and all that she did for him in that lifetime. She needs not fear. She is greatly loved. She is greatly protected. She must have absolutely no doubt.

K   How can the subconscious help her with her feelings of doubt?

SC As she reviews this message we bring to her ... she will accept it.

K   Thank you. Emma spoke of destiny and free will. Can the subconscious explain this?

SC Everything is not written, but there is free will. And yet there is a destiny. When you have a blueprint, let us say, for a house. You can never change the structure, the foundation of the house, or the house will fall. But within that house you have a kitchen, there are things you call aesthetics, that can be changed, but the solid foundation of the house should it be changed, would make the house collapse. The blueprint, the foundations, is the contract. We have you understand, if a partner refuses to honor the contract, another will come in to help you with that contract, your purpose, your destiny. Someone will come in to assist to fulfil her destiny, her path.

I found this to be a wonderful explanation of destiny and contracts. There were many other questions and healings that were addressed which was unrelated to her lifetimes with Jesus, therefore they are not included.

Note: The Joseph Emma spoke of in that lifetime, appears to be the Joseph Arimathea mentioned in the Bible. *In Luke 23:50, it states, "Now there was a man named Joseph from the Jewish town of Arimathea. He was a member of the council, a good and righteous man..." He was considered very wealthy at the time. Joseph asked Pilate for the body of Jesus, and provided his tomb. Sometimes, people were mentioned in the Bible, but not much else was told about their relationship with Jesus and the family. It was also thought that Joseph had vessels for trade. In the Bible, there are many references to Jesus on a boat as he was traveling from one location to another. Also in Dolores Cannon's* Jesus and The Essenes, *her client said that Jesus traveled with Joseph so he could expand his teaching to other parts of the world at that time.*

Emma's Impressions after Her Session

Emma came out of her session enthusiastically saying, "I love it here! I feel great!" She said she felt it important to stay in the body, even though she could feel herself trying to get out of her body. There was a sense of a pressure in her head and then came a like a "whoosh" sound, when healing was taking place. She said it was so strange. Emma said she was surprised that she felt comfortable saying things she wouldn't normally say to others due to their negative reactions.

Reflections after a Few Years

When I asked Emma how she felt the session had helped her she said, "For one thing it did help me to better realize why my strong connection was with Jesus, and now I feel I can talk to him more as a friend then some far away entity. I am accepting that maybe I was his Uncle; based on your session and a reading I got that stated the same. And this has helped me see myself in a much better light. I have a more peaceful attitude about my life. I have had, in my meditation, what I believe is flashback visions of us together traveling. And I also had visions of me as Joseph taking the family to another land that was safe." Emma was very happy to hear about my experiences with other clients who had verified that Joseph was Jesus' uncle, and had taken Jesus to various locations on his boats.

Chapter Six

"Some people in life and there are not very many, but there are people whose hearts and minds meet and resonate at center point, and then reflect that lightened vibration. You could not be in his presence and not feel Light energy. It was of Him and you felt and you knew you were close to God."
GRACE

GRACE

Grace previously had a past life regression with another past life therapist. She explained that she was looking for someone who was trained with the Quantum Healing Hypnosis method, and a friend told her about my work. At that time she was a successful business owner. When speaking with Grace before her session, she indicated that she has experienced vivid dreams about a lifetime with Jesus. Clients will sometimes tell me they have had dreams of other places and other times. These types of dreams generally are more detailed having realistic and vivid images, unlike a dream many of us experience nightly. These vivid dreams of other places and times are a way of the soul recalling and remembering lifetimes from their past. In our conscious mind, we sometimes deny and doubt what we are experiencing.

In her second past life experience Grace began by saying, "I'm Mary's sister." She said that she was Mary's older sister. She described herself wearing thin sandals with a leather band around it, wearing a long light blue gown. Grace indicated that she had to work very hard in that life. In the session, she continues speaking with great confidence that she was Mary's sister.

The Past Life Session

K You stated that you are Mary's sister. Are you Mary's sister, the mother of Jesus?

C Yes. That makes me very happy. She greets me as "sister."

K What is your name?

C Terese. (*Sounded like*)

> *Grace being unfamiliar with the name, had difficulty with articulating the name. Names can sometimes be difficult for clients to recall when there are differences in pronunciation. In researching the names Teresa or Tereza, I found them listed as Hebrew names.*

K You spoke of working hard, can you explain?

C I work in the house. [I work] much with my hands, much cooking ... healing, with family ... that's what we do.

K Were you close to Mary?

C Oh yes! I'm now 26. Oh! I have pain here, that's interesting. ... Oh, I lost children! (*Spoken with great sadness.*)

> *She indicated pain in her lower abdomen area which was later healed in her life review. Clients while in their past lives, are able to feel physically what is happening in their body.*

K How many children did you lose?

C Oh! I'm very sad. Oh! It's very hard. I'm very sad though. (*Spoken with deep sadness as she indicated she had lost four children, but has a daughter.*) ... It's very hard.

K Are you close to this daughter?

C Oh ... yes! And Jesus plays. They play together. My daughter Sarah is six and they play, and they get dirty together and play. They get very dirty ... very dirty. Just [having] fun with sticks and balls. We call them ... and they're late. And, "Where are they?" It's a big community and we all cook together and eat together. It is all very good. (*She indicated that Jesus was six years old.*)

> *As in Tiffany's session, she also describes young Jesus playing and having fun with his friends. She says "I feel dusty, dirty" when playing with her friends. And in Joy's session there is another confirmation of this*

account when she says," I see a stick."

K What is the community you spoke of?

C Many comings and goings ... teachers come and teachers go. The men talk all the time in circles. Family is a much bigger term in this life. I like this much better, we all take care of each other. The men will take off and some men will stay. We all take care of each other. It's a very good life. It's a kind and loving, peaceful life. Outside the wall ... are not so ... but that's okay.

K What is on the outside that you were speaking of?

C We are lucky from most of people. Most people don't want what we have.

K So do you live separately from them?

C Yes. Well we're close by, but again, we do not have a lot of wealth nor do we want a lot of wealth. So people leave us alone, because they don't want have what they want and that is by design. That keeps us faithful. It's a good life.

K What type of house or dwellings do you live in when in that life?

C They're all kind of connected ... with open windows. Cooking gets done off the back, kind of like a compound. Because there is a big common area with rough tables and benches and with many private areas off shooting from there ... that are each family's little sleeping space. You have rooms off the common area. There is a teaching room for the children. And then Elders have a fire area. They have their own area for meetings and readings, and sharing of knowledge, and community meetings. There are a courtyards. There is a teaching area for the children. Then there are the Elders. They have a fire area for meetings at night for sharing of knowledge and community meetings.

K What did they teach the children?

C The reading room is for the children. Because children must learn readings of our faith.

K What is your faith?

C It's of God and connectedness to the Earth and honoring the sun, moon, the stars. All of them are given by God. It's a give and a take between us and All of That Is. And the children learn early. We are pretty peaceful. (*Long pause*) We're a reverent group and a peaceful group, if you live from your heart. You do call us Essen-sits (*Essenes*) today. We have old wisdom. An old wisdom that will be preserved … yes.

> *Many clients speak of a connection between Jesus and the Essenes. Grace goes in great detail explaining how Jesus and Mary were involved in this community, including details about their beliefs and the differences from the other groups at that time. She also spoke of things being very secretive which may explain why this was not common knowledge for many in that lifetime. This aspect of the secrecy around the Essenes was also conveyed in Emma's session.*

K Did you notice anything different about Jesus as a child?

C No, but we knew he was groomed for learning from an early age. He was very bright but not in your ways. (*Suddenly, without being asked the question, she very fervently began with the following statement.*) Immaculate Conception is just silliness … right! He was destined for his path. Immaculate Conception is just silliness … just put on.

K Can you explain this?

C He was destined for his path.

K Did they know he was special?

C No. But Mary and Joseph and our community did. And it didn't matter, as it was from his time of birth. His destiny was driven by his heart in a beautiful way. And his passion grew with time. But he had a normal childhood … yes, [he was] a very normal child. But his capacity for knowledge couldn't be met without sending him away to learn.

K Where was he sent?

C To places, they were long and far away. [It was a] long journey by boat ... by sea ... long journeys. By fourteen years he was gone. He was traveling.

> *The* Bible *doesn't mention anything about Jesus' life from 13 to 30 years of age. The last reference of the young Jesus was at 12 years old, was when his parents took him to Jerusalem and then found him listening to the teachers at the temple in Jerusalem. There were many clients who said that Jesus traveled to many different places with Joseph. In her experience she said by the age of 14 he went to faraway places.*

K You said by boat, did someone take him?

C Oh yes, he couldn't go alone he was too young. There was a man ... he was one of the Elders. He was Joseph, a holy man that was of our community that took him south, and then he went somewhere were the mountains were. But they were on Joseph's boats. They were under Joseph's protection. We were blessed to have him. But we didn't know that Jesus was who he was to become. But it became clear when he came back.

> *There were three other clients that spoke of Joseph taking Jesus with him by a boat to different places. She also speaks of Joseph being Jesus' protector, as Emma also indicated in her session.*

K Did many know who he was to become?

C I didn't know. So when he came back ... Oh my goodness! I feel it all through my legs. (*Her present self began speaking of her leg discomfort. I then gave her a suggestion that she would feel no discomfort in her legs and then the discomfort was released.*)

When he came back from his journeys, there was passion in his heart ... a very strong passion in his heart. And he knew what to do, and in that he went to her and asked Mary for her understanding, knowing no mother wants to watch what was to become. But he did know at that time what was to pass, and he asked her to give him the strength. He actually didn't know exactly what would happen, but knew it wasn't going to be good, but knew it was important. And so he asked her... Oh! And he was so wise, he knew that if he asked her to hold that strength for him ... she would. Joseph, his father had passed by then. It was just Mary and me! Oh! He was so smart because she had to hold the strength for him. She couldn't go to her own sorrow because she was holding it for him. It was so wise of him ... it makes me cry, because it was so hard. But it was good work, and we knew we had to do it. It was so sad. Oh! Before he was going to die ... to be sending him before he knew he was to die ... to be him sending him this Power!

> *This is an amazing story of Mary holding the strength for Jesus, and how difficult it must have been for her and her sister. I could feel everything she was saying as it was spoken.*

K Was everyone in the community aware of this?

C No! They could not know ... they would have been in danger if they knew.

K Why would they be in danger?

C Oh! My goodness! The dangerous ones ... the less they knew. Our community could have been decimated and he didn't want them to be hurt. He wanted them to be safe. Many could not know and so many could not keep secrets.

> *It is reasonable to assume there was secrecy surrounding his connection to the Essences. Yeshua would have wanted to protect the community from harm. He also speaks of Jesus being groomed for learning, which was mentioned by several other clients. There seems to be many secrets kept for everyone's protection.*

K So Jesus never spoke of being in the Essence community to others. Is that correct?

C Oh, they knew who we were. They just didn't understand who we were, and it was best that way.

K Who are the others you speak of?

C The rest in our community could not know Jesus was to die. It didn't make sense.

K But did they know who he was?

C They knew. Jesus told them and it's the truth, that he was not alone of God ... that we are all of God. And so he never made himself different ... only us ... we did. It was hard not to sense and know his power ... Mary knew. He told Mary that he was to sacrifice and she went to God for that.

K Why was he to sacrifice?

C Because the message had to be carried forward in the world. It was all about his message. That he came to carry the message. But he had to do it ... if not another would be sent to do the same. It had to happen. Not all of us ... but in our circle we knew to hold the circle of light. And there was much work that Mary could do. Mary Magdalene brought much to that.

> *Previously, she mentioned there being an Elder's circle. She again speaks of a circle where they are holding a circle of light. This once again speaks of the power of the light and holding the light for others.*

K Did Jesus know Mary Magdalene?

C As an adult he did of course.

K How did he meet her?

C He came back from his journey. Mary was there. There is an awful lot of energy between the two of them. She wasn't around when he was young ... until after he was fourteen. He went away, and then he came back and then she was there.

K Was she in the same village?

C Yes, and it was fun because they would spar together. (Smiling)

According to Mary's sister, Jesus and Mary Magdalene knew each other before, and were friends when they were children in their village. Perhaps others may have not been aware of their earlier connection at that time.

K So you could see their connection?

C Oh yes!

K Were you aware that they were ever married?

C You know ... marriage in today's world is different from marriage back then. They were together and so ... actually he needed her for part of ... there is a part of the heart ... energy transfer. Part of the prayer work had to be done between the two of them together and they did it, and you could feel it, and it was palpable. Mary knew how to do that too ... my sister.

She said it was difficult to explain what we call marriage. Many times certain words in the past cannot be understood in today's language. Other client's said it wasn't marriage as we know it, but that they felt that they were very connected.

K So did you know Mary (*her sister, Jesus' mother*) was special too?

C Mary was pure of heart. She was of service ... well we were all of service ... to be of service that is who we are. We all are and it comes through our mother. It comes down through that ... it came from our lineage. Yes ... it's good!

In this statement she is speaking of Jesus' grandmother being of service to others as part of her lineage. According to the early Christian text of the Gospel of James, and Islamic tradition, Saint Anne or Anna, was Mary's mother and the maternal grandmother of Jesus.

K Did you ever hear Jesus speak? What did he say that resonated to you?

C Oh Yes. Well, he believed what I believed. We all believed the same, we still do.

We are one with God. And through the route to God, is from within ... through quiet and counsel. And some of our priests in our community are too harsh ... too stark. They believe that comes as getting closer to God is through harshness of self and others. That's not God. God is a loving God.

K You spoke of priests, so are there priests in your community?

C They are not priests, they're Elders, but some of the Elders are not in our community like us. But the other communities are harsh.

> *Grace initially called them priests from her current understanding of their religious role. However, it was made clear when I asked her about what they were called in that lifetime she then indicated they were called the Elders.*

K So there are other Essene communities?

C Yes, very much so.

> *This can help to explain some of the differences in people's impressions of the Essenes.*

K How many other communities?

C Let me ... look here ... (*She began counting*) Seven. Some are many hours away.

> *I felt Grace was accessing the Akashic Records when she said, "Let me look here" for additional information. The Akashic Records are the etheric records of everything that has been experienced, thought, spoken, or felt by each soul which is recorded for all time. Sometimes clients while in a very deep state are able to access these records. Edgar Cayce was able to access the records of peoples' past lives by accessing the Akashic Records. Besides Edgar Cayce, Helena Blavatsky referred to the tablets of light which recorded all human thoughts and actions, both in the past, present and future. Everyone can access the Records when seeking*

information, if it is for their highest good.

K So are there many differences of belief from those in your community?

C Oh yes! Some are very strict and that's how they think things should be. And other ones sell their soul. Some of them do commerce in a way to get coin, but it compromises them. So we stay in poverty because it stops that desire. It stops that humanness. (*Long pause*) Human nature that takes us away from God and the Earth and stars, and what's natural and how we are to be. If you add all of that [with the others], it gets complicated and takes people away from God. But we all believed it … yes. Now where Jesus brought back different wisdom that I didn't understand … it was when he came back from the mountains, there was like, meditation work that he knew how to do that I didn't understand.

> *It is interesting to note that when she spoke of selling their soul, she used the phrase "to get coin" which is a phrase that wouldn't normally be used to speak of selling and buying. In many sessions, clients refer to certain phrases or words that would be appropriate to the times, but would be out of character in their current life.*
>
> *Once again, she refers to the connection with God, Earth and the stars which suggests that there was a love and reverence for nature and the stars, as well as God. And she explained when Jesus came off the mountain she didn't understand his meditation method, which actually may suggest that he was accessing his subconscious.*

K What did Jesus say about meditation?

C He didn't say … he just used it. Jesus was a teacher. He truly was the most gifted teacher on Earth so far and that was how he understood how to put God's message to the man … to all men at all levels. Through the vibration of his voice, they would hear God. So it was something with the vibration. But He didn't teach it … He was it! (*What a beautiful statement.*) And I didn't know how he did it … we just knew he came back with the light and he could do it. Now, what was interesting, Mary Magdalene in her women's work, couldn't do the same. Mary couldn't do what he did, but she could add to it vibrationally … being plugged in. So, she could recharge him.

K Was there times when Jesus was tired?

C Yes, but sometimes he would get frustrated. So when he got frustrated, she could calm him down. She could help him to use Earth energies to regenerate. So she was always about the Earth energies. She also was an incredible healer. He didn't understand healing as she did. She could heal the bones … that wasn't what Jesus did. Jesus would heal the mind. She would heal the bones and the heart … so they worked together beautifully.

This was an interesting observation concerning Jesus' and Mary Magdalene's healing gifts. In Ellie's channeled session, she also spoke of Mary's healing abilities. Mary is never mentioned in the Bible as a great healer. This may be due to the fact that women were not considered as important as men at that time in our history. In those times women were considered to subservient to men, and in their religious practices they were separated. According to their religious law, women were subordinate to either father or husband.

In the GNOSTIC GOSPEL ACCORDING TO MARY, *it was stated that even Peter did not consider Mary Magdalene to be as important as they were and not be taken seriously. In one of the passages Peter answered and spoke concerning these same issues, "Did He really speak privately with a woman and not openly to us? Are we to turn about and all listen to her? Did he prefer her to us?"*

K The Bible speaks about Jesus healing lepers, the blind and many others physical and emotional difficulties. Is this true?

C Yes, he would do that. It was mind energy. That is what people made decisions about themselves. Then Jesus would clarify and release, and that was through their electrical body.

> *Here is where she clarifies that Jesus possessed the understanding that one's physical difficulties are brought upon by their own selves. I found this to be true in my work. Once they understand the emotional reason for their physical issues from the past, they were able to release and heal the body.*

K Did they have groups of healers that helped in your community?

C The women did. Mary taught the healing works. Mary traveled after Jesus' passing.

K Did Jesus teach others as well?

C Yes, so many of us learned. Again, they taught on different things. He taught of understanding God. The men would not hear her. She knew God as Jesus knew God. But it was Jesus' job to have men teach the men of God ... of what God was. They wouldn't listen to her. It didn't matter because she was about healing the heart and teaching the women. Mary also had her miracles, but they are not spoken of.

> *As mentioned previously, women at that time were not taken seriously, and the Bible was written by men, it would make sense that these miracles by Mary were not included. In Ellie's channeled session, Yeshua confirms this by saying, "There were other disciples, my students, those who followed me, who did miracles even beyond what I did in that time. They are not written about."*

C My job was to be by Mary's side. She is my sister. I loved my sister.

It was very clear from the beginning, that she deeply loved her sister.

K Did you ever travel with Jesus as followers?

C We're family, so we don't follow! (*Laughing*) We would still take him to task …
in that work. He is still was a man, so you take him to task on occasion, or if
you didn't serve his mother properly. And sometimes we would be caught up
in his work and he had to be taken to task to be reminded … to serve his
mother. It was not for Jesus to lead the other Elders to provide supportive
directions. He needed to care for her. He needed to give direction to voice.
Instead, he would get caught up in the politics of the day and his mission and
not [her]. And she would make excuses for him and then I would take him to
task … and that was okay. He would have such great passion.

*This paragraph demonstrates that Jesus also had to be aware of his
impact on his family according to his aunt. She also explains that she felt
he should be taken to task by his family. Again she shows her devotion to
her sister Mary. These statements show us the human side of Jesus and
his family, which is not often spoken of in the Bible.*

K So did we travel with him?

C Sometimes we traveled with him and sometimes he traveled on his own. And
people followed him and he had a following. We knew where to find him.

K Did you hear things about Jesus while he was traveling from others?

C Oh yes, there was so much traveling with and between our groups and them.
We would have travelers from afar that would come and ask for validation of
things they heard. And that was good, and it was important to carry that on.
But Mary wouldn't speak of it.

K She wouldn't talk about his travels and what he did?

C No. She would never … justify … not right word … she didn't care of what people believed or didn't believe. And she knew once they were in the presence of him, they would come to understand what others spoke of. So she didn't get into it because it could be exhausting.

This is an interesting observation about Mary not allowing others to dim her light.

K You spoke of being in the presence of Jesus, how did you feel in his presence in that lifetime?

C Some people in life and there are not very many ... but there are people whose hearts and minds meet and resonate at center point, and then reflect that lightened vibration. You could not be in his presence and not feel light energy. It was of Him and you felt ... you knew you were close to God. And people at that time needed that, and so it was a lovely thing to be able live with that kind a person around, and to be touched by God all the time.

What a beautiful statement!

K Did you actually see a light around him, or were there others that saw the light?

C You would feel it. You could feel it. It's a resonance.

K What is your description of Jesus appearance?

C (*She began laughing.*) You paint him more handsome than he was. Well, he was handsome by terms of that day but not of today. It is different than your pictures or statues. He was quite flexible. He was quite healthy because all the things he ate were blessed by Divine light because he drew the light into it. He could do that, and he taught us how to do that.

K Can you explain blessing your food?

C But it's more than blessing your food. It's drawing the light down in and up and in, because part of this comes up from the Earth and its understanding at the point of intersection how that creates a different level and dynamic that's been lost today. So it's like today when you bring down the light, you got only have half the equation. You missed the other half ... drawing it up from the Earth because that's where the communion point is. Jesus and Mary knew how to do that and taught us how to do that.

This is an interesting statement concerning blessing our food. It is reasonable to assume that Jesus would bless his food. Many people today bless their food by saying blessings and prayers before meals.

K What was his father's occupation?

C Carpentry ... [There are] big buildings, compounds. Oh ... I see! Something fell on him. He had a back injury. It didn't kill him but it really slowed him down. There was discomfort when he traveled but he still could move around. (*Long pause*) I get the sense ... it's interesting ... when Jesus went to the cross, I don't feel Joseph's energy there at all. Joseph passed, because just before Jesus left there were sadness in his heart before he left. Many of us were there to support Mary about that as well as the community. We kept Mary busy to help.

She indicated Jesus was about fourteen years old when Joseph died. She said Joseph was eight years older than Mary.

K What was Jesus's most important message that he wanted to convey?

C God's most important message, "Love one another as I have loved you."

K And did everyone respond to that message positively?

C In our community ... yes. Others didn't understand, but they wanted to. Many wanted to ... that was part of the sadness. But life was hard then ... very, very hard. To give up what little many had to follow Jesus knowing that the power in the world at that time was very different than that, you didn't do that.

K But there were followers?

C Oh, yes!

K Did some followers come for a period of time, and then some leave and come back?

C Well, the community was very transitory. In our community there was much in flux because we were also trying to preserve some of the Ancient Knowledge. Some of it we were trying to keep away ... keep it safe. That time period was all about control of information and history, and so we were still trying to preserve and protect.

> *In this statement it was clear how important it was to the community that the "Ancient Knowledge" be preserved and safe. Many clients felt it so important to preserve this knowledge by hiding it in order to keep it safe.*

K Who wanted to control the information?

C Oh, the power of the time and the ones that had the money... the Pharisees. So our job was to preserve ... to protect and spread.

K In the Essene community did they have a book or scroll of knowledge?

C We used many scrolls. Our belief was that the word of God came from many forms throughout the globe, and to have an open sharing across all of those.

> *This was a very different concept, considering the times when the Jewish religion was very rigid and there was only one way of thinking. In this community there seemed to be an acceptance of all faiths rather than just the one.*

K So you had variety of many scrolls from different places in the world?

C Yes. They moved from community to community. There wasn't just one way. God's word showed up in many places.

> *This was an important statement about this community, that there wasn't just one way, but other sources of spiritual information was accepted. Unlike today, some view the Bible as the word of God, and no*

other sources are accurate in their eyes.

K Was the Essene community different from those around you?

C Oh, very definitely! We were a poor community. We were not the moneyed, nor did we want to be. So there was the moneyed Jewish faith. Their belief in God looked very differently.

K And how did it look different?

C Oh! It was loaded with money ... so I see lots of gold coins and I see lots of exchanging. It was the political structure ... so it became the politics, it wasn't religion. It was just politics, and it was power and cronyism and injustice. And all in the name of religion which had nothing to do with love and God!

It is interesting to compare this statement with what we hear today about religion in the world being more about politics and not love and God.

K Did your community have strict rules?

C No! It all depended on who had the money. They just chose to listen or not listen, depending upon the need of that time or what the community wanted. So there part that they would pay attention or not pay attention to.

K When was the first time you would hear Jesus speak?

C Well he grew up with me. Many would come to our community at night to hear him at the dinner hour and he would talk. I did not go out and I wouldn't go to see him speak. It would be informally in the courtyard after dinner and then there would be many. But what was interesting in those times, is that within our community he would come in our community and he would teach after dinner. And many would come to hear him. And the women and children would also listen as well. In terms of him speaking ... much of what he was teaching was what religion was not but God's message. He was trying to correct the damage done in the outer community. Letting people know that

God was in each of our hearts, and that if we went inward through prayer, and if we did not fill us up with ourselves ... there would be room for God. And money complicates things and not unless it's given back. And how do we treat each other and even what many call enemies. And he tried to help. So then when he was teaching the apostles, he was teaching at a higher level because again they were taught to be teachers. That was a different lesson all together than when he was speaking to many.

> *In many years of working with the subconscious, I have found this to be true that there are different levels of awareness, which is dependent upon the level of understanding of that person. So when teaching the apostles, she explained Jesus' teachings were at a higher level of understanding than the masses.*

K So were you privy to this information?

C Oh yes! The information is the understanding of how to raise the minds of common man as well to raise our own vibration ... as you call it vibration, raise our vibration so it can be better heard, and then to be aware of how it's landing to be able to read that. And that was difficult work for quite a while for some of the followers to get out of themselves and understand what he was trying to teach them. But it was important that they learned, because if not, his work would stop, so they were to carry it on. So there was a certain amount of pressure to make sure they truly learned the skills to become, and know their message had landed and to be birthed in the followers.

> *In this statement she spoke of the importance of higher level awareness in order to teach others the messages of Jesus. This was also confirmed by other clients.*

K How was he able to accomplish this?

C Through speaking and then by exercises ... by checking and their learning and to read their own body. There was also telepathic piece to this, something with ... here. (*At this time she began pointing to location of her third eye.*)

K The third eye?

C Yes, but a resonance ... being able to open it ... communicate it, and then have it mirror back so that you know, and then look to the heart and closing it again. Oh, and many more of these kinds of the things of which ... some I was good at and sometimes I was not.

> *The third eye is your connection to spiritual wisdom and insight. By opening up the third eye, it allows you to access various psychic abilities for deeper spiritual guidance. The location of this chakra is located in the middle of your forehead between your eyes.*

K What were you good at?

C Vibrationally I was very sensitive, so I could pick up from quite a distance. So Mary and I would use this to communicate across distance ... so Jesus taught us.

> *Another interesting statement that is not included in the Bible and something that Grace would not have known previously.*

K Are you speaking of communicating telepathically?

C Yes, through long distances.

K How were you taught this?

C It came through deep prayer work, where you are deep cleansing. You know the diet of today doesn't support that kind of clear work. You really have to have your system has to be quite clear in order to send and receive.

K Are you speaking of having a vegetarian diet?

C Yes. Not a lot of death in that body.

K Did you learn anything different from Jesus that you didn't learn in your community?

C Part of my work in that life was to hold up the energy. That was part of my work and Jesus knew it.

K What energy did you hold up?

C There was a certainty of the path ... that if you picked up on the humanist is of that time. If Jesus didn't have people surrounding him that were really strong in understanding the bigger picture and holding God's Light ... that vibration of those times of terror and just putting upon people would have undermined him. And so he would have to run or there were a lot of things he could have done. So my place was to be holding him ... you don't have words for it, sending him the loving vibration, so he could stick through it and knowing he wasn't going to be painful for him. He didn't leave the body, but he was such a powerful ... he could hold himself inside, so none of that entered him. We also had to take on some of [vibrations] ... there is a transmuting of the fear ... that's why. So as the time approached and the natural humanist of the fear of what lay ahead ... came to Jesus. Our job ... me, Mary [and] three male Elders ... our job was basically to take the fear out of him and to transmute it. Oh! I am not sad. Oh! God's energy to protect ... to pull it out, and he counted on us for that, and he felt our Love.

K How was this accomplished?

C Through very intense prayer work ... circle work. It was done with very peaceful grounded circle work. And it was good and it was done. And it was such a painful time for the community. They felt they lost all hope. It was a difficult time and it was very difficult afterwards.

> *In these statements it appears that Jesus had a great deal of help to hold his light from those who truly loved and protected him. It was also interesting that Grace, Mary, and three Elders would help Jesus release the fear by holding the light through prayer and circle work.*

K Did Jesus know what would happen?

C Yes. It was very clear. He knew he was to come to create the story and that's what he did. Then, what we did with the story was up to us. Some of it has been good and some of it has not been so good.

K What is the least accurate about the life of Jesus that you call not so good?

C Man's way is to be exclusionary. So all of the exclusionary parts of any of God's story, is human!

> *This explains the concept of separation is from a human perspective, and not the belief in Oneness spoken by Jesus.*

K So all of those parts of the *Bible* are not correct?

C Well, it was made by humans!

> *In this statement she speaks of the* Bible *being made by humans therefore not being totally the Word of God as some believe.*

K Did the Essences believe in life after death and reincarnation?

C Yes. They knew it was a journey.

K Did Jesus speak of his other lifetimes?

C In the world today that is kind of like an entertainment piece ... that was just a way of being in those days. So it just was.

K Did you feel kindness around Jesus?

C Oh yes, passion, passionate kindness. It you follow God's path ... your step each day is divinely given and clear. But you must say well rooted and not removed from it for it is very easy and not to wonder.

> *This appears to be another explanation of being grounded.*

K Was Jesus arrested? Did you hear or were you aware of him being arrested?

C I heard. Again arrested wasn't the word being used then. He was captured ... he was imprisoned. He was driven by those that were afraid of the following that he was getting. Many of the working class were following him, and any kind of coordination for the workers ... worked against the political direction. Oppression wouldn't work well.

It was quite interesting that another client spoke of him being captured, and didn't like the word "arrested" being used to describe what was happening to Jesus.

K So Jesus had a large following?

C Yes, but it was not well coordinated ... just because [it was] all through word of mouth and word of heart. There was a knowing that he was coming. There were people that were watching and waiting. And it wasn't just in that small community, and that it was throughout a great geography.

K So did he go to many lands?

C And even if he hadn't, the work that he accomplished had been tried prior in the past and didn't come to pass. If it hadn't work with him, it would have been tried again and again ... would have been tried one more time, so it was by design!

K You called him Teacher. Did anyone else call him by another name such as the Messiah or Son of God?

C He wouldn't allow himself to be called the only Son of God. It would have made him angry. Yeshua, um ... that's it!

After initially calling him Jesus, when asked "What was his name?" she called him Yeshua. This was another confirmation that "Yeshua" was the name that he was called at that time.

K Did you ever meet any of the disciples, apostles, as we call them presently?

C They were all in the learning. They all came along through the passages of his life. They had to learn so they came and they lived with us. Some I liked and some I didn't like.

K Who didn't you like and why?

C (*Long pause*) Something about Mark ... didn't work for me. I just know. Peter was noble in his ideas and intent, but it wasn't sound.

K Which one did you like?

C John. I get a very warm hearted feeling.

K Was Judas responsible for Jesus capture?

C I don't get the negative from him. I didn't get that sense. I feel I have done enough ... I feel like I have no more. I'm wearying.

> *Sometimes clients express being tired and wanting to end the session. I respect their wishes. I then ask if I can continue to ask a few more questions. So permission was granted. She then wanted to access her subconscious, so we needed to move ahead from that lifetime.*

K Just one more question. Did Jesus come to those after he died on the cross?

C You mean did he resurrect?

K Yes.

C See again, it's a story that's told in its own version ... in a common man's version. In terms of vibrational understanding of what happened, you know he never dies. He never did die. His body is gone at that point.

K What happened to his body?

C I don't know.

> *Many times you hear from a client that they do not know the answer, which validates the session, since they will not say anything that they have no previous knowledge of at that time.*

Grace in the Subconscious

K Do I have permissions to speak with Grace's subconscious?

SC You can. (*Breathing very heavy*)

K Why was the lifetime with Jesus shown to her?

SC It has been time and she is aware of that, although she was not ready until now. There is integrity in the understanding, and understanding what her place today is, in that a piece of who she is today ... that needed more time to materialize in her current life ... in order to understand and honor who she is at this time on the planet. This is the beginning of a different layer of work for her and she is now ready for that new layer of work. She would always honor it with integrity but because of the lack of self-confidence ... she would not have been able to give it its full breath. She is ready now!

My subconscious also explained that it was time for me to know. Therefore when it is time for us to know the information, it will be revealed.

K Was everything completed and released from that lifetime?

SC Very much so! There will be more clarifications over next several days!

When communicating to clients, the subconscious will convey to them that there will be greater understanding and clarification even after their session. However, clients need to be open and listen to that voice within for greater understandings and healing to occur. There may also be signs given or dreams that will reveal what needs to come forth. It is always a choice to become more aware.

K Can subconscious explain why some people have different interpretations of the events in the life of Jesus?

SC Once again, all of us have filters based on our humanism and our position. There was much fear on the planet at that time, and this individual did not hold fear like many did, so her viewpoint will be different. Her job was to hold that strength for Jesus and her sister.

The subconscious explains that there were different perspectives at that time, as well as different experiences creating our reality. It was interesting to find the subconscious explain that fear was also a factor in those times of great fear. The present world situation can also be described as a time for fear, so it is important for all of us to hold that strength in bringing light to the planet.

K What spiritual Masters guides her?

SC Joseph of Aramethia is a part of that community, and continues to guide her spiritual progress.

K Was Joseph of Aramethia the Joseph that you spoke of that took Jesus to other lands?

SC Yes.

Many clients described Joseph of Aramethia as the uncle who took Yeshua to other lands. It is fascinating that he is her guide in this life.

K Was he a relative?

SC Yes, a family member ... an extended family member.

K So was she connected to Joseph of Aramethia in that lifetime?

SC Yes.

K And how was she connected to him?

SC Through a relationship. He was part of the community and they respected each other greatly.

SC There will be more clarification in the next few days.

K Why was it allowed to be so different than it really was?

SC Because all our listenings are different, so to have it broadly across a large population ... what that one hears and lights up from it, is going to be different.

SC Thank you for honoring us!

K Thank you for honoring me with your wisdom.

Grace's Impressions after Her Session

Grace said, "It's funny when I think of him. I see him as a nine year old playing with my daughter. I vividly remember, so there was none of that mystique around him. Before he went to the cross, Mary was at his feet and I was there. I do remember, the scene kept flashing in my face." Many times clients are not telling me everything that they are experiencing. After the session they are given the opportunity to recall other events or feelings that took place in that lifetime which were not expressed in the actual session. Some clients convey more information after the session, while others need more time to process without much discussion. Grace was able to speak clearly, but at times could not find the correct words to convey her message.

"I just remember willing his strength and courage. I didn't have this incredible sorrow, mourning. It's like when you have contrary emotions to what's happening. It validates it in a way. That part was interesting. He knew how to communicate with people on fifth grade level because that is where some people are. And that was a gift as a teacher was to be able to be heard for all these different levels of people." Again this is interesting observation about their understandings of what Jesus was trying to convey to people on their level of awareness.

Grace also said, "It explains the whole feeling of being aunt-like. You know when you're an Aunt, it's like not on a peer level. I was with his mother and I had no idea it was like that, but that makes but that makes sense now. Mary was very powerful. But Immaculate Conception...hogwash!" In Grace's session she was very adamant that Immaculate Conception is a false narrative.

Chapter Seven

"But the Counselor, the Holy Spirit, whom Father will send in my name, he will teach you all things, and bring to your remembrance all that I have said to you." JOHN 14:26

".... do not be anxious how you are to speak or what you are to say; for what you are to say will be given to you in that hours; for it is not you who speak, but the Spirit of your Father speaking through you." MATTHEW 10:19; 20

RUTH

Ruth was referred to me by a friend. At the time of the session she was a stay at home mother, working part time with her husband's business. She came to ask questions about her guides and angels to gain greater spiritual understanding. She has a very uplifting and positive outlook on life.

In Ruth's Life between Life Session (*LBL*) Ruth was guided to the interlife between incarnations to review her past lives with her Council of Elders. The Council members offer only encouragement and advice, there is no sense of judgment. More information about the session is provided in the Chapter, *The Process Explained*. One of her questions was to ask if she could channel Jesus. Later in the session she was later able to access the subconscious where she began to channel Jesus. Ruth was my first client who channeled Jesus.

The Session in the Life between Life Spiritual Exploration

K What was Ruth's most significant life?

C In the presence of Jesus.

K Does Ruth want to review that lifetime?

C I want to … but I don't want to make it up.

K The Council is not going to allow you make it up. They will show this lifetime on a type of screen.

> *During the Life between Life sessions, clients sometimes describe seeing their lifetimes unfold on a type of screen, like a movie. Once given*

encouragement, Ruth began to speak freely allowing her story to unfold. When the conscious mind begins to doubt there is a blockage to the information and clients need more encouragement to continue with their life story.

C (*Long pause*) "I see a boat. I'm at the edge of the water."

K What is happening? What are you experiencing?

C It's basically what you would think of for a sermon.

K Is it like the Sermon on the Mount?

C It's kind of like that. Not sure if it is that one. There are crowds of people down here at the water, and the place is filled with love and joy. And I believe I'm a woman. I've been tired of feeling how I've been feeling. I'm just worn out.

K How did you hear about this gathering?

C   From another woman, like an aunt, or grandmother. Some woman above me. She heard about Jesus and encouraged me to stay here and to listen what he has to say. And as soon as I get there … you don't even have to hear a word … it's just being there, you can just feel it. So that first and most important message … now the Council is reminding Ruth … is that what she does know is true! That's Jesus' message that we can all do exactly what he has done! He totally understands what happened, that to get the message across, people are so amazed by it that they looked outward before they looked inward and when they looked outward, they put them up on a pedestal. He totally understands why it happens. He didn't think it would be so many and so few that really remembered the truth of it. He thought it would get passed down. Just being in his presence … I'm like, several hundred feet away and I can literally feel the warmth of his heart. I can't even see him, but I can feel him, but I know exactly where he is in the crowd because I can feel it coming through everybody. And it's almost as though it catches all the other hearts with it and it just keeps growing more and more. And the mind gets sucked into it like a magnet and you get attached to it too ... and this is what he is showing us. This is what he wanted everybody to do. This is what he was hoping we would do. He did do his work, he just misunderstood that his work wasn't meant to be completed then. He thought his work was over and done. Not that it would take millennia for it to be understood completely by the masses.

That is what he wanted to show us that it's like putting a toy ... where you put it together and make a bigger and bigger sphere. Maybe it's just like a big mass of magnets. He is a really strong magnet just because he understood heart ... as any Master truly does. But he found a different way to talk to people about it. There has been so many Masters on the planet ... than anyone has ever realized ... but not every Master knows how to share the information with the public. The Council thinks it's funny to say, (*Laughing*) ... but that's part of being human in that experience, and communication is part of it. Some Masters could have been more masterful by realizing that they were in the presence of another heart and joined theirs, it would be more amplified than they felt it in that moment. So Jesus understood that.

> *This is a fascinating observation that Jesus had such a deep connection with people that other Masters did not seem to possess. There has been a consensus among clients about Jesus' charisma. I found the similarities interesting between Ruth's description of Jesus being a strong magnet to people, and when Ellie explains our connection to God is like being drawn to a magnet.*

C We are near the water and it goes up a hill a little and the water goes out. It's almost like a part of peninsula ... it's like a mountainous peninsula. He's going up the hill. It's like the masses are coming down. And it's like a party and everybody is happy. (*As Ruth is speaking she's actually making you feel like you are there as she moves to various locations.*) It's like fishes and loaves ... but no one is starving. It's almost like everyone there is working together. We made the food, we created it. It wasn't just Jesus.

It was like a group miracle!

Unlike the Bible's *interpretation, Ruth calls it a group miracle.*

K So they all created it?

C Yes, Jesus started it and everybody fed into the energy. He was the spark of the energy, because people have more problems with spark. Because his spark is more like a fire ... it's so much easier to attach yourself to it.

K Did you follow him or just listen to him that day?

C I wanted to follow him. My time with him was very short, but I wanted to follow him and be in his presence all of the time because it felt so good. But I didn't need to. It was after a very short time ... the number 3, I don't know if it was 3 years, 3 months or 3 sermons. I was to go off do my own work ... my own ministry.

K And what was that ministry?

C Showing how this heart magnet thing works. So that is what I'm supposed to do now. In using that and also the idea of the individual and the group, so maybe by bringing the heart magnet piece. It's a missing piece of the puzzle. So I can see myself walking around. I have very dark hair ... it's very long. I feel like a type of band on my head, and I put that as decoration in my hair. I just loved it! I did have sandals ... which seems like someone gave them to me as a gift.

K Did you walk alone?

C I felt like I went door to door in a village for a while, and then some people would say, "You should come to another town with me and sort of be my guide for a while." And those people would fall off and another group would form. I was with a few people at one time, but always different people. I would be with two or three people for three weeks and we would go all around the town. And the next group would show me around, and then the original ones they would go back to their homes and spread the teachings that way. It worked, but why did it die off?

K Why didn't this progress? What does the council say?

C It did work. I became disenchanted somewhere.

K Why did you become disenchanted?

C I didn't quite understand the benefit of ego yet. So I got so fed up with ego. I didn't bless it, so I got caught up in hating ego. So unfortunately I stopped my work. (*She began to cry.*) I don't know if it killed me or I forgot about it and detached.

K What does the Council say?

C You convinced yourself it was a dream. You convinced yourself that it wasn't real.

K In that lifetime?

C Yes, as that lifetime ended. Because I lived for a very long time. So Jesus became such a distant memory that I convinced myself it wasn't true.

K Do you need to release any of those feelings?

C Of course it is always a good idea. Let go of when you just gave up on yourself. That you gave up on the whole picture and that you gave up on God in a way. You gave up on the perfection of God and the perfection of this whole thing. This whole drama.

K Can the Council help Ruth understand? Does Ruth understand now?

C We understand why it happened. She understands ... as the Council helped her to understand.

Ruth's Impressions after Her Session

Ruth felt that she already knew some of the information provided, but by having this experience it helped her validate her feelings and validate those experiences. She said it was a perfect time for her to come and have this support in order to heal. Ruth also felt I asked her some questions that she would not have asked herself. She said, "It feels much better you were reminding me not to judge what was coming through." Many of us tend to judge our experiences and feelings and not believe them to be true. Ruth also felt it was helpful to have someone guide her through the experience in order to have a greater sense of that lifetime.

Ruth's Second Session While in Her Subconscious and Channeling Jesus

"They weren't so much changed as they remembered!"
RUTH

Ruth decided she would come back for another session to access her subconscious for more answers. She felt she wanted to know more about her lifetime with Jesus. After experiencing another lifetime, I asked Ruth's subconscious to come through at the highest level of understanding and wisdom. In her first session she asked if she could channel Jesus, and I agreed. I am always open to new avenues of learning. Jesus came through in another channeled session with Ruth.

Ruth in the Subconscious

K Do I have permission to speak with Ruth's subconscious?

SC Yes.

K How was Jesus's incarnation different from the other Masters?

SC He appeared to each of the Masters.

K How did he appear to them?

SC He wasn't in those lifetimes. Sometimes he appeared quite often, almost as often as a playmate.

K Is he appearing to any Master now?

SC I can't answer that!

> *Sometimes we are not to know everything and the subconscious will not answer the question.*

K Did Jesus ever incarnate as thinking of being separated from divine love?

SC NO! That's what makes it different! He had the question of understanding everyone around him then and that a little more of Jesus' path. It was never about being separated, but of understanding everyone thoughts of others being like the opposite ... not understanding. Coming to that understanding ... Jesus over here and everyone over there ... complete understanding and no understanding. So you first understand ... so they don't get this then move to this, and hopefully they will understand what he knows.

K In one of her questions, she wants to ask Jesus directly. Can we speak with Jesus?

SC Yes!

K And how does the subconscious accomplish this?

SC Because we are all connected!

K   So we would like to speak to Jesus now. Is that possible?

SC Through me ... yes!

Channeling Jesus

At this point in the session Ruth began to channel Jesus.

I will continue using the C for the client even though Jesus is speaking through her.

K Did you rise in the body? Did you ascend?

C Yes.

K Was it agreed upon?

C It was agreed upon.

K Did you reincarnate before?

C Yes.

K And who were you in those lifetimes? Can we know this?

C Not Yet! (*Jesus spoke with a firm tone in this statement.*)

K Were you other Masters?

C Masters you don't know.

K Will you literally be back on Earth?

C Yes.

K When and how soon will you come to Earth?

C Soon. All that's not necessary for you to know.

   Once again certain information will not be given that is not for us to know.

K Will you come as Jesus?

C Yes. To the masses, quietly. That is why you and Karen experienced that life of

James and it will happen more and more. That is why she was shown this before.

Ruth is referring of her past life experience with James when James came to her in spirit. So I am assuming Jesus will come back in spirit.

K Thank you!

C Thank you for your gratitude.

K What was your life on Earth really like?

C Like playing a game. It was fun … just like playing a game despite the stories of sorrows.

K I have heard from other clients that you laughed a lot. Is that correct?

C Most definitely. Don't you laugh during games? But there is fun in the games. There is still fun and some strategy but there is no losing here.

K Did you remember from the start that you were created in divine love?

C I was never separated from it. But just as Ruth was questioning why others didn't understand, there was a little difficulty. I had difficulty understanding why not everyone understood as I did.

K What was your childhood like? Did you have what we call a "normal" type of childhood or was it different?

C It was special, but it wasn't as different as you might have thought it may had been.

K Why was it special?

C Because there was a lot more light. Because even in dark moments, there was always so much light!

K What were the dark moments?

C Just comparatively speaking, how other lifetimes have darkness and heaviness and sadness. Even if I was around others who felt that, I was always connected to my light, because I did not know separation.

K Did you die on the cross for our sins?

C It was for example ... for understanding. Despite the worst thing that could ever imagine ... there is still more.

K There is still more, can you elaborate?

C Despite all the negative things that go along with dying on the cross ... the pain ... the torture ... the complete opposite of love ... there is still love. That does not kill love. Love still reigns, even amidst the worst the physical could imagine.

K Were you able to leave the body before the pain got too difficult for you?

C I could have, but I didn't.

K Why did you choose to experience the pain?

C For the experience!

> *Years later, Tiffany also spoke of Jesus' experience in that lifetime as a learning experience.*

K And what did that experience show you?

C To be compassionate to the pain that others feel, so I could understand more.

> *Jesus provides us with a valuable insight in this statement. When having a challenge and difficultly in a lifetime, the soul can learn greater compassion. By experiencing the same feelings associated with difficulties in life, you can walk in the shoes of another with an understanding on a deeper level than if you had not experienced the same difficulties in your life. But I found it rather interesting that Jesus expressed this as a learning experience.*

C But that was to actually understand the physical.

K So that was something for your growth to learn?

C Yes. I might be Jesus, but I have more to learn too! Yes. Everybody has a path. There is ascension in all of us!

K What would happen if we didn't incarnate?

C I have something to tell you, but you might not understand it. I am one of many. There are others throughout the universe like me.

> *After the session she spoke of a feeling and the experience of seeing many stars. She said, "I was not sure I should say it, but felt she (Karen) would understand." … "I felt like it was a big secret."*

K On other planets?

C Yes. But not sticking to one or the other, but traveling. And that's the connection to divine love from the start. Not ever knowing separation.

K As a group, do you have a name that you are called?

C No we don't need a name.

K Ruth wants you to tell us a story we haven't heard about you?

C As a baby I could float!

> *I found Ruth's question truly insightful, in asking Jesus to tell us a story we haven't learned. And her response was quite fascinating explaining Jesus could float when he was a baby.*

K Did your parents see this?

C My mother did, but then she asked me to stop doing it! (*Laughing*)

K Why did she tell you to stop?

C It would scare people. She was very proud of me and I understand with my wisdom now … but I didn't understand then. But I knew enough. She asked me in such a sweet and loving way, "Wonderful job, but you will do so much more if you keep your feet on the ground." And she was right … for me to do the work I needed to do because I needed to be on the ground!

> *After the session, Ruth said she felt Mary's responses to Jesus levitating was spoken with such love. She had a strong sense that Mary was so gentle and kind in her response to Jesus.*

K So you needed to be grounded?

C Yes.

K Did she know ahead of time that you were special?

C Yes.

K Is the Immaculate Conception correct?

C Well how do you understand it to be?

K There are a couple of different ways people say that happened.

C When you say immaculate ... Mary was pure of heart. She did not have ego herself. She was aware of ego, but she was able to see ego and put it to the side. She was actually invited as a child, to be my mother. So when she was brought the good news ... it was exciting and she had sort of forgotten the prayer...the invitation, but it didn't take long for her to remember. So that's how she knew it to be true because she had offered this as a gift. Because she knew it wouldn't be easy, but she knew it would be helpful.

K So did she know the outcome?

C Not so much my death, but she knew that because there were so many wonderful things, they would be balanced out by the things that were difficult too. There is balance in everything.

K Did Jesus come before they were married?

C Not exactly. There was already intention. They already had a deep attraction to each other, but they didn't understand it. Joseph was much older than her.

K Were they a part of the group called the Essenes? Did they live with the Essenes?

C Not all the time but later on. It was very close to before his birth. The openness that they experienced as part of this group ... the love, the connection ... the divinity, is what made them be prepared and remember that prayer they had as children.

K So the group helped them?

C Yes, because they didn't just become … it's like they were on the outskirts and then became more involved. Before it was like watching and listening … not participating … but within their hearts participating but not outward … not spoken.

This secrecy might explain why their involvement with the Essenes were not known by many. This sense of secrecy around the Essene connection has been once again confirmed by many clients.

K Were the Essences persecuted as a group as we have heard?

C Much was kept quiet so they wouldn't be persecuted so they could understand and experience. And there was knowing of when you're doing things differently. But, there were some that could not keep the joy within.

K Within the group?

C Yes. So then they would be persecuted for their outlandish blasphemy! But it was not necessarily based on these. There were some other reason for them to be taken. But that also showed the group how special it was … what they were coming to understand. Some of the others that I was telling you like me were also part of this group.

K So some of the others were with you then?

K Did you travel to other countries?

C Yes.

K What countries did you travel to?

C Just as you suspect. I did go to India.

I found it interesting that Jesus could read my mind about my feelings of his travel to India. In THE UNKOWN LIFE OF JESUS, by Nicolas Notovich he found this statement in the Tibetan manuscript given to him in India by the monks, "Then he left Nepal and the Himalayan

Mountains, and went towards the west, preaching to diverse peoples the supreme perfection of man."

K Did you also go to Egypt?

C When I was younger. Not on the same time period.

K So what other countries did you go to that were helpful to you?

C I could travel all over and places I could not name. Sometimes just pop in and pop out. It's not necessary.

K Did you learn anything from going to those places?

C Well of course! It's all learning ... it's all sharing.

K So you also shared with them?

C Yes.

K So can you tell us a good story?

C I thought telling you about levitating as a child was a good story.

Judging from this statement, Jesus appears to have a great sense of humor.

K Yes it was a good story, how about a good story when you are older?

C But if you see me with crossed legs like in India just like the monks do it, like floating up in the air.

I found this to be a fascinating statement concerning Jesus' influence of the Indian culture. It appears that Jesus is explaining that he had the ability to float in the air like the monks. There have been many clients who said he traveled to India, therefore this could be another explanation of this connection.

K Were you taught this in India or remembered?

C I remember it. Not like I didn't remember it. I just toned it down. In lots of the lost years, I was just popping in and out of places.

K Did you go to the mountains to obtain even greater spiritual guidance?

C Many times.

K And what did you do on the mountains?

C Talked to Source, Father.

K So you like to talk to Source on the mountain? Couldn't you talk to him anywhere?

C Less distraction … less noise. And the energy from the Earth helped me to stay connected longer … just like it does for all of you.

K In Karen's work, there are sometimes differences of interpretation of some of the events, particularly concerning the crucifixion of who was there at the cross with you. So what is the true story and why the differences?

C Their perceptions makes a difference. So their ego sometimes creeps in. So they are excited about being there. They are excited about your work.

K But they were really there at that time, but sometimes they get confused with details?

C It's easy to do.

K Karen felt a few clients did not actually live in that lifetime with Jesus that are not included in this book. Was what she felt correct?

C They might have popped in. Some weren't living that life. If you go to a place where there is a lot of energy on the planet … to a place of high energy … you can sometimes on purpose or by accident tap into that energy. Not knowing. So if they have been in a past life experience or going to look or review … they might get to come. We can all pop into any period of history. Maybe they didn't live there, but were able to experience it and witness it in a different time. Just another way of traveling and experiencing. As you know there is no time.

> *Jesus speaks of pop-ins many times in this session. After the session Ruth said she felt it was from different timelines in the ethereal realm. Jesus*

explained that sometimes "pop-ins" would come just for the experience. This was information was new to both of us.

K Some of my clients felt there were groups of healers that you taught healing as well? Is that correct?

C It was a sharing about healing.

K So you shared your knowledge about healing?

C Yes, turning on the circuits so they could all tap back into it.

K Clients said they were changed by being with you.

C They weren't so much changed as they remembered! Everyone's essence is the same ... personality is not the same ... essence is, yes.

K Why wasn't reincarnation in the Bible?

C It was taken out.

K What would Jesus like to say?

C I love you! Always when there is an opportunity to say I love you.

K Thank you! What would you say about finding our true essence?

I actually could feel his love when he spoke those words.

C The misunderstanding of the God above ... versus the God within. Spirit is ... God is ... all love ... everything. Whatever is without is also within. Whatever is within, manifest without. So if we all go within, we can manifest without on the outside.

Ellie and other clients also makes a very similar statement that God is within rather than above.

Feel free to always use my name Yeshua, for you Karen. Always remember to pray from Love, not fear. You're healing and you're healed. Just remember if you don't see it manifest in the way you expect it, doesn't mean it hasn't happened.

K Yes it is confusing for humans.

C Yes. Game may not be the right word maybe it is the activity ... play time. But only because you ask for it.

K Were you married to Mary?

C Not officially.

K Were you and Mary soul mates?

C Yes.

K Did people come and go to be with you at different times?

C Yes, people could come and join our group whenever they wished. Sometimes it was happenstance.

K Is there anything that Ruth needs to know about that life with Jesus that would be helpful to her in her current life?

C (*Long pause*) Not everyone that was there was living in that time frame. Some from other times. They were called in with that energy.

> *When speaking about the loaves and fishes, she had called it a group miracle. So Jesus is saying that the energy was called in by many in spirit form. This was something that Ruth was unaware of in her conscious mind.*

K Can you explain further?

C They were just popping in on that energy. Some from that lifetime and some between lives. So when she was talking about having the energy of the whole ... it was really their energy that kicked it into high drive. We all had our high part.

K So that is why the subconscious says, "we"?

C Or "I"... it all comes back to One. We are all One ... there is no separation. But we like to use "we" for humans that are Earthbound to understand for better illustration for you.

> *This was confirmation that clients were still in their subconscious*

even if they had said "I." I will always ask for confirmation that the subconscious is still present when they say "I," as sometimes it can be an indication of the conscious mind entering. But if clients say "I think," then I know the conscious mind has entered because there is no thinking in the subconscious, only the knowing.

K Why does Karen feel a stronger connection with the name Yeshua rather than Jesus?

C Time that you lived. Not many knew his name.

K Thank you.

K Can you give more information about the disciples? Did you have lifetimes with them?

C My group of disciples ... I had always connected energetically and in many lifetimes. It's like having neighbors ... living in a neighborhood. I was more connected with them and traveled many lifetimes. I am actually speaking of living in a body on Earth. I'm just a tool for others to get to Source within them. Some people prefer my tools and some people like other tools.

K Like some of the other teachers?

C Yes. Same when the story gets mixed up, and causes violence.

K Can you tell us the best way to access our True Self?

C Best prayer is to invite love and ask others to invite love in yourself. Inviting them to tap into the love that already is there. Inviting them to tap into the love that is within. Or by your actions. The river of love within.

K How can we better connect with you?

C To be quiet. State your intention out loud but then feel it in your heart. ... When you are only stating it out loud, so it makes it real faster because you made it real. Your mind versus your mind and your spoken word, increases with your energy ... when it spoken. Always do it in love, not fear.

K Were you ever afraid?

C I did have moments when I was afraid on the cross. So I was also grateful for it so I could understand it better.

K Who was there with you at the cross?

C Barabbas … he felt bad. He was the one they let go. He didn't want to be the one to let go.

> *This was fascinating detail about Barabbas, which is not addressed in the Bible. Ruth said she had no prior knowledge of the man called Barabbas in her current life, and was surprised about this detail. In the* Bible, *Barabbas was a criminal in prison for murder and insurrection, but was released by Pontius Pilate due to the crowd's choosing Jesus to take his place. It was the custom at the time that a prisoner would be released every year before Passover, so Yeshua was not the one chosen to be set free.*

K So he was with you when you died on the cross?

C Yes!

K Was Mary there too?

C Not the whole time, but it was too hard.

K Were the disciples there?

C They took shifts. There were people there, but it was also very quiet.

> *This is an interesting statement explaining that people had taken shifts at the cross, which may explain why some people say they were at the cross.*

K Is it true that the Romans didn't allow everyone to come?

C Yes. They didn't want a mob scene. They didn't want them to come and free me or overrun them. Because instantly everyone knew how incorrect it was. Like Barabbas snuck up there. He was cloaked, so they didn't know it was him.

> *This is another fascinating observation concerning Barabbas, when he*

was "cloaked" at the crucifixion so no would recognize him. It also makes one wonder if Barabbas knew Jesus was someone special.

K Did he say anything to you?

C He actually didn't want to be free because he knew the benefit of my experience. It was not easy for him to let it go.

This is fascinating statement about Barabbas feelings about the experience. This explains the belief that we come into various lives for the experience.

K Did he know who you were?

C Yes, we had been together before. We made an agreement before.

Jesus is speaking of a contract made prior to them coming into that lifetime. From my experiences in working with clients for many years, it is my belief that we make contracts with those in our lives for various lessons and experiences before we come into a lifetime. In Ellie's channeled session, Yeshua explains, "So the child creates the contract before it is born. When it decides that it's going to experience a temporal life and it decides where it is going to live, where it is going to be and what it wishes to experience."

K Did Judas betray you as we were told in the Bible? Did he tell the Romans where you were?

C He was tricked. Someone else tricked him into saying it. He was trying to safeguard it.

K Did he take silver coins from the Romans?

C No. He was not greedy.

K Why did history make him the betrayer?

C To help explain a story to give an example of what to be and what not to be. He doesn't care about what was thought of him. He loved me very much and he wanted to protect me.

K Did all the disciples love you?

C Yes, but Judas especially loved me.

> *This is an interesting take on Judas, which gives us an entirely different perspective of his role in the life of Yeshua. This was also confirmed in Rose's session that Judas loved him more.*

K Why did some people call you the Son of God?

C It was a name they gave to me. I didn't stop them from using it. It just better illustrated to have them learn. Going back to whole idea, that knowing that there is no separation at all. Separation … knowing it was an illusion, but thinking it would be a useful way for them to understand. They will all know some day that they all are Sons of God … a Child of God. So it wasn't just for that time. So they misinterpreted it as blasphemous.

K What did the followers call you?

C Beloved. If they didn't know me as well … they called me teacher. In trying to explain or illustrated that my gifts were the gifts of all. I tried to dissuade others from putting me above them. So once they were closer in the group, we were all each other's beloved.

> *This was such beautiful statement regarding Jesus not wanting to put himself above others. This was also confirmed by the many clients that he didn't want anyone to put him on a pedestal.*

K They all knew you were different. Is that correct?

C The only difference was I didn't have the same hiccups. The same darkness of ego to cloud my judgment. There were times that I could try it on but I knew where I could wear the mask of ego a little bit of time if I wanted, if I wanted to get angry … if I want to tap into what that energy was like, but I never wanted to hold onto it very long. Where if someone else held onto anger... they didn't know they could turn it off anytime they wanted. Ruth's body is tired.

When clients speak of being tired, this informs me that the session needed to end soon. I asked if we could continue with a couple of more questions, and he agreed.

In discussion when asking the question about our water.

C Intention ... to put love to it, put strength, put resolve, or whatever you want into water. It's just another tool. Take 3 deep breaths ... have intention whether it's your water or a word and practice that over and over. And naturally fall into a rhythm you have never known.

The subconscious spoke of having intention to put love, strength and resolve in the water, and using this method as a tool. This was a subtle reminder of when I spoke of intention being important tool when healing in my session. There have been many confirmations from other client's statements which can't be ignored.

K She wanted to know the best way to facilitate healing within self?

C Just what I told you! Think about the goals of the day. Put discipline in the water.

K Anything else Jesus would like to say to her?

C Just, I love you. There is nothing more than love.

K Will I be able to connect with you through other clients?

C Yes, but let them come to you with the understanding that all is One first and once they understand that all is One ... then you can tap into other voices.

Ruth's Impressions after Her Session

After the session, Ruth elaborated on some of her experiences and feelings during the session, when she channeled Jesus. She said she definitely felt like a witness. In accessing the subconscious, she found it difficult finding the words to express it in human terminology. She felt Jesus wanted to speak with us in a way that we would understand his words in our current time frame.

Ruth found it interesting that she had seen pictures of stars when speaking of Jesus being one of many. She had the feeling that it was a big secret, but she needed to say it. When speaking of Jesus levitating as a baby, she found it interesting as well. Before her was a scene of Jesus levitating in the kitchen area, and Mary's response was so loving in her explanation of why Jesus shouldn't show others what he could do. She said this felt very real to her.

When speaking of pop-ins, Ruth said this was definitely never anything she had thought of before and something entirely new to her. In describing the feelings about pop-ins, she said she felt it was before or after on a linear scale. In the ethereal realm, souls might say, "Let's check it out … fascinating."

Third Session with Ruth in the Subconscious Channeling Jesus

"Jesus said to them, Walk while you have the light, so that darkness will not overtake you; he who walks in the darkness does not know where he goes. While you have the light, believe in the light, that you may become sons of the light."
JOHN 12:35

Ruth expressed interest in accessing more information about her lifetime with Jesus. At this time she was aware that I was writing this book, and gave me permission to ask some questions that I had about the book. When I asked her subconscious about the truth of Jesus' birth, there was a response, "There is more of us here." It also explained that Ruth was having some difficulty letting go of her conscious mind. It was explained that "It takes a lot of energy for her to step aside." After helping her to once again connect to her subconscious, she was then able to move quickly into her subconscious.

Ruth in the Subconscious

K Can the subconscious explain the truth of Jesus' birth?

SC The light within Mary was able to manifest into the Light of Jesus. But it was the light that already existed. But it's her intention as to do with the light that created the intention.

K Another client spoke of Jesus being one of many, can the subconscious explain this for greater understanding?

SC There are other Souls of Light that are bright. That light that understands from the beginning of time and has incarnated. There are many others throughout the universe. He chose this plane.

K Why did Jesus choose to come to Earth?

SC Because it was hard.

K Why was it hard?

SC Because there is so much darkness that gets in the way of the Light.

K We have heard much about sin. What does the subconscious say about sin?

SC The choice … the free will you've been given allows you to make the decision … to step into love or turn your back on it.

K How did the concept of sin become so confused?

SC There's a density that's different here, so it was chosen more and more. Once chosen … once love is not chosen … it's less and less because it wasn't seen. More is being seen again. Because when it gets too imbalanced, the tide will always turn.

K So the Earth is in a state of balancing?

SC Turning back toward love. All that ever was!

K Did Jesus ever speak of sin in his teachings?

SC No.

K So that was a manmade concept?

SC Yes.

K Did he speak of darkness?

SC Not being in the light. Either accepting light or not stepping in a stream of light … a never ending light! You may ask for Jesus now.

Prior to this, the subconscious indicated it was not time to access Jesus. My impression that there were other issues which needed to be addressed before the client was ready to channel Jesus.

Ruth Channeling Jesus

K Welcome! How is the subconscious able to connect with Jesus?

C We are all of One … love. (*Breathing very deeply*) What would you like to know, Karen?

K When one of my clients was speaking to me about this book, she began to speak what seemed like an ancient language that we both were unfamiliar with. What language was she speaking in?

C The one you suspect, Aramaic.

K Were you connected to the Essenes?

C In my heart.

K Did you come in with great spiritual knowing or did you learn from others and their teachings in other places?

C I did both. I had a great deal of information. I came in with knowing. My experience was reversed from yours. So I would go to others to know how they felt disconnected. I came in with everything I knew as to oppose to you choosing to come in not knowing.

K Why did we choose not to come in with knowing?

C It's a greater path! You have the greater gift!

K Can you explain this?

C Everyone thinks I am the gift, but they are. They're the gift of God to understand … God's greatness.

K But you helped us with greater understanding?

C I just helped you remember what you forgot! (*Beautiful!*)

K Why were you called by so many different names, teacher, Beloved, the Master, Son of God, and many more?

C Because it's always easier to see the truth when it's outside yourself. It's always easier to see that first … for someone that is not remembering.

K So these are just labels?

C Yes.

K What would you like to be called?

C You … we are the same. I didn't want to be different.

K Did it bother you that you were called by these names?

C No. I understand their need.

K I feel that the name Yeshua resonates to me more than the name Jesus. Why is this so?

C Yeshua is how my mother called me.

K Did everyone call you Yeshua or just a few?

C Every one of my time.

K Did you have more incarnations, other lifetimes?

C I understand what you're asking, but it is difficult for you to understand. But you will understand.

K So can you explain the truth so Ruth can have a better understanding?

C I am that ever was and will be … that is you. There is no separation … there is no separate experiences. You can step into my experience any time you want to. It just takes a little practice and discipline and acceptance. That discipline is acceptance. Step into love. You speak of fear … there really isn't fear, you just haven't stepped into love. I have been here before in different times and different forms. It is difficult for you to process what I mean. You do not remember all of my forms. But I was in the garden. I was in the beginning.

> *When Yeshua speaks of being in the garden in the beginning, it gives us confirmation that he was the man we call Adam in his first incarnation. Edgar Cayce also spoke of Jesus having various incarnations; first as*

Amilius (Adam) in Atlantis, Enoch, Hermes, Melchizedek (King of Salem), Joshua (One who also helped to led the Israelites into the Promised Land), Zen (founder of Zoroaster), and then Jesus.

In early Christianity there was a belief that Jesus was the reincarnation of Adam. This was referred to as "Primal Adam" ideology. One of the decrees of Emperor Justinian in the 6th century was written, "If anyone shall say that Christ, had different bodies and different names, became all to all … let him be anathema." If the church acknowledged this belief with this anathema, then it must have been a commonly held belief among various groups.

K What happened in the beginning?

C I allowed myself to have the experience to choose not remembering. I allowed myself to choose … not love.

K Others have said you had five children, is that correct?

C I had five stars. Stars are beings that have the same density and lightness as me … you have.

K They were with you as children?

C Yes, although I have a daughter. Let's fill this room with love. Can you feel the room getting warmer?

Jesus moved from the question I was asking, to stating he was with us and giving advice about this book without me asking.

C I'm here! I love what you are doing … I'm grateful. You are not responsible for your work … it is just your hand. Step into knowing it's already done … its already amazing, already saving lives. This is not your book … just starting typing, writing. Let your hand move. It's not your book. It is just an opportunity to be a part of it. It already exists … which is what you asked for.

K When Karen had the experience where Yeshua raised his hands up in the air with palms outreaching, she became very emotional. Can you explain why Karen felt such emotion?

C   Because you've attached to that experience. Seeing all that moment you were reconnected. You remember everything at the moment you are clear on everything ... nothing blocking you.

K   Was Ruth in the subconscious when speaking of the lifetime with Jesus in the previous sessions?

C   Yes. Just because the conscious mind comes in sometimes ... it doesn't mean it's not the truth. It's just a harder time to speak words.

K   Was Joseph of Arimathea your uncle?

C   Yes.

K   Did he take you with him to various places to speak?

C   He helped me around my local area, but encouraged me to discover more than he could help me find. I had my questions to experience like everyone.

K   What else do we need to know about the Bible?

C   Actually would be useful to you ... seeing with different eyes. All useful to someone at some time ... seeing with a different light. What rings true to you is a clue.

K   What about the concept of the devil? Is that useful?

C   To someone who is not ready to see the complete truth.

K   What is the complete truth about the devil?

C   As you can understand it now ... when a choice is made to back away from light, in essence one is choosing darkness. In essence there is no darkness to choose ... it's just a stepping away from light. There is a new energy. All energy has a frequency and these frequencies are attracted to similar frequencies.

K   Is this when we speak of energies attracting each other's energies either positive or negative?

C Correct. So, once there was a choice to back away from light … there was an opportunity for that to grow. It's easier to explain it to someone who has forgotten everything and make it external and give it a personality.

What he is explaining is that humans sometimes give personality to something we can't explain in human terms, which is similar to giving evil a name and calling it the devil. This explanation of what we call "evil" has been confirmed many times by the subconscious.

K So what you are saying is, there is no devil?

C There is darkness and it can be strong … you can feel it. There is no soul that has lost all light.

K What about a Hitler?

C That is a good example of fear. That is a good example of magnetizing others. (*At this point breathing is very deep.*)

K In her session, Karen experienced a voice coming out of her saying, "His stomach is responding to the truth." Was that my subconscious or the collective?

C It is the collective consciousness. Just as I am speaking to you now it is the collective, but you can personalize now. As the Spirit you once walked with, that you miss so dearly now. But I tell you now … there is no separation. So when you miss a single soul, you miss everyone.

K Thank you. Beautiful!

K Karen has always wanted to understand why her session was not recorded.

C It wasn't time. The way you remember it and the way you interpret it is best.

K It was always interesting to Karen, as to why her session with Yeshua was while she was in her training to be a past life therapist?

C It was time to know. Every time you put a request out, it is always answered and it's answered with the amount of energy it's given out.

K I wasn't expecting or aware of that lifetime. But was my subconscious aware?

C Correct ... correct.

I explain to clients that your soul is calling forth for you to remember. Sometimes we are not aware on the conscious level, but our subconscious always knows and guides us. It is like when I accepted the library book that was different from what I had reserved. My subconscious was always guiding me to where I needed to go. The important aspect of this, is to listen to the voice within and thereupon act on the guidance given. Some people say they would not have taken the book. Therefore if I hadn't listened to that inner voice, my life path may have taken a completely different path.

It has been my experience in working with clients, that we are given options for our life plans for certain events in the interlife prior to our incarnations. As we are given free will, our life paths can change depending on our choices in life. We are unaware of these options on the conscious level, but there is always guidance if we listen to that inner voice within.

K In Ruth's session she spoke that there were many Gods, is this true?

C There is only one Source, but many aspects of it. You could put a personality to study an aspect. It's like looking at a set of books with many volumes, which book you want to study, but their all part of the collection. There is but one Source. It's all that will ever be. It will never change. Source is love and light.

K Ruth and others spoke of The Way, can you explain?

C The way of experiencing back into truth ... remembering.

This is an entirely different interpretation than what was taught in religious institutions. In this beautiful statement, Jesus is speaking of the Way, is our remembrance of the truth. He spoke earlier in the session he said, "I just helped you remember what you forgot."

K What were the secrets revealed to the disciples?

C All is light. There is nothing you need. Ask and it shall be given. This is why there is nothing you need because all it takes is creation.

K Is that why Karen was drawn to that concept of ask and it will be given?

C I know your intention before you ask. But the secret is in the power when the light has been divided into individual souls or spirits. There is still a power within that light that is what you call free will. That's the choice to bring your light into light or continue to keep it separate.

K Is this what you explained to the disciples?

C So you have to understand that their understanding was so different from your understanding now. They did not understand these concepts then ... all [are] One Source. What direction do you want to see today ... whether it is compassion, empathy, forgiveness, gratitude?

K Did Judas betray you?

C He picked that lifetime, as it was incredibly important. Of course he didn't remember. It would be incredibly difficult to remember.

K Was he tricked?

C Yes. It was difficult for him. You see him as a betrayer, I see him as a lover.

> *This is an important statement of how we perceive others without understanding their true purpose. This misconception of Judas is based on people's perceptions, and may not be entirely the truth of who he was. Many times we need someone to blame without the true understanding of what actually occurred. In both Rose's and Ruth's session they indicated that Judas loved Jesus more than the others.*

K Did you die on the cross or was it the appearance of death as some have felt?

C I did leave my body and then returned to my body. I showed them ascension so they could see what I could do. Everything I can do you can do.

K Did they understand?

C No. But starting to understand what they needed to understand.

K Were you married to Mary Magdalene?

C I was committed to her. What makes a marriage ... it was commitment.

K Can you give us more information on the five stars?

C They're from stars. They came with us. She gave birth to them. They spent time with us until it was time to move on to other places on Earth and other places.

K You also spoke of having a daughter, did she have the same knowledge as you did?

C Yes. But she didn't have the same knowing. She was filled with Love, but did not have the knowing. Her experience was to experience a family with true love.

K Was Mary Magdalene a prostitute? Although it was never proven to be true, some in the church claimed she was the prostitute in the Bible.

C There were things that were not accepted. Reason for having a reputation. It is always worse than it is.

> *This statement seems to validate Rose's session when Mary spoke of being a healer and having an inappropriate relationship with a man. Again it is about people's perceptions of the truth.*

K How did others perceive that reputation?

C Sometimes she made choices that she was not in love and when you're not in love, you do not know that you are worthy. She picked that experience to see what she would do, and then she decided to wake up.

K So she did sleep with other men?

C She wanted to feel love.

> *What a beautiful demonstration of non-judgment.*

K When was the first time you met Mary?

C They were throwing stones.

> *She indicated that this happened many times without the same intensity spoken of in the* Bible.

K When she saw you, did something happen?

C Yes. It was like turning around to see what you haven't seen.

K So you have the ability to show others what they haven't seen?

C I have the ability to come when I'm called. When you are the most desperate with a shred of hope. I have the ability to hear that call. I enjoy most amidst the desperation, there is still hope. Anyone not connecting to hope ... it feels like an earthquake. Our intention for compassion is all of us showing up, that is the call ... we call to do that. Do you want to be one who is understood or one to understanding? You do not exist ... you and me are we. I get less lonely when we are we.

K So you experience loneliness?

C I have experienced it. I have put it on. I enjoy relationships more. Be focused on relationships, consider who you are relatively to me, to a flower, to family. There is no experience without relationships.

Ruth's Impressions after Her Session

Ruth said that she felt differently and more like a medium in this session. But she felt the truth was coming through even though she wasn't as deep as she was in this session. She described the feelings as, "It's like one more layer coming through, rather than a direct signal. Instead of you watching a TV, it's me describing what's on TV. Sometime you see TV directly and sometimes it's me describing what is on TV." When Jesus came through, there was the feeling of a more loving and sweeter presence. Although she was able to remember most of her session, Ruth could not recall certain information when asked about her impressions of certain events in her session. When asked if she thought the session was helpful, Ruth felt the session was very helpful and profound.

Chapter Eight

"The first lesson should be, One—One—One—One; Oneness of God, oneness of man's relation, oneness of force, oneness of time, oneness of purpose, Oneness in every effort—Oneness— Oneness!"   *EDGAR CAYCE READING 900-429*

ELLIE

Initially, Ellie came for a past life session to find answers to her questions about finding her purpose and to gain healing and peace. She decided to experience the Life between Life session. She also wanted to know if she had a lifetime with Jesus as she had a deep connection with him. There were a couple of years between her first session and the Life between Life Spiritual Exploration session. Feeling called by her guides, she felt it was time for her to come for a session. Her boyfriend recommended her to come for a session. At the time of her first session she was a program analyst. Presently Ellie is a compassionate, gifted psychic reader.

Ellie experienced two past lives and then was guided to her Council of Elders in the Life between Life Spiritual Exploration Session. In her first past life session there was no mention of a lifetime with Jesus.

Life between Life Spiritual Exploration Session

In her Life between Life session, Ellie explained that there were six Council of Elders members. She described them all circled around her as she was in a laying position while suspended in the light and resting, and saying, "They want me to rest while talking with me." A leader on her Council came forth saying, "There is healing you need to go through." Clients are asked to bring in questions to ask their Council. One of her questions was if she had a lifetime with Jesus.

When we are between lives, we always go before our Council of Elders to review our lifetimes. This is a place of reflection and guidance without judgment. The Council is a group of highly evolved spiritual beings who offer us advice and wisdom. *(For additional information go to the Chapter, The Process Explained.)*

Ellie with Her Council of Elders

K Ellie would like to know if she had a lifetime with Jesus.

C Yes.

K Is it important to review that lifetime now?

C Yes.

K Who was she in that lifetime?

C She was a girl.

K When was the first time she met Jesus?

C She knew him as a boy.

K Were they friends.

C Yes ... as a child.

K Did she notice anything different about him?

C Yes ... his eyes!

K What were the color of his eyes?

C Light green, blue sparkly, and they changed colors.

K Why did they change colors?

C The sun. They were bright and vivid.

> *This may be an explanation of why some say Jesus' eyes are blue and others describe them as blue green.*

K When you looked into his eyes, what did you see?

C Light. It felt warm, unconditional love, and happy.

K Did you have psychic gifts in that lifetime? Did you see things, know things?

C Yes.

K Did she feel that connection with Jesus?

C I would get visions. I know when something was going to happen. I have a very strong third eye. It wasn't always pleasant ... sometimes very hard.

K Did you see the future as to what was to happen to Jesus?

C Yes. I got glimpses.

K Did Jesus and you discuss this?

C He said he knew.

K Did he ever tell you why he came?

C To bring peace.

K Did you know his parents?

C Yes. Mary was beautiful, loving, generous and kind.

K Was Joseph the father?

C Yes. He was charitable, honorable, very intelligent, educated and well respected and strict.

K Did you live in a community?

C Yes.

K Did the community have a name?

C It was the Essene. I feel I shouldn't say.

> *This is another confirmation of Jesus' connection to the Essenes, and the need for it to remain a secret.*

K Why shouldn't you say? Was it a secret?

C I have heard that before, but it's okay now. It's time to come out.

K What don't we know about the Essenes?

C (*She began crying.*) Well ... we feel an obligation to bring peace and Light to the world. Not just this region or this country, but Mother Earth and all its people.

K Did others accept this community?

C No.

K Is that why it was kept secretive?

C We knew it was important to be quiet ... to live quietly ... to walk quietly and to be peaceful.

K Can you describe the actual community?

C It was very self-sufficient ... very communal.

K Was it like a commune?

C Yes, but not everyone had owned a home and owned animals. Not everyone, but many did. We shared everything. We went fishing and we shared the fish. We shared toys, we shared tools, and everything we had ... we shared. Nobody was poor, we shared everything with everyone. No one was left alone when they got older. We took care of everyone. They all had a place.

K Were there other communities like your community?

C There were others like our community ... other places and even in other countries which I was told.

> *This appears to validate that there were many communities which called themselves Essenes. Philo believed that there were large Essene communities in many places. Additionally, according to the Jewish historian Josephus, there were a large number of Essenes in many cities and villages around Judea.*

K Was Jesus born of Mary and Joseph?

C Yes. He was special because of his star he was born under. I didn't know what star... that's what they say.

K Moving to an important day, a day that you consider to be important in that lifetime. What is happening? What are you sensing? What are you experiencing?

C There is a big celebration.

K What kind of celebration?

C A wedding.

K Is it your wedding?

C Yes, I am marrying Joseph. We were friends forever. He was in my community.

Ellie recognized that Joseph's energy was the same energy as her current boyfriend. In a past life regression, many clients can recognize the energy of someone in their current life. We carry the same energy from lifetime to lifetime.

K Was Jesus there?

C Yes.

K If you heard your name what would you hear?

C Madeline.

K Were you related to Jesus?

C Yes. I feel related, like cousins.

K Did Jesus say anything at the wedding?

C He gave his blessing. Everything was radiant ... beautiful, and a fun day.

K Did you eventually follow Jesus?

C Yes ... we followed him, but didn't go with him everywhere. We had a family, so we stayed home. In the beginning we did follow him, then later I had a family and couldn't go.

This was another confirmation that some followers came and went and not everyone stayed with him all the time. As presented in my session, many people had responsibilities with their families.

K What was Jesus' teaching that resonated to you the most?

C Love your brother as yourself, that we are all one family. All cells are in body of God ... not his exact words.

At this point in the session, she said she had some doubt. I asked her to go back to her Council, and gave her the suggestion that they were helping her without interference with her conscious mind. I asked if we could continue and the Council said "yes." The Council indicated everything that was spoken previously was correct.

K Will she believe it?

C Yes.

K Did Jesus travel to other places?

C Yes ...Turkey, Tunisia, Egypt, Iraq, Europe.

K So I understand that he traveled extensively. What type of transportation did he use to travel? Did he travel by sea?

C Yes.

K Did he travel by sea with anyone?

C Yes, his Uncle Joseph.

> *This is confirmed in Emma's session when Joseph says, "He travels with me. I take him to different parts." In her session Joseph also states, "I am the Uncle." This has also been confirmed by other clients in their sessions. None of these clients were acquainted with one another, nor did they have any knowledge of what was said in other sessions.*

K What was his most important message?

C There are many messages. All are important ... forgiveness.

K Did people understand it at that time?

C No.

K Did Mary Magdalene understand forgiveness?

C She grasped it and she understood it conceptually. She did her best to apply it in her life and when she did, she felt good.

K Was this a new concept?

C Yes, forgiveness as a discipline. Yes ... as a spiritual discipline.

K What other messages did he give?

C We're all One. There is no division ... no separation ... all are One. What I can

do, you can do. What I have you have. It lets you hear the Voice of
God. Go to that peaceful place that is your central being and peace. You're One
with your brother… you truly are. This is not something that we just say to
make you feel good, to make you feel ashamed. There is no shame in love. Love
is the glue. It's what you are!

K Is there something we don't know about Jesus?

C There are many things you don't know of Yeshua.

*She initially referred to his name as Jesus, but in this statement she
switched to calling him Yeshua. I will now refer to him as Yeshua in her
session, since she began to call him by that name.*

K What is important for us to know?

C He is in every one of us. The spirit he attained by going within himself is
the spirit that exists within every one of us. He will help you find that spirit
in yourself. If you reach out your hand to him and ask for his help, he will
reach down and lift you up, and help you, and lift you up into that spirit of
Oneness … into that place!

K Did Yeshua receive any messages or did he already know everything?

C He truly experienced himself as connected to every blade of grass, every leaf,
tree and every hair on a caterpillar. He was consistently conscious and in that
state of awareness. His auric field went out for miles for at least five miles.

K Beautiful! … Did people see that?

C Yes … they could feel it … the radiance … the energy.

K Did all of the people feel that energy?

C They all felt it … yes, but it irritated some.

K Why did it irritate some?

C It made them feel something. They felt foreign to what they were experiencing
… fearful. They felt they were being judged but they were just judging

themselves. By the light it made them look at their actions. They didn't know. (*Very interesting statement.*)

K So it mirrored them?

C It was a lens. It was a light that showed their dark places that was uncomfortable for everyone some time. It was only truly comfortable especially when his voice was with it, and he would talk and you would hear the softness in his words.

K Did you hear him speak in large groups?

C Many times.

K What happened when he spoke?

C Peace fell upon everyone. Peace came over everyone like a spell. It made everyone love each other.

> *As she spoke I was reliving that same feeling I had experienced in my session when Yeshua spoke to the crowd.*

K How beautiful! Did those feeling of loving each other continue with everyone?

C Yes. It had a lasting effect. ... It stayed.

K Is there anything incorrect about the life of Yeshua?

C There are accounts of him being angry, scornful, casting out demons ... that's not how he did it.

K Was he a great healer?

C Yes.

K Were you a part of a group of healers?

C I was not one of the healers, but I did hear that he would go to the Father and through his Oneness with the Father, he would bring the other to himself. He would insure to dissolve their perceived separation between them and see themselves as One. And when they see themselves as One, the person would see their Oneness with the Father.

K Beautiful! ... Thank you.

K K Were you aware of others that also did healings?

C Yes.

K Did he show them or teach them healing?

C They wanted to learn. It was in their heart to do that.

K Did you personally see healings?

C I saw some healings. A broken bone was healed. I saw it being healed ... it was a bone coming through the flesh. It was very bad. And then it was perfect after the bone was not going through the flesh. There was no blood. The bone was perfect. It scared people.

K Did he heal the blind, sick and disease?

C Yes.

K When it was spoken about casting out demons, was that an expression or understanding during those different times?

C It was the manifestation of the sins the person felt they committed in a raw, unfiltered form.

K Did they have a "fit," like it was explained in the *Bible* of today?

C That would become a manifestation. It was a manifestation, it was an expressing. It was like taking a pimple and squeezing it and bringing it to a head so all the fierceness of the guilt would come to a head and it would be squeezed out. Sometimes it took a squeezing out to release it, so the person could let it go ... like a purging. But it wasn't done in a judgment or rage. It was a healing of love and kindness and forgiveness that guilt couldn't handle and it would get fierce, and it would fight the forgiveness ... that's a fierce love!

K Jesus was called by many names, what was he called?

C Yeshua.

K Was he considered a great teacher, a Messiah?

C Yes.

K What did "Messiah" mean?

C Savior. He wasn't saving people... he was saving people from their illusions.

   Once again, I believe it is important to clarify client's interpretations of the names describing Yeshua at that time. In calling him the "Messiah," her interpretation speaks of saving people from their illusions which has a different meaning than what is presented in the Bible.

K Was it felt that he was going to change everything?

C Yes. Some wanted him to fight the politicians and the leaders. Some wanted him to take down the structures and destroy.

K So he was called by many names?

C Yes.

K What did you consider him to be?

C A friend. A great teacher.

K Did he teach you anything? And what did he teach you?

C Yes. By watching him ... I learned a lot by his example.

K What was the most important thing he taught you?

C To forgive myself. We can only forgive ourselves. We cannot forgive another if we can't forgive ourselves. We have to forgive ourselves. As we forgive another we forgive ourselves.

   When we forgive ourselves and others we free ourselves and there is peace where there once was anger.

K Did Yeshua die on the cross?

C Yes.

K Were you there?

C No.

K Did you hear about this?

C Yes.

K Did you hear that he resurrected?

C Death could not hold him.

K So did he come to others after his death?

C Yes.

K When he came to others, did they say what he told them?

C Yes. They said he came to show them that even death is an illusion. Even death is not real. No one really dies.

K Did they understand this at the time?

C They didn't understand because they could only see the death of others, and it must be that he was somehow a God.

> *This fascinating statement explains the perspectives of his followers who were unable to comprehend the true meaning that there is no death. They interpreted his resurrection as being God-like. This could explain some parts of the Bible, and its interpretation of who Yeshua was to them. This may have contributed to the perception that he was God-like.*

K Some say he walked the Earth and some say he ascended?

C He stayed for a while … for three years

K Where did he go?

C With everyone who followed him.

K So was he in Spirit then?

C Yes.

K And could they feel his presence?

C Yes, very strongly.

K When he first came to others, was he in Spirit or human form?

C He came in a human form to show that there is no death. But the form dissolved. It was a collection of matter, and then it dissolved and that presence continued.

K Did you ever hear why he needed to die?

C To show us life could not be killed. Life continues, where before no one believed that.

K Before that did they believe in reincarnation?

C Yes.

K Did Yeshua believe in reincarnation?

C Yes ... that we all lived before and we all walked Earth before. We were plants, trees, animals. We all have taken on many forms, and like the clouds form and disappear and come in another form. All are a part of the experience of density.

> *I have personally had clients speak of lifetimes as trees, plants, dolphins, fish and many other forms of life. I believe the soul will choose what form they would like to experience.*

K Did Yeshua speak of other lives he had lived?

C He was in Egypt, Sinenda (*It is written as spoken.*) He was on other planets and other solar systems.

> *She indicated that Sinenda was an ancient culture.*

K Did he understand and speak of the other planets he was from?

C We aren't supposed to talk of it. It was in a solar system we aren't conscious of.

> *Many times clients will not speak of things the clients or mankind are not prepared to understand at this time. In THE SPIRITS' BOOK this was also confirmed in the statement, "On Earth, God does not allow everything to be revealed to them."*

K So was he a volunteer?

C Yes. He came to remind us of our abundant nature. And also, to realize that we are loved by God and that we have everything we need. And that we should be appreciative and talk with God. Everyone can talk with God and give thanks and gratitude. And in giving gratitude … we multiply what we have. It's that simple. He would say, "It's that simple. Give appreciation and gratitude for the gifts you have, and more will be brought to you."

K Some people think Yeshua was saying we need to be poor to be spiritual?

C NO! (*Very loudly spoken.*)

K Then where did that belief come from?

C The Romans! They could see the followers of Yeshua and appealed to their belief and twisted it to control.

K Who were the ones who had Yeshua crucified?

C It was the Elders. The Romans were interested in it also.

K Why were the Elders concerned about Yeshua?

C They were jealous. They didn't like the following he had that undermined their authority. His teachings were opposed to many of their teachings.

K What did they oppose what he taught?

C It opposed going through anyone to speak to the Father.

K So they wouldn't have the power?

C Right!

K Were there any secret teachings?

C No … there is nothing secret. Everything is out in the open. It is the way he spoke. Everyone got what they needed.

K How many years were you with him?

C Four or five years.

K Did he have anyone special in his life?

C Yes. His wife, Mary Magdalene.

K What were your impressions of Mary?

C She was very protective of him. She was very strong. She had very dark skin, dark features and she was beautiful.

K Can you describe what Yeshua was like?

C He was beautiful!

K Where did the belief that he was not married come from?

C That came later in the writings.

K Were there the disciples as we know them?

C There were disciples.

K How did you feel about them?

C I did like them. They are brilliant. But they're brilliant in their spiritual understanding. They understood him.

K Did you have psychic gifts in that lifetime?

C Clairvoyant, psychometry ... a knowing. I could feel it in my body.

K Was the life with Yeshua complete?

C Everything is perfect.

Ellie's Impressions after Her Session

Although Ellie remembered much of the session, she felt that she had not remembered everything. She found it interesting that she was a cousin of Yeshua. She understood she could now go to him and talk with him in her current life. She felt there was releasing in her body when she released the issues in the past lives. When I asked if she found the session helpful, Ellie said she felt it was a unique experience and found it to be helpful in her current life.

Ellie's First Session Channeling Yeshua

*"To you has been given the secret of the Kingdom of Heaven,
but for those outside everything is in parables,
so that they may indeed see but not perceive, and
may indeed hear but not understand."*
MARK 4:11-12

Ellie contacted me to say how the session had helped her. She also indicated that she is connecting with Yeshua/Jesus daily and receiving messages. She said she felt he was very close to her now. I felt drawn to ask her if she would be open for another session where she would be able to channel Yeshua, since he was coming to her daily. Ellie said she was contemplating the same thing, and was excited at the prospect of being able to channel Yeshua. In this session Yeshua came through. One of most fascinating aspects of the channeled sessions was when Yeshua came through using stories to explain various spiritual concepts. These stories were used quite often by Yeshua to convey his message so it could be understood by the common people. These stories are called parables in the *Bible*.

I will continue using the C for the client even though Jesus is speaking through her.

K At this time is it possible to channel Yeshua? Do I have permission to speak to Yeshua?

As I asked permission to speak to Yeshua, I felt a tingling sensation in my body. After the session Ellie said she felt something in her body as well.

C Yes.

K Do I have permission to ask questions?

C Yes.

K Was this supposed to happen?

C Yes!

K Yeshua are you here?

C Yes!

K We thank you for coming.

C Thank you.

K What message do you want to convey to Ellie?

C Blessed child, know that I am always with you. You are never alone. I hold you in my hands and I give you my energy field. Take refuge in me dear child. You are loved. I tend after you. I look after you. I share myself with you. Come unto me and be healed. Come into my energy and know you're true whole. Blessed child ... child of God ... we are One. We are all One with all of life ... all of nature ... all of the Universe. There is nowhere you must be. Not in the future, not in the past ... now! For where I am, you are. There is no separation. Blessed child, I hear you! You hear my voice ... it is true. Listen ... peace be with you. Yes Karen, thank you for bringing me here. So grateful and so happy to be with you now ... thank you. What can I do for you?

K Thank you. Do I have your permission to ask questions?

C Yes. I come to bring light so that all may see more clearly their Way ... the Way of Truth ... Way of the Light. There was no light upon the world at the time I came.

K You said there was no light. What happened to the light?

C It was deep within the Earth, below the surface and hard to see. There was great confusion ... great misunderstanding. The fear of life ... the fear of death

... fear in general and the fear of darkness.

K Is there a lot of fear and darkness now in the world?

C Yes. The time for light has come. The dawn of a new era is beginning. Many are waking up ... waking up to see.

K Did many wake up in your lifetime?

C Many began to wake, yes.

K Were you married to Mary Magdalene?

C Yes. (*Confirmation of last session*)

K Why are there differences in whether you were married or not married to her?

C They aren't listening to their truth. They are not listening. They are only repeating what they heard.

K Did you have children?

C It was seven.

K What happened to the children?

C They had families of their own.

K Did some of the children have gifts like you?

C Some did, yes.

K After the crucifixion, what happened after the death scene?

C The question you asked was not an accurate explanation of what happened?

K Can you explain what is accurate?

C Much focus is placed on the crucifixion. There is no judgment. It is a fascinating phenomenon for many to imagine that it's possible to nail a man to a cross at all. That this could be done is unconscionable. That any being could be nailed to the cross and be put up to suffer, is unfathomable. Yet it was done in that time. Now the suffering of a body in that manner was part of the lesson that there is no need to suffer. There is no need to punish. There is no need to torture. It is not necessary to put one's self through agony for any reason whatsoever. And yet there are those that feel suffering must come before joy. Suffering must come before Heaven. Suffering must come before reward, but the Father demands no suffering. The Father expects no torture. It is your right to live now, to experience now without the need to suffer. All is given now! Free yourself from your suffering … free yourself from your torture. You do it for no reason and no gain. It is not a righteous act. It is not a wise thing to do and it's not necessary. Do not condemn. Do not punish. Do not damn.

K Did you suffer on the cross and if so why did you suffer?

C I needed to suffer to show there is no need to suffer and that life is eternal. You don't have to suffer to receive God's gift of life. It's not necessary. How did this give people the need to suffer because I died on the cross? It is surprising, but it is not too surprising.

> *It is my impression that Yeshua is explaining there is no need to suffer physically in order to prove that one is righteous. The way in which it is explained if feels like he is speaking of those who die for their beliefs, similar to being a martyr. He was explaining that he was not trying to be a martyr as the reason for his death, but to show others that life is eternal.*

K Did you ascend?

C Yes. I was always alive. I never died. This is what I was showing that there is no death.

K Did you show yourself to others after your crucifixion?

C Yes.

K   Did you go to France or any other counties after your death scene?

C I ascended unto the Father.

K So you no longer continued in the body on Earth, is that correct?

C That is correct!

K Were you receiving training in other spiritual beliefs in other countries?

C Yes.

K What was the most influential?

C Africa... Egypt area, Tunisia, and the Tibet area.

K Why did some of Karen's clients have different viewpoints in your lifetime and death?

C There is a great amount of myth that have been interwoven into the historical accounts of my lifetime on Earth in the life of Yeshua. There is a great deal myth, there is a great deal of misinformation. The message has been changed in some ways to suit certain intentions that aren't necessarily what my intention was. So there is some confusion and some of this carries over even in the regression, on occasion. And not just the conscious mind, but there are certain imprints that are left on the subconscious can be interpreted by the subconscious a certain way.

K So are you saying that if someone thought you were God and not a man in that lifetime, then that would be imprinted on their mind?

C Yes, that is a good example.

> *This is an interesting statement concerning the discussion of imprinting. This is similar to saying that what you believed in the past lifetimes, may be your perspective in the current lifetime. This is important information how we can retain the same perspectives from one lifetime to the next.*

K Why did these clients choose to come to that lifetime with you?

C The meanings of the reasons for lifetimes are so varied that it depends upon the individual. However there is something to be learned, something to be gained, some experience that was necessary ... evolution for reconnecting.

K Are there more people who will come with lifetimes with you?

C Many more Karen, there are many more coming. I see twelve more that are not necessarily all at once for one book.

K Are clients called to come to Karen as others have told me?

C Yes.

K So the book will take a little longer than she originally thought.

C Yes. You would like to see it finished in seven months, but that is not going to happen. Three years maybe for it to be complete. Don't worry. You are supported in this book. I am guiding you! I am a very strong guiding force for you.

> *There seems to be a consensus among client that I am supported in writing this book. This book has taken almost five years at this point due to various challenges. It has been difficult at times, but it has always been a labor of love. I held the belief that this book would come out when it is the right time. I now understand why certain events occurred which has held back the publishing of this book.*

K Is there anything else you would like to explain about the book?

C You will take it one step at a time as it been unfolding for you. Take your time. Do not worry about linearity. The only purpose for dating it is just for you to keep a record for yourself. They don't necessarily flow in the order you receive it.

K Thank you. What does Yeshua wish to speak about healing? Is it pure intention or something else I need to understand?

C Healing ... it is not just intention. Healing is making whole ... what is already whole. Healing is recognizing the wholeness that already exists. In order to heal it is important to first experience one's wholeness and feel and know the wholeness. And then in the state of wholeness ...of Oneness ... direct one's attention to the fragmented area that appears separate from the wholeness and then see it as whole.

K Beautiful. So can everyone heal?

C Yes everyone can heal. There is no lesson in illness. Illness is the perception of separation.

K What about young children with disease, are they teacher souls?

C This is some of the misunderstanding. Everyone learns from each other. Everyone is a teacher and a student. Often when a child comes in and experiences illness it is own soul created separation, a sense of separateness … fragmentation … that needs wholeness. And sometimes the only way for this soul to experience the wholeness is to entirely depart the physical plane to return to wholeness. The intent is to experience the wholeness in all planes of existence. Some planes are easier than others. Some planes are much more difficult.

K Is Earth plane the most difficult?

C It is just one of the more difficult and for a Whole Soul, a Soul is on all planes of existence at one time. The Full Soul focused in the Earth plane, can enter the Earth plane, not with a sense of wholeness and immediately manifested disease, which is what happens often with a newborn. It is not in a state in experiencing wholeness and it must depart quickly if it wishes to, or remain to try to bring an expression into a fuller state of wholeness. It has a choice. It is not for the purpose to teach a lesson. It is doing its best and those beings that are around the soul that is experiencing this, may gain enrichment in their wholeness and may learn the importance of wholeness, or may choose to suffer for it, which is not desirable. Or they may create less wholeness in themselves or a sense of less wholeness, we should say. What every being is striving to create greater wholeness … that is its natural tendency.

Yeshua speaks of the Whole Soul as being on all planes of existence at

*one time and says the Full Soul is focused on the Earth plane, which
can create illness if it chooses. So if we can remember our Whole Soul
then healing can occur. When clients are healing, I ask them to go
to their original blueprint of perfect health. Yeshua explains that we
must remember our Oneness in healing which also can be explained as
remembering the Whole Self.*

K So when you were healing, you were showing them their wholeness?

C Yes. When I would say, "Come with me, I am One with the Father. I am One
in my wholeness with all Creation. Join me in my Oneness." And in joining in
my Oneness ... it supported the other in experiencing their Oneness.

If you could imagine liquid mercury and there is a pile of liquid mercury
and other beads of liquid mercury around it. The liquid mercury in its bead
form may feel separate. It may tell itself "I am separate, I feel insignificant and
small." Although it is mercury, it is the liquid mercury in its existence, but
it sees separation. It could perceive itself as weak and could attribute itself a
disease. It could say "You are weak, "and tell itself this. In its weakness it
could create a vulnerability. In its vulnerability it could open up to a sense
of lack. It could open itself up to a sense of dis-ease ... uncomfortableness,
unhappiness and despair. It could split apart into other tinier pieces. Still, it
is no less liquid mercury, but I would say, "Come unto me," and invite that
piece of liquid mercury to join with me in my Wholeness and Oneness which I
share freely. And as it joins with me, it feels its own Oneness and Wholeness.
And it knows it is not even apart from the Father liquid mercury, or any other
pieces of liquid mercury. It now feels at peace and whole. This is much like an
example of the metaphor the healing that I did. It is bringing a sense of
wholeness and Oneness with the Creator... with Home.

This is such a beautiful metaphor to help us gain an understanding of our

Oneness with God, Source. Yeshua continues to use metaphors or stories similar to the way he conveyed his teachings to others in order for his message to be understood. In Matthew 13:13 Jesus says, "This is why I speak to them in parables: because seeing, they do not see; and hearing they do not hear; nor do they understand."

K Thank you! So did you perform many healings?

C Yes.

K Did you teach others healing?

C Yes.

K Are there differences in the way people can heal?

C Remembering your Oneness with the Father. The origin from which you came, for all who came ... from all who came ... is essential for the healing process. Knowing the Oneness ... knowing that there is no separation is essential to a perfect state of healing, because in that state of Oneness; anxiety, fear, and worry are dropped and gladness takes hold ... joy and peace take over. The harmony is restored and everything can mend. Add to it a picture in your mind of wholeness and perfection ... that is true Oneness. It's beyond this appearance of the separation. This too is important and vibrating ones energy to the frequency of wholeness means letting go of appearance.

What is true beneath the surface of everything ... sink into the truth ... sink into the unifying vibration of the universe ... sink into the fabric of the universe ... sink into the one tone that is the underlying, subtonic One to all creation. Here is where there is Oneness ... here beneath the surface appearance where the truth lies. Here is where pieces of God sink into the plane of existence that is Unity ... that is Oneness. It feels like all worlds are united. Heal the Oneness and feel the unity. Now once you're in this state of being, you may feel your hands tingle. You may feel clarity ... tranquility ...

peace beyond the world you see. Here is the truth of your existence. There is no need to force anything. Just feel that source of your being. Affirm it and claim it as truth and then let it go. It is very simple.

I was curious about the word "subtonic" as it related to the statement "sink into the one tone that is underlying, subtonic one to all creation." It is the seventh tone on the musical scale and a step below the tonic. This is quite interesting as it does relate to the meaning of the sentence. I believe that the collective will sometimes give us a word or information that the client and the therapist does not know in order to validate what is spoken through the channel.

K What was the most important message you gave to the people?

C Unity ... Oneness ... the Christ is the one unifying spirit.

K When others spoke of you being the Son of God. Did you have a normal birth? How were you conceived? Was there Immaculate Conception?

C No. There was no immaculate conception as some would wish to say, because God could not conceive a man. And many wish to give me the title "God." I am no more God than anyone is God. We are all God. We are all One with the Father. But the title "God" that was given to me was meant to create a higher hierarchy and that is not what we wish to teach. It was a normal conception.

K Thank you.

C Gabriel did tell Mary she was to have a child. This is true.

K Were you a part of the Essences?

C Yes.

K Was this kept a secret?

C Many things were kept secret at the time to preserve the teachings.

This could explain why so many clients said the Essenes were secretive.

K Were there secret teachings?

C There was information that was shared with those that were able to understand it.

> *Again confirming other client's statements that there was information given to those who were able to understand advanced teachings. In Naomi's session she said, "Many in our group though are not at the same level."*

K So it depended upon where they were and what they were ready to understand?

C Yes. The teachings went all the way to China and Asia. The teachings went across the world.

K So how did the teachings get so confused?

C Well, it is a matter of communication ... translation. In many it was interpretation. Sometimes there is a context already in existence that some wish to reinforce with interpretation that reinforced that context.

K So people will find what they need to support their belief.

C This does occur.

K Will there be any documents to come out the will speak of the truth?

C The truth needs no documents! (*I loved this!*)

K Thank you.

C It is known in the heart.

K Is the reason Karen and others didn't relate to the church?

C Yes. Follow the heart. It is the center of your being ... the Source that gives you life.

K Did the people who followed you understand about energy, and the chakras?

C Yes, they understood. It was actually easier to understand than now. People were much closer to the Earth. They were much more sensitive to the vibrations of the earth, of the rocks, the trees, and the air. They could feel it more acutely in their being.

> *This is an indication that there was a greater connection to nature and the Earth during those times.*

K Did you volunteer to come to Earth?

C Yes. (*This is a confirmation from the last session*)

K Why did you decide to volunteer?

C To bring more light to the Earth, so that others could see the light within themselves. It was that piece of mercury ... One with the Father. Magnetic in my ability to bring other pieces of mercury to me, to expand the mercury and this is what I did. It created more Oneness and Wholeness. More were brought unto me and therefore brought unto the Father. And this is what we are still doing. We are bringing awareness, consciousness ... waking awareness unto the Father. We all join in the sea of awareness ... the sea of light with our eyes open to experience our fullness, our wholeness, and our Oneness with all Creation. And this expands and expands. It is expanding constantly and its light radiates out.

> *I found it fascinating that he described that Yeshua was magnetic in his ability to bring people to their Oneness and many clients said they were drawn to him as in this observation, "you were pulled to listen, as though you were pulled away."*

K Did you have any other incarnations on Earth?

C Yes.

K Was Edgar Cayce correct about your other lifetimes?

C Yes.

> *This was also confirmed in Ruth's session about Yeshua having many lifetimes.*

K When you were discussing that we are here for the experience, am I correct in saying we are also here to learn lessons?

C It is not the way that it has been explained. There are many that feel this is no more than a school. That is not entirely true. This is an expression of being … a creativity of joy and celebration. It is an expression of love. A painting is beautiful when it is viewed in its totality … in its essence … just as it is! If it is taken and broken down and broken in parts and analyzed, it loses its beauty. Life is the same. It is not always to be analyzed. It is not always to be decided if this is a lesson or not. It can be just experience without anything more than that.

> *In Yeshua's response, there is a bigger picture than a soul just coming for the learning of lessons. He says that sometimes when we tend to analyze it can then lose its beauty. Sometimes we decide to come just for the experience. He stated previously that we are learning lessons.*

K So it can also be just the experience, is that what you are explaining?

C It is about the essence of life … the essence of what is life. What is life? Life that brings forth and blossoms that plays and dances and celebrates, and expresses itself in countless and innumerable ways. It needs no interpretation, it needs no formality. If one were to let themselves be, and just experience in their being, and feel within their being the expression of life in every moment, then they would naturally blossom in their greatest glory and beauty and be One with God their Creator. Do not be concerned with ascension. That is missing the point … that is something man made. Creator would have you as the hummingbird and have joy in your being … thanksgiving in your expression of life. Life is everlasting … life that does not die. As you do that, as you celebrate the joy of living … the joy of life that is in the core of your being, naturally without any work or effort, you blossom and you will evolve. It is not work!

K Then why do people come in with such difficult lives?

C They choose it.

> *I believe that we choose and plan our lifetimes before our entrance into this world or other worlds. After working with clients for many years, this has been confirmed many times.*

K What is the reason why they would choose it?

C Because they think they must make it so in order to evolve. They decided there must be a struggle in order to grow. They have created this themselves because they have decided there must be suffering. The suffering of me on the cross ... they projected it on to me because it helped them justify their suffering, which they felt was necessary. It wasn't! They must feel the guilt that they created in themselves and then feel the need to punish themselves for the guilt, and create a set of circumstances that allows for the suffering to make the guilt go away. But it is a never ending cycle of bringing suffering, and bringing guilt and bringing pain, until they finally learn to give it up and letting it go. (*Interesting statements*)

K So aren't they learning something?

C It is a natural course of learning. But it doesn't have to be, Karen. It is not necessary to go through lessons to learn to be. That is what we need to remember that the natural course of life is to thrive and not struggle and strain.

K So are you saying, it is our own belief system that creates struggle?

C Yes.

K So can you explain the current world situation? Again is that a collective belief system which creates killing and chaos are on Earth?

C Yes. It is one thought ... an erroneous thought that gets picked up like a virus by the thoughts of others which is really One. It is held onto for a while until it is let go. It is all creative expression. It is all a creative way of perceiving life. Sometimes the soul may want to express itself as not life, to experience what life is! It is all okay ... it is all acceptable.

K So how can we change this virus?

C The best thing anyone can do is remember Oneness! Take the focus off the virus. Take the focus of what is not wanted entirely and focus on the unity and the Oneness with the Creator and with the joy and harmony of that and that will change ... change everything around it. It's like a ripple in a pond.

Nearing the editing of the book, the coronavirus became a major pandemic for the world. I found it particularly interesting that Yeshua choose to use the word "virus," when referring to humans not remembering the Oneness. In these times as a nation, there is so much division and the forgetting of our Oneness. I have a feeling that this message has an even deeper meaning than when it was spoken five years prior to the coronavirus coming to Earth.

K In the *Bible* it speaks of evil and sin. Can Yeshua address this?

C There is no evil ... no sin! (*Loudly spoken*) Again, it is the state of discomfort from being out of alignment, which is the natural state of being. It is going against the natural flow of life ... that is all. It takes on all manner of form and all the gruesome form it takes on, but remember it is an idea that is not permanent in the mind of the Creator. And remember, the tendency of the soul is to have fun ... even when creating a situation to scare itself. It's for its own joy and amusement. It is for the experiment of being afraid. And sometimes the fear becomes more interesting and it is let go. Very little needs to be done to force that shift. Allow its life, its expression and it will soon pass out of boredom, and put the attention on what is really more pleasurable. That is all.

According to THE GOSPEL OF MARY it was written, "The Savior said,
"There is no sin." There were several clients who said Yeshua did not
believe in sin. In Naomi's session she said, "There is no sin! There are only
burdened souls who have for some reason come into a situation where
they are not as aware of the light and the love, and the peace."

K Is there something about your life that we don't understand?

C There are many that believe I came to Earth on a spaceship. A star seed. This
is true.

K But were you still conceived by Mary and Joseph?

C Yes.

K Then can you explain when you spoke of coming to Earth on spaceship?

C Oh, that was a metaphor. Just that I was of another solar system ... not
sprouted forth from the Earth. As many have come from other solar systems
to be on the Earth ... so have I. We have all lived on other places at other
times. Yes, so I was in a more evolved state when I came, with the explicit
purpose of bringing more light to a higher vibration than had been on the
Earth before to help illuminate ... to help wisdom and enlightening awareness
for the evolution of the planet. And yes, I came with an expression fresh
... no more evolved than you are. The only difference was that it was a time of
great darkness ... much more darkness. (*Sigh*) And with that kind of light ...
that kind of high vibration ... miracles occurred which got a lot of attention,
which is necessary to help shift some focus.

In Adam's session he confirmed that Yeshua lived on other planets with
this statement, "But he has traveled to other planets."

K Are there other volunteers coming to Earth? Karen has had clients say they are
volunteers from other planets. Is that correct?

C Yes. They volunteered to bring different fragrances.

K Can you explain?

C Perhaps a different frequency. Imagine a symphony and there is a song. So they volunteered to bring a particular tone to the symphony. Sound is vibration that creates and this is why they needed to bring a different tone to create differently. So perhaps there might be a new direction ... a new experience the Earth is going in, a new expression. And it seemed at the time, that particular sound was needed to create what needed to be created. So many heard the call as they say. Many heard the song and they would say our sound would fit well there ... it would be beautiful. The harmony we could create!

K Beautiful! ... Some who came seemed to be confused?

C Yes. Some came and they were very comfortable in the song they were used to hearing and the new song they were hearing was disorienting. They wished to be back in the song they heard before. It was more comfortable. The new one was more volatile perhaps because of the particular place in the song that was being played. It needed that kind of tension before it could move into a smoother place. They came to gather up what they could as well with this new song imprinting on their soul, because they were changed by it as well.

Once again Yeshua made use of stories or parables on numerous occasions to help his followers understand his teachings. Although they may be different stories than what was in the Bible, I found it fascinating how Yeshua also used these beautiful metaphors or stories many times in Ellie's sessions for our understanding.

K Are there more volunteers coming?

C We are all volunteers.

K So everyone is volunteering?

C Yes.

K But some are volunteering with the intention of helping others, mankind?

C Everyone is volunteering with purpose of healing. Some egos get in the way. Only those who wish to experience the song of the Earth come ... only those who wish to experience it. Some have been here before and some have chosen to stay for a while. Some have never been, and some are attracted to the song and come here. Each one is contributing to the shaping of the song and the expression of that. Each one may come and find it is not to their liking, by their own hand if they wish. There is no wrong or right way and there is no greater value than another. That is ego only. There is only contributing to the symphony of Earth and the symphony of any other galaxy beyond. It is all beautiful and all perfect and they go places. And so some are a attracted to different places and they come here with a whole different tune perhaps, it is new. It hasn't been played in the symphony ... a different note and it can, if played correctly, influence that direction the music is going, but I assure you it will never end. It will never end. It will always find expression some place, somewhere. It is eternal and it is continual. There is no end. There may be a crescendo ... there is a beautiful high light, but it will continue and the dance and the song continue.

K Beautiful ...Thank you.

C This is what I meant when the Father comes unto me. It is a metaphor I gave you before, like the mercury. Life attracts life. Life is a common thread in everything. It senses its own and we are all One. We are all One Karen, and we can find me in you as well. You just call for me and I am already there. You may imagine that my auric field is around you. I am her big brother ... your big brother ... I am your big brother nonetheless.

K Thank you.

C Yes.

K Ellie would like to know how she can connect with her Higher Self more, and where the truth lies.

C Call her to become still and say "Higher Self." It is important to remember that the Higher Self doesn't mean higher above. Actually that is an inaccurate description of what Higher Self is. It is more accurate to describe it as the inner self. It is within ... so go within. Because within the core Essence of them, is their Higher Self. Like the sun and the system in the galaxy, that is where the Higher Self is. The term the "Higher Self" has impressions it brings that is somehow above and must reach for it but, it is more of a sinking into the Inner Self ... this is more accurate.

It is also my belief that the Higher Self is within. However, humans seem to have a need to think of higher when accessing greater spiritual awareness and knowledge. In this book, I am using the subconscious to describe what many call the "Higher Self." It also has been referred to as the Inner Self or the True Self.

K Are there levels of the Inner Self?

C Going within is also confusing. It is difficult for some, because they have difficulty and tend to believe God is not within. They tend to feel God is above. The center of life is within. This is what we must change. This is what we must change for the human race for the human to become empowered. We must learn to realize that God is within them. God is in their heart. Every cell has a point of light in it. Every cell has a God spark within it. The heart of the healing ... the beating heart and the breath center of life is within. God is within the Higher Self ... the expression of the God within ...turning within. Realizing the Source is within and not outside of you is a great step toward empowerment. (*Beautiful*)

K So that is why the "Kingdom is within" resonated to Karen?

C Yes, it is true the Kingdom is within. Heaven is within. All realms are within. When a person chooses to die they choose because death is a choice. It doesn't have to be. The person goes to a portal within. When you look at a galaxy it goes within ... it expands out. The calm within the center of hurricane. These are metaphors and expressions that reflect and mirror back to you truth ... the truth of your being.

K Thank you,

C Yes.

K Thank you for coming to us today.

Ellie's Impressions after Her Session

When I asked Ellie what was her first impressions she responded, "That was wild." She felt all of her responses were based on her impressions and feeling that Yeshua was conveying to her while in this altered state. Ellie felt that she had received very specific information coming through Yeshua. When Yeshua spoke of the lessons, he felt there was too much emphasis on the lesson, and that it's really just the experience of life. I do feel that lessons are a part of our spiritual growth, but it may not be giving us the total picture of why we came to this plane. In the experience there also may be a lesson as well. I felt that is what Yeshua was trying to convey. My feelings about learning lessons were later confirmed in the next session.

Ellie also felt that the analogy of mercury was "cool." She spoke about feeling a tingle in her fingers when Yeshua came through. I felt a tingle as well, but in my body. We both felt this loving presence in the room. When Yeshua came through, Ellie said she felt an overwhelming sense of love that took over her and she said,

"There is no faking that." As Yeshua would speak to the crowds at the level of their understandings during his time on Earth, Ellie felt that he was talking to us on the level we could understand. This has been verified by other clients as well.

Ellie's entire session was around five hours long, so she was in a very deep state of hypnosis. There was a softness in her voice while speaking at a slow pace with many pauses in the subconscious. I didn't include all of the pauses, as it would be difficult for the reader. At times it was difficult for me to remain unemotional when Yeshua was speaking.

Ellie's Second Channeled Session with Yeshua

"Truth is all within ourselves. We don't need to find it from outside ourselves. We don't have to go to someone else. We have the power ourselves."
HARMONY

Ellie while in her subconscious state, was told to go to her Council. Once in the Council, I asked her subconscious how they were going to help her channel Yeshua. Immediately she said, "I am here now," as her head turned toward me. This was a sign that Ellie had begun channeling Yeshua.

C I am here now. It is good to be here with you.

K It is good to be with you again and we want to thank Ellie.

C We bring peace and love.

K Do I have permission to continue with questions that were prepared by Ellie?

C Yes.

K Do I have permission to ask about Edgar Cayce?

C Yes.

K Was Edgar Cayce correct in his messages of learning lessons?

C Many of things Cayce brought forward were correct ... yes. He was helping people.

K Can you explain his connection with The White Brotherhood?

C Edgar has had lifetimes with some of these beings. Yes, some are connected on inner planes, and he created his group of advisors because they were so helpful to him, influential. They left impressions on him and asked if he could share his knowledge with others. They said he could.

K Thank you. Can Yeshua explain darkness?

C Yes. Darkness is an illusion. It is an illusion.

K Why do we sometimes pick up that energy of darkness in others?

C Most of this was contracted for learning ... for the growth as an opportunity to see what it is so vastly different from what you are. It is part of the exploration and eventually you get tired of it, and life is harder with it.

> *In this statement Yeshua does explain that there are things that are contracted for our learning.*

K So darkness is an illusion that we must experience to learn?

C Yes.

K You spoke of contracts. Can you explain who created the contracts? Do we as souls create our own contracts?

C It is the soul that creates the contract, yes. So the child creates the contract before it is born. When it decides that it's going to experience a temporal life and it decides where it is going to live, where it is going to be ... what it wishes to experience.

> *In Ruth's session, Yeshua also says that we create contracts as a type of an agreement made before coming to Earth. From my work with clients, I have found in my work that we create contracts with those in our lifetimes for various lessons and experiences.*

K And the other persons are agreeable to this contract?

C This is why it is a contract.

K Why is a contract needed?

C This is beyond your ability to understand exactly, but I will try. Imagine that there is something in the body. It is not the body itself, but of a part of the soul. This is like a homing pigeon. It is given its instruction and it ventures out and it's going to meet at a particular grid and particular physical location. It is as though the soul ... the part of the soul, is deciding to do that, to reach out and meet at a particular location at a particular time ... at a particular date or window, and this is what happens with the contract. The soul remembers the agreement to be at a particular coordinate, but it isn't time driven. It is different. It is more event driven than time driven. But this is well beyond your ordinary ability to understand.

> *This is such a wonderful explanation of our contracts. It is similar to what Emma spoke of in her session, "The blueprint, the foundations, is the contract." And once again, Yeshua says this is beyond our ability to understand. I am assuming there is even more that we do not yet understand about our contracts.*

K Did you call certain followers disciples?

C All of them that followed me were disciples.

> *Clients often spoke of Yeshua having many followers.*

K So it wasn't just one special group?

C No.

K Was there anything else that the disciples meant at that time?

C The disciples also taught. They would learn and teach. It was the purpose of the disciples to go into the world and teach. They taught the principles I taught.

K Why were there different viewpoints of your teachings?

C Just projections from others of what my teachings were, and what I was teaching.

K What was the greatest misconception of your teachings?

C There was no misconception. My teachings always stand for itself in this time.

K Why are there different opinions of what you taught?

C There will always be different opinions in anything that is taught as people refer to their egos.

K Did your mother Mary and Mary Magdalene have the gifts of healing as well?

C Yes.

> *In Grace's session she also confirms that Mary and Mary Magdalene were also healers.*

K Did your disciples?

C Yes.

K Did you come to Mary and the disciples as an apparition or in a body after the crucifixion?

C My physical body… my physical form from their perspective. What they would see was solid. They needed a form. It was not enough to experience me in spirit … for them to understand that nothing dies.

> *We are given only that which we are able to understand at the time. Therefore, Mary and the others would have to see the physical form of Yeshua in order to believe that no one really dies.*

K Did you ever go to the pyramids in Egypt?

C Yes.

> *This was a confirmation in Gina's session, when she spoke of Yeshua*
> *going into the pyramids and saying, "He was drawn to the pyramids."*

K Were you drawn to them?

C Yes I was.

K What were you feeling in the pyramids?

C I went to help cleanse the dark energy that was there.

K So there was a dark energy that was there?

C Yes.

K What kind of dark energy was there?

C Kind of dark energy that could be disastrous to the planet. There was a focused energy that, as you know, that went through the pyramid with Gaia.

K I had a client that went to recharge in the pyramid as she said there was an energy flow that was positive. Was she correct in that feeling?

C The energy flow when I went there was corrected.

K So, when did you go to correct the energy flow? Was it in the soul state or before?

C No before.

K You spoke of traveling to different places, is that correct?

C That was correct.

K Did you go to learn spiritual concepts?

C Yes, I did. I studied. I gathered knowledge. ...I remembered.

K So you were gone quite a few years then. Is that correct?

C Yes.

K Did you travel by ship to these places?

C Yes, that is correct.

K Did Joseph of Arimathea take you, or did someone else take you to these places? Who took you on these travels?

C Joseph did take me.

Another confirmation of Yeshua traveling with Joseph to different places.

K Can you give more information about the Essenes?

C What would you like to know?

K Was the community kept a secret or did everyone know?

C It was kept secret ... but many knew.

K Were you born in the Essene community?

C Yes, I was.

K Were your mother and father a part of the Essene community before you were born?

C Yes.

K What did that mean to be an Essene?

C The answer is not straight forward. There was a community familial lines ... passed down from generation to generation and that they married amongst themselves. And the principle was one of giving and receiving. There was sharing, it was very much communal.

K Was it a poor community?

C It was not poor. It was said to be poor ... only from the perspective of wealthy Romans.

K Were the Essenes separate from the traditional Jewish community?

C It was.

K What did the traditional Jewish community think of the Essenes?

C The regular Jewish community acknowledged them. Yes they saw them as their brothers, but they saw the Essene community almost in a bubble ... its own little world protected. They understood that it was a pure line of DNA.

A pure line that needed to stay protected, untouched and undamaged. And they understood this. There may have been other factors … perhaps from a sense of jealousy … the lower ego minds, influence. But Essenes were seen as the seeds of humanity. It is necessary to preserve those seeds. There is a purity of the DNA … a purity that would allow for what you call miracles. This is very important. It was protected for many millennia and the community helped ensure that. The community lived intentionally an unremarkable existence. They did not want to draw much attention to themselves if they could be viewed as poor.

K What was the principle of their beliefs at that time?

C That they were the chosen children of God. But when we mean to say "chosen," we don't mean excluded. We understood the purity of the DNA. The blueprint for all of humanity was stored in the Essenes.

K What happened to this DNA, as the Essenes community is no more?

C The DNA continues. It is still present.

K You spoke of the DNA creating miracles. Is that correct?

C This is correct. Just a gift of prophesy, a gift of clairvoyance … a gift of miracles … yes.

K So psychic abilities are in this DNA. Is that what you are saying?

C Yes.

K You spoke of having children with gifts, can you explain?

C Gifts of the Holy Spirit, clairvoyance, gifts of speaking in tongues.

> *It has also been interpreted by some scholars that speaking in tongues during the time of Yeshua, was actually intuitively speaking many languages without any training. And there are others who would say that it could have been translated as speaking in an ancient language. There can be different interpretations of words in the Bible since there*

were various interpretations from the original Aramaic language that
was spoken at the time.

K Did your children go and speak of your teachings?

C Yes they did. Many had to go into hiding for a very long time.

K Are we aware of them? There is no mention of them in the *Bible*.

C No, this is not in the *Bible*.

K You also spoke of being from another planet?

C Yes.

K What was the name of the planet?

C Not that you can discern.

K One client described it as the Planet of Light. Is that the planet?

C Yes, this is one of the planets.

K Can you describe the Planet of the Light?

C Planet of Light is truly of the light ... everything is light. It is difficult to describe because it's not like anything you have ever experienced or seen in this physical world. It is pure light. It is the brightest of light, beautiful beyond description. There is a body, but the body is the light body. It is what you call a "Light Body," but it is beyond that. It isn't the light body that you know from the physical form. It is more like crystal, but pliable but flesh ... but not flesh. It is transparent, and what you see when you look at this body is like a glass body with a light radiating within in its center ... its core. There is no need to cover up with clothing ... there is no need for adornment ... no need for protection. Everything is radiant.

   I had two clients from other sessions describe similar experiences in the
   Planet of Light.

K Does everyone go to this Planet of Light?

C No, not everyone. Those whose inclination is to evolve in the light. Those who choose to go, and many do.

K Does every soul experience some type of experience on other planets?

C Yes they do.

K It has been said that Venus is the Planet of Love, is that correct?

C There are many planets of love. Even this planet is a planet of love. It's intended to hold the energy of love to dominate all the energies of the other planets. This is part of what everyone wants to be a part of. Venus, is a planet that followed very much the same steps of Earth. There was a great love presence anchored in the planet of Venus, and it was a catalyst in many ways for the successful seeding of Earth.

K Are you saying that Earth was seeded by Venus?

C It was part of the process. Those on Venus were involved in the seeding of Earth ... yes. Not exclusively.

K What were the other planets involved?

C Venus was not the only planet in our solar system that was involved. There were other planets from other solar systems that were also involved, and there were other energies not exclusive to a particular planet that were involved as well.

K How was God involved with creation of the Earthling? Did God create us or beings from other planets?

C It's important that God works through entities. These entities are the Hands of God ... the God Source ... God Intelligence. God Light is in everyone when they choose to listen to it. Those that listen to it and hear its voice can be the Hands of God ... the Voice of God. God is omnipresent ... everywhere ... everyone ... not an isolated entity. So these entities, these beings involved in seeding the Earth, are just as One with God as you are. Although different and have different ideas, but the spark of light within them is the same spark of

Light you carry. One of the things that we are here to learn is accepting all forms and realizing all forms, all beings are a part of the One. The One is God ... yet One with the One Creator.

K Beautiful! Why did beings seed Earth? What is the purpose of this?

C There is no one reason. There are many, many species that come to create Earth ... many.

K Were they in conjunction with each other or were they separate?

C The most amazing beautiful gift, the most amazing beautiful project, for a lack of better word, ventured forth. If you can imagine many warring, in some cases galaxies, planets and species deciding to come together ... one planet for peace ... for love ... for life ... that's what Earth is. Earth is not just symbolic in its purpose. Earth is the hope of the entire universe!

> *In Jacob's session he confirms Ellie's channeled statement that Earth was created "to bring about love." It is also very similar to Ellie's last statement when Jacob says, "This planet is one in a billion. There is much interest in this planet. Many planets have a vested interest in it."*

K You spoke of Earth as a planet of peace and love, then why do we still continue to have wars?

C Let us explain. I am giving you relevant information that takes time to communicate to Ellie. Some of the information I am trying to send her takes a while to transmit ... it is slow, but we are doing the best we can but right now. It is slow and we stretch for the right words.

> *At this point in the session, Yeshua was explaining why it has taken time for Ellie to answer the questions as Yeshua. The responses from a client's subconscious many times will come through at slower pace, as the subconscious has difficulty expressing certain wordage and is communicating at the level of the client's current understanding.*

C Earth is the hope for the galaxy. There have been wars. There have been wars beyond your comprehension. There has been devastation and destruction beyond anything you can begin to conceive of. There have been solar systems completely obliterated with no life left remaining ... entire solar systems. In this galaxy there are millions of solar systems. In these solar systems there are varying levels of intelligence, life forms and some are the most rudimentary, simple cells with intelligence. Some with the intelligence and ability to create miracles, even though the simplicity structure you might liken to poison ivy or some other small plant. Yet that plant has the capability and ability to create miracles in everyday life. And then, there are some that are so simple that there are no miracles. There is not much for even you to notice.

And then there are some that are very war like in their expression that are hostile, aggressive, heartless, and ruthless. And others that are meek and gentle, peaceful. This mixture of cell structures, of instructions and templates, is what has come together on the planet Earth. This mixture of cell structure to simplify the terms, was brought together in a laboratory ... again I am using a metaphor. And a new template was created that contains and combines all of these predispositions. All of these at its core ... the filament, is the God Source ... the Light Eternal and this is what was placed together into Earth. And this is why you see such varying degrees of behavior.

You don't see this on other solar systems. You don't see this varying vast spectrum of behavior. This is why you are told this is a planet of free will. A planet of free choice, because every entity has the choice to experience and express any multitude of behaviors created from this hybrid, homogenous, template. Now, when we say we have a planet of love ... infinite love, infinite peace, it is because the structure of the cells of the DNA have a predisposition for this. There is also a disposition for the aggressive. There is also a disposition for the meek. As the energies in the galaxy influence the Earth, you have heard of photon band [belt?], for example. As the energies interact with the earth plane, the magnetic, the electromagnetic crystalline grid of the planet, the varying energetic layers of the planet, and the varying energetic layers of these DNA, light up. Some other layers become dormant and some light up. This is the part of the awakening process we talk about. As these new layers of DNA light up and activate, new behavior comes through. You have seen this slowly happening because this does not happen immediately. But every human being on this Earth possesses this DNA. This DNA that is long extensive and fully packed with this homogenous mixture from all across the galaxy. And the experiment, as they say, is not an experiment as you would think of the terms of an experiment, but it is the most beloved endeavor of all those who hope for peace throughout the galaxy. It is almost akin to the world in olden times when countries fought with each other. One of the ways to ensure peace was to marry into another's country monarchy. It is very similar in its concept. They all agreed to come together and invest their own aspect of DNA. This world ... this Earth, is the only place where all the galaxy, aspects of DNA are brought into One.

It is hoped that with this success of Earth ... there will be peace throughout the galaxy, because everyone will begin to realize they are One ... they are truly One. It is a part of the process for realizing and recognizing the Oneness in all entities, and recognizing Oneness is the first way to bring about peace. This is why Earth is so important. This is what most people don't know. They have no way of knowing. This is why everyone wants to be a part of this Earth. Everyone wants to be a part of this. From the far reaches of the galaxy comes a being who wants to be born on Earth. Once you have lived on Earth, and you have experienced the vast range of emotions, the vast range of feelings and expression ... the vast range of belief and attitude, you now will know that when you meet any other entity from any other solar system, how it might possibly be, to be that other species. That is so vast.

As the Earth awakens and wakes up ... as humans begin to venture into space, into the galaxy, they will carry the seed, the imprint of every species in the galaxy. It will help them to bring peace further throughout the galaxy. This is why they say that humans are the hope for all creation. It is true ... when you say you only see war, you only see the hideous side ... you are seeing part of that growing process. It is necessary as the human evolves, the human will recognize that warring creature. I say creature because I want you to think when you first meet this other being on another planet that is all about aggression, and he will know a part of him is with you and you will know a part of you is in him, and there will be greater opportunity for peace. It is a beautiful design. It is also at its very essence, a way to recognize the Christ ... the Christos, which is the One Spirit that we are a part of. We already are One in Spirit.

This gives us a fascinating insight into our DNA and the nature of our planet. Although this is quite a lengthy statement, his words ring true to me in his beautiful explanation. I decided to include this entry for the reader to make their own decision.

K Thank you. Is there anything else Yeshua wished to talk to us about today?

C We wish to continue with these visits and the ability to channel me. Use the post hypnotic suggestion and call my name three times and I will come through. You do not need to go to a past life. Bring her to the Collective and in the Collective to free her mind enough to be open to receive me. I will come through her ... she needs to be in a receptive state.

It was quite surprising when Yeshua was giving me instructions for

Ellie's post-hypnotic suggestion to assist her in helping him come through quickly. This has never happened before in any of my sessions.

K What was the purpose of this channeling?

C It is for your book. Use it for your book and we will develop Ellie as a channel. As we do this she will be able to bring herself to this place.

In this statement, Yeshua was giving me instructions to include Ellie's channeling in this book for the reader.

K Thank you.

C Yes. We wish you blessings and peace. Oneness to feel Christ Oneness yourself and in all beings.

Ellie's Impressions after Her Session

Ellie said she remembered the discussion about Earth describing that it was the hope of the galaxy, and felt like she wanted to cry. She indicated that she "never imagined it was so vast," as it was the whole galaxy, and the whole solar systems that was involved in the seeding of the planet. When she thought of the part about our DNA being from all parts of the galaxy and beyond, she said she was "blown away."

When channeling, Ellie felt it was not her anymore, and had a sense of joy coming through. She also felt the vibration. In listening to her last session, she explained that there was so much she didn't remember. It was also surprising that Yeshua gave me instruction for her post hypnotic suggestion. The entire session was once again very interesting and informative.

Third Session with Ellie Channeling Yeshua

"When I would say, "Come with me, I am One with the Father. I am One in my wholeness with all Creation. Join me in my Oneness." And in joining in my Oneness ... it supported the other in experiencing their Oneness."
ELLIE

This was the third channeled session for Ellie. In her last session, I was instructed by the subconscious to first contact the Collective before channeling Yeshua. She went very easily into a deep state of hypnosis with the suggested post-hypnotic suggestion. This was quite interesting when Ellie's subconscious instructed me how to begin the session this time by contacting the Collective first. In this channeled session she has covered many different subjects.

Ellie in the Collective

K Does the personality of the soul remain once the soul is with God?

C Yes. God is everything and just as each snowflake is unique and is a unique expression of the drop of water, so too each soul has its own unique expression, even when it's filled up with and breaming over with a piece of God. It is its unique expression, beautiful, brilliant. Extending the piece of God, sending it out, and shinning like an echo reverberating, bouncing off other pieces of God. You are literally a piece of God and the piece of God.

K Is the Collective pieces of God?

C Yes. The collective is the One being expressed in many pieces, but yet One. Yes, the Collective is God. Yes there are many names that are called the Collective but the heart it's the same. ... The Sea of Awareness, Infinite Light, All That Is, God ... many names for the nameless. Every being has the piece of God ... which seems to be a piece of God there is a reflection in each being of God. There is a mirror that sees God ... and sees God everywhere and in all things.

K Can everyone channel?

C Yes, anyone can. However not everyone is ready. Ellie has fortified her being to be able to hold the vibration of light coming in and bringing it into the Earth plane uncorrupted. It is like being able to hold electricity, it needs a direct path and it needs a path that is sturdy enough and wide enough to be able to handle the frequency. If the channel is not ready, it simply will not work. If the channel is partly ready and not properly grounded or anchored ... there could be great discomfort, possibly injury. It is best to work to develop the channel first to make it strong.

It was stated that Ellie's other lives as a channel was a preparation for this lifetime. I have heard similar statements from other clients that their previous or present life is a preparation for their next life.

K Why do Angels, Ascended Masters and other spiritual beings resonate to different people?

C For each soul these beings ... these Ascended Masters and Angels are quite literally a part of that soul, are quite literally one with that soul, facets of that soul. If you imagine each soul as a diamond and there are many, many facets on that diamond, and so the soul will want to explore them all. They will look to what's capturing its attention ... its awareness, and helps it to feel uplifted ... a sense of belonging, a sense of home ... comfort, but more importantly a sense of unity with the rest of its beingness. And then that part of that soul that has taken on the image of Angels will communicate from the far reaches of the soul sense information that it has gathered that is concentrated and shared with another part of the soul that is seeking it. It is all the same soul ... all One but it is the soul. The light ... it's being shone between the very aspects of the soul and it becomes lit up and the dialogue is happening like a synapse in the brain, it is very similar, but still one brain but coming from different parts ... but still the brain. It is very similar when you conceptualize the vastness of the soul. It can seem as one aspect that it is seeking are far more advanced and somehow separate but they're not, they're not. They are One with the seeker of the information. The seeker of the information has found a way to retrieve the information.

K So when the seeker is ready for the information it will come?

C It may come in the form external to the seeker, but it is still the seeker answering itself.

K So the seeker already knows the answers?

C The seeker has the answers. It's just finding a way to bring it to itself. It could get the answer directly. It needs not the other form to get the answer. As the seeker begins to remember its Oneness with all Creation, as it begins to remember ... it knows the answers as well as the question. It will no longer need form to support itself.

K Why did the seeker not remember the information as humans?

C This question cannot be answered at this time. (*Long pause*) It is not that you are not to know. It is beyond the ability to explain it in a way that will make any sense to you.

Once again, it has been explained that the information is not always available to us and it is not time for the information to be given.

K It is my understanding that there is learning in between lives. Is that correct?

C Oh, yes.

K Why is there less learning that does not occur with some souls in the afterlife, where other souls are able to learn and heal?

C It is ultimately the willingness of the soul.

K Doesn't the soul want to know?

C The soul is exploring and experiencing what it wants to explore and experience. It is may not be willing or ready to move beyond what it is focused on. It is still learning about what it wants to learn about ... still remembering and exploring. It may not be ready to move out of that and to look at something new.

K Did she have another lifetime as a channel? Can the Collective tell her about those lifetimes?

C Yes. There were a few lifetimes where she practiced channeling, opening herself up to Spirit, to entities, to be able to communicate with them ... to be their voice. It was very troublesome for her as she felt that once the door was open, she didn't feel that she had any authority of what was expressed. She felt violated. She felt that she was just a vessel and that those conscious spirits that wished to be heard, and took over and didn't respect her boundaries. Which she allowed.

K How can they help her with this?

C Always ask for highest vibration with peace and love. Always ask specifically for any expression of spirit to communicate through her, that they are only the highest light vibration to be to communicate to her. Some information she would not normally would know, however the vibrational frequency she allowed to resonate with her body, her vehicle, was too low which created illness in her body, and anxiety, mental distortions, illness. She lacked awareness and knowledge and it was very hard for her. She vowed she would not channel after that, because she did not feel safe and she resisted channeling for a long. Now we would like her to be a channel once again. We are now calling her to channel light beings, to channel messages. To channel information for those who raising their vibrations. Your natural inclination which is to channel, just tell Spirit, that only the highest and best, most beings of divine love are free to communicate through me these vibrational beings.

I felt this is a cautionary explanation for those who wish to channel. There needs to be boundaries set and working only with those beings of the highest vibration. It was made clear that channeling should only to be a way of accessing spiritual information from those light beings of the highest vibrational level setting the intention for the highest good of all.

K So will she be able to safely channel from now on?

C She will release the fear as she does this. She must face what she is afraid of and do it again. And she will know, this time she will do it properly for the express purpose of sharing and shinning the light that these divine beings are wishing to bring to Earth. They need channels to do this.

K What would the Collective suggest? Should we remain in the Collective or go to Yeshua at this time?

C It is best to go to Yeshua at this time.

Ellie Channeling Yeshua

K Thank you. Yeshua are you here with us?

C I am.

K Do I have permission to ask questions?

C Yes.

K Ellie's question is what is the Holy Spirit?

C It is conscious awareness. The Holy Spirit is the Voice of God. It is the active interaction between the Son of God, the person and God. The Holy Spirit is the bridge … the communication link between the Father and the Son. It is the means by which, the Father and the Son communicate. When I say Father… it is the Creator. When I say son, it is all humanity … all life even the animals. It is the one word for all.

K Can you explain the Holy Trinity?

C Yes. It is a metaphor and it is an image to hold when understanding creation. Everything is interdependent … the Father, God, Creator, His Son, His Creation, the Holy Spirit, the translator between the upper and lower realms, for communication. The Son … being of the lower realm in substance only, to act out an existence that seems separate from the Father, from the Creator. To explore the denser regions, needs a way to communicate with its Source, its Creator, The Father. Some would say the Mother, but it is of no consequence, it is only a term. But it is used to help remember the love and devotion a father has for its son, a mother for its child … deeper and deeper than that kind of love. But the communication from the Source to the creation is needed and that is the Holy Spirit. The Holy Spirit is the bridge, between God and his Son … the Creator and His Creation. The Holy Spirit … the Trinities, other component only emerged when the experience and acceptance of a separate existence occurred in the Mind of the Creator. It was not and will not be needed when there is no longer an experience of separateness. Everything is experiencing this differently all the time.

K Can you explain the voice within?

C This is the voice of the Holy Spirit.

K Does Yeshua also speak to us?

C Yes. Yeshua is … to put this in a way that is understandable in Spirit, Yeshua is One with the Holy Spirit. The Holy Spirit is "wholly" in meaning. It is all encompassing and whole. It is much like the Collective, and that all beings that are of the Spirit are One with the Holy Spirit. But the Holy Spirit is also its own being … its own entity … its own quality. It is the Great Spirit. It is what some would call "innate." It is the communication link. It is the bridge … it is the conduit. And yes, entities such as Yeshua, and other Divine beings, which you are also, that are in their Spirit form … living in a higher vibration, may tune into the Holy Spirit to communicate. So you see, Yeshua is in the highest planes right now from your perspective, yet Yeshua is not the Holy Spirit. Yeshua is the Son of God, as you Karen are the Son of God, and Ellie is the Son of God. But to communicate with Yeshua, Ellie or you, would need assistance of the Holy Spirit. And to communicate with God you need the assistance of the Holy Spirit.

> *It appears when Yeshua is speaking of the Holy Spirit he is really speaking of the Whole Spirit, relating to Oneness. Therefore our interpretation of the meaning of Holy may have an entirely different meaning than we think when he speaks of Wholly Spirit.*

K So are we communicating through the Holy Spirit now?

C You are right now. We are all communicating through the Holy Spirit.

> *There can be many definitions of communicating with God, this is just one of them.*

K Thank you. Is Yeshua still with us?

> *I was making sure that Yeshua is still with us for the following questions.*

K Can you give us some information on the Arcturians?

C The Arcturians are here surrounding the Earth. They are Guardians of the Earth. They are the oldest of Creator Beings. They are very ascended, very light, very high energy. They are living in an energy of love and peace. They are intent on helping Gaia ascend, humanity ascend. They are your older brothers and sisters. They have been around longer.

K So they are the ones that helped seed Earth?

C Yes. They are a part of the process for seeding the Earth.

In February 1931, Edgar Cayce speaks of Arcturus in Reading 311-2 ... "as an entity passes on, as has been given, from this present or this solar system, THIS sun, THESE forces, it passes through the various spheres - leading first into that central force, through which - known as Arcturus, nearer the Pleiades." It is fascinating that he also says that they are the highest civilization in our galaxy.

K Are there any other lifetimes that are important for Ellie to review?

C It is not important right now, we do not need to review any lifetimes further. We are in the now and this is where we need to be. This is where the future experiences are created. The Arcturians are in the now. They live very present in the now and can teach this switching off. Shutting down off the left brain hemisphere and switching on the right brain hemisphere ... further enables the remembering of how to live in the now. With the left brain switched off, it is not going to be possible to dwell in a consciousness that is focused on the past and future. It will be present which is also helpful. All power of creation is in the present moment.

We ask you to observe to see what happened to Ellie as she switched off the left brain and switched on the right brain. Observe ... it may be helpful in your practice. We now go to Ellie's subconscious. In her subconscious she sees a circuit breaker of a pane, l for there is a circuit breaker for her left brain, her logical or linear brain. When we say "logic" it is not accurate ... for the ego function for the linearity of past, present and future. And we now recognize that she has a panel control for the left brain. We also see the panel control for the right brain, which is her multidimensionality, her spirit, her True Self and her gifts of the Spirit, clairvoyance, clairaudience, and clairsentience. All of the gifts of the Spirit that do not require linearity. It is her multidimensionality self we now switch on with the circuit breaker. Her right mind hemisphere we switch them on. We now switch off her left brain hemisphere and her left mind we switch it off. We now see that Ellie is functioning with One mind only ... her right brain hemisphere. With this she will now experience greater clarity, greater beauty, greater divinity, and her multidimensionality. Everything in love and light will be enhanced. She will not lose in any way anything that helps her function well in day to day life. Her genius will blossom now because all she has to work with now, to work with is her genius. And she will also have a permanent capacity installed now that allows her to expand and continually enhance and develop her experience and appreciation of her multidimensionality and light. And she will see this light and multidimensionality in her brother, in all she meets. It will allow her greater God capacity, Oneness with her Creator in ways beyond what she has not experienced up until this point ... Amen.

This is such a fascinating explanation of the subconscious turning off her left brain and turning on the right brain. This was something neither Ellie nor myself were aware of previously.

K Thank you.

K What is the greatest difference in the current Bible from what you taught?

C The contrast between what is written in the pages of Bible and what I taught ... there is not much that is different truly, much is quite accurate. Many miracles that were expressed are there. Many of the conversations, my teachings are there. The reliance on relationship of God is there. The emphasis on those gifts being available to others is there, but what seems to be missing are the examples of those who walked as I walked ... who were able to do feats as I was able to do feats. They were not expressed there and this is a phenomenon that occurred. The *Bible* makes it appear as though I was the only one able to express Spirit through the physical and give what you would call illusion or miracle ... its day in the sun. But there were others that were able to do so. Not just my disciples, that were there and whose books are written about in the *Bible*. There were other disciples, my students, those who followed me, who did miracles even beyond what I did in that time. They are not written about.

> *Clients confirmed there were many followers that were able to heal, including Mary and Mary Magdalene. Yeshua is confirming that there were many others that also could perform miracles.*

K Why were they not written about in the *Bible*?

C It is important for the church to portray me as the only Son of God, and important to show not that all of you are Sons of God. Had there been examples written about others that perform miracles, it would have given people the notion that they could do the same. This the church did not want that. The church wanted people to feel powerless, to demand that the church care for them, and to give the church power over them so they could feel safe and protected, instead of claiming the power that they are also Sons of God. This the *Bible* does and omits the information for that reason.

K What were some of these miracles they performed?

C They healed and they performed miracles. Growing plants out of dry ground before your eyes and bringing rain.

K You previously stated that you were married to Mary Magdalene. Why was that not included in the *Bible*?

C The *Bible* was not interested in showing I was a man just like you, that had remembered my Oneness with God ... my relationship with God. It was not about building your relationship with God. The book wanted you to build your relationship with me, with Jesus which is wonderful, but each person must build their relationship with God directly.

K You spoke of the pyramids in a previous session of having a dark energy connected to it. Why did the dark energy and who created that dark energy?

C Yes. During the seeding of the Earth. There were beings from other galaxies that came into Earth's atmosphere and entered the Earth with the intention of making Earth their home and a place to live. Their environment, atmosphere demanded a certain level of negativity. A certain level of negative energy balance to facilitate life for a species, and so that contributed to the energy of negativity that was prevalent there. They were drawn to Egypt and worked to cultivate that energy at that location.

K Why were the pyramids built? Was it to house energy?

C It was not built for negative energy ... built as a transmitter. An energy portal existed under the pyramids in the Earth. The pyramid amplified that energy and sent energy into space as a signal to hone in on, to locate Earth, to locate that particular location, but mostly to locate Earth. Many planets have pyramids for that purpose. It corresponds with the natural energy reservoir in the Earth has a particular kind of energy, quality, frequency of energy. And pyramids are built on top of that.

> *This sounds similar to what Nicola Tesla constructed in 1902 called "Wardenclyffe," which was a massive transmission tower using Earth to conduct the signals for free energy. Unfortunately he was unable to complete his work due to financial and political pressures from those in power who did not want to give people free energy. Also there have been*

several theories speaking of the pyramids as transmitters of energy. Christopher Dunn has written THE GIZA POWER PLANT on the subject with evidence supporting this idea.

K It sounds like it was a positive thing?

C And remember, these beings came after the pyramids were already built. They were attracted to the beacon and worked to cultivate a home for themselves which required a deposit of a particular negative frequency.

> *In this statement it appears that the pyramids are much older than previously thought. Although archeologists date the pyramids between 2589 and 2504 BC, it has also been explained that samples 50,000 years and older do not give us accurate results for radiocarbon dating. I have always believed the pyramids were much older than when the archaeologists have indicated that they were built. In Gina's session she confirmed that it was a power source. But she also said it had "lots of energy," and was used for healing. In looking at the statements by Yeshua and Gina, the pyramids could have had many different functions throughout its long history.*

K You said it was corrected in the previous session.

C It did, hijack the frequency … the natural Gaia energy. It disrupted it and corrupted it, and it was neutralized in some ways. Some of the potency, the amplification of that positive energy, which could have been more beneficial to humanity tens of thousands of years ago.

K Was there a time when all souls understood they were One? Was it in the beginning?

C Yes. Well … there is no the beginning. It is a hard concept to comprehend, but it is a good point to start this discussion. So when a soul is experiencing its multidimensional self then yes … it's experiencing itself without time. What happened is, the soul knowing itself, knowing its Creator looked at itself and saw itself and began to dream it was something other than itself. It's the only way to describe it. It felt into a dream ... a deep sleep, in which it dreamed it was something else. Many souls are still dreaming they're something else, but they're still a soul. You sometimes remember when you're awake what you experienced in the dream and sometimes you don't. Sometimes you don't remember at all. So it for the soul. That is a metaphor. When you sleep at night that is truly what happens to you. You feel asleep and in your sleeping dream, you are something other than what you are. And you will awaken and you are awakening ... all will awaken to a beautiful dream. It will always be a dream while you are in physical form. You will be awake in your dream. Lucid dreaming is also a metaphor for this ... becoming awake in the dream. You are dreaming and you don't know it and you are calling to be awakened in your dream.

K Did your mother Mary help you to understand your gifts or did you already understand them?

C You can tune into anyone ... any friend, family member, people you know, and you think about them. How is this possible? Are you not in a dream? Your minds are One. They think of you and as you think of them. When your dream is of suffering, your dream can be of joy. You give your dream to the Holy Spirit and ask Him to change it for you, so you can have a happy dream. So in your happy dream you will be walking on clouds into Heaven. The happy dreams replace the unhappy dreams, but they get you closer to your memory of your Oneness with your Creator.

K Is it true you said "My Father's house has many mansions?"

C Yes.

K Are you referring to the levels of awareness, and can you explain?

C Yes. It is very much the many levels of awakening. We are all awakening. The Earth is waking up. Everyone is waking up. Some are choosing not to. Some will go further into madness. Some are afraid it's too much light and it's frightening [to them]. They should be left to sleep longer until they're ready.

   I found it an interesting statement that there is an awakening, however some of afraid of too much light. They choose to remain frightened and are not ready at this time. He even goes on to say they can "go further into madness," which can explains some of the madness and despair found in today's world.

K Can you explain further about the need for some to hold on to the belief that suffering or to carry burdens in order to be closer to God?

C There are some that do. It is about a desire to be closer to God. But as long as there is a belief that God will punish and forgetting that God is nothing but love, some will choose to punish themselves to mitigate whatever punishment they feel they deserve from God. So they choose to punish themselves, looking for leniency from a God that doesn't punish because of the myth they bought into and believed. There are many that feel guilty and they blame themselves, and so they choose, "I will punish myself God, and save you the trouble." And so they punish themselves for no reason, but their guilt.

K In the *Bible* you spoke of sinners when before in the session you said there was no sin, can this be explained?

C There is no sin. There is no evil. Sin is man made in that the church needed something it could control people with. The belief that there is death when there is no death, is also a problem. We wish to be able to show that there is no death. Death is the byproduct of a belief in sin. If there is a sin ... something that is permanent ... a mark on the scale to say ... this is a bad thing. We will give you two points toward time in hell and put it on the scale for you. But to go to hell, you must die. So we will give you the illusion of death so that all who witness this, who you wish to have to carry that sin with you will see that they are no longer here. They must be dead and make them fear that they will have the same fate, and so they believed in boiling for eternity for no way to escape. It was probably many of these that were destined for hell that came back in the next lifetime because there was no hell to go to, and they wanted to work off that sin that they had made with their brother so they went back and had another relationship ... continued the fight and the struggle and compounded it further. Two more points on the scale ... such is the wheel of Karma. Such is the wheel that man-made ... that needs to be let go.

I also believe there is no death as the soul is eternal. We always will be in some form or another. He speaks of the wheel of Karma created by man, and it is the beginning of the Great Awakening to recognize this misconception.

K So is the Great Awakening about our need to release Karma?

C Yes. Because it is never ending. There is no escape in one's mind who believes that they have to pay the price for something they think they did ... that God would punish. God is not the punisher, so they punish themselves. Eventually they see several lifetimes ... several demerits. "I guess I will punish myself and inflict punishment and that is way to look at it." We make light of it because it is not serious. It is only imagination ... it is not real. We would have you know truth what is real. What is truth? It is not these made up stories that inflict suffering. What is it? This is what you must ask yourself over and over again.

K So once we decide as a soul, that we no longer need to reincarnate, we can choose not come back? Is that correct?

C That is correct!

K But as long as we feel we need to finish something, we will continue to reincarnate. Is that correct?

C Yes.

K Is that what you were explaining when you said we should not concentrate on the lessons learned?

C Yes.

K Are there what we call Angels from God as well, like Archangel Michael, Gabriel, etc.?

C They are messengers. They are teachers but they are advanced souls that are what you might call "extraterrestrials." They are not winged beings. They can give the appearance when they come to you and visit you. They are pure light. They don't have bodies any more ... only when needed to help you feel safe around them. When you sense their presence, they look pretty harmless. But they are advanced, highly evolved beings, teachers ... comforters.

K So in the *Bible* was much of the things explained really related to the extraterrestrials?

C Yes. But that was not discussed in the *Bible*. In *Genesis* there was not much discussion of it either. But there is a big component of that has been sealed away.

K Where has it been sealed?

C Many have been sealed in scrolls and the Vatican.

K The Vatican knows this?

C Yes. The visits at Fatima spoke of extraterrestrial contact from Divine advanced beings. All of this has been sealed. Humans in their limited perspective, assume they are the only beings in the galaxy, and so they make up stories that are nonsense to make them feel this way. It is not to be. They are upset over this lack of accuracy in the recording facts and history. Nothing can prevent the truth from coming out.

K Is this a part of God's plan that extraterrestrials are helping us?

C It is part of helping humanity and Earth to ascend ... yes!

K Do these extraterrestrials have what we describe as death? Do they reincarnate or remain the same?

C There are ways that they transition into new experiences.

K Have some come here as humans?

C Yes. But for some to transition to a higher frequency, they must shed their body, and they do it in a conscious way where they don't have to go through a trauma and cause pain. They are able to lift up off their body in love.

I have had clients who have come to help our planet from other planets that speak of the difficulty adjusting to the density of Earth. They have told me that it was very painful for them when they came to Earth because the energy is so dense.

K Can humans do this as well?

C Yes humans can, once the awakening is clear and they know who they are with their relationship with God and they are clear. They can and some have.

K When asked about your disciples, you said there were many not just the ones we have heard of, John, Matthew, Mark, etc. Were they considered the special ones?

C They were equal. They just had different abilities. Some had spiritual gifts of miracles and could perform miracles. Yes, but it is interesting is it not? This is not in the *Bible*.

This was confirmed by several clients that others had different abilities. But once again he is speaking of others performing miracles.

K What else is not in the Bible that needs to come out?

C We are all connected, you are all connected and the fact that you're asking the questions, you know on a deep level that there is misinformation from the *Bible* because the *Bible* is viewed as such a Holy Book. So much is tied to the *Bible* in daily life and you turn to it as comfort. But knowing that, a good 40% more could have been written and was intentionally not put in there makes you realize, that the *Bible*, while helpful to many, is also has some means that are less than honorable.

K Is this true of the other holy books of different religions?

C Yes.

K Can you explain Christ Consciousness, the Christos?

C The Christ Consciousness is a Consciousness of Oneness. Again as we spoke of in the beginning, there is a piece of God, which is the piece of God in every Creation of God. God did create you. This is true.

K I think some people may have difficulty understanding if God created us, how does this align with the seeding of Earth by the extraterrestrials? Can this be explained?

C Yes, that's a good question. When it comes to expressing that awareness that came out of the creation by the Father, it becomes something different altogether. You are born into being a permanent Child of God. That can never, ever change. As this permanent entity. As this permanent Son of God, you can express yourself in any way you want. You can be a part of the seeding of a planet. You can be a part of the first to live on the planet. As a Son of God you are endless, timeless, and eternal. That is what you are, that is your core essence and true of your being. As core essence, you can communicate with other souls that are also of the same core essence. So you can express yourself in form. So being a part of the seeding of Earth and another planet ... remember you are infinite. There is no time in which you began ... you always were and you will always be. As civilizations come and civilizations go ... you still are ... you don't die ever. The true essence, the True Soul is always there.

K So our True Essence is our soul?

C Yes. It is one way to say it.

K So you are saying we can choose to come in any form?

C As long as we choose form ... yes. There will be a time, and we use time here, again it is illusionary, linear, as long as we are experiencing that. There will be a time when form will not be necessary and you will be viewed by others as an angel.

K What would be the best way to manifest healing in others and self?

C Look to the core of the being ... the piece of God that is at its core and remind them of that. Remember, everyone knows at the deepest level, that they are a piece of God. Everyone knows this.

K How did you heal while on Earth?

C By seeing the truth within each person, by seeing the piece of God within them and holding that for them to see also. Reminding them, they are at the right hand of the Father... they have never left. This is the illusion. This is not real. They are reminding them so they can have that clarity. It will dawn on them they will remember. (*Beautiful*)

K Did they understand this?

C There is a way to communicate energetically, but my energy, my presence knew it and because I knew it with all clarity and certainty, it influenced their ability to know it.

K Not everyone knows this on a conscious level.

C That is the thing, not everyone is conscious of it, but on a deep core level everyone knows and you are programed. You are Spirit. One with God. You sit at the right hand of God, you have never left ... ever. But for the experience you have chosen a body, chosen a form. In that form, in that body, you may have a

DNA program to seek God, and so you seek God.

> *I found this an interesting concept that we can program our DNA to seek God.*

K Can you expand on the concept of forgiveness, as humans have difficulty understanding true forgiveness for someone that has committed horrible crimes against another?

C Remember, on the third dimensional plane is where you are; and the fourth and fifth, it fades away a little bit more. In the third dimension reality that you experience, it may take more repeated efforts at forgiveness to say, "I don't believe, you are not real." That is what you are saying when you forgive it … it will heal and this is what happens. It can happen in an instant … the change which we call a "miracle." Because the truth comes rushing in so powerfully and present. Because it is true and never was not true. And with that knowing, that it is not true, and you build up the skill. You build up your ability, and your confidence in the untruth detection in telling it's not true. That is how you learn to perform miracles. Some miracles can happen instantly. The change will happen instantly when you can forgive. You may not see it immediately. The more you do that, the better you get at it. You'll begin to see the changes happen more rapidly and they will be more of a contrast in the truth in the lie. The truth will rush in and the miracle will be visible to others and yourself. You must build up this skill and you must practice it. You must forgive the heinous crimes along with the petty lie. You must forgive it all because they are no more important than the other.

K Did the disciples understand the concept of this being an illusion?

C Not exactly. It is a skill you must practice. You must forgive the Hitlers. You must forgive the man who killed others in mass shootings. You must not hold out one offense as more valuable to hold onto than another. They must all be given up. It slows your progress when you don't do that. You free yourself when you forgive. The Child of God is free. You are free. You are just claiming your freedom that you already willingly entered into an illusion. You willingly choose to let yourself sleep. You're not a victim ... remember that.

It is interesting that Yeshua spoke of that feeling of freeing others and yourself when one forgives. This is exactly what I found to be true for those who released forgiveness of self and others in a past life or the current life. They would always have that sense of freedom and a feeling of being lighter once it was released. The weights of the past are no longer present. And there are no victims.

K So if it is all an illusion, can we change that illusion to be a more positive experience?

C Yes. Remember what illusion you see in your awareness is only there because that is where you put your focus. Put your focus on illusions that feels better, ones that make you happy and lift you. Ask for the help to transform your illusions into happy illusions. You don't have to do it all by yourself. You don't need to suffer in your illusionary state. You have God to talk to.

In a letter written by Leo Tolstoy in 1904 he speaks of his life being a dream, "The dreams of our present life are the environment in which we work out the impressions, thoughts, feelings of a former life. As we live through thousands of dreams in our present life, so is our present life only one of many thousands of such lives which we enter from the other, more real life and then return after death Our life is but one of the dreams of that more real life, and so it is endlessly, until the very last one, the very real life, the life of God. I wish you would understand me: I am not playing, not inventing this: I believe in it, I see it without doubt."

K Are there any messages for Karen?

C The work you are doing is valuable. Do not underestimate it or feel in any way that it is all for nothing. You are following your inspiration which comes from God. There is a purpose. There will be those that read your book and are transformed by it. It's going to be important. You are not alone. You are free to ask for help at any time. The help is always there. You are supported. Everything is always there.

I decided to include this statement about the book, as this was one of the many messages of encouragement from Spirit.

K Thank you.

Ellie's Impressions after Her Session

Ellie said she heard herself talking, but felt asleep most of the time. When Yeshua assisted in switching off her left and switching on her right brain, she said "it sounded crazy," and initially doubted the information. She spoke of the clarity in which the information was coming. Some of it was difficult for her to understand. While in the Collective she felt it was different than when channeling Yeshua. In the Collective she said it felt like floating in space and being super expansive. She felt it was more focused when Yeshua came through. Ellie was surprised that Yeshua's disciples also performed miracles. A lot of the doubt comes from our conditioning. The emphasis on the Holy Trinity she felt was interesting and surprising to her. Ellie also found it fascinating about the pyramids being built as a transmitter.

Ellie's Fourth Session
Channeling Yeshua

I was instructed by Ellie's subconscious to say Yeshua, Yeshua, Yeshua, to easily guide Ellie to channel Yeshua directly. I begin by asking permission to speak with Yeshua. I always ask permission to ask questions prepared by the Ellie. Permission was granted. Yeshua began to explain to Ellie that there should be no fear of losing herself, that she merely step aside and she can observe and listen. Yeshua instructed her to become a tiny fragment and allow let him come through. I did not include very personal questions in any of these sessions.

C You want this to merge with me fully, to express me. You want what I offer which is you joy, peace, radiance. I am you in your highest expression. Let it resonate in you. I am but a higher expression of her, and you, and all. There is just one voice for many. Step back, allow. I am ... I am. Let this resonate to you. This we will have you do now."

K Is Yeshua totally here now?

C Yes, Ellie has totally stepped away now.

C Yes ... Karen you have more questions?

K Why does the subconscious come through the client with a drastically different voice?

C Often times the change in voice it is to let you know, yes there is a shift. It is more symbolic than anything.

It seems logical when the voice changes, the client would be aware of a shift in consciousness. And by stating it is more symbolic, it would help clients to understand there is a shift if they need confirmation of the session. In Ellie's session her voice and tone was very different from her normal speaking voice.

K Why are there different versions of the truth?

C On occasion, it is because their framework that they are getting information from ... it is limiting what is coming through. Other times they are hesitant to share more of the picture to understand its ability to be comprehended and understood. Other times they do not receive all the picture because they are not able to ... for whatever reason.

What is the truth? There is only one truth. In order to know the truth one has to be able to be familiar what is not the truth. Anything that is transient and changing, is not true. Anything that is constant, and unchanging, is true. How do you know what is true? It is in your heart ... you feel it, you know it ... it is true. The truth is something that you will access moment by moment. There is not just one truth or many truths. There is not several versions of the truth. There is just what you know in the moment. Because it is constant. It feels true, because it is constant.

K Edgar Cayce as well as other spiritual leaders thought they knew the truth, and other religions think they know the truth. So the truth might be different from another. Can you explain?

C You were told by someone to write the truth. Trust what feels true to you. Go with what feels true to you, Karen. Tune in to ask, is this true? Trust that you will know. If there is not, in world of form, many people feel they have the truth or their story is the truth. They are but perspectives, perspective is not the truth. When you have the plaintiff and the defendant, everyone is looking for the truth. What you hear is perspectives. Where is the truth? In all of it is truth. Is one true in all of it, where is the truth? Truth is sublime. Truth is perfection. Truth is real ... sublime, heaven, bliss, life, peace, kindness, love

... that is true. In the world of illusions where you live, there are perspectives. It is way of seeing from a particular angle, people mistake it for the truth. They say this is truth. What is true is love? What is true is peace? It is constant and unchanging, that is true. Many people feel creation is truth. It is what they were told ... and they think that is truth. That is not truth, that is only perspective. There is great differences between truth and perspective.

You will be able to discern the truth of how you feel. Does this feel as though as love is coming through, does this feel as kindness is coming through? How do I feel with information? Does it feel genuine, does it feel uplifting? Or does it feel fearful? That is your discerning of the truth, and even that can be misleading in a world of illusion, in a world of duality you will get perspectives ... truth lies beyond that. Ask ... is this something beneficial? And trust what you get. It is not for you to judge. You must follow the guidance you are given, which is most important thing. It is not easy, you understand that. That is all.

I found this to be an excellent example of the true meaning of the truth. Those things which Yeshua spoke of love, peace, kindness; those are the real truths. So we must ask ourselves if this feels true, if it is love coming through, and not our perspective or based on fear.

K Thank you.

C You are welcome.

K You spoke about seeding of the Earth, can you explain it in more detail?

C This is why we are less interested in the seeding of Earth. It is not about being on Earth and continuing in other dimensions or other form based worlds. This is why it is continuing into other dimensions ... it is but a distraction. It just continues the egos dramas. It is a distraction from the one true goal which is to wake up from the dream of illusions in all its forms and return to the

Father. Return to the Oneness ... pure ecstasy ... a pure everything, which is what you want.

This is not what you expected or imagined that would be expressed on the pages of your book. It is not something you thought would get into but it is what is needed is what's needed to be expressed! It is going to help many people. Even Ellie was not expect this.

We both found this fascinating when Yeshua spoke about Ellie and myself not expecting what was spoken. We did not expect this!

K Why do we choose to forget who were are?

C How is that we have forgotten. It is a matter of how long you choose to take part in that process. It is not easy to explain and hard to comprehend. We use metaphors and symbols. This is difficult for many to understand because it is not aligned with the thought system you were born into. The thought system you accept is true but the thought system you accept as true, but it is not true at all. It is a lie and accepting this and seeing the lie for what it is. It's necessary to truly awaken in the Christ Oneness. That you all, that you will remember who you are ultimately. That is all.

K When experiencing past lives, are they stored for us to access?

C What you call past lives, of course is simultaneously. It is an amalgam of experience. When you tune into a lifetime you pick up a piece of it, and shake the dust off and look at it, and it may bring you to time in your Earthly history that is a reference point ... a context. It is an opportunity for that limited self that we talk about ... that sees itself as not whole, not One with God, but separate to indulge in times in the world of ego or choose to return to God, the choice is always there. With what one does with the experience of the lifetime, there is no judgment. It is a matter of what is being heard at that time. It takes some practice, but eventually lets ego knows it is not the ruler of the world.

K In a previous session, you spoke of not concentrating so much on the lessons, but you also stated we were here to learn something when we come to Earth. Can you explain? So are there lessons?

C Yes, there are lessons. We just want you to know while there are lessons to learn, you must not take life so seriously because it is all made up. You will not necessarily remember the lesson or lessons, but you find by learning them, you will not repeat them.

> *Yeshua clarifies that there are lessons to be learned, in order to not repeat them. And if the lesson is learned by the soul, than the lesson will not be repeated.*

K When you were in that lifetime as Yeshua, did you understand this concept?

C Yes. There is no need to come back.

K Are there souls with God totally, that no longer are in the illusion?

C If an idea sees itself as a soul, it is not yet 100% connected. There is no separateness. Once the connection is made with God, there is only One. Imagine yourself as a layer cake and there is only the one layer of frosting on top and many layers underneath it. All those layers are separate and distinct, but there is but one unifying layer ... the layer on the top that encompasses the entire cake as a metaphor. Once that unifying layer of cake is unified, joined all the other layers are meaningless ... they don't see themselves as separate. There is only the One. Yet they are all already One, but they see themselves as separate. As long as you see yourself separate in any way, you are not free of ego. This is ego's fear that it will be obliterated, that it doesn't want to be One. But to be One with God is never ending. It is in a perpetual state of nirvana, bliss, ecstasy, that goes on and on without ever fatiguing ... without ever not wanting to be there. Because it is the most exquisite, amazing, ecstatic experience imaginable beyond your imagination ... that Oneness with God.

It is not even remotely possible to understand it from this perspective, yet you have glimpses of it, only glimpses with what that truly is. Nothing can compare … nothing.

K Once with God, do you merge with God, Source?

C You merge totally … there is no separateness whatsoever.

K Do I have permission to speak about your life on Earth as Yeshua?

C Yes.

K Were Mary and Joseph your biological parents?

C Yes.

K Why was it portrayed as not true?

C It was necessary for the folklore … for the fairy tale to make Yeshua special as if he was the only Son of God, which is not true. He had to have been born in an unusual way.

K Why was Yeshua the one that was more famous, or we hear more about him than the others you spoke of that could do the same as he did?

C It served the purpose of the church to exalt Yeshua to make him a God, a deity, so he needed a back story. He was a man who walked the Earth. But a man that was wise and One with the Holy Spirit who listened only to the Holy Spirit for guidance. Yeshua was an example of what all humanity is becoming. He paved the way … he showed the Way. He taught what that you can do what I can do and this the truth. There must be willingness … there must be desire. He had lived many, many lifetimes seeking, learning and growing. Many lifetimes focused on just that … of forgiveness, understanding, how the world works, what the world is and what God is, the Father.

K Was Edgar Cayce and my clients correct about his learning in Egypt?

C Yes. They are too vast to go into here. By the time he went to Egypt he was teaching. He was sharing what he knew. He was demonstrating what he knew.

K Does the Vatican have information about Yeshua's travels that they are not sharing?

C Yes of course. There is information that is not being shared.

K Was there a lot of information not shared?

C No, because a great amount of information that was available was destroyed throughout history in various ways. The truth cannot die.

K So can you share some more information about life as the Essenes?

C The Essenes were master record keepers. They chronicled information meticulously. I learned from them and shared with the Essenes. It wasn't just all learning, it was also sharing what I knew as well.

> *This statement is similar to Adam's session as Yeshua's teacher. He said, "So even though I was teaching him as a young boy, I was learning from him. His answers were so profound and beautiful and sometimes made me think a different way."*

K Were they open to your sharing?

C Not entirely.

K Edgar Cayce spoke of Mary being chosen by Essenes for the birth of Yeshua come through. Is this true?

C Yes, this is true. When they say she was chosen, they don't mean that she was selected by them but they predicted it.

K There is much speculation what happened after the crucifixion and what happened to your body in the tomb. Can you explain?

C What is important to know is that I did manifest physically before my disciples. The body never resurrected. The body was still a dead form, but the mind being free, not being a body. But was able to project a body for others to see that was physical. It is the mind that is free ... the mind that is resurrected, not the body.

K So the body remained in the tomb?

C That is correct. You have you ever heard of by-location for being to be able to project its physical form in more than one location that is similar to what occurred. What happened with showing my disciples when I projected my physical form to show them I would not die. It was the only way they would know that I continue. They needed to see the physical form. That was to show them because they could not see my mind which continues on after the physical body died. It was only to show them what was necessary. If they could perceive my mind without the body there would be no need to project a body. But the projecting of the body, which to show them I am not dead. I will be with you always until the end ... which is what I meant. The end will come with joy, and radiance, as everyone returns to the Father. The end of time and space and illusion and I, will be with you until the end. I will not forsake you. I will not leave you. I am always here and you can call upon me at any time. I am with you in mind. Always we are One. And they needed to learn this so that they could call upon me in their heart and in their mind and then when they heard me ... they heard that I was always there. The image of me is helpful as to remember that I, like you, walked the Earth at one time ... actually many times. But there was one time when I left the body and returned to the Father to the no formless place where we must go ... where we all want to go, and are resisting the lane.

K When we are with the Father do we still remember our lives?

C When you are One with the Father, you will remember everything, but it will be meaningless. It will be but a dream you will forget until we are all One with the Father. There will be no need of me to communicate to you.

K Is there any other information that needs to be brought forth at this time?

C Do not be saddened by the information that you have received. Do not to be troubled by it. It is not intended to frighten you or worry you where you are going ... it is new information. It is somewhat confusing. We ask that you take whatever you're unsure about and offer it to me, and ask that we take it from you and return it to you in a way that will make sense, in a way that lift up your heart and give you peace of mind. As you do that, the pieces will fall together. Offer it to me and I will explain it to you.

Ellie's Impressions after Her Session

Ellie said it was like a dream, and a little fuzzy. She felt there was a great deal of information given to her in the session. It was interesting that Yeshua seemed to know my feelings before I had a chance to ask the questions. Ellie stated that "It flips everything upside down." She also said, "Today I listened to my CD and it was fascinating to hear what was said, and hear and feel the difference between my voice when describing the past lives and my Higher Self communicating. And I was so wise. I am feeling so grateful for the messages I've been receiving from the session with Karen." It is my opinion, that not every spiritual book written can tell the complete truth, as perspectives can sometimes enter in the work. Yeshua stressed this point what we must realize what truth is not. And that we always go with our inner self for those answers to what Truth is, and not with our ego and perspectives.

Ellie understood that we choose death as a transition. "We have tombstones, everything is expressed as death ... a shrine to death that is a fictitious experience we are not aware of it." Ellie is now channeling spontaneously when at home. She is feeling more comfortable with the process and her abilities. She said she felt good about the session, and it was helpful.

Many Years after Her Session

Ellie is currently utilizing her spiritual gifts to help others in her work. She also expressed that many new awakenings have occurred and she is feeling comfortable with her spiritual gifts and knowledge. Many times greater healing and understanding can be awakened after listening to their CD once again.

Note: In Corinthians 12:7-11 there is a description of the various spiritual gifts given to those who have special psychic abilities, "To each is given the manifestation of the Spirit for the common good. To one is given through the Spirit the utterance of wisdom, and to another the utterance of knowledge according to the same Spirit, to another faith by the same Spirit, to another gifts of healing by the one Spirit, to another the working of miracles, to another prophecy, to another to distinguish between spirits, to another the various interpretations of tongues. All these are inspirited by one and the same Spirit, who apportions to each one individually as he wills."

Chapter Nine

"Though free to think and act, we are held together, like the stars in the firmament, with ties inseparable. These ties cannot be seen, but we can feel them. For ages this idea has been proclaimed in the consummately wise teachings of religion, probably not alone as a means of insuring peace and harmony among men, but as a deeply founded truth. The Buddhist expresses it in one way, the Christian in another, but both say the same: We are all one."
NIKOLA TESLA

NAOMI

Naomi came from another state which was some distance to travel for her session. She found me through a recommendation from a friend. She came to learn more about her spiritual work and healing relationships. Naomi's occupation at that time was working with others to help with literacy issues.

When Naomi came off the cloud to the surface she responded that she saw a very crude cart. She then described herself as middle aged male wearing sandals and said she felt dirt under her feet and felt it was very dry. She then described herself wearing a long white robe while some of the others wear brown robes.

The Past Life Session

C Some people wear brown.

K Does it make a difference why you are wearing white and others are in brown robes?

C Yes ... I have greater wisdom.

K Are you in a type of community or village?

C Yes.

K Does the community have a name?

C I can't pronounce it. Ess ... en ... es.

> *Many times clients have difficulty pronouncing words or names due to the differences in languages and their sounds. It sounded similar to Essene, but she indicated that it had a different sound. She explained that the language of the word was different.*

K Do we know them as the Essenes?

C Yes.

K What does the word Essene mean to you?

C Bringer of the Light.

> *This is a new definition of Essene that I have not heard previously, but it is similar in meaning to "expectancy." Edgar Cayce spoke of the interpretation of Essene meant "expectancy" in Reading 254-109.*

K Is everyone in that group Bringers of the Light?

C Yes.

K How many people are there in your group?

C Twenty some.

> *In Dolores Cannon's book, JESUS AND THE ESSENES, her client said that the majority of the Essenes did not live within the community walls. And there was housing for the families that lived outside the main complex. This might explain that the Essenes were the Wise Ones, and perhaps the others in the communities may have been considered Essenes, as a way of life.*

K You spoke of having more wisdom than the others. What kind of wisdom are you speaking of?

C I understand things that others don't understand. Many of the people with me understand more than I do. We learn from one another and we share. We give, we love one another. Jesus is the embodiment. He is the Way.

K Is Jesus among you?

C He is not here right now.

K Was Jesus an Essene as well?

C He has been with us.

K So do you learn from Jesus?

C He learns from us.

K What does Jesus learn from you?

C When he was young he learned quickly ... he's a natural. He is the embodiment of light and love ... all that is pure. He is completely selfless.

K And this is what you felt from him?

C You can tell being near him.

K How do you feel when you are near him?

C I admire him.

K Does he have a presence around him? Can you describe this?

C It is beautiful ... serene ... peaceful ... patient. (*She is in awe.*) His demeanor does not change in spite of anything. That is how you know he is of the light. We are all of the light, because we are all God.

K Does Jesus talk of this as well?

C Yes. So many people don't understand. Their lives are so hard. They struggle to exist. But we are all One. We are One because we are all God. God is the essence of love and life and it flows out, expands and manifests into individuals. And when you are learning of your awareness of the light and who you are not just within but, what you are ... when you become Christ- like.

K Did Jesus talk about being Christ- like?

C No, he is humble! (*Spoken in with great strength*).

K Did you understand about being Christ-like at that time?

C I do. It's the full awareness of who we are. That we are him. And it's when we think of ourselves and our troubles and who we are, and worry about things of this Earth ... of these societies, of the others around us, that we sometimes are turning away from the truth of who we are. And people separate themselves from the Divine that is within them. But it's there! It's in all of us. And it's not just a group of individuals that are One, we are the One ...

and it splinters out for us to get to see, to recognize and know that. And then it strengthens and it strengthens within each of us, and the light and the love grows. Jesus is the embodiment. He is the Way.

According to many clients, Jesus spoke of the importance of Oneness in his teachings.

K Was Jesus' mother and father Essenes?

C Mary was not an Essene. Joseph was an Essene.

K Did she join them?

C But they are mostly men.

K Did they view women as equals to men?

C Yes. We did not have women in our group.

K Are there women in your community?

C There are not women in our community.

K Are there women in other Essene communities?

C Not at this time.

This was similar to Jacob's session when he said they were all men.

K You spoke of teaching Jesus, can you explain?

C Part of our group did. We've have to move.

K Why did you have to move?

C We need to be in nature and in peace. We are a peaceful people. People find their way to us.

K So people come and stay with you?

C Yes. They are always welcome to stay with us.

K Does that include women?

C Yes. We help everyone.

K Are you considered an Elder?

In other sessions, there were confirmation of Jesus being taught by

Essene teachers.

C Yes.

K So you are not like the Elders in the Jewish state?

C No!

K What is different about your community?

C Many of the Jewish faith are very tied to rules. They are more worried about the letter of the law rather than the spirit of the law.

K Why did Jesus decide to come to you?

C There are people in our group that knew him when he was young. I think he was about 9 years old when he came.

K Did he stay with them?

C He met with them in town at that time or on the outskirts of town, and he then would come to them and learn from them what I have heard. I can see him sitting around them, and he stands in the middle of them and he gets it.

K So it's a remembrance of what he knew? Did you have a premonition that he was coming?

C It's the way it is for all of us.

K Did your group know that he would come before he came to them?

C Yes.

K Did you have gifts at that time?

C Oh yes.

K What are your gifts?

C I have the ability to see and understand that which is within. What is in the heart? What troubles the soul? I help reconnect to the light so those struggling can find peace through understanding and through Love.

K Wonderful. Thank you.

K Does everyone in the group do the same thing?

C   We all have deep wisdom and understanding. We love to sit and share and talk and figure things out ... the mysteries. We elevate each other. We are human. The wisest of all of us, not matter how connected you are to your truth, there are moments when you are disconnected and need your fellow ... your compatriots, your group members, your brothers to remind you and you do the same for them. We understand there is so much we sometimes we take it for granted. We don't understand how people can be so disconnected ... it's quite sad. And it's a beautiful thing to share Love with them, a meal ... compassion. They need compassion. When you see it from their side and they feel that you do, it helps them to move forward.

K   Thank you. Did you feel Jesus was the most special?

C   Absolutely! He came young but he didn't always stay with us.

K   Did you know if he traveled?

C   He traveled quite a bit. He has been to so many places and he met so many souls along the way. Some he benefited from them and some he always benefited them. But he grows in his practice of what he knew innately and he learns from others.

K   Did he bring back information or learning from his travels?

C   Not to me personally, but to the group ... yes. He has been to so many places it takes a long time to travel and he meets so many souls along the way. Some he benefited from them and some that he always benefited them. But he grows in his practice of what he knew innately and he learns from others. Because within each culture there is a facet of understanding that may be missing in another. He gathered so much of it and brought it together.

> *In this statement it appears that Jesus touched more lives than has been portrayed in the Bible. He also speaks of Jesus' travels and learning from different cultures. It becomes apparent that Jesus gathered various*

knowledge and wisdom from those cultures, which would eventually
have influenced his teachings.

K Did he come and talk with you?

C We were brothers. He joins us. He does not hold himself above others.

K Does he talk of spiritual ideas with you?

C Always!

K What was the most important thing that he spoke of that resonated to you?

C That we are of God. That we are all One. All glory be to God. He is uncomfortable with people calling him God.

K Why did this happen?

C Because it is clear to so many that he is not like everyone else. He radiates. He is a beautiful soul.

K Does he radiate light?

C Light and love.

K Can everyone see the light?

C You don't physically see it, but you know it's there. It's like walking out on a beautiful morning after a storm. You feel in his presence how much he loves. His demeanor does not change. It's fascinating! When people would tend to be frustrated or mad ... he's still was there, patient and loving, serene. No one that I know can maintain that all the time like he does. Many in our group though are not at the same level. But we are a gentle people.

K Are you secretive of who you are?

C Well, people don't understand us ... so you meet each person where they are and you know how to speak to them. That is speaking heart to heart. So when you meet someone of a particular religious mindset or a particular absence of religious mindset, you know who they are. But you know there is good, you see the Love, and you speak their language to help them be connected. And then they think you are one of them, but of course we are. But they see it in a more individualistic way. Quite often it broadens, it elevates and it causes them to think. Thinking is good. When you stop and you think about what you are really feeling ... when you feel the love, and the beauty around you, and you can think of how it is all connected ... it is so beautiful!

K Yes, it is beautiful!

C Do you have any gifts of a psychic nature?

K You know ... sometimes I do.

C Did you see what would happen to Jesus in the future?

K I feared for him. But you don't have to be psychic to know that it's a dangerous time.

C Why did you feel it was dangerous?

K He threatens the church. He speaks the truth and they are political. They want power and they want money for their church.

C What would Jesus say about the church?

K It starts out with a pure intention and then people get in their own way. You know it is written, there are so many people that try to be good throughout time, but there is only One Way, One Light ... One Truth, and we each must find our own way. Guidance is good, but each must have his own path and when others try to dictate what that path will look like or how you are to look on that path ... well ... that doesn't work so well.

K Are there any writings about your beliefs? Any scrolls or books?

C Yes, mostly scrolls ... books not so much. You need to think about what it creates ... a book have to write so many pages and keep them together.

This was an interesting observation as it must have been difficult keeping books together during that time. In Jacob's session he speaks of hiding these scrolls in caves.

K Did you have scribes then?

C Yes.

K You spoke of the truth. What is the truth?

C The truth is our awareness ... complete unadulterated awareness of the divine that we are. And when you are in the complete understanding, which that is the goal ... we are enlightened and there we find peace, wisdom, understanding, appreciation, gratitude and connectivity. We're putting the pieces back together ... that is our mission. As a society ... as each of us knows the truth and knows who we are, it all comes together like pieces of a puzzle ... like droplets of rain coming back to form the pond.

> *In Ruth's session Jesus says," It is the way of experiencing back into truth, is remembering."*

K Did Jesus ever say why we lost our way?

C It was intended for us to lose our way.

K Why was it intended?

C That's where we learn our lessons. It is the path and the opportunity to find our way back. That it is in that ... we grow and we love, and that is the only way for humans to reconnect fully.

K What are some of your other observations that you can tell us about Jesus?

C He speaks quietly. He does not speak a lot. He speaks when there is a need, he mostly observes. He mostly feels his way through and understands. He knows and he says ... what we need to hear. He tells stories ... not just to us, but look at those stories closely ... [there are] so many levels of understanding. So if you are in one place in your journey, you get what you need. Someone else is in a different place. They have evolved into a deeper understanding and they can hear the same story and still come away with something they need. And this the beauty of it. Those who are out to get him do not realize he is helping so many people. (*Smiling*) They think he is just telling stories because they're not open to the meaning of the stories and it just sounds like stories. And so, he is safe and it keeps them from arresting him.

> *He reveals that Jesus was speaking on the level of awareness and understanding of the person before him. And he explains there are multiple levels of understanding when Jesus speaks in parables, depending upon what the person is ready to hear at that time. And in return, everyone will get what they need.*

K You said he came about nine years old. How old were you when he came?

C I was not in that group.

K How old are you now?

C I don't keep track of that. Life is eternal. To count the suns is a waste of time.

> *This makes perfect sense, as there were no watches or clocks, so they would use the sun to determine days and times. It can explain why some people do not know their exact age during those times.*

K What did Jesus talk to you about that was new to you spiritually?

C It's not that he tells me things ... it's that he shows me things.

K What does he show you?

C He lives it! I should not say this, but between you and me (*Laughing*), it's easy to be good in this community. (*I thought this was a point well taken.*) But to be the embodiment of all that I know and understand in the worst of conditions ... that is truly enlightened! Most impressive!

K Does Jesus speak of God?

C The Father. He is Father to us all. And if you think of a father ... there's wise counsel, unconditional love, guidance, generosity [and our] needs are met.

K You spoke of others calling Jesus God. Do they call him other names?

C Oh they give him a lot of titles. Well, those that adore him ... they give him many titles ... the Savior, the Christ, the King. He never accepts that, but he gently and humbly says, "Oh give what belongs to God, give it to God, and that belongs to God."

K Do you hear stories of him healing others or do you personally witness healings?

C Yes.

K How does he heal?

C We all have that ability, but his belief and his understanding, his connectedness to the Divine is so great that it heals physically, but that it heals not just physically [but also] emotionally.

K What was the most beautiful healing you saw?

C A woman brought her child. He was ravaged with fever. He had sores. He looked to be dying. She had no family. She gave herself to her son. She loved her son. Truly he was her life. She traveled so far. Her clothes, her body bore the brunt of her travels. Many would not want her in their presence. There are people who had compassion to help her get in to see Jesus. There were crowds and when Jesus heard of the stirring, he knows things. He sensed something, "What is going on?" People were trying to keep her out. He would tell them, "Stop! What is going on?" And he allowed her to come forth and she wept just to be in his presence. My heart was really full for her and Jesus touched her on the head and he whispered some things to her and she wept. She felt unworthy. And then he laid his hand on the boy. It was a miracle! It was a miracle! It was not like he jumped up and everything was fine, but suddenly you could tell that a transformation had occurred and you could tell a burden had been lifted from this child. And I wonder if it was not only Jesus' love and belief, but also that of the mother. The child was healed. He looked better, but still was weak. But I know her will recover healed!

K Were you aware that there were other healings that occurred?

C Oh yes! We are all aware of that!

K Were there others in his group that healed as well? Were you aware of this?

C I know some can, but some say they can't, and some can't.

K Did Jesus have disciples?

C Oh yes! So many people chose to be followers.

K Is it true that some followers came and went?

C Yes, but they were human.

K You have said that Jesus knew everyone. Was he picking up their true essence?

C Yes.

K How was it made clear to you?

C Well he knew me! I knew him and he knew me.

K Did Jesus ever talk about past lives?

C We had talked about that. He tells us that we do have many lives … some more than others. It is to fully fulfill our understandings and lessons to grow. He has times where he is goes into the woods and the mountains and he meditates and prays. He communes with Spirits.

K Did he tell you what spirits come to him?

C Moses speaks to him. There are others. He does not share all of that with me but I know that it is what he does. He gives insights. Sometimes even when you are with Jesus, there is so much burden to help.

K Did he feel that burden?

C At times he did and so he would find time to pray.

K Did he learn meditation from another country?

C Yes, he was in the Orient for a while. He was in the Tibetan area for sure. He was even in the Celtic regions you know.

K Did Jesus ever talk about sin?

C Sin, as it was spoken of by others ... by those in the church. Those of other understandings. They're more concrete in their understandings and so as they look at sin ... they look at as a flaw. The minute you call it as sin you are judging! There is no sin! There are only burdened souls who have for some reason come into a situation where they are not as aware of the light and the love and the peace. They get caught up. They try so hard to do the right thing ... even the murderers. Those filled with rage ... those filled with anger are the most closed to their divine aspect.

> *There are other clients that say there is no sin. They explain that sin is when there is a disconnection from God. In Joy's session, Jesus explains they are misled, "And that they do not sin." In Ellie's session Jesus says, "There is no evil ... no sin! Again, it is the state of discomfort from being out of alignment, which is the natural state of being. It is going against the natural flow of life ... that is all."*

K Was Jesus able to release that anger and rage from others?

C Yes. You know sometimes just to be near him changed them. You can't help it. It feels so good to be near him. You want more of it. You want to be it! (*This is such a beautiful statement.*)

K So were you with Jesus often?

C Not a lot. You don't want to crowd him. Give the man a break! He comes and finds respite with us.

K Did you know if Jesus was married?

C (*Smiling*) Yes ... Mary Magdalene.

K Was it kept a secret?

C It was a secret.

> *Some of his followers may not have been aware that Jesus was married, because it was kept as a secret.*

K Did you know if they had children?

C Yes, I have heard.

K Did everyone in your group feel the same way that you did about Jesus?

C Yes. We are fairly enlightened people.

K Did you come in that way?

C Yes. And that's how we find each other. And I think that's why Jesus liked to see us.

> *I have found in my life and work, people are drawn energetically to each other when they are spiritually connected. And I feel my clients who had lifetimes with Jesus found me as well, as we all had a connection with him in that lifetime.*

K Did the people who didn't understand him call Jesus names?

C They thought he was a traitor, maybe that is not the right word ... he was turning people away from the established church and the government, because government wants the power, the money. They want the statues. They want to build their beautiful things. But they're things!

K So it is my understanding that you had other people stay with you?

C Yes, but they were not Essenes ... but they were among us.

> *This is new information that that the Essenes were Enlightened Elders and had allowed other people into their community.*

K So your group was called Essenes, but not everyone that came were Essenes?

C People come and travel to be near us to learn from us ... to find refuge with us ... a safe place to be.

> *This might be one explanation why people said they were Essenes, but they might have just stayed in the community to learn. Because of that learning, they may have considered themselves Essenes.*

K Did the church try to shut you down?

C Yes. We've moved. We had to move.

K Why did you have to move?

C They would imprison us!

K Where did you move? Can you describe it?

C It's very remote. There are mountains and there are not many trees, and there are caves.

> *I have personally visited the region call Qumran, and this area is very similar to what he is describing. This area is very dry and hot. There are numerous caves that would be very difficult to access. Archaeologists have associated these ancient texts to have been written by the Essenes. The texts date from 1,800 to 2,000 years old and comprise of the oldest known Biblical texts found at this time. According to the archaeologists, the Essenes lived and later hid The Dead Sea Scrolls in these caves for safe keeping. The Dead Sea Scrolls number close to 900 scrolls and are older than the Bible. They were discovered between 1947 and 1956 in eleven caves in and around the ruins of Khirbet Qumran near the Dead Sea in Israel. As the Essenes were fearful of being imprisoned or killed, they wanted to preserve the scrolls for future generations. I have found that many of my client's recollections are not always what the archaeologists assume to be true.*

K Did you stay in the caves?

C They were great shelters.

K Did you have houses or complexes?

C We did in the last place, but not in this place.

K So how did you survive? How did you get food to eat?

C People would bring us things and food. You are always given what you need. Sometimes it seems that we do without quite often.

K What was the most important thing Jesus wanted to tell others?

C To be loving, and live compassionately. And when we are told to love him first, it is not to make him an idol. It is to make him a model.

Like many others have said, Jesus was the example, the pattern, the example of how we should live.

K Was Jesus conceived by Joseph and Mary?

C I believe that is true.

K So he was not conceived literally by God?

C I do not believe it as they say, but aren't we all conceived of God. And that's what people don't understand. So when they tell of this … angels come and tell you … as they often come and present themselves in dreams … or they materialize near you. And so we knew this child was special before he was born.

He is explaining that this was a belief by some that Jesus was quite literally conceived by God, but that they didn't quite understand the entire picture that we are all of God. One could assume this is the reason it was written in the current Bible, since the belief was based on perspectives at the time that Jesus was conceived by God.

K Do you feel Mary was chosen to be his mother?

C Of course! She is a gentle soul. She allows him to be who he needs to be. She gives him what he needs and the understanding what he needs and was very supportive.

K Did you hear of Jesus' death or were you there when he died?

C (*Becoming very emotional.*) It was horrible! So cruel. How do you do that to anyone? He's so good. (*Crying*) I saw them take him down.

K Did you take him to the cave after he died?

C I was not there.

Again the client will not give information if they are not aware of it. This to me is a confirmation and proof of the authenticity of their session.

K Did you hear if Jesus rose from the dead?

C We all rise again! And that is an important piece of this. People have to believe that. But, I understand that maybe … (*Almost in a whisper*) it is not as it appears.

K So there was an appearance of death?

C There was an appearance of him disappearing and the assumption is he rose, but a physical body does not rise.

> *In Rose's session, she gave a more detailed description in her observation, "He had powerful, powerful drugs in his system that others were able to arrange somehow."*

K Did he go somewhere else?

C Oh yes … he did! Mary went with him. There were no children at that time. They came later.

K Did they go to a different country?

C Yes. It was very far away … it had to be. They went at night … he was hidden.

K I had heard from another that he had taken a drug to have the appearance of death. Is this correct?

C I am not sure of that, but it wouldn't take much to look like he died after that. He was weak. He lost much blood and the mental anguish.

K Were you aware of a trial for Jesus?

C I don't know of the trial.

K How did you hear that he was going to be killed?

C They had been after him so long. That is why he spoke of his stories … that way they didn't know. They were just stories to them. He could feel the waves of those who were against him and he knew what he had to do. He knew how it would end.

K Did he ever tell you why it had to end that way?

C He sacrificed himself. He could have changed what he said. He could have changed what he did ... but he had to be who he was. He had to remain true to the light and to God and to that which he is. And by doing so he gives hope to others and shows others how to hold onto their faith ... he shows us. But had he done anything differently ... he would not have helped the millions and billions of people that he has the potential to help. He's been through to many lands ... [telling] the stories ... the travel.

K When you spoke of him in the mountains, did he ever speak to you about talking with Buddha?

> *I asked this question since he said Jesus had meditated. It was expressed by many clients that he travel to India.*

C I know he spoke to the Enlightened One, a meeting of the minds. They have known each other before, I'm sure.

> *Another client, not in this book, described this connection with Buddha and Jesus as well.*

K You spoke earlier of his belief of past lives. Did Jesus ever speak of his past lives?

C I have heard him say that but he did not speak of those lifetimes ... not to me anyway.

K Did he speak to you differently than when in the group?

C I am not aware of his private conversations with others or I don't know how to compare or contrast that. In a group we share ... we learn from one another. We share different philosophies and our thoughts.

> *Once again the client is not speaking of that which she has no previous knowledge of at the time.*

K But did you speak with Jesus individually?

C Yes.

K I assume you never married.

C No ... No.

K Did any others in your group marry?

C No. Some are quite close. You know what I mean, and that is not okay.

K In your group?

C Yes, I know of two.

> *He seemed somewhat bothered by not approving of a relationship*
> *happening within his group.*

K So I can assume Jesus was aware of this, as he knows everything.

C He loves everyone. It's not a problem for Jesus. It's a problem for us.

> *This was very clearly stated that Jesus had no judgment of others, only*
> *unconditional love. This was such an important part of the session*
> *making us aware of his teaching in loving all without our own judgments*
> *and perceptions of right and wrong.*

K Is there anything else that's important about Jesus that would be helpful for us to know?

C You know it's hard to put it into words because it is not like the things from Earth. He is so divine! It's hard to capture that which is so perfect in so many ways.

K Did anyone write down what Jesus had said?

C Yes. We write it down. He guides us.

K So there is in written form what he said?

C So some of it is what he says and some of it he has guided us and so we broaden our awareness and our understanding, and our learnings are captured and written. So some of it is interpreted ... some of it is what we have come away with ... but in any form of communication with Jesus you run the risk of not having the words that best and most accurately portray his message because you end up putting a human spin or interpretation of it. Although we are fairly good at this understanding, because he doesn't say a lot. And then we find ourselves kind of going to a new level, and it's so beautiful.

In many of his observations, it is easy to comprehend the scope of his spiritual knowledge and wisdom. This was a wonderful explanation of how Jesus' words could be misinterpreted depending on the person's perspective at that time. He speaks of there being some confusion since Jesus may not have expressed everything he taught, but lived it in his daily life. Interestingly, this may have been the reason for some of the confusion and misinformation of his actual teachings.

K Does Jesus talk of the different levels of awareness?

C Yes. We are each in our own place and based on our experiences ... we either take on things that are unhelpful or we take on things that further us. And the unhelpful things can further us as well as long as we are open to learning from them.

K Thank you.

C The broader and deeper your understandings and the more connected you are ... the more your awareness grows. The deeper your level becomes, it's easier to apply when it becomes so deeply understood in your brain.

K You spoke earlier of Jesus speaking in stories, parables. What story do you remember that resonated to you the most?

C When you build your house on the sand and you build your house on a rock ... you need a solid foundation or the sand can wipe away.

K And did you understand that story's meaning?

C My foundation, my core of who I am, my strength ... all comes from my connection to God. And when I put that understanding first, everything else comes.

K If you were to hear you name called what would they call you?

C Equanknea.

> *He had difficulty pronouncing his name, so I asked him to just give me the sounds of what he hears.*

K Does your name have a meaning?

C Bringing of love.

K Beautiful.

K What was your relationship with your parents?

C They didn't always understand me. I was not tough. I spent a lot of time as a youngster... I appreciated beauty ... I liked to think ... I liked to be alone. They wanted me to do hard labor ... to work hard.

K So what changed? How did you come to be in that community with the Essenes?

C I met someone. There was a little gathering with three or four people. And I would listen to them, and I kept listening, and I thought, Yea, Yea ... that it made sense!

K So what they were saying resonated to you?

C Yes! There is somebody like me! And I was drawn to everything they said and I hung onto every word. It wasn't always what I had been told. A lot of things that others had said were harsh, but I didn't believe God was harsh.

K Did your parents eventually take you to them or did you go on your own?

C I was in town. I was running errands for my mother and I saw them, and then I heard them. You know when you are walking by and you kind of catch their attention, and just notice [and are] tuning in. I kind of went on my way through the market and came a different way ... kind off behind them. They caught me and I said, "What are you doing?" And then I said, "What are you talking about? ... What are your saying?" And they looked at me and we talked a little more and they could tell I was pure of heart. I had a genuine interest because I wanted to learn more. I understood so much. They were explaining things I already knew. They put it into words because I was confused because I was young. I was a boy.

K So did you just drop everything and go with them?

C Not at first. I met with them a couple of times. Then one day I left with them.

K Did you tell your parents?

C No. I left with them.

K Did your parents eventually know where you went?

C I don't know. I had to walk away. It was not good for me to stay there. They were hard on me. They loved me, but they tried to make me something I am not! But you know it's not uncommon for a twelve year old to walk away.

K So you were at peace with your decision to leave?

C Yes, it's okay. My brothers were just what they wanted.

K What were the circumstances of your death?

C I was connected with Jesus. They wanted to stamp out anything that was connected to Jesus.

K So did they come for you?

C We were there. We were confused with things that happened. I saw them take him down off the cross. There were rumors. We didn't know what was going on, but we understood who he was and we understood how it works ... the soul. I knew he was or thought he was a peace at first. Finally the suffering had ended, but it was tragic and so hard to be a part of. And it was so hard to look at. (*Crying*)

K You need not look at it any longer. Just remember his love. So how did you die in that lifetime?

C They killed me! (*Crying*). The soldiers killed me! (*Crying*).

K Did they kill everyone in your village or just you?

C They killed many people.

K How did they find you?

C I was not in my village.

K Feeling no discomfort in the body. As the soul releases from the body what is happening? What are you feeling?

C There is such death and destruction and pain.

K Are you looking down at the scene?

C Yes.

K Now let's move away from that scene. Is there anyone to greet you?

C Michael. (*It was spoken very softly with such love.*)

> *When she said Michael was there to greet her, she was speaking of Archangel Michael. Clients often speak of angels helping them when they crossed over.*

Naomi in the Subconscious

K   Do I have permission to speak to Naomi's subconscious?

SC Yes.

K   On Earthly terms what level of the subconscious is Naomi on now?

SC Three.

K   How many levels are there?

SC Eight.

K   Can she go to a higher level?

SC Okay.

K In reviewing the lifetime with Jesus, why was it important for her to review that lifetime?

SC She needs to spread the word of love and to heal them. It is her destiny!

K What does she need to understand?

SC She needs to step out of the way. She gets in her own way and when she learns to do that, she has great gifts to share. Her gifts are greater than she knows. She skimmed through the last part with Jesus in the death part. She reveled in the part when she was with Jesus and she could learn and feel all that it made her. It grew her in so many ways ... her understanding, her heart, her love ... her capacity for love. But the death scene she skimmed through. She still cannot look at that.

K What does she need to understand to look at that is blocking her from the death scene?

SC She feels guilt.

K Why does she feel guilt?

SC She feels she is partially to blame for something?

K What does she feel partially to blame for?

SC She feels she is partially to blame for Jesus's death.

K Why would she feel this?

SC He was in her community. He had been in her community and she had been about and she confided in someone, and they knew more how to close in on him. She did not deliberately betray anyone. Her love for him is immense. She did not realize someone overheard her.

K Now it is time to let go of that guilt.

SC Yes. She needs to let that go.

K She needs to remember what Jesus would say to her. What would Jesus say to her?

SC "My child you are forgiven."

K Will she be able to remember those words and release the guilt now?

SC She is feeling it in her heart right now.

K So the subconscious is going to help her release that guilt now?

SC Yes. There has been a lot of work done to get to this.

K So this is the main reason she came?

SC Yes.

K Where did the guilt manifest in the body?

SC In her ears.

K So that is why she didn't want to hear. (*She had indicated to me before the session that she had difficulty hearing.*) So can her hearing be restored now?

SC Yes.

K That was a big lesson about forgiveness.

SC Yes. He (*Jesus*) knew it in her heart. He appreciated her heart and he came to her sometimes to let her hear.

K Sometimes Jesus came to her?

SC Yes. He came to her. She was a good friend.

K Is it completely gone now?

SC She is feeling relief.

K Is it completely gone? Is the hearing is healed?

SC No. The guilt is gone. The pain is receding.

K I understand the subconscious is very powerful. I also know that it can be completely healed.

SC Yes. Her heart is bursting open ... wonderful! She's been through so much and she's been trying to prove herself ever since. She doesn't always feel worthy of love.

K Where did that feeling of unworthy of love come from?

SC Because of the betrayal of Jesus. That is where her pain has been ... her troubles have been.

K Now that she understands this, it will no longer be an issue.

SC That is correct. Once there is understanding ... a transformation.

K This is wonderful. I know she will appreciate this immensely. She's been waiting for this quite a long time hasn't she?

SC Yes, she has. She deserves this.

K Definitely! (*There was quiet as healing was occurring.*)

SC It is complete.

K Thank you.

SC The love that she speaks of ... the love that she gives to others, she must also give herself.

K Why did she find it difficult to love herself?

SC She did not feel worthy.

K But now she is not going to find that she has released this completely?

SC She sees it now.

K Wonderful! Thank you.

Naomi's Impressions after Her Session

When coming out of hypnosis, Naomi's first response is "Wow, wow, wow." She said that she remembered most of the session, but after I asked her questions, there seemed to be less memory of what transpired. She said, "I deeply experienced bursts of Light in different places, I went and then I could feel it." I believe Naomi was at a very high level of awareness when she was in the lifetime with Jesus, as there were times when she didn't know how to put into words what she was experiencing. The tone and cadence of her voice changed as well. When I asked her if she felt that lifetime was real, she said "yes." Naomi also explained so beautifully, "There was an essence, and I felt things, beautiful, feeling unearthly, bliss and peace."

Chapter Ten

"While ye have light, believe in the light, believe in the light, so
that you may become sons of light"
JOHN 12:36

"To you has been given the secret of the Kingdom of Heaven,
but for those outside everything is in parables,
so that they may indeed see but not perceive, and may
indeed hear but not understand."
MARK 4:11-12

TIFFANY

Tiffany had previously seen another past life therapist in her area. She came to me in order to access her subconscious in the Quantum Healing session. She wanted to learn about her life purpose and to work on healing. At that time she was a Reiki light worker in this life. A friend of hers referred her to me for the session.

Many times in the client's session it is not immediately apparent that they are with Jesus, but Tiffany responded immediately that Jesus was with her. In session she describes herself as a childhood friend of Jesus becoming a follower in later years.

The Past Life Session

K Coming off the cloud down to the surface, very gently coming back down on the surface. Tell me the first thing you become aware of as you come back to the surface. What is your first impressions?

When Tiffany came off the cloud and came down to the surface, she immediately began to speak.

C I'm in a room with Jesus at a table with my friends.

K Who are you with at a table?

C With Jesus and the others. It's loud. There are people laughing ... lots of laughing and joking.

K What were they joking about?

C We're laughing. Someone said a joke and it's funny. We were just making fun of each other, because they were friends. I feel sandals on my feet...also my robe. ... I felt dirty, dusty. And I hear outside it is loud, like a town. It is boisterous and a lot happening ... selling sheep, and yelling ... selling breads, chaos, laughter, but not in a bad way.

K Are you male or female?

C Male ... in my 20 or 30's.

K Why are you at the table with Jesus? What is your relationship with him?

C A friend ... him and I are good friends.

K Have you been friends a long time?

C Yes, we love each other. I feel like we knew each other for a long time. We played. We jumped in puddles, trees, and ran, and laughed and rode donkeys, played with chickens, and got into trouble. Always laughing.

> *He indicated he and Jesus played together as childhood friends. Joy made similar statement about being a childhood friend with Jesus, saying they played together and laughed. Grace's session is also very similar when she spoke of Jesus and her daughter in this statement, "My daughter Sarah is six and they play... they get together and play...they get very dirty, very dirty....just having fun." This sounds typical of the kind of things children would do in that lifetime.*

K Did you know he was special as a young child?

C No, we were just were friends.

K Did you know Jesus parents?

C Yes.

K What were your impressions of his parents?

C I loved them both. I loved his mother. She was beautiful and kind and caring. I'm feeling his dad is quiet and strong, stoic kind of, but he was kind. His mother was just love.

> *There seems to be a consensus with clients who said they knew Mary,*

that she was kind and caring.

K Can you tell me about your parents in that life? Were you close?

C I am not feeling them.

K What type of dwelling did you live in?

C Stucco ... [made of] mud, grass ... very simple.

K Did you live near Jesus?

C Yes ... down the lane. I lived in town and he lived down the lane and out of town in the country ... not far.

K Did you have brothers or sisters?

C No. I feel my grandparents raised me. I feel like an orphan.

K When did you begin to follow Jesus?

C When I was 15 or 16 years. I knew he was special.

K How did you know he was special?

C He talked in kind of stories and parables, and taught me. He was just so kind. He loved everyone so much. I feel like we used to say, "You and I, we must make a pact to bring salvation to those who were hurt."(*Crying*) They don't understand they can heal themselves. But they are broken. Whether it is anger or hate, we still love them. We do it through love and kindness. It is never through force. It's always kindness. He taught me this. (*Crying*) I tell my son this. (*She indicated that it was her current son.*)

   Tiffany had come to the awareness of where this understanding was established of teaching kindness to her current son. Many times while in a past life regression, clients will come to an understanding as to where their ideas, thoughts and feelings have originated from. And these thoughts and feelings from the past have been brought forth into their current life.

K You spoke of having a pact to bring salvation. What does salvation mean to you?

C To bring God here on Earth, and get rid of all the hate and the distrust.

I am always curious to find out what a client's interpretation of various Biblical words and terms mean to them at that time with Jesus. This was again an interpretation that differs from the Bible's *meaning of salvation.*

K What did Jesus talk about?

C He talked about the light that never dies. It might get so tinny, a flicker and it's my job to see that in others and in myself. I must see it in myself, then I can help others. I feel it almost goes out and then it lights up the night.

Many clients spoke about the light within as well as seeing the light in others.

K You mentioned you were with the disciples. Were you close to them or anyone in particular?

C Maybe John. I see John with a dark beard. I was younger than them. I am in the room with them. They were older than me.

K How did you feel about Judas?

C It's like I want to hold my heart and guard myself, and I want to guard Jesus. (*Crying*) Jesus told me that was the way it had to play out. It was God's plan. Even though I knew it had to be ... it was very hard for me because I loved him very much.

K Were you aware there were women around him?

C His mother. I see women washing his feet ... not his mother. It was a regular thing people were washing feet a lot. Everyone washes others feet.

I found this to be an interesting statement, since the Bible only mentions Jesus' feet being washed. According to her statement, the washing of feet was a common occurrence. During Jesus' lifetime, it was common to wash your feet as it was very dusty, however there strict rules in who should wash another's feet based upon their status.

K What are the most important words he said to you?

C Have mercy, grace … above all love. There is nothing above love. There is nothing that love can't cure or heal, or brokenness. Love will never fail you. It's the light within you!

K Did Jesus ever speak of the light within?

C Yes, there is darkness around us. (*Crying*) Though we walk through the valley of death, it is not who we are. God guides us through the light. It's never far and he wants me to know it's my job. It's that I sit with people in the dark, but we don't stay, we walk through. I hold their hand. I carry them, but we don't stay.

> *This is a different interpretation of the Psalms 23:4 Bible verse, "Yea, though I walk through the valley of the shadow of death, I will fear no evil: for thou art with me; thy rod and thy staff they comfort me."*

K Can you explain why we don't have to stay?

C Because we are light. We are not there to stay. We are there to learn.

K What are you to learn?

C The lessons of the dark, whether it's hate, jealousy, brokenness. Whatever the lesson, whether it is pain, grief, mourning, but you don't stay there. You let it teach you and you go and get out.

> *This concept of learning various lessons has been expressed by many spiritual teachers. He expressed an important message about when you allow the lesson to teach you something, it is then time to release it and move forward.*

K So did Jesus come for lessons as well?

> *In Ruth's session she also said that Jesus came to learn lessons.*

C Yes. ... I will be tempted to say, why do you forsake me God? Why did you turn your back on me?

K Who said these words? Did you or Jesus say this?

C I said that.

K What happened to you that made you say those words in that lifetime?

C I felt unloved and cared for ... different, shunned maybe.

K Why were you shunned?

C Something my parents did?

K What did your parents do that caused you to be shunned?

C Ostracized ... [about] some moral issues. Something with money ... stealing ... a betrayal of the greatest kind. (*She found it difficult to find words.*) Betrayal of trust ... trusting somebody. That's why I want to trust my husband. ... I tried to learn the lesson the first time.

> *When Tiffany came for her session, she indicated that she had strong feelings related to being betrayed. In her life review, she was able to release feelings of betrayals from her past life that had manifested in her current life. This often occurs when we can carry our thoughts and patterns from our past lives into our present life.*

K So people blamed you because of what your parents had done?

C I don't know if it was like bribery, stealing. Was it church money? I don't know but I was ostracized by their mistake. It was a moral of falling short because of their mistakes. I feel like they were stoned. They are dead.

K Were you young when this happened?

C Yes. Jesus loved me even though they had done something. It didn't matter.

K Jesus loved you unconditionally.

C Yes. He loved me even though it happened. It didn't matter.

K So when did you decide to follow him?

C When he left town I wanted to go.

K So did Jesus said you could come with him?

C Yes. He said it would be hard sometimes.

K Why did he say it would hard sometimes?

C Because he would be crucified. He would be terrorized, betrayed, attacked. He said it would be very hard.

K So Jesus knew that he would be crucified?

C Yes. He knew he was going to be betrayed. I think his mother knew. She was so sad when he left. It was almost like a death sentence he was walking into.

K Did you travel with Jesus?

C Yes. We would go to towns and feed people. We laughed a lot. We joked and we healed people. He was the greatest healer that ever walked the Earth.

K How did he heal? Did he tell you how to heal?

C He touched people with his hands and he asked God ... "May their affliction be healed and their pain be eased and erased." It's about love.

K Were you also a healer?

C I did.

K Did he teach you how to heal?

C He showed me and placed my hands and helped me.

K What did Jesus say about healing?

C It comes from God. It's from God ... [it's] not about me. It's love!

K Did he say everyone can be healed?

C No ... not everyone.

K What was the reason why?

C They have to feel their pain ... it's their path for whatever reason. It's their path, and it's not for us to determine. We can't heal everything.

This is another confirmation that not everyone can be healed, since it is determined by the soul's journey.

K Did you know this before?

C No.

K Did he have a group of healers that went out to heal?

C Actually there was a group. We would lay hands on people. Sometimes is was physical affliction ... sometimes it was mental. Sometimes it was just pain, grief or mourning or hurt or loss.

  Not only was this a confirmation that a group of healers did exist, but other clients said that there was mental and emotional healings as well.

K Did you ever see Jesus heal?

C We're on a dirt road ... it was dusty ... burning hot. I was so thirsty. We came across a man who was filthy and dirty and he could walk and he reached out his hand to Jesus. I think he was a leaper ... there's like sores oozing. It was even painful to look at him ... the sores were crusty like yellow seeping, bleeding. So I felt so sad for him. (*Crying*) He smelled, but Jesus didn't care. Jesus hugged him and Jesus smiled at him and placed his hands on his face. He just said greatest of these is love and it was as if everything came off the man ... like he was clean. He went from unclean to clean. There were no sores. It washed away his sins ... although he [Jesus] said there was no sinner. That is not of God's love. God loves from the worst of man ... rapist, murderer ... it makes no matter what you did. God can heal you. He loves you and then it was gone. It was like magic. He fell to his knees and he was clutching Jesus's feet, he was crying so much and thanking him so much. He was so grateful, it doesn't even explain it. Not even the physical pain it was the pain inside. He healed him of that burden. (*Crying*) Jesus hugged him. It was as though I didn't know what to think. It was amazing! And it was just so real and yet so not real. And then we just kept walking, just as though it was another day. I see the donkeys walking in the distance. It was chaotic but peace in the chaos. *She was extremely emotional throughout this entire statement. Her recollection of the healing with Jesus was very specific. I felt as if I was there with her when she was speaking.*

K Were there a large group of people watching this?

C Maybe a handful of people. And we walked on. We just kept walking ... just like every day. We kept walking like it was just another day.

K When Jesus spoke to the crowds were you there? Was it a large or small group?

C Large crowd. I feel like I was there when we fed the people. There were fish.

K What happened with the fish?

C He puts his hands like John ... there was fish. The fisherman caught it and everyone was hungry and complaining. He put his hand over it and I think there was bread. It was hard to explain it ... it was there. It was like a miracle! Everyone had food ... children who were hungry. There were grumpy people who didn't believe.

K So there were people there who didn't believe?

C They weren't causing problems, but I feel it wasn't in their heart. And then it happened. It wasn't like a flash or thunder, it just happened. But what I loved about it was, it wasn't like a flash or thunder. It was amazing! It was just there!

K When Jesus began to speak to the crowd, what did he do?

C He put his hands up to God. He always gave the glory to God. It was not him, it was God. He always gave the glory to God. He never saw himself as anything more. ... I feel like I might have been there when he walked on the water. I see him in the boat. I feel like after that we had to go to a wharf somewhere ... Galilee. We needed to be somewhere. It was starting to storm. It was dark and scary and lightning. They said we shouldn't go but we had to go. I could feel water coming into the boat and he said it would be fine. I just see him and he just got out of the boat and just walked.

K What did you think about this?

C I have to say, I wasn't that impressed. It was Jesus! I just laughed to myself. I was in awe of him always. It is hard to describe. It's like a difference. He inspired me. He never pressed me. I see him walking and liked calmed the waters. We went to Galilee … that was chaotic.

K Why was Galilee chaotic?

C There was just a lot of people. I see a town. People were watching for his arrival. I see a town with houses on the hill built into hills. Lots of people waiting for him to speak. There were some haters. It might be the first time I felt frightened for Jesus.

K Why did you feel frightened?

C I felt their hatred. I think I felt their mistrust, and betrayal coming. I never felt frightened for Jesus until that time.

K At that time were you an empath?

C Yes, I feel it. My legs hurting around my knee.

K Is that related to that lifetime?

C Yes.

K How did that leg get hurt in that lifetime?

C I feel like, we came ashore at Galilee. Maybe there was an argument or fight.

K A fight with whom?

C I think I might have been protecting Jesus. I say to them, "Stay back." I didn't want them to hurt him. I think it is like an altercation [which] was the result of my leg hurting. It's really hurting.

I gave her the suggestion that her leg will be released from any discomfort from the past life, and that she no longer needed to feel that discomfort. The discomfort was then released.

K Does anyone else protect Jesus or was it just you?

C We all gathered. It was like we met people who saved us. They took us to a safe place. They kind of brushed us aside. I feel like we were shuffled quickly ... like, "Come this way quickly, this is the way." And we find safety here.

K When you spoke of sin, what did sin mean to you at the time? Did Jesus talk about sin and what it meant?

C Transgression about your fellow brother ... against God ... not being pure of heart ... not loving your fellow man as you love yourself, stealing, coveting, adultery ... adultery. "Not a big deal"... he said.

In her experience she felt Jesus' feeling about sin was not viewed as horrific as sin is viewed by many. Another client said Jesus didn't think sin was a big deal.

K Did he feel everyone sinned?

C Yes, each and every day.

K Did Jesus feel he had sinned?

C Fell short of God's expectation ... he felt it.

K How did he fall short?

C He felt human. Sometimes humans ... having human needs of food. I think he judged himself for being human sometimes. He forgot he was so connected to God that indeed he was a human when he was here. He was a spiritual being in a human life.

This is a fascinating observation about Jesus' feeling human and the difficulty of being a spiritual being in a human life.

K Did Jesus feel he was special?

C No, he was never greater than anyone.

This has been a fairly common theme among clients, that Jesus did not feel any more special than any other person.

K What did people call him?

C Messiah.

K What did Messiah mean to you at the time?

C Coming of God to this Earth.

K So people thought he was God?

C No. They thought he was God's Son.

K Did Jesus believe he was God's Son?

C Never! He didn't want to bring attention to himself.

K Why not?

C It's not what God wanted. It never was about him. It was about God. He was here to teach people lessons that God wanted them to know.

K What did God want them to know?

C Faith, hope and love and the greatest of these is love. I feel like my name begins with M ... Michael.

K Did Jesus talk about Angels?

C I remember when I was younger, Jesus told me ... he said I was an angel. He said "You're an angel and you are here to provide comfort to people's in the darkest of night. When there is no hope you will come. When there is no hope you will shine like a diamond in the sky. The sky may be dark but there is always hope." And he resides in my heart and in all peoples' hearts. Jesus is in your heart.

K Did you know if Jesus was married?

C I see women washing his feet and men too. He loved his mother.

K Were there people who followed Jesus coming and going or did they stay?

C People ... disciples ...we would go to towns and speak with people. Sometimes it would be small crowds and sometimes it would grow and we would go to the next town. And sometimes people would throw stones at us and spit on us. There was hate there. I remember one time when Jesus needed to be alone. He was alone a lot actually ... going off by himself. I missed him so much when he went off ... that was selfish. But I knew he needed time to be with God for days and nights.

K Were you aware that he went to different places?

C I felt when he left us that he went to a place and stayed. I don't know where he went.

> *Again the client will not speak of situations she was unaware of at that time.*

K What surprised you the most about Jesus?

C His realness. When he smiled at me, it was real ... there was no agenda. It was pure, divine love of the greatest kind. I've never seen it since and I don't know if I will see it again.

K Yes I agree...how beautifully stated.

K Can you tell me a story we don't know about Jesus?

C He played with the angels. Like Jesus, we love to joke ... but good natured teasing ... making fun of each other. He just was happy and pure. It radiated out of him like sun beams.

K Did you see a light around him?

C No. He was normal and real. He was handsome, striking, and tall. I feel it's odd when I touch his face and feel his beard ... long hair. I see him when we were children. We played with chickens and see their feathers flying as we chased them. I see that.

K Was Jesus crucified?

C I see him walking up the hill with the cross. It was a pain that I never felt before. (*Crying*)

As he was describing the pain as something he never felt before, it reminded me of the same horrible agonizing pain which I felt as I witnessed him carrying the cross.

K After death, what happens?

C I went to his mother and Martha and I were comforting them. It was a pain, you can't take a breath. It was as if God abandons us. But I keep saying this is what Jesus told us, it's going to happen. But I didn't believe it at the time. We had to have faith and hope. It was just black and the sun didn't come out … darkness. I remember holding her hand. I doubted it and my heart was dark … terrible pain.

I also experienced that it grew dark the day he was crucified.

K What happened to Jesus' body?

C I don't remember what they did. I remember him being wrapped in white. There was a tunnel in the cave. (*This is another client who spoke of there being a tunnel in the cave where Jesus's body laid.*) I didn't want to leave him. Falling to the ground and then I remember praying to God, "This can't be the end. It couldn't end this way" … yelling. Then the sun came out and I remember seeing him. He came to us. He was so bright!

K Did Jesus say anything?

C It felt like he was a real person … his Spirit. I knew he was going to go. We had to bear witness to what we saw. It was amazing, but frightening at the same time. It was so hard to see him go. He said he would see me again.

K What happens to your life after this?

C We were exhausted and had to fortify. It took a while to heal from that. We went to the countryside and I feel like we were all together. Time of joy and of pain. Good times … last night we were together, the disciples were around fire.

We had a mission to do. We were to teach people of God's love. Shepherds took me in at night. I lead a simple life.

K How did you die in that lifetime?

C In my bed. I had something written comforting me.

After the death experience, Tiffany is guided to a place to review that lifetime with greater wisdom and knowledge from a higher spiritual level of awareness. This is a place of self-reflection. Every soul has a life review after each lifetime.

Review of that Lifetime
from a Higher Level of Awareness

K Now let's move to that peaceful place to review that lifetime, where you have more wisdom and knowledge available to you than while you were in that lifetime. Just rest until I call you back.

K What gave you the greatest happiness?

C Jesus when he smiles. I see pure joy here on Earth now.

K What was the most difficult time in that lifetime?

C When he died and took his last breath.

K How does that lifetime affect the current life?

C I didn't stay in the darkness, and I am not staying there now.

K Do you need to forgive yourself or anyone else in that lifetime?

C I need to forgive myself. I doubted a little bit, but never gave up. I needed to feel more joy. I don't access it.

Forgiveness was complete when using the method previously explained.

Tiffany in the Subconscious

K Do I have permission to speak to Tiffany's subconscious?

SC Yes.

K I know the subconscious could have brought forth many lifetimes, why was the lifetime with Jesus shown to her?

SC It was the happiest time. And the healing time to be a healer in this lifetime and connection to others with God. All forms of healing.

K What is her purpose in this lifetime?

SC To heal and to bring light to others.

> *Tiffany's subconscious spoke of her being the Queen of Light Workers to gather and inspire others. It was then explained that it's like a queen bee, where they are all working together. I thought this was a beautiful analogy.*

Tiffany's Impressions after Her Session

When coming out of hypnosis, Tiffany's first impression was that, "It was pretty crazy". She said it was like right here, but in the beginning she just couldn't get to it. And then she felt she was able for her subconscious to come up to forefront. She indicated that her lifetimes were clear. Tiffany felt that she knew she was always close to Jesus, but didn't know she had known him personally. Tiffany felt her subconscious came through as being very strong. She realized it was always there, but she just didn't listen to it. She said she was happy with the session and indicated the session was very helpful.

Chapter Eleven

"For this I was born, and for this I have come into the world,
to bear witness to the truth. Everyone who is of the truth
hears my voice."
JOHN 18:37

GINA

Gina decided she wanted to come for a Quantum Healing session to answer questions about her relationship issues and her purpose in this life. She presently works in the health care field. Among many of her questions, she asked if she could understand her life purpose. She wanted to know if she was called to dance in order to help others utilize dance therapy for healing. After her session she said she had no idea she would have had a lifetime with Jesus. As she had a strong Christian belief, much of what she said in her session was not part of her Christian belief system. Later she indicated that she had difficulties with some of the information. Since her past life experience with Yeshua was vastly different than her current Christian beliefs, it would be reasonable to assume that this would be a confirmation of her session being authentic.

This session was unique in comparison with the others in that she spoke of Yeshua's connection with the pyramids. Gina explains that Yeshua spent time in Egypt, which has also been confirmed by clients. Interestingly, she describes her close connection with Mary Magdalene and their love of dancing. Mary's love of dancing was later confirmed by Rose in her session, who said she was Mary Magdalene in her past life with Yeshua.

Gina described herself in Egyptian life as a female around thirty years old. She made jewelry where she traded them in a type of market place in her village. She said she was not married because she described herself as being "too headstrong."

The Past Life Session

K What type of jewelry do you make?

C Necklaces and bracelets ... using mostly black stones and other colored stones.

K Do you also make them using gold?

C Yes.

K Where do get the gold?

C I go collect it ... deep in the pyramid.

> *This is something that she nor I had never heard of before.*

K Do others know about the gold in the pyramid?

C No.

K How do you know the gold is there?

C I explore the pyramid.

K Can anyone go inside the pyramid?

C No.

K How do you get to go in the pyramid?

C I'm not afraid.

K Are others afraid, and why are they afraid?

C Its dark ... there is no light. You have to bring your own light.

K What do you bring to give light?

C A torch.

K So when you are in the pyramid, do you sense anything else?

C I sense orbs ... light beings ... energy and they help guide me too. I know they are there. If my torch burns out, they will show me the way out.

K That must be wonderful to know that.

C Yes, it is.

K Have you always seen these orbs inside and outside of the pyramids?

C They are stronger in the pyramids.

K Why do you think they are stronger in the pyramids?

C Because it's a power source. They are safe there and it's dark.

>   *In Ellie's session Jesus spoke of the pyramids as an energy source.*

K You said it is a power source, can you explain that further?

C A lot of energy.

K Did you know who built these pyramids?

C People … but they had help.

K Who helped the people?

C Big Spirits.

K Where did they come from?

C They are always there. They came out of the sky. They are always around.

K Do they look like you?

C No. They are mostly light … effervescent … wing like. They bring the wind with them.

>   *This is an interesting observation in saying that "they bring the wind with them." One could offer another explanation.*

K So did they help build the pyramids?

C Yes.

K Do you have any contact with these winged beings of light?

C I saw them as they were helping build the pyramids. They don't speak … they just are. I always felt [what] the orbs left behind are their gift.

K You spoke of people being afraid of going inside the pyramid. Are people afraid of these beings?

C   Some are and some aren't. I surround myself with those that aren't fearful.

K Do you have anyone close to you in that lifetime?

C I have a good friend. She is a female and she lives near me. She is similar in age.

K By what name would she call you?

C Sarah.

K Is there anyone in authority?

C Yes, but I don't interact. I am poor.

K By what name would people call this person in authority?

C Pilate.

> *Even though I had my suspicions that she could be in same time period as Jesus, it is not my place to assume anything. It is important to allow the client to continue their session without any interference from me.*

K Now let's move to an important day. A day that you would consider important in that lifetime. What is happening? What are sensing?

C Lots of people running … .scared, [and] fearful for their life.

K What is happening? What are they running from?

C Another tribe … a warring tribe … trying to take over the village. They are coming on horses, camels. They are coming through the wall. There is a wall around the village.

K How did they get through the wall?

C They climbed over and then opened the gates and I ran. I knew where to go. I went inside the pyramid. (*Crying*) I took my friend with me … her name is Rebekah. Now I know she is safe, so I run to get the children and bring them into the pyramid.

K That was very brave of you.

C So everyone's safe. We're all just huddled and quiet.

K So eventually do these people leave?

C Yes. It's still standing, but everything is toppled over. People are missing … a lot of people.

K Did they take some of the people with them?

C Yes. They took some and some got trampled. Rebekah and I try to help find their parents. Some we find ... others we take them in. We clean up.

K Moving to another significant event in that lifetime as Sarah?

C There are crosses ... there are a whole bunch of crosses.

K Why are there crosses?

C There are a whole lot of people on the crosses. They were stealing for food to survive. They were saying things ... people in power didn't like.

K What were they saying that people in power didn't like?

C They were talking about equality. That everyone should take care of one another, and to help those that are not as fortunate. That those in power knew that when the people got stronger, they would be threatened ... so they tried to keep that down.

K Did you know the name of the person or did you ever meet this person talking about equality?

C Jesus.

K Did you follow Jesus?

C Yes.

K And when you were with Jesus, how did you help with this journey?

C I prepared meals.

K Did you travel with him?

C Yes ... for several months.

K And how did you hear about Jesus?

C From some of my friends.

K Did you go to where he spoke?

C Yes.

K Can you describe that event?

C He was speaking in a garden. (*Breathing heavy*)

K What did he speak of in the garden? What resonated to you that he said to you?

C His message of love and non-judgment ... acceptance. That we all make mistakes, but what is important is what we learn from them. And then I was there when he came through.

K Was that in Egypt?

C Yes. I was there when he was carrying the cross and bleeding. And I didn't know what to do. There were so many yelling at him.

> *For some reason she jumped to the time when Jesus was carrying the cross and then she became extremely emotional and crying.*

K What were they yelling?

C Hate ... because they were afraid.

K Were there some yelling in response to their sadness of what was happening?

C They were crying. I was there at the crucifixion.

K Were there many others there?

C Yes. (*She begins crying all the time.*)

K Did the soldiers allow you to come?

C I watched from behind them, and I stayed till the end. I felt like he needed my energy. He needed light and sunshine. (*Crying*)

> *This is an interesting statement because in Grace's session one year earlier, she spoke of Mary and her holding the light for Jesus. There must have been many who held the light for Jesus at that time.*

K Did he say anything?

C He was quiet at that point.

K Did he die on the cross?

C I helped take him down. There was a group of us. Rebekah was there. We took him and cleaned him. We hid him in the tomb with a large rock in front, because we were worried others would take his body. We felt like his Spirit was still with his body.

K So you didn't think he was gone?

C Not completely. There was still connected ... there was still a connection. He hadn't completely transformed into the light. And we felt it was important to protect his body. He didn't completely leave until we moved the rock and then he left.

K Who moved the rock?

C The spirits that helped build the pyramids. He fully joined them ... because there is not one God. There are many that make up the whole.

This is an interesting statement about her view of God, where there are many that make up the whole in light of her strong Christian belief. This was also acknowledged by Jesus in Ellie channeling session.

K So did you see him after he transformed?

C I just felt it was okay.

K What was the most important thing he said to you?

C Always love and to do everything out of love. And where ever there is darkness send the light, because no matter how dark things are there is always light in the darkness, even if it's just a flicker.

K Did Jesus explain why he came?

C For that and that alone ... because the world was dark and people needed a reminder.

K A reminder of what?

C Of love ... because there is evil, but only if you let it be evil. We have the power to change that.

K So the evil is within.

C Yes. People create evil.

K Did Jesus ever explain why?

C Because they are afraid. They let power take over, and the ego and greed. (*She began breathing very hard at this point.*)

   This is another explanation of evil that differs from the Bible.

K Did you witness Jesus healing others?

C I did. He healed many people.

K What was the most powerful healing you witnessed?

C He healed children that couldn't see.

K How did he heal them?

C He touched them.

K Did he say anything while healing them?

C He was very quiet. I couldn't hear him. It was like the transference of Light.

K Did he speak to you or others about the ability to heal?

C Yes. He told me that I could heal others through dance and my jewelry making.

K So you danced in that life?

C I led a lot of the dances for the village. I think that's why a lot of men were afraid of me, because I could dance.

   It is interesting that one of Gina's questions was related to her dance therapy and if that was her purpose in this life. It is apparent that her love of dance was connected to that lifetime with Jesus.

K Why would they be fearful of you dancing?

C I think they liked it. (*Laughing*) They like it a lot. I also did belly dancing, and I think they were intimidated. There were other women who danced.

K You said when you first met Jesus, it was in Egypt. Is that correct?

C Yes.

K Did he ever say why he came to Egypt?

C He was drawn to the pyramids.

K Did he say why he was drawn to the pyramids?

C Only that they were special and he was drawn to them.

K Did you feel he was special?

C Yes.

K What made him special?

C He was simple. When he smiled you knew you were safe and when he touched you, you knew you were safe. He didn't need anything. He just carried his message and his healing powers, and then he was cared for by the people who followed him.

K Was this a large group of people?

C Yes.

K Did some stay and some leave?

C Yes, not everyone stayed. Some would come and then go back to their lives and took what they needed, and then they left.

This appears to be the consensus of the clients that not everyone was able to stay all the time with Jesus.

K Did he have disciples as described in the *Bible*?

C Yes, but they weren't all men! It was a blend of men and women.

When asked about the disciples described in the Bible, *she acknowledged that there were also women who were disciples. This is another example of statements made by clients that are different than what was portrayed in the* Bible.

K Was there one he felt very connected with?

C I think me, because I danced (*Crying*)... and he knew I had pure joy.

K Did you have a connection with Mary Magdalene in that lifetime?

Before her session the client spoke of feeling a strong connection with Mary Magdalene. Many times clients feel a connection with certain time frames or people, as these are the memories of other lives surfacing to their conscious mind.

C I did!

She became very emotional, when asked the question.

K Why is there so much emotion connected with Mary?

C In some ways I feel a deep connection with her... almost like I was her, but I was not her.

K Now move to the time with Mary. Were you observing her or were you her?

C I saw them together.

K Why was the connection with Mary Magdalene so strong?

C She was a teacher.

K Like Jesus?

C Yes. I feel like she was a mentor to me. She lifted me up and inspired me.

K What did she say to lift you up and inspire you?

C She was the one that encouraged my dancing. She was like my mother ... but she wasn't my mother.

K What happened to your mother?

C I feel like I was an orphan... something bad happened.

K So she took the role of your mother?

C Yes.

K How long did Jesus stay in Egypt?

C He was there maybe a year and he came back ... at different times.

K Did he go into the pyramids?

C Yes.

K And did he experience the same things you did?

C Yes. I took him through.

K What did he say about that?

C He just reveled in their beauty and their power. He put his feet in the stream that ran through. The stream was deep underneath the pyramid.

K What does this stream do?

C It just keeps the flow of the energy, because it's constant and it cleanses.

> *In recent years, the pyramids in Giza have been found to have a vast network of underground chambers and water tunnels.*

K So the pyramids are a source of energy? Was there anything else that you can explain about the pyramids?

C There's people that were there. People would gather often and go there to pass and transform into the next lifetime. Animals would go there too.

K How did they transform?

C When it was their time to die, they would go there because it was safe ... closer to the energy source ... and also to give birth.

K Was this a place of healing as well?

C Yes.

K Did you ever go into the healing pyramid?

C Yes. I went into all of them, and I moved easily throughout. They were all same ... just different.

K Were there healers in the pyramid?

C Yes.

K Can you describe the healing?

C A mixture of people and sometimes they had animals with them in the healing pyramid. And there were lights ... crystals ... sacred rocks, that would hold their energy and they could transfer their energy into the rocks, and place them on people or on their hands with the rocks. Sometimes the priests would wear the jewelry I would make. And in the one there was a midwives helping to give births. I did help and I danced too.

K You mentioned beings who came from the stars. Were they from other planets?

C Yes.

K Did they describe the other planets or tell you anything?

C Just stars ... just lights.

K Did Jesus talk about them?

C Yes. They were from a planet that was just water.

K Was Jesus able to communicate with them?

C Yes, he pulled all those energies. He pulled from the water, the stars, and the trees. Because the trees are the connection between them.

From this statement, it explains how Jesus is connected with nature and the stars.

K So did he travel extensively?

C He traveled all over. I didn't go with him, I knew my place was in the village. I stayed near the pyramids.

This was another confirmation of Jesus' many travels.

K Were you a follower?

C When he came through.

K How did you learn he was going to be crucified since you were in Egypt?

C Mary came to me. She called me, because she needed help too. She needed my strength.

K Did you feel they were connected in marriage?

C Yes.

K Did they have children?

C Yes, five children. (*Again mentioning five children*)

K Was that well known or was it a secret?

C It was kept a secret … only a select few knew.

K Why was is a secret?

C Because it felt safer. Many people questioned a lot. People were scared when he performed miracles and healings, and people sometimes thought it was bad energy because they didn't understand it, so they went into fear.

> *Once again another client saying that it was a secret that Jesus' had children, for reasons of their safety.*

K What miracles did you personally experience?

C I knew he could walk on water.

K And what was the purpose of him walking on water?

C Showing the power of your mind. He said that if you believe strong enough … you have the power to shape your environment, your surroundings … your well-being.

> *I found this to be both an interesting and believable reason why he decided to walk on water. I believe we are much more powerful than we know, and Jesus was trying to show us that power we have within us. He was not only teaching his lessons through his words, but also he was a demonstration of the meaning of his words.*

K Did he explain why he didn't use that power when he died on the cross?

C He had to die because it was his time. Everything has to shift and change. And he couldn't stay because he had completed his purpose. It had been fulfilled. He had to die on the cross because of the directions … the north, south, east, west … above and below … all the different directions that are spirit that are connected.

> *I found this a fascinating statement concerning the directions and their connection to the crucifixion. This was something both Gina and I had no*

previous knowledge of at the time.

K What was his physical characteristics?

C He was dark skinned with long hair and a beard. His blue eyes, which was unusual. It was one of the reasons he stood out.

This is another confirmation from a client that he had blue eyes.

K When he looked into your eyes, how did you feel?

C They were always captivating! Full of energy, life and light and joy.

K After his death what did you do?

C I was grieving. It was difficult to not have him physically there.

K Moving to an important day. A day you consider important in that lifetime. What is happening? What are you sensing, feeling?

C I am around a fire. It's a huge bon fire. We decided to bury things not serving us any more ... to help them shift and change. Possessions aren't serving us anymore.

K Why was this done?

C We needed to leave and find a new village.

K Why did you feel you needed to leave?

C To deliver the message. It was Jesus' message.

K What was Jesus' message?

C To be in a peaceful community that could be self-sustained. And so we burned everything that didn't serve us and left.

K So did you find a new village?

C Yes, we built a new village. There were twelve of us. It was a day's travel away. But Rebekah didn't come because her place was in the other village.

K So you created a new community? Were there disciples who came with you?

C Yes, one or two. Peter stayed.

K What are your impressions of Peter?

C He was young still. He had the right intention, but he needed to still grow up. I felt he had a little too much ego ... but he didn't like to feel.

K Did Jesus ever address this with Peter?

C He tried to tell him it was okay to feel and that was the only way he could heal, to be empathetic. Matthew was always real serious. He was older and always the analytical one. He was really brilliant and had good ideas.

K Did they write down Jesus' words?

C Yes.

K What happened to them?

C They were placed in a book ... but then they were altered over time. We buried them in area around Egypt.

> *Perhaps these could be the writing found in Egypt in the present day. The Nag Hammadi Gnostic texts were found in Nag Hammadi, Egypt in 1945. Included in the scrolls found were, The Gospel of Thomas, The Gospel of Truth, and The Gospel of Judas.*

When I asked about Gina death in that lifetime, she described her death when she was very old. As her soul left the body, she spoke of a feeling warmth and a pulsating sensation, along with a sense of peace and freedom.

After the death experience, Gina is guided to a place to review that lifetime with greater wisdom and knowledge from a higher spiritual level of awareness. Each soul has a life review after each lifetime. This is a place of self-reflection.

Review of that Lifetime
from a Higher Level of Awareness

K Now that you have more knowledge than while you were in that lifetime, what gave you the greatest happiness in that lifetime?

C My dancing and knowing it can help heal. I could move through energies and move through all the different pyramids, because I understood they were all the same ... just different energies in each one. Death was birth ... birth was death and learning was both of those.

K What was the most difficult aspect of that lifetime?

C Knowing that there were some people that can't be healed.

K Did Jesus address this?

C Yes, because they weren't ready, it wasn't their time. They weren't ready to receive. But I always want to hold hope.

K How does this affect the current life?

C It's hard for me to walk away from people.

K What would Jesus say about this?

C He would say, "I give until I know it's hurting me, and when I identify it's hurting me ... I have to walk away."

> *I found this an interesting statement when Jesus explains that if the healing is detrimental to him, than he needs to walk away. This is very much like what today's energy workers explain about healing others whose energies who are detrimental to their own energy.*

K Did he also have that feeling that sometimes he had to walk away?

C Yes, he was better at it than me.

K Did he say it could hurt you physically?

C He said I always gave too much of myself and opened myself up too much.

K Does this affect the current life?

C Yes.

K It is time to release it and move forward. What part of the body did this manifest?

C The pelvis.

K Are you ready to release this and heal the body and the soul?

C Yes.

K Then give it to Jesus, the angels or whomever you wish to help you heal and release this so you can move forward. That was in the past and no longer needed. She then said it was completed.

K What did you learn or accomplish in that life that can help you in your current life?

C I remember one night when Jesus would be teaching, after he talked, we heard music and we would dance, and Mary would dance. She was one of the women. I taught her. I felt healing through dance. Jesus confirmed this as he knew it would bring happiness.

Two years later Rose would come for a session, and would go to her past life as Mary Magdalene. And in that session she said she loved to dance with other women. There is no mention of Mary Magdalene dancing in the Bible, *which indicates to me that this is another confirmation of both sessions.*

K Were there lessons learned in that lifetime?

C To never lose sight of my True Self and not let other people's opinions influence me and take me off my path. But to be true to me!

After experiencing another lifetime, I asked Gina's subconscious to come through for even a higher level of understanding.

Gina in the Subconscious

K Do I have permissions to speak with Gina's subconscious?

C Yes.

K (*At this point she began coughing.*) Is there a reason why she is coughing?

SC She holds back a lot.

K I know the subconscious could have chosen any lifetimes, why was this lifetime show to her?

SC She needs to remember that she's a healer. She's here to bring beauty and heal through dance. She is here to inspire other people to find the beauty in themselves, no matter what shape or form that takes.

K Does Gina need to go a higher level of the subconscious?

SC Yes ... now going higher ... she is flying and floating. (*Long pause*) She is on the back of a hugged winged bird. She is flying over land and valleys and trees. I am looking down ... knowing all is okay.

The subconscious also worked on personal issues related to her other lifetime. And I will only concentrate on the lifetime with Jesus for this book.

K Why did Mary Magdalene come into her current life as a friend?

SC To be a mentor.

K Has she been with Mary in other lifetimes?

SC Yes ... in Spain.

K Were they friends in that lifetime?

SC She was a governess and I was a child. She had a strong connection then too.

K When she went to the lifetime with Jesus, was everything said correct?

SC Yes.

K Can the subconscious explain why some events are different with other clients when speaking of their life with Jesus? Why are differences in their experiences?

SC Because we still have free will and our thoughts. It's hard to completely separate all the time. So sometimes the conscious mind sneaks in.

K Is the subconscious here totally?

If I feel the answers come from the conscious mind, I will always make certain that the subconscious is still present. Sometimes the conscious mind will enter, as it thinks it is protecting the client. I can usually tell when this happens and redirect the client back into their subconscious.

SC Yes.

K So did Jesus die on the cross?

SC Yes.

K What else is important for her to know about the lifetime with Jesus?

SC (*Long pause*) Symbols hold a lot of significance.

K What type of symbols?

SC Triangles, circles, spirals, ovals, and stars.

K What do these symbols represent?

SC Triangle is mind, body, spirit. ... Circle is infinity. Oval is infinity ... Stars are light.

This was something new to her when speaking of symbols. This correlates to when Jesus used the circle to indicate to us that his circle was complete.

K Did Jesus speak of the light?

SC He said that everyone has the light and should be treated just like that. Life is fragile.

K What did he say about those in darkness and finding their light?

SC (*There is a long pause*) They need to find a way to create their own light versus taking it from other people. Reality is what we create. We all believe what we create ... what we believe.

K When she was with Jesus, did she ever feel alone?

SC No.

K So she needs to remember that feeling and keep that with her.

SC Yes.

K What did Jesus say about manifestation?

SC We must think it, to then believe it, then for it to happen. Things will happen when they are ready. You have to go out and make it happen and achieve it. You can't just sit back.

K Is there anything else important in the life of Jesus that is important for her to know?

SC NO! (*No was forcefully spoken.*)

Gina's Impressions after Her Session

After the session Gina said she felt a lot more open. She also had the feeling of being very warm. Many clients speak of feeling hot or very warm, which can be caused by the high level of energy in the room. A few times my computer has turned on and off by itself because of the high energy level in the room.

When I asked Gina if she had ever felt that she had lived a life with Jesus before coming for the session, she said she did not. She also said that she struggled with thinking it was real or just made up. "I was raised a Christian and I questioned, "Was this a myth? And then as more time passed and I experienced more, and said no, it really existed. ...There was much there!" I found it fascinating that she had a strong religious faith, but was able to give such an enlightening account of her lifetime with Jesus from a different perspective than her current beliefs. There were many experiences and statements which were not included in the Bible.

During the session there were several occasions when she was coughing, and I then asked the subconscious to explain what was happening. It was explained that it was a way of releasing past issues which she had held onto for a long time. When clients release issues, many times there is releasing through coughing, itching and/or having to use the bathroom. Gina also stated, "I've honestly still been processing a lot of the lessons I gained from the session with you."

Later after Her Session

Gina later wrote me that she had definitely walked away with was a sense of peace in terms of the relationships she had been struggling with. She said, "I truly felt like I was able to let go of a lot of things. Physical ailments I've been struggling with are no longer with me." I was happy to hear she has been completely healthy ever since, in all the areas we worked on. She indicated that she is reconnecting with her dance as well creating more avenues for performing her aerial acrobatics. Gina felt that this was extremely exciting for her.

Chapter Twelve

"A new commandment I give to you, that you love one
another: just as I have loved you, you also are to love one
another. By this all people will know that you are my disciples,
if you have love for one another."
JOHN 13:34-35

ROSE

Rose came for a past life regression to work on her feelings of betrayal. In her current life, she has the gift of psychic abilities and described herself as a healer and spiritual teacher in this life. She explained that three different psychics told her that she had a lifetime as Mary Magdalene. Rose indicated that she hadn't experienced that lifetime previously, but wanted to know if it was true. I specifically did not ask her to go to a lifetime with Jesus, as I wanted her to go to the most significant lifetime for her highest good. Immediately after coming off the cloud, she began to describe the lifetime with Jesus. I always ask for the lifetime which would be the most beneficial for the client at this time. They are then guided to the lifetime that is the most important for them to review for greater understanding and healing. I believe their subconscious will choose the lifetime that is for their highest good.

The Past Life Session

K Tell me what is your first impression, the very first thing you become aware of when coming back down to the surface.

C OH! OH! OH!

At this point she was extremely angry and almost uncontrollable upset at what she was experiencing. Rose began reaching up with her hands high and having a claw like motion with her fingers.

K Tell me what is happening. Everything is alright, you are always safe and protected. Everything is okay.

I began repeating those words over and over to help her calm down.

C At first I was in the Mediterranean, and then I just hear Judea. I am a woman wearing a draped like robe. I feel powerless. They are not protecting him. They are not protecting him. The pain is almost unbearable!

K Moving back in time in that lifetime to a happy day. What is happening, what are you feeling, sensing? Now moving to a happier time in that lifetime... What is happening?

> *I felt I needed to help her leave that scene of tremendous upset, and take her to a calmer time. Many times clients experience great emotional responses to what they are experiencing. Later in the session we returned to that event associated with the difficulty in order to release and heal the wounds of that event.*

C (*She began to breathe heavily.*) I am just sitting with him and touching his feet and had my hand on his foot. And I feel so safe and secure, and I feel just pure love.

K Who are you with?

C Jesus. He is coming through town and I was drawn to him like a magnet.

K What drew you to him?

C He was emanating such light.

K Could you see the light?

C I felt it and I knew that I wanted to give all I had ... and yet at the same time I was scared.

K Why were you scared?

C I was scared of losing me, turning into nothing, dissolving. Afraid of the unknown.

K What caused you to have these feelings?

C It was just an inner knowing that my whole life was going to change.

In this lifetimes Rose had psychic abilities as well.

K Did you ever speak to Jesus about this inner knowing?

C He knew … I didn't need to say anything.

K So you just started to have a conversation with him?

C He asked me what my names was.

K What was your response?

C Mary. I asked what his name is, and he said, "Jesus." And he said, "Would you like to come with me? Would like to walk with me?" And I said "yes." … Then we came to a gathering and people started gathering. People just wanted to listen and it was quiet. I just sat there and he began to speak and I was mesmerized.

> *Adam also describes his feeling about Yeshua when he says, "He mesmerizes us." Again I found it fascinating that both clients used the same words describing their impressions. I have found on numerous occasions that clients have used similar words, or even the same words in their descriptions. It is important to remember that clients had no prior knowledge of what each one had said in their sessions.*

K What did Jesus talk about?

C He spoke of our Heavenly Father.

K Did it make sense to you at the time?

C It was such a longing and so deep inside me to hear these words. That I didn't even know I had that longing before. He said my Father has many mansions. All of a sudden for the first time ever, I didn't feel worthy.

K Why didn't you feel worthy?

C I felt like there was never enough that I could do for him, to be worthy enough.

K You spoke of him saying my Father's house has many mansions. Did you have an understanding of what that meant?

C When he said it, I felt this vastness, and that's when the unworthiness kicked in.

K Did you ever discuss not being worthy or being enough with Jesus?

C I felt guilty because I had things that other people didn't. I was financially secure and I was a beautiful woman. I felt like maybe I wasn't doing enough to help the less fortunate.

K Did Jesus speak of helping others?

C He talked about being humble ... I felt ashamed also.

K Why would you feel ashamed?

C (*Long pause*) I had a transgression in my life before I met Jesus. It was a secret transgression.

K Were you married at that time?

C No, I was a healer... I healed.

K How did you heal in that lifetime?

C Healing took its own form, but I used crystals, and sometimes I just used my body as a healing vehicle ... light touch ...sound. And a man came to me for healing and I abused the power because I was attracted to him.

K Did you tell Jesus of this transgression as you call it?

C I felt he could see through me ... that he already knew and so I felt ashamed.

> *Once again she speaks of Jesus knowing things about her. Other clients also said Jesus had this knowing about them. In David's session he said, "He knows me," even though Jesus did know him previously.*

K Did he feel this or address this with you?

C He would look at me with such compassion. It's like he could forgive me and yet I couldn't forgive myself.

K Why couldn't you forgive yourself as Jesus was able to forgive you? What was so difficult for you?

C I felt like I hurt someone.

K Who did you hurt?

C I hurt the man. He trusted me for healing and used that trust. He was in agreement but I was in the power position.

> *In this fascinating statement, Mary give us a completely different interpretation with regards to a certain relationship with a man. The portrayal of Mary Magdalene being a prostitute was first introduced at an Easter sermon delivered by Pope Gregory in 591. Pope Gregory I (The First) spoke of Mary Magdalene as a "sinful woman," who anointed Jesus' feet. In 1969, Mary Magdalene was officially cleared by the Catholic Church of being the "sinful woman by Pope Paul VI. To this day many people still believe that she was a prostitute.*

K Now move to an important day, a day that you consider to be important when something important is happening. What is happening? What are sensing, feeling?

C (*Long pause*) I'm just witnessing him on the cross and I feel like this is so wrong and yet at the same time I understand it is the divine plan. I'm having tremendous duality in myself.

K Where you there at the cross?

C (*Crying*) Yes. A few other woman near me. I'm to the right, some type of gathering on the other side. I'm feeling men.

K Did Jesus die on the cross?

C No ... he didn't completely die. He had powerful, powerful drugs in his system that others were able to arrange somehow.

K So what happened?

C (*Long pause*) He cried out in pain at one point. I wanted to die. I didn't want to live. ... I thought it was my fault.

K Why would you feel it was your fault?

C I don't know. I felt I could have prevented it ... if only I had been better or something.

K Been better at what?

C Better at using my power. I feel like this is. (*Having difficulty speaking about something.*) I don't want to admit this.

K It is okay. You are safe.

C I feel like I betrayed him with another.

She had some confusion as to when this occurred.

K After they took him off the cross what happened?

C I see this big strong armored type guy ... just ordering everybody and he doesn't have a clue. He's just like a robot doing his job. Ordering other people in lesser position than him.

> *This was an interesting observation about the strong armored man doing his job like a robot and ordering others. In Lily's session she described herself as a strong armored Roman being very stoic. She said she was the Roman advisor who was at the crucifixion. I am not certain that this was the same person, but it does sound very similar.*

K What is happening to Jesus' body?

C I see them taking him and I just want to die, and I don't want to live anymore. (*Having difficulty talking*) I feel they just toss him out like a piece of garbage.

K What is the guard doing now?

C (*Having difficulty speaking.*) He's not letting me in to see him, his body.

K Does he take the body somewhere else?

C I feel so alone ... I feel so lost.

K Were you close to any others in the group?

C Close to his mother. She was at the cross. I feel her presence at the cross. Now

I feel so alone and abandoned and alone and the light has gone out. The light of my soul has gone out. The light I used to be able to access. I just feel I can't access the light now.

K Are you aware of where they take the body eventually?

C I feel like he doesn't die. The drugs make him look like he is dead. Somehow when the guard isn't there, we are able to take his body ... and he comes back to life.

K Does Jesus come back in spirit or in the body?

C In the body.

K What is happening next? Where do you go?

C (*Long pause*) I feel like there is group of us that steal out of town and go to some distant place. And I feel like I have a child with him.

K What do you do in that distance place?

In Naomi's session, she also said that he did not die on the cross, but went on to live another life in a different country.

C Living a householder type life.

*I found this to be an interesting word ... "householder." Sometimes clients will use words that are no longer used or uncommon to present day language, which indicates a confirmation that they were in that past life. In researching the word "householder," I found that there are five references using the word in the Bible. In Matthew 20:1 it states, "For the Kingdom is like a **householder** who went out early the morning to hire laborers for his vineyard."*

K Does Jesus go on with his teachings?

C He keeps a very low profile.

K Why does he keep a low profile?

C Because it is somehow part of the Divine Plan that he was to die as people's savior and have them believe. Whatever it was to be, it was. I feel it was downloaded with Jesus. That this was all to happen and to set humanity back on the right tract.

I have had clients on many occasions downloading information while in their session.

K So were just a few that knew he did not physically die on the cross?

C Yes his mother, not with John. I'm feeling so much dissension.

K What was the dissension about?

C I get this feeling like ... not with John, not with Peter, for me, but Andrew yes.

K What about Judas?

C Judas loved Jesus so much!

In Ruth's channeled session Jesus said, "He loved me very much and he wanted to protect me."

K So he didn't betray Jesus?

C He was just part of the plan. Only someone who loved Jesus could take on that role.

Sometimes souls have taken on an assignment for the greater good, even though it may not appear to be what is actually happening in that lifetime. This statement speaks of Judas' taking on the role of his betrayer, when actually he loved Jesus so deeply that he chose this difficult path. This love of Jesus with Judas was confirmed by two other clients.

K Did he understand that role?

C I think so.

Another client spoke of Judas being part of the plan. This would be something the clients would not be aware of in their present life experience.

K It was felt by some that some that the others were jealous or didn't respect you, is that true?

C They were jealous of me because of my closeness to Jesus. Because I was a woman. I had inner power. They would not admit that but they sensed it.

K You spoke of your healing ability. Did Jesus also heal others?

C Jesus healed all the time just by him being Jesus. Yes, he definitely healed.

K What was the most powerful healing that you saw?

C (*Long pause*) How he would be with children that needed healing.
I loved him so much for that! (*She began crying with this statement.*)

K Did Jesus work with other healers? Were there other healers?

C I am feeling that. Some of his people didn't really understand who he was, they didn't really get it. It's weird. People that weren't so close to him got it so much more and because of his influence, others did become healers.

K Did he speak about healing to you or others?

C He spoke of the breath of life ... in this energy one can heal.

K What were the most important words Jesus spoke that resonated to you?

C He spoke of love. When he spoke of loving everybody and God's love and l loving the lowliest of the lowest and loving the ugliest, but not condoning their behavior and yet still being able to love.

K Did he have many followers that followed him? Did some come and some stay?

C Yes, all of that.

K After the crucifixion did Jesus have followers?

C After the cross episode, it was much more low key ... no fanfare. We settled down. I see it, but I don't know where it is ... it's a farming community. Lots of open land and people around us. Life became normalized.

K Did the disciples know about his life after the cross?

C A lot of them did.

K Did some continue his work?

C Some, yes. ... Some were there because they were really there because of the teachings, and some were there for ulterior motives.

K Why were some there for ulterior motives?

C It was that their hearts weren't that pure. I don't know how to describe it.

K You spoke of Jesus having this knowing. If he had this knowing, why did he choose those who didn't have a pure heart?

C He worked with what he had, and he saw that. You know people always had a choice. He didn't feel perfect himself. He just didn't. He wouldn't claim perfection. He was doing his best to follow his Father's will.

K Did he receive messages from the Father?

C He would just commune and go off?

K Did he go to other places to learn that you were aware of?

C Yes. I am getting Kashmir for some reason. I don't know for sure but that name kept coming in.

> *She didn't have any knowledge of the connection with Kashmir at this time. In 1887 Nicolas Notovich, a Russian Journalist traveled to Himis a province of Ladaka in northern Kashmir. A Lama told him about a manuscript that spoke of life of the prophet called Issa. He spoke of these scrolls containing the Buddha Issa who taught and preached the Holy doctrine in both India and Israel. After persuading the Lama to show him the scrolls, Notovich was allowed to translate the Pali scrolls into Russian. He went on to write the book, THE UNKNOWN LIFE OF JESUS in 1894.*
>
> *In 1922 Swami Abhedananda traveled to the Himis monastery where Nicolas Notovich said he found Tibetan manuscripts about the life of*

Issa. Issa is the Indian name for Jesus. He went as a skeptic but was able to verify Notovich's findings. He was able to confirm Notovich's accountings and was shown the same Tibetan manuscript by the lamas about the life of Issa. Then in 1929 Nicholas Roerich came to the same conclusion as Notovich and Abhendananda when he was shown the same scroll containing the life of Issa which was Jesus. In THE LOST YEARS OF JESUS by Elizabeth Clare Prophet, she spoke of Madame Elisabeth Caspari and her husband on a pilgrimage to Tibet in 1939 where they stopped in Himis. There they were shown an ancient manuscript. It was stated that the librarian at the time said to her, "These books say your Jesus was here."

K How old were you when you met him?

C I met him later. I had time with him before the crucifixion.

K What did he confide in you that he didn't confide with the others?

C He had concerns about his mission. He had concerns if he was really up for the whole thing. He would get distressed about the squabbling. He would look to me as a salve.

K What was the squabbling about?

C It is so petty.

K Did Jesus ever talk to you about his early years in his life?

C He talked about how he loved his mother and how special his mother was. How he learned everything about love originally from her. She just had this spirit of unconditional love.

K Did he have any brothers or sisters?

C If he did they're not in my picture. I seemed to feel there was family, but it is not coming into focus.

K Did you have children?

C I think I had a few children. My babies, I love them so much!

K Did they have gifts like Jesus?

C They were the joy of my life! They were kind of like minister's kids. I loved them very, very, very much!

K Did Jesus ever say why he came into this life?

C He needed to do this mission to get humanity on a different tract. A tract that was God oriented ... not all this my ego ... selfish ... power trip.

K Did he feel he accomplished this?

C I feel like he was at peace. And I feel like he knew the story would be written.

K Did he ever hear stories about his death on the cross?

C We were somewhat isolated from that, and yet we knew stories were being told.

K Did any of his disciples stay in touch with Jesus either physically or by other means?

C We stayed in touch. We think we saw some physically. I am seeing a man not with a full beard, dark curly hair ... just radiant blue eyes, like full of diamonds.

K Are you describing Jesus?

C At first I wasn't sure, but I feel this must be Jesus! I just want to hug him...hug him.

K Did Jesus die a natural death?

C Something happened. It wasn't an unpleasant death, it was fairly quick. It was natural.

K What were the circumstances of your death in that lifetime?

C I feel like I could no longer absorb moisture. I'm feeling alone.

No one was with her at her death. Jesus had died before her.

K Now it is time for your soul to release from the body. Moving away from the body. ... You may say goodbye to the body. What is happening? What are you feeling?

C I feel there is an angel guiding me ... I'm not completely free. I don't know why.
Many times if things are unresolved or there is a strong emotional attachment to an event the soul will not feel at peace. But as the soul gets closer to the higher level of awareness, the peace and joy return.

After the death experience, Rose is guided to a place to review that lifetime with greater wisdom and knowledge from a higher spiritual level of awareness. Every soul has a life review after each lifetime. This is a place of self-reflection.

Review of that Lifetime
from a Higher Level of Awareness

K Now that you have more knowledge and wisdom than while in that lifetime, what gave you're the greatest happiness in that lifetime?

C Meeting Jesus and having my children.

K What was the most difficult aspect of that lifetime?

C I've not done a lot.

K Is there a need to forgive self?

C There is some residue.
Rose was able to release and forgive herself and others.

K Is there anything that needs to be released from that lifetime that is affecting the current life of Rose?

C Feeling worthless, feeling not good enough.

K Where do those feeling of being worthless and not good enough manifest in the body?

C Somewhere between the naval and my heart ... the solar plexus.

K If that was a color what color would it be?

C I feel reddish brown. (*The healing was complete.*)

We worked on many other issues that needed to be released and healed. Some of the issues addressed were feelings of abandonment, dehydration, feeling alone and the feeling she didn't want to live. All healings were complete.

K What would you like to bring into your life?

C Times of tremendous laughter and joy.

K Just like we can release things, we can also bring forth positive things from our past. Would you like to bring that laughter and joy back?

C Yes!

K Is there anything else you would like to bring forth from that lifetime?

C I loved to dance then.

In Gina's session when speaking of her friendship with Mary Magdalene, she spoke of them loving to dance together. This is another confirmation in the sessions. These clients did not know each other, and their sessions were years apart.

K Did you dance in that lifetime?

C I did a certain feminine type ... flowing ... beautiful.

K Did you dance with other women?

C Sometimes I would dance with others. I would have a feelings of abandonment ... letting go ... being free ... taking flight like an eagle. I would love to bring it into this life.

When Rose spoke of finding joy in her ability to dance, there was such tremendous joy in her tone and being.

Rose in the Subconscious

K Do I have permission to speak with Rose's subconscious?

SC Yes.

K I know subconscious could have brought forth many different lifetimes for her review. Why was that lifetime with Jesus shown to her? What did that teach her?

SC To help release all that angry energy. In that lifetime it was the apostles. In this lifetime with her brothers ... those who worked with her. It's time to completely letting go of any judgment, not condoning them, just forgive them and to release that energy.

K How will the healing be accomplished?

SC It is being accomplished as we speak because she now has the awareness and the desire and understanding to let that go. It served its purpose. It's no longer needed.

K Thank you ... I know she is going to appreciate this. Is everything totally released from those lifetimes, or is there more to be released and healed?

SC As the Higher Self, I would like to review the Jesus lifetime again, allowing major learning that would like to come forth right now. One of the reasons that lifetime came up was to come into complete self-acceptance, self-love, self-worth, and that is now time to completely 100% embrace all of that, even if mistakes are made, to keep that in the forefront of my consciousness and be a leader in that area.

K   Subconscious are you still here?

SC Yes. We will be there right by her side.

K   What is the learning that she is accessing?

SC To stand in my truth … to stand in my own God given brilliance and not to worry what others think, and to value and trust myself.

K   Trust seems to be an issue with Rose and I know the subconscious can back the feeling of trust to her.

SC As her Higher Self I would like to say she is completely worthy of her own 100% self-trust and to release. Now assisting her in any self-doubt, self-worry, anxiety in regards to her identity in this lifetime.

At this point in the session I was checking the subconscious if she was in that highest level in determining if she could go to that higher level of awareness. Then the subconscious instructed me "We can go higher."

K   Is there anything that needs to be completed and understood with both of those lifetimes?

SC Like to say to those lifetimes, you are loved so much, you have always been loved and even if you didn't see it or feel it at the time…you are loved and held each step of the way. And all mistakes are just lessons to be learned and all mistakes didn't even need to be forgiven because you did nothing wrong. Just learning to walk, to sprout your wings. What I encourage is to keep working on complete 100% self-forgiveness in all lifetimes including this one.

K   Can the subconscious help her with self-forgiveness? I know the subconscious is very powerful.

SC Yes. We will be there right by her side.

K   Will she believe this to be true?

SC Yes.

K   Wonderful! Thank you.

Rose's Impression after Her Session

Rose spoke about not expecting Jesus to come through. She said it was a big surprise when she felt she was in Judea. She said Judea just came out of my mouth from nowhere. In the very beginning of her session, she explained that there was such a strong sense of anger at the men for what they were doing to Jesus and that it was difficult to contain her emotions. Rose was also surprised to hear that I was writing about my clients' experiences with Jesus. When a she was a teenager she indicated there was a time when she asked Jesus to come through. Rose felt the session was helpful, and there also was a sense of feeling lighter.

Years Later after Rose's Session

Rose emailed me back and said, "I have fond memories of our session and meeting you in your "sacred place." She also said she had finished reading her transcript and it was very healing. I recommend clients listen to their session again. Sometimes after listening to their session after a period of time, clients may gain greater insight from their session that they may have forgotten or not understood at the time.

Chapter Thirteen

"Those who have failed to work toward the truth have missed
the purpose of living."
BUDDAH

"What you think, you become. What you feel, you attact.
What you imagine you create."
BUDDAH

ADAM

Adam was a college professor in his current life. He was aware of my work, and decided he could hopefully gain more understanding and knowledge from the Quantum Healing Hypnosis experience. Adam has been a seeker of spiritual knowledge for many years.

In his first lifetime, Adam was monk leading a very spiritual existence. Adam's second lifetime was in ancient Lemuria at a time when Earth was a place of love and peace. Edgar Cayce spoke of Yeshua being Amilius in an ancient civilization. I have included most of this session, so the reader can have a sense of what this community was like during an earlier incarnation when Yeshua was present. Later in this session, she was a teacher of the young Yeshua in one of his lifetimes on Earth.

Adam described himself as a female in her mid-twenties, wearing light clothing from the shoulders down. She lived with her mother, father and three siblings and was very connected to all of them. She described her wedding as lasting ten days with great celebrations with the entire community present. She described her community as having around eight hundred people. Her description of the community was that of being advanced and communal.

Past Life Session

K Coming off the cloud down to the surface, very gently coming back down on the surface. Tell me the first thing you become aware of as you come back to the surface. What are your first impressions?

C I'm a woman! (*Adam was very surprised that he was female.*) And it is an ancient civilization on Earth ... but it is very advanced.

> *Many times clients are surprised to discover that they were the opposite sex in a past life. We have lifetimes of both male and female bodies.*

K Does this place have a name?

C Lemuria. It's very peaceful and very, very advanced to what we have today.

K Do you have a body?

C Yes.

K What is a typical day like for you in that lifetime?

C You can do whatever you want. Everything is abundant. We can go out, we can swim, and we can learn stuff. We know how to levitate objects ... so we have games with it which I play with my siblings.

K That must be fun.

C Yes. ... Basically you can do whatever you want to do from morning to day. We understand that whatever we do, we share with the entire city. Yes everything is shared in the city. We know a lot of people. There is no money.

K So how do you get your food? Is there a place or do you create it?

C Some people create their own food ... they are more advanced. We go to a place to get our food. Some people don't even need food. You see you get all the energy you need from just meditation. If you believe that you can sustain on just meditation, then you do not need to eat. So a lot of people just meditate.

K Do people meditate all day?

C No ... not really. They meditate lots of hours but they also spend time with family. They play with their kids. It's a very loving, peaceful community.

K Is this a community on Earth or on another planet?

C It is on Earth?

K Can you create things or just those who meditate a lot?

C I don't think I'm that advanced, but I can do a lot of things.

K Do you have the ability to levitate objects?

C Yes.

K Were you taught this?

C It is very natural for all of us. It's not something that can be taught in schools or whatever.

K Do you have spiritual beliefs in that lifetime?

C Yes ... in the belief that we are all aspects of God. And that we are all expressions of God, and we understand the interconnection of one another.

K The Oneness?

C Yes.

K Do you have a place of worship?

C There are some places where you can go, but it is under the clear understanding that what you perceive is what you project ... which means you can either go inward or connect with God within you, or you can connect with God outward that is outside of you to connect with God. They are one in the same. There are places you can go, or you can meditate and go deep within. There is no separation between the inner world and outer world.

K Do people live a long time in your community? Do they have long life span?

C Yes ... a lot of them do. I know an Elder who lived seven hundred years and he is still living.

K Does this Elder ever talk about what happened previously?

C Yes ... he talked about lots of stories. He talks about the power of crystals.

K What does he say about crystals?

C They are like a life force. They are not simply stones. They have their own consciousness and they understand you ... so we can get in touch with them and communicate with them. And they tell you a lot because they have been living for thousands and thousands of years. If you want to know what happened for hundreds of thousands of years, you can ask the crystals and they will tell you.

K Are some of crystals more powerful than others?

C Some are more powerful. But each is unique and brings their own knowledge and wisdom, and you can learn from almost any one of them. You can learn anything from them, and they are very powerful.

K You spoke of crystal being in your apartment. Where do you get the crystal?

C They just come ... I don't know.

K What else do the Elders say about previous years? Does he talk of previous civilizations?

C A little bit ... but not much.

K Does he talk about other planets and other stars?

C Yes ... there are all these connections from other civilizations, planets and other stars. They are all very astrologically inclined, so they know the positions in the stars.

K What else did the Elder say that resonated to you?

C He doesn't tell you much, as he lives on his own. But if we want to get some advice we go to him sometimes, and there are others as well who are very wise. There is a special place for him where he lives ... not in the same compartment as me, but we all are the same community. He lives in a slightly remote area, but he does come and [he] blesses our marriages.

K Why did your marriages last ten days?

C There are some astrological things. But the most important thing is when someone gets married, there is an entire community that is filled with joy, happiness and love. It is a testament for being in a community.

K So this community is full of love, there is no strife?

C Yes.

K That sounds like Utopia.

C It does. It is!

K Moving to an important day, a day that you consider to be important in that lifetime? What is happening?

C We are just having a philosophical discussion. You see there was this person who came from a different place ... from the east. We know people from the east, but this is also a new person.

K What is the philosophical conversation about?

C It was about the universe. We talk a lot. There is something about him. It is a very deep energy. He mesmerizes us.

> *I find it interesting that she explained her feelings of Yeshua with the statement, "He mesmerizes us," which was also expressed in Rose's session. I found it quite interesting that they both used the same word, "mesmerize." Rose said, "He began to speak and I was mesmerized."*

K What does he speak about?

C He is very intrigued about our civilization, with our community, and he talks about life on other planets.

K Is he from another planet?

C No, but he has traveled to other planets.

K How does he travel?

C You simply have a body that is basically light turned into matter. So, you can travel anywhere in the universe with just your breath and your mind, your thoughts. So he is one person who can travel.

K Does this man have a name?

C No.

K Do you recognize his essence?

C Yes, he is Yeshua.

K If you heard your name being called, what would your name be?

C Melos.

K What else does this man from the east speak about?

C He says we can do what he does and that we can travel as he does. He manifests things very easily ... easier than others. He just got an apple like that out of thin air and he gave it to me. It was very juicy.

K Does he come and speak your group often?

C Not often. But he has come here twice or thrice, but not often. I know him.

K How do you know him? Were you with him before in another lifetime?

C Yes. I think I knew him in Venus, but have known him in other lifetimes on Earth. He's a very loving energy. And he attached my pineal gland and completely activated it so my meditations improved. I've had visionary experiences in that lifetime.

K So were you able to do what he did?

C No ... because I didn't believe in myself.

K Why not?

C That is something I have to work on to believe in myself. There were only a few who could do what he did. But he did things with so much ease. And he talked about God.

K What did he say about God?

C How loving God is. We are one with God. We are one with Him and so if he can do it, so can we.

K Does the whole community listen to him?

C Yes, because he has that energy about him. Everyone is intrigued when he comes. I just wish he would come more often.

K What does he tell you that is powerful?

C He told me to believe more in myself. To trust in my own abilities and he also said he and I will have lots of lifetimes together.

K So he could see this?

C Yes.

K Did he speak about being with you in between lives, in the interlife?

C Yes. I've been with him in between lives too. He says that I have all the knowledge that I need myself and he asks me to teach others of that knowledge. He says that's my purpose in many lifetimes.

K Do you teach in this lifetime?

C Not the way [he is] being a teacher ... but I teach it in a different way than he does.

K Can you explain?

C That particular lifetime, we were all open to these ideas but I couldn't travel to other planets. So in that lifetime things were easier to explain because everyone had a higher level of spiritual comprehension. In this particular lifetime it is a very materialistic world ... so you have to use a different way to express ideas and you express them by not activating the pineal gland, but show them love, forgiveness, and do a lot of service. You treat everyone with compassion, with love, kindness, forgiveness.

K Did he teach forgiveness?

C You see forgiveness was a shadow because everyone loved each other ... it was a more open community.

K So forgiveness was not necessary?

C We didn't need to forgive anyone.

K That sounds wonderful, Thank you.

K Now moving to an important day, a day that you consider to be important when something important is happening in that lifetime? What is happening?

C I'm old ... I'm not sure but I think my husband has left his body, so I am also considering leaving.

K So you have that ability to consider to leave the body?

C Yes, usually when you decide to leave ... you just let go of your body. Very few people have an understanding of the process of death. Most just let go of their body. I am considering leaving as my daughter is happy. I don't think there is anything more in this lifetime.

K Can you tell me what is happening as you leave the body?

C My energy is filled with light. There is only light.

Adam in the Subconscious

K Do I have permission to speak with Adam's subconscious?

SC Yes.

K Do I have permission to ask questions?

SC Yes.

K Why was the second lifetime shown to Adam?

SC It was shown what it means to be in a family. He loves Yeshua. In that lifetime they connected very deeply.

K Has he had other lifetimes with Yeshua?

SC Yes.

K Is it important to review a past lifetime with Yeshua?

I always ask the subconscious if it is important to review a lifetime if more understanding and healing is needed. If the lifetime is needed to be reviewed, the subconscious will access that lifetime for the client to re-experience.

SC It was the lifetime in which he taught Yeshua.

K What did he teach Yeshua?

SC Many things. It is important to know that Yeshua is always with you. He thanks you for that lifetime when you taught him. He is always with me teaching in this lifetime, and I am thankful for that.

K Were you his teacher when Yeshua was young?

SC Very young.

K What was your name?

SC Kashabah. (*Sounds like*) I was a Yogi in the Himalayas.

> *This seems to be confirmed with the eye witness accounts of Nicolas Notovich and Nicolas Roerich when they were shown various ancient scrolls indicating Saint Issa (Jesus) was in the Tibetan area in the Himalayas during lost years of Jesus. The scrolls said that Issa left Jerusalem at the age of twelve, "intending to improve and perfect himself in the divine understanding and to studying the laws of the great Buddha." It also stated that Issa was a great teacher of the people "preaching to diverse peoples the supreme perfection of man."*

K How long was Yeshua there?

SC Not for long … for about nine months he was with me. But there were others too, not just me. There were nine people.

K Didn't Yeshua already possess great knowledge at that time?

SC He did.

K What kind of things did you teach him?

SC We did. Every day there would be a huge session with all of us circling around him. He would be in the middle and he would be asked highly philosophical questions of the universe and he would come up with the answers and those daily questions helped him with his own understanding.

In Naomi's session, she also was a teacher to young Yeshua.

K   How old was he at this time?

SC He was around twelve or thirteen ... very young. And that he came back later in that lifetime when he was much older. He came back to teach at the same place at thirty-six. That would be much later after his resurrection.

K   So did Yeshua actually die on the cross?

SC No ... he would come back. He would also actually bi-locate he would have another body in front and another body here in India where he taught. So he was able to do that. And not everyone understood.

This could explain why some clients received various perspectives on his death or life after the crucifixion if he was able to bi-locate.

K   Can the subconscious explain how he could be in two places at the same time as you say "bi-locate?"

SC You see all of us can do it because it is not any more different than manifestation if you want to manifest a life for yourself. If you want to manifest your life ... you do so with your thoughts, your emotions, and your actions. The first thing is to feel is that you are not entirely this body but pure consciousness, which means you can go anywhere at any time. And Yeshua was doing that ... but I didn't know how to do it in that lifetime.

K   So how did Yeshua know to go to the Himalayas?

SC He was brought by someone ... but that wasn't his life spot. He had to learn from the Masters at the Himalayas. But we taught him only philosophy. There were others that taught him deep yoga and pranic techniques. He could let go of his body at any time and come back at any time. I believe that is what he used during his crucifixion.

K   Thank you. So were you aware about what happened later in his country?

SC Well ... he came back and he told us about his life, about the crucifixion and the Romans. And he would tell us to forgive them.

K   Did he talk about him healing others?

SC Yes.

K   Did he also speak of others healing people?

SC Yes ... he would teach us. So even though I was a senior, I was learning from him.

K   Was there a time when he could levitate?

I asked this question to receive confirmation of the session as his Aunt said he had levitated as a young child. In Jacob's session Yeshua also spoke of his ability to levitate.

SC Yes.

K   Was he able to levitate things as well as in the lifetime in Lumeria?

SC Yes. But I couldn't levitate in that lifetime.

K   You said you taught him, but did you learn from him as well? If so, what did you learn?

SC Yes ... a lot of things. Sometimes when you teach ... you don't know who is the teacher and who is the student. So even though I was teaching him as a young boy .... I was learning from him. His answers were so profound and beautiful and sometimes made me think a different way.

K   So how did he help you think a different way?

SC There isn't one specific answer, but sometimes the way he looked at things was slightly different than the way I saw them, and it allowed me to open up to a different perspectives.

K   Did he talk about perspectives?

SC Yes. He said that you create your reality based on your perspectives. They are not formed from external experiences ... but they are internal and they manifest the reality you want to live in.

K   Thank you. You spoke of forgiveness being an important teaching as well can you explain?

SC   Yes, he told us to not be angry at the Romans ... to forgive them. And not only at that time but he already knew what the Romans would do 200 years later with his teachings, and he said that everything needs to be forgiven.

K   Did he explain why some people are cruel and do harmful things to each other?

SC   He said they do it because they experience lack of love ... or at least they think they experience lack of love, but they are always given love by God. ... They don't remember or recognize it. And he says that the only way to show them the light, is for us to send more love.

This is such an insightful statement confirming many of the client's thoughts about sending more love so others can remember their light.

K   You said that Yeshua went with Mary Magdalene. Were they married?

SC   Yes, he did marry her and they have a daughter, Sarah.

K   Did his mother and the disciples understand he was still alive and didn't actually die on the cross?

SC   Some of them did. But some of them only believed when they saw. You see the entire thing was a lesson to show people that you are beyond your physical body. That was the greatest lesson of the entire crucifixion and later the resurrection. That was his mission to show people consciousness ... that you're beyond your body. And some people only believed it when they saw him later. It was a time in which when people only believe in things when they can see it and he showed it.

Other clients also spoke of the crucifixion being a lesson so that people could see that we are beyond our physical bodies. I also feel that it was a great lesson which helps to remove the Christian myth that he died on the cross for our sins, which never made sense to me.

K Thank you. Is there anything else Adam needs to know about that lifetime?

SC Just to know that Yeshua is always with you, and he will always be with you. Wherever you go you can always draw from his teachings, because you are one with him and he is one with you. Understand this.

Adam's Impression after His Session

Adam said the session was "awesome." He felt it was huge that he was able to let go without analyzing. He stated that he was very analytical in this lifetime and sometimes it was difficult to let that go. He said that he loved both of those lives and saw a flash of light. Although he unable to visualize in his session, he said that he had a knowing. He also stated that the lifetime in Lumeria was a surprise for him and that he never could have imagined being there. He spoke of the importance of family and community that was present in that life, but that he hasn't had that in many of his other lifetimes. Adam spoke of having a daughter whose energy felt like his mother in his current life. When in a session, we can recognize the energy of a person in our current life. Adam felt he remembered some of his session, but not all of it.

Chapter Fourteen

"After this the Lord appointed seventy others, and sent them on ahead of him, two by two, into every town and place where he himself was about to come."
LUKE 10:1

PAUL

I first met Paul through a mutual friend. He is currently retired from a successful career as a professor at a well-known University. He came for the session to find if he had a lifetime with Yeshua. He had previously been told by many psychics of having a lifetime with him. So he was seeking confirmation of this. In his current life he is extremely intelligent, but in his session he speaks in simpler manner. Many times clients will totally take on the way they spoke in the lifetime they are re-experiencing. Paul has been a seeker of spiritual knowledge for many years.

Past Life Session

K I want you to tell me the very first thing you become aware of as you come back down to the surface.

C I think I am a young man, a young boy.

K I want you to look down at your feet and tell me what you are wearing on your feet, what type of footwear are on your feet. Or are you barefoot?

C Sandals.

K And type of clothing are you wearing?

C Just what boys wear ... it was comfortable, not fancy.

K Is there anyone with you or are you by yourself?

C Just a few other boys. We just joke and laugh around.

K What type of dwelling did you live in that lifetime?

C It was a simple house ... one story and some windows.

K And I want you to go inside. What is the inside of the house look like?

C Some tables and I slept in the corner.

K What type of foods would you be eating?

C Vegetables. There was a garden. We get breads from the market.

K You spoke of "we." Do you have a family?

C Mother and Father, sister and brother. I was older ... my sister and brother younger.

K Did you recognize the energy of anyone that is in your current life?

C Maybe my sister ... she was the little sister and is in this life as my sister. She was nice.

> *Many times clients will recognize the energy of someone in their current life in the session. We may look differently in each lifetime, but we carry the same energy with us from lifetime to lifetime.*

K Let's move to an important date in that lifetime? A day that you consider to be important in that lifetime. What is happening?

C I think that's Yeshua is down the road ... there are a lot of people around him. I didn't know him at the time. I am older, but Yeshua is older than I am.

> *Once again another client saying his name is Yeshua instead of Jesus.*

K What is happening?

C They were all crowding around him. I said, "What is going on? "Who is this?"

K And what did they tell you?

C They said he was a teacher, and so I just stood on the edge and watched. And there were some older men with them, and other followers. I was just one of the followers.

K So you were a follower at this time?

C Well, we were just hanging around, watching ... observers. I didn't even know what they do.

K So you heard him speak? What resonated to you that he spoke of?

C He was nice. He was ... peace and he was wise.

K What did you understand?

C He spoke in simple terms, about life, and about living. It's a good life. But he spoke of these temple things I didn't know.

K What kind of temple things are you talking about?

C What the priests all spoke about.

K What did the priests speak about that was similar?

C All the stuff that was in the books.

K What books?

C They have these books in which were written things. And this man, Yeshua, he knew that stuff. And the people following him, they … well they sort of knew that stuff. But he knew it and he knew it well. I hadn't read those books.

K Could you read in that lifetime?

C No.

K Did most people read or not read?

C No. Not many of us, only the priests and a few others, the tax people, and some of the military. Not many people could read and write.

K Did he speak about the priests?

C He would say, what the priests would say, but then he would say what it really meant, and not what the priests said. He gave a deeper meaning.

K Can you give me an example of that deeper meaning and what they would say?

C It was like they had these laws. But Yeshua said it was about the Father.

K What was about the Father?

C The statements that the rabbis and the priests said … it was more about how God wanted things to be. But Yeshua spoke about the Father.

K Did he say why he called Him the Father?

C I think it was meant, because we have fathers, and we know what a father is … maybe we don't know what God is.

This is an important statement about how Yeshua was trying to help people have an understanding of God that was relatable to them at that time.

K And so it helps you understand what God is?

C Yes.

K Move to another important day in that lifetime, a day that you consider to be important, when something important is happening. What is happening?

C Yeah, there's Mary.

K Mary, his mother?

C Magdalene.

K And what is happening with Mary Magdalene?

C And I'm talking to her. And she's telling me or explaining to me things about Yeshua.

K What is she explaining to you about him?

C About what he is doing and how he's training these people to be teachers. That's who are following him and how he was trying to change the people's thinking … about the Father.

K About people's thinking about the Father?

C Yes. And she asks if I'd like to help. I said, "Sure, what can I do?" And she would tell me where they were going, and could I go to where they were going, and speak to some people who would … well, where they were going and to let them know that they were coming and when they would be there.

K So you prepared people for their entrance to their villages?

C And I could run.

K Oh, you could run fast?

C I was a young man, and I knew where it was. And so I would run to get there and tell them that they were coming.

K And what did the villagers say? Were they happy that they were coming?

C Yeah! They were waiting for him!

K So they knew he was on the way?

C But they didn't know when he would be there. So I would tell them. And I would go too. I would ask where these people lived, so I could find them and tell them.

K So they knew the people ahead of time?

C Yeah.

K Did he stay with those people?

C Yeah.

K Did he stay overnight?

C Yeah. Well, sometimes longer... and so I would follow. I would be there with them. And there was food so I could eat. I didn't have a job so I was their runner. And when they would come ... I was already there. You could see them coming and the people would go and meet them, and I think mostly I talked to Mary Magdalene.

K Oh, so you were connected with her?

C Every now and then I would talk to Yeshua.

K Did you have a crush on Mary?

C No, she was older than I was.

K So was she more like a mother figure?

C Yeah, maybe an older sister.

K And what were her qualities?

C She knew what to do, and she would see to it that it got done.

K So she was kind of a program person or organizer?

C Yeah. And she knew what Yeshua was doing. She understood.

K Do you think they were married?

C She was just with him all the time. You could say ... she generally stayed out of the way. There were all these men around Yeshua.

K Were there other women there?

C Yeah, there were a few who followed. So I would generally hang around her, waiting for my next assignment.

K So why do you think she chose you?

C We were friends.

K Did you knew her before?

C No, we just became friends.

K So you had talked to her way before she asked you to come?

C Well, she saw me hanging around with the other boys, and she figured she needed somebody who could go to the next village.

K Now, if you could hear your name called, what would your name be in that lifetime? What do you hear them calling you?

C I just heard the name Joel. Huh, that's my brother's name.

K Joel? Was that your name?

C Oh in this lifetime, as Paul, and I have a brother named Joel. So yeah, we just became friends. She was older and I understood what she wanted me to do ... and she was like a sister.

> *Paul said that Joel was his name in that lifetime, and his current brother is also named Joel. In the past life session, we can recognize the energy of people in our current life since our energy always remains the same.*

K When you were in the villages, did you listen to Yeshua?

C From a distance. There were older men always around him. But I would try to listen.

K And what did you hear him say?

C You should love the Father, like you love your father.

K Did you love your father in that lifetime?

C I had a good father!

K So you understood that kind of love?

C Yeah, I did. But he was speaking of something bigger, like the Big Father.

K Did you understand that?

C I didn't have much schooling, so just knew what the boys I knew, and I never went to school. So I could understand the simple parts.

K Did he speak of anything else besides loving the Father that you understood?

C He smiled at the kids.

K He liked children?

C He liked the kids.

K Did he say anything to them?

C (*He began crying at this time.*) He just loved them.

K Did he love everyone and talk about love?

C With the kids. It was different with the men though.

K Why was it different?

C We were simple. And the men, they spoke a different way... a different language.

K What kind of language did they speak?

C Like the priests.

K So it was more difficult for you to understand?

C Yeah, and maybe some laws. I didn't know what those laws were. I didn't go to the temple.

> *This would be understandable since he was a young uneducated boy at the time. As previously stated, Paul is highly intelligent in his current life.*

K Did Yeshua go to the temple?

C Yeah, he would go. And he would talk with the priests.

K And did you arrange that as well?

C No.

K What were you doing when you weren't arranging things? What kinds of things were you doing?

C I just hung out with the followers. And ... so he was off having his meetings and just waiting for the next thing to do. I knew where to find Mary.

K Were you close to any of the other followers besides Mary?

C The name Judas comes to mind.

K And why, were you close to Judas?

C He was smart.

K And does he tell you anything about Yeshua?

C He tried to explain what he was doing, or trying to do.

K What kind of things did he explain?

C How he was trying to get him to change their thinking about the laws. But I didn't know what the laws were.

K How he was trying to get Yeshua to change?

C No, how he was trying to get the people to change their understanding of these laws. That the priests and rabbis felt it meant this, but that Judas and Yeshua ... it meant something different, something deeper. And so there was disagreement. And the rabbis and the priests were pretty determined in what they thought. And Yeshua, would try to explain what it really meant. And Judas knew, he knew what it meant.

K Did the other people, followers understand as well?

C Only a few.

K Were you aware of any, what we call miracles that Yeshua performed? Any healings? Were you aware of that?

C I wasn't around.

K But you heard things?

C Yes.

K What kind of things did you hear?

C There would be sick people, and they would get better, and somebody couldn't walk and they could walk. But there were crowds, always crowds, so I didn't see anything. I just heard.

K You stood in the background?

C I never saw what he did or how he did it.

K Did you believe that Jesus was special? Did you feel that?

C He did what the Father told him to do. He did what the Father wanted him to do.

K So how did you feel in his presence?

C Well, when he was with these older men he was just a teacher. But when he was with us kids ... (*Crying*) he was our friend. So he was two things.

K What does Yeshua look like?

C Well, he was taller than I was, and he was ... he was a good looking man. He walked straight.

K What did you mean, he walked straight?

> *I found this to be an interesting observation when Paul described Yeshua walking straight in his session as well. I am assuming that not everyone walked straight during these time. This may have been due to the fact that people working hard in that life may have had back issues. Also he refers to Yeshua being strong and young, as opposed to an older person in his description.*

C He didn't lean over or limp.

K Did you lean over?

C No, I was young, I was strong. I was a runner.

K But there were other people that you saw that were leaning over?

C Older men, with canes. So he was a young, strong man.

K Can you see his eyes? When you look in his eyes what to you see?

C I see that ... how he looked at us kids with such love?

K So you could feel that love?

C Yeah. (*Crying*)

K And what's that feeling?

C He understood us.

K And what did he understand about you?

C Everything. He knew.

K So he knew who you were?

C He knew who we were, and what we were. And it was it was okay. (*Crying*)

K Now you talked about the kids a lot. Did any of the kids follow him too? Or was it just you?

C Well, there were kids everywhere, everywhere he went. In the next village there would be even more kids. But the other ones had to stay in the villages. And there might have been a few of us who would go from village to village.

K Let's move to another important day in that lifetime, a day that you feel was important to recall. Moving to that important day. What is happening?

C There's a lot of people.

K And what are the people doing, listening to him again?

C They all wanted to come and listen. Boy were there a lot of people! Wow!

K Where was this held? Was it in the village?

C No, on some, on some hillsides. They couldn't find a place in the village where they could all stay ... so they needed room, so they went out. Wow, there were a lot of people! All I could do was look at all the people.

K Were you impressed that there were was that many people?

C Wow! I had never seen so many people.

K Did you come before and set that up?

C No. They knew he was going to be there.

K How did they know if he was coming you didn't tell them?

C Word got out that he was going to be there.

K So he speaks in front of the crowd? Is that correct?

C Yeah.

K What happened?

C They were quiet.

K It was very quiet?

> *Once again it is mentioned about the crowd being very quiet when Yeshua spoke to the crowd.*

C And I couldn't … I was too far away.

K Why didn't you get closer?

C There were too many people, so I was in the back.

K So could you hear him speak?

C Only barely.

K So what did you barely hear?

C He spoke about love.

K And what does he say about love?

C It was important, and it should be what they thought about in their life. And not so much about other things and about what they were told they didn't have to be told how to feel … you can feel, and that's the Father's love. You didn't need anybody to tell you this.

K So everybody had that already?

C Yes, and they needed to listen. And they were quiet, and they were thinking … Wow! They were so quiet! So they could hear him, I guess. And it made sense,

I think!

K What made sense?

C What he was telling them ... about love.

K Was that the most important thing he said that you remembered?

C Because ... they sort of know about love. They did need it to be told to them from somebody like him, because the priests didn't speak of this. They spoke of the laws, and what you should do, and not do. But they didn't speak of love. But he spoke of Love. And that was new, and that they could understand. Yeah ... there should be no hatred ... no hatred.

K And did the people understand that?

C They knew, they knew about hatred. They didn't like the Romans.

K Did anyone ask questions of him?

C When he had finished speaking.

K What were the questions?

C The people would all get up to leave and some would stay by. And he would talk to them.

K Individually?

C Or in small groups, because the rest were now leaving and it was getting noisier, and he needed to go speak to some.

K Did you hear what he said to the small groups? Were you there?

C No, I was still way off, and they were all leaving, and I just knew if I was going to be needed, I would be close enough.

K Did you ever talk to Mary about what he spoke about? Did she explain it to you so you could would be clearer?

C I think Judas did.

K What did Judas explain that you understood better?

C Judas was smart, so ... I liked Judas. He would try to explain it with examples.

He would say, think about how you might react in some situation. So these were examples of what Yeshua had been saying to everybody. So he could give me examples. Simple examples. I say, "Oh I see, that's what he was saying." And he would say, "Yeah." But I knew there was a bigger meaning. But he was giving it to me so that I could understand it. And I appreciated that. I liked what he told me.

K What was the most important thing he told you?

C Well, what he was telling me was to try to relate simple statements about love and Father to situations in your life, things that happen to you. And are they similar? Oh, I see, so that would make it relevant to what I did, rather than what the priests and the rabbis did. And Judas was willing to explain this to me.

K That was very kind of him, wasn't it?

C Don't know why he would talk to me.

K Why do you think he did talk to you?

C Maybe I just understood him. There were different groups of the disciples that would have hung together in little groups. And I could see him talking to Yeshua, just the two of them.

K Did Yeshua ever talk to you?

C I was a boy. But Judas was willing to speak to me about what Yeshua was saying.

K So he interpreted what Yeshua was saying for you?

C He took me under his wings, so to speak. And I could tell that he and Yeshua had a good relationship. And a deeper one.

K More so than the others?

C But Judas had his own … he had his own thinking, his own way of looking at things. And it wasn't quite the same as Yeshua.

K Why not? What was different?

C He was educated, and he was relating it to … more of the political situation. He wasn't a fisherman.

K And were the others fisherman?

C Some were. There were farmers … for everybody was picked for a reason, I guess. I didn't know what the reasons were. But I could see Judas and what he was valued for. So he would explain things to me. Yeah, I liked that!

K Were you aware of Yeshua working with others and teaching healing, to other groups? Did he have a group of healers?

C Mary comes to mind. Mary knew about healing.

K So Mary helped with the healing?

This is another confirmation of Mary being a healer.

C Yeah … Judas wasn't … he wasn't into healing.

K So was there a specific group, who were designated as healers, as well?

C I think he was trying to teach some of the disciples to heal.

K Did you hear what he said about healing?

C No. I didn't understand about healing.

K You said that there were followers. Did some followers come and go?

C Yeah. It depended where he was going.

K But some had families, is that correct?

C Oh yes! But they liked him. They followed him as they could. Yeah, they had families. But there was only this smaller group that went wherever he went. So he had many followers, but they weren't with him all the time.

This was confirmed again that some of followers had families and were not always with Jesus.

K Did Judas or Jesus or Mary ever discuss his earlier life? Yeshua's earlier life experience?

C No, I didn't know about ... he just came in that one day, and there he was for the first time, and I think I just knew Mary Magdalene and Judas.

K And now we're moving to another important day in that lifetime with Jesus, moving to that important day in that lifetime. What is happening and why is that an important day?

C They told me he was dead. (*Spoken with such sadness.*)

K Who told you he was dead? Who told you this?

C Some of the people. They knew that I was one of them, and they said he was dead. And I was [saying] ...." no ... no, he's not." They said, "Yes he is." "How do you know this, I said?" They said, "Well, everybody knows."

K Why didn't you know? Where were you?

C I think I was back in my village, my home.

K Did you stop following Yeshua?

C Well, I was home and he was away.

K So, you didn't always go with him then?

C No, at this time, I was back at my home.

K Did you hear about it in the village? Did the people in the village tell you?

C Mary said he would be busy and I could go home. And so I did. I said, "Could I do something? "And she said, "That's okay, we'll let you know." So I went back home.

K And then you heard it from the people in your village that he had died?

C Yeah.

K And how did that make you feel?

C I didn't understand. I mean ... why?

K So you didn't understand why he would be dead?

C Why would he be dead?

K Did they say how he died? Did they tell you that?

C They said they crucified him.

K And did you ask why?

C Why would they do that? What did he do?

K And what did they say?

C They didn't know the reason, they just said that's what they heard.

K So they didn't know the circumstances of why he died.

C No, nobody knew in my village.

K Did you ever find out what happened?

C Sometime later some people came to the village.

K And what did they say about his death?

C They said they had found him guilty …. Oh! He was saying the wrong things.

K Did they say what he said that was wrong?

C No that was the reason why they and I didn't know what he could have said that was wrong! It didn't make any sense. (*Crying*)

K It's okay. You are very sad and I understand. Did you ever see any of the other followers after that? Did you go search for them for answers, or did you just stay in the village? What did you do?

C I saw a couple of the older men who knew more.

K What did they speak of? Anything different than what you heard?

C They just talked about what it was he had come to tell us, and they understood it.

K And what was that? Why did he come?

C There needed to be a new way, a new way of thinking about things, a new way of relating to the Father, a new way of treating people … and that's what he would be remembered for. But he hadn't done anything wrong to deserve this. (*Crying*).

K Did you ever see Judas again? Did you ever hear from him?

C No, when they sent me back to my village, they were all gone. I never heard.

K So you never heard from any of them?

C Just these two men who came back, and they knew that I had been with him as his runner.

K Had they been with him too?

C Well, they were ... they were sort of followers. (*Crying*)

K They had seen you there?

C (*Crying*) They thanked me.

K What did your parents think of all of this? Were they supportive?

C Yeah, it was okay, it was good.

K So they liked Yeshua? They felt he was a good man?

C Yes, (*Crying*) they were proud of me. He was a good man.

K That was nice. What did most people call him? Did they call him teacher, Master? What did they call him?

C Different people called him differently. Some just called him "rabbi." We thought of him as a teacher.

K Did anybody call him the Master?

C Some, who knew him better than most. He was our teacher ... us boys.

K What did Master mean in that time frame, when he was called Master? Do you understand what that meant?

C That meant that he was a big teacher. He knew more than teachers know. He knew ... he knew a lot! Yeah!

K Did everyone in your village follow him? Did they like him?

C Yes, we liked him.

K So did he had a big following then?

C In my village, yes.

K But not in the other villages?

C Not in Jerusalem.

K Why not in Jerusalem?

C They were with the priests. They were powerful.

K You said you heard the Romans killed him. Did the priests have anything to do with it? Did you feel or did you hear anything?

C Yes, it was the priests who did it. And they turned him over to the Romans, who did the job.

K Did they say anything about Judas?

C I never heard about Judas after that, the last time I saw him. I don't know what happened to him.

K Did they say what happened to Jesus after he died?

C Some said ... I thought this was strange ... they said they thought they saw him after. They said over someplace, several people claimed that they saw him. I said, "Well that can't be true, because he died!" They just said they saw him, and they didn't ... that couldn't be possible.

K So you didn't believe it?

C So it must have been somebody who looked like him. That's what we thought. Yeah, that's what they claimed, but you can't believe them.

K Why do you think they claimed that?

C It must have been he looked like him, and he spoke like him.

K So what did you do after he died? You said that you stayed in the village? What did you do in the village then?

C I grew older and I took a wife.

K Did you love that wife in that lifetime?

C She was nice. (*Smiling broadly*)

K Did you have children with her?

C Yes ... I think two, one of each. She was nice.

K So that was a happy life then?

C Yes. She didn't know Yeshua.

K Did you tell her about him?

C Yes.

K And what did she say? Did she believe? Did she understand what he was saying?

C Kind of.

K She was accepting of it though, is that correct?

C Yeah.

K Did you talk about him a lot to others too, as well?

C I told the story when I was older.

K To the children, or other people?

C Everybody, they knew that I knew him.

K That must have given them comfort too?

C And they knew that I knew, I told them I knew Judas, and I knew Mary Magdalene.

K Did you ever hear what happened to them as you became older?

C They just said that Mary went away. They never told me where she went.

K What about Judas? Did you hear anything about him?

C The last I saw him that one time, and I never saw him again.

K So the end of that life then was very happy?

C Yes, it was. Yeah, I had a good family.

K How did you support yourself then?

C I worked. I think we made things. We built things.

K As someone like a carpenter?

C Yeah ... kind of. I was a worker and I made enough. Yeah, I made things.

K Were you aware that others spoke of Yeshua? Did it talk of his teaching travel, his words?

C We all knew he had been there and he was remembered.

K Were there any books about him or scrolls?

C We didn't read. But the stories were told. And I think some of the stories were changed.

> *Another confirmation that many people did not read at that time. He also explains that the stories changed which again addresses the authenticity of the Bible as we know it.*

K Why did you think the stories changed?

C Well, one person tells someone, and then someone changes it slightly, and then that one changes it, and over time. So there were the healings, but the details got forgotten. But they remembered that he had done healings and ... so there were just memories. But life went on, and those memories would be passed down as stories.

K And did you tell your children?

C I did.

K What were the circumstances of your death in that lifetime? How did you die in that lifetime?

C Oh, I think I just got sick.

K Where were you sick? In what area of the body?

C I was just ill with a fever.

K Was your wife with you?

C Yes, they were sad.

K Were you much older then?

C Yes.

K Were there any final words to yourself to your family?

C [Crying] I love you. And I held her hand.

K Did you decide to go or did you decide to stay for a while?

C I went.

K Is there anyone to greet you on the other side?

C No.

After the death experience, Paul is guided to a place to review that lifetime with greater wisdom and knowledge from a higher spiritual level of awareness. Each soul has a life review after each lifetime. This is a place of self-reflection.

Review of that Lifetime
from a Higher Level of Awareness

K What gave you the greatest happiness in that lifetime?

C Jesus and the kids ... and my wife.

K Do you understand that type of happiness in the current life, as Paul?

C No.

K What was the most difficult aspect of that lifetime?

C Hearing that he died. Where it was a good life. I had some happy times.

K Is there a need to forgive anyone in that lifetime, or forgive self?

C No.

> *Many times clients have already forgiven others in their previous lives, and forgiveness was complete.*

K Did you bring forth anything else that needs to be released from that lifetime that's affecting the current life of Paul?

C I just regretted I didn't know more, what Judas and Mary Magdalene were telling me. I didn't understand.

K You weren't able to understand at that time, were you?

C No.

K Do you need to forgive yourself for that?

C No, it's just regret.

K So now you just need to let that feeling of regret go. Because you were at a point in that lifetime where you didn't have the knowledge that Paul currently has, is that correct?

C Uh hum.

K Have that knowledge that you were assisting Yeshua in many ways.

C In simple ways.

K Beautiful ways. So what did you learn or accomplish in that lifetime that can help you understand the current life?

C It was about love.

K What about love?

C That it's real and it's important and it heals.

Paul in the Subconscious

K I know the subconscious could bring forth many lifetimes so why was the lifetime with Yeshua shown to him?

SC The wisdom of the heart. It's all about love. In that lifetime his heart was open and in other lives it was not. This was the one life of greatest openness and those feelings could be rekindled.

K Can the subconscious rekindle those feeling now?

SC Yes. (*The subconscious indicated that his friend will help him.*)

K He wanted to know if the lifetime with Yeshua was true as it was given today.

SC Yes.

K Are there any memorable experiences with Yeshua that would be helpful for Paul to remember?

SC He did speak to Yeshua.

K What did Yeshua speak to him about?

SC He did not understand but the seed was planted. He will remember.

K What does he need to know?

SC He is loved.

K Is there anything he needs to remember that Mary Magdalene spoke to him about?

SC She spoke to him about his exuberance and the need to control it.

K Did he heed her words?

SC Sometimes.

K Since I understand the subconscious knows everything, did Mary and Yeshua marry?

SC Yes.

K Did they have children together?

SC Yes.

K Did Yeshua appear to some after his death?

SC Yes.

K Why was Yeshua sent or to volunteer to come to Earth during that time?

SC Yeshua is of the comrades of Venus and volunteered for this very difficult assignment. He needed to be trained.

   Clients sometimes speak of being trained for their next lifetime.

K When was he trained? Was he trained before he came to Earth?

SC Yes and during.

K And what was Yeshua trained in?

SC Sacred Knowledge .... powerful knowledge known by few. Which must be carefully taught and understood to work miracles. He needed proper control of his body. He needed to establish connection to Higher Source.

K Didn't he already have that connection?

SC It took training to establish this once in the body.

K How is it that more people are not given this Sacred Knowledge?

SC This knowledge is very powerful.

K So it doesn't want to be misused?

SC That is correct.

K Is there anyone on Earth today with the Sacred Knowledge?

SC Several.

K Will they come forth soon?

SC When it is time. ... Yet to be determined.

> *The subconscious will not always give us specific time frames for an event in the future.*

Paul's Impressions after His Session

Paul explained that he didn't remember much of his session. He spoke of not knowing this information previously. Clients will give information in a session that they previously had no prior knowledge of. There was a feeling that this was different from what he expected, which is a very common response. He also spoke of others perspectives that may have been different from others. Paul seemed to be processing the information and was unable to talk in great detail, which is common for some clients.

Impressions One Week after His Session

Paul said "How can one ever forget such a session?" He explained that he was surprised about how much emotion was brought forth in the session and released. He also was surprised at how many emotions were buried in our soul, where sometimes we carry the baggage of traumas from long ago.

Impressions One Year after Paul's Session

"Seeing Yeshua for the first time in my regression, when he came walking down the road, surrounded by so many people, all wanting to hear him and just be with him. The discussions were quite animated at times. What stood out for me was his incredible peace, calmness, patience, and even serenity, coupled with profound wisdom. What a perfect teacher he was!"

"Seeing Yeshua turn his attention from the crowds of people to take time with us kids was such a joyful memory! It was as if he needed some light relief from the pressures of the day, and our presence enabled him to express a different kind of love to us. The phrase, "Suffer not the children to come unto me" was perfectly clear to me."

"I could see that Mary Magdalene was one whirlwind of activity; Yeshua's executive, or administrative assistant, always arranging and organizing things behind the scenes. But there were those infrequent times when I caught a glimpse of her just talking quietly with Yeshua. And it was easy to see that those moments were much needed for both of them."

"My friendship to Judas Iscariot came as a huge surprise. Why did he take me aside and teach me things about what Yeshua was saying? I was very attentive to everything he told me, even if I was struggling to understand the full import of Yeshua's teachings. But Judas did not mind my questions and was very patient with me. He became a very good friend to me and I always sought him out. You could see that Judas was smart, and had a mind of his own, however. And there would be moments when he and Yeshua would have these discussions where those differences were apparent."

"And, for sure, completely unexpected was the revelation that I married in that life a simply wonderful woman! The depth of her love for me in that life was something that I have rarely felt in this lifetime. The time when I witnessed Yeshua speaking to a few thousand people was unforgettable! When does anyone these days ever witness such an event?"

"One of the most significant takeaways I had from that regression was how uneducated, and young I was, and this did not enable me to comprehend the import of Yeshua's messages and how, even now, I regret missing that opportunity. But I was not much different than thousands of other people in the same respect, for they too had trouble fully comprehending the import of his teaching. It was only later that I learned from Yeshua that it did not matter that much that they did not understand, for he had planted the seeds of understanding would grow over time."

So you ask, "How did this regression affect my current life." Your regression gave me mental pictures of scenes in that life, like watching a movie that gave what Yeshua has told me, a kind of reality. Thinking of that regression is like turning on a spiritual light bulb that reveals deeper truths than the written word."

Chapter Fifteen

"Remember, healing--all healing comes from within. Yet there is the healing of the physical, there is the healing of the mental, there is the correct direction from the spirit. Coordinate these and you'll be whole!"
EDGAR CAYCE READING 2528-2

"And he said to him, (a leper) "Rise and go your way; your faith has made you well."
LUKE 17:19

HARMONY

Harmony is a sound healer in her current life. She said she was drawn to learn more about her past lives as well as accessing her subconscious for greater healing and clarity. She spoke briefly about a lifetime with Jesus in her previous session, and she wanted to know more about that lifetime. After reviewing Harmony's past lives, I asked her subconscious to come forth. She went easily into the subconscious.

Harmony's Session in the Subconscious

K   Do I have permission to speak with Harmony's subconscious?

SC Yes.

K   In her last session, Harmony spoke of having a past life with Jesus. Is that correct?

SC That is correct.

K   Can the subconscious give her more information about that lifetime with Jesus?

SC They grew up together in the same village. Their mothers were friends. Before she was born, Jesus gave her a light initiation.

K   Can you describe that to us?

SC As the bellies of the mothers touched ...the inside my mother's uterus was charged with the light and filled with the light and from that moment forward until she was born.

> *What a beautiful and fascinating statement about the power of our light energy touching another.*

K   Did they know each other? Were they sisters?

SC Yes, but not sisters, just friends in the village.

K   Did she grow up with him?

SC As much as he was around, but he wasn't always around. There were time he was gone.

K   Where did he go?

SC They took him to school at different times at different temples and different villages.

K   And what did she notice about Jesus? Did she feel he was different?

SC Yes. She knew from the time before they born that he was meant to bring peace. He helped her find her way in those times that were not always nice to women. He helped her to see herself as beautiful soul, and to be free to live with love. To open her heart and teach others to do that. That is part of what Harmony brings to this life.

K   What kind of difficulties did she experience as a female?

SC They had to take her away to schools and hid her in order for her to learn and in order for her teach the children. They did not believe in having women having knowledge ... it was very much a man's world.

Once again this supports the fact that women were not considered to be equal to men at that time. Another client spoke of how the others felt about her in this statement, "Because I was a woman. They didn't like women hanging around."

K   You spoke of teaching children. Can you elaborate?

SC She was teaching the children. She taught them of the ways of Jesus ... of the way of God ... of the way of peace. She taught them to find joy, to laugh and sing. It was not out in the open.

K   If you could hear your name, what do you hear?

SC Isabella ... as a child Bella.

K When she was with Jesus was she a follower?

SC Oh yes! He was charismatic. There was just something about him that just brought your heart open (*Sigh*) and wide and flowing. And just life was easy and beautiful.

K What was the most important thing that he told her?

SC To never forget to love, to be kind, and to see God in everyone she met.

K What did Jesus say that was the most important message to the world?

SC His message was love and to always put love first ... to be loved ... to show love and to see love in everyone.

K When she was with him what did she do? What was her position?

SC She was his support ... she was there to hold space for him. She was there to help others that may not have understood, when they were fearful and to hold their hands.

> *This is very similar in Grace's session when she spoke of his mother, Mary saying, "She was so smart because she had to hold the strength for him. She couldn't go to her own sorrow because she was holding it for him that she held a space for him with her and Mary's energy."*

K Why were they fearful? Was it his teaching that caused the fear?

SC Because for some people it was so different. It was so not the normal that some were afraid of him at first, but after an afternoon with him, their fears quickly went. But she was there to hold that space, to help the space around to stay clear so the message could be taken in their hearts.

K Were there other women around him?

SC There were!

K What did everyone think about that?

SC Again ... the women had their place in that time, and women that were around him were seen as followers.

K So were many women around him?

SC There were many.

K And did some of them come and go?

SC Yes.

K Were there times where Jesus worked with others on healing?

SC Absolutely! They were taught to heal ... as he healed. They were taught to use their hands to send their energies to activate Divine Source. To open their hearts to help them with all their physical ailments as well as their fears.

K And did she see him heal others?

SC Yes. She saw him heal the lepers.

K Did you go with him?

SC Yes she did.

K Did she work with him?

SC Yes, she did.

K Were all the lepers healed?

SC Not all.

K Why weren't they healed?

SC Because they didn't believe. They would see and yet they wouldn't believe it was for them. There were feelings that, "They were special and I am not."... "I don't deserve that."

> *In my work I have found that many times illness cannot be healed due to various factors such as learning a lesson, for the experience, teaching others a lesson, or belief that they cannot be healed. Myself and others, spoke of Jesus saying that not everyone could be healed.*

K So you are speaking of self-worth issues?

SC Yes. I don't deserve that.

K   Did Jesus say that it also could be their lesson?

SC Sometimes, it could be their lesson.

K   Describe what Jesus looked like?

SC He was rather ordinary looking. His eyes, however were mesmerizing. They were definitely different than anything I've ever seen. They pierced you and they looked into your soul. And they held you love with kindness. That's what emanated through him. His hands would be warm and his voice was soft. There was a resonance to his voice that when he spoke, you were really pulled to listen. It was as though you were pulled away. He had brownish hair and a beard most of the time.

> *This is similar to how I felt when in Jesus' presence. When clients responded to the question about Jesus' eyes, there was a feeling of unconditional love when he looked at you. There were two other clients who spoke of Jesus' eyes as "mesmerizing."*

K   We have heard many stories that he was married, is that correct?

SC Yes. He was with Mary Magdalene.

K   Did he have children? If so how many children?

SC Yes he did. I see five children.

> *This seems to be the consensus with regard to number of children. For those who say he had no children or were not married, they may have not known this as it was a secret as Harmony explained in her next statement.*

K   Was everyone aware of this marriage or was it a secret?

SC It was kept a secret … that is why it is not written. It is how Mary wanted it. She didn't want the children to grow up with the persecution that was felt by Jesus. It was protection for her family.

> *This is a real possibility that it was kept secret by many, due to the*

tumultuous time in which Yeshua lived. This was also confirmed by several clients that it was kept a secret.

K   Who did Jesus say he was? We have heard different variations?

SC He would call himself Yeshua.

Again she spoke of his name being Yeshua and not Jesus.

K   Why was he called Yeshua? Karen and others would call him by that name in their sessions.

SC Because to him that was his name! (*Spoken with great conviction.*) That is what his mother called him.

K   Thank you. Some people called his the Son of God, the Messiah, can the subconscious explain this?

SC He knew what his journey was to be. He understood that he was serving mankind for many different reasons. He did not see himself as the Messiah or the Son of God ... he saw himself as just another human being. But one that was enlightened to know the importance of love, the love of God and what that brought into your lives.

K   Why did he feel that he came to that particular time in history?

SC To help the evolution of man. He understood that deep down.

K   Did he consider himself as a great teacher?

SC He considered himself as a teacher and a healer, yes.

K   Did he speak about his birth being different?

SC I have never heard him speak of his birth.

K   Did you ever meet his mother, Mary?

SC Yes, I have met Mary.

K   What can you tell us about Mary?

SC She was gentle and so kind. Her job as his mother was one of the hardest jobs ever ... to be that giving and understanding. She too understood his purpose and understanding. She protected him when she could or felt when she should. But also allowed him the wings to fly when he needed. Her prayers were so great, that is what helped him throughout his life the way he did. She was the incarnation of Divine Source Energy. Joseph was the grounding that grounded the center... that was centered. And from the two of them he came as this beautiful incarnation of a soul, centered on our Earth and yet guided by Source Energy ... that is what he was able to do what he could.

This was such a beautiful explanation of Mary. It is also was another instance of a client speaking about Mary being so gentle and kind.

K   Did you ever meet Mary Magdalene? Can you describe her?

SC She was different than Mary. She was gentle but she hung back. She was full of gratitude. She was full of gratitude. Her piece was the gratitude piece for being forgiven for so many sins and for non-judgment.

K   What was her sin?

SC She was a prostitute before she met Jesus.

K   What changed her?

SC He did. He saw her heart. He forgave her.

K   It is my understanding that the church told this story and it was not true. It that correct?

SC That is incorrect.

K   Why are there different versions?

SC In today's world like you have different versions of the news, stories, back then it had the same.

K   So was it to protect Jesus that this was not spoken of?

SC Yes.

In Rose's session as Mary Magdalene, she described herself as a healer and felt tremendous guilt of taking advantage of a man. Therefore, she may have been seen by some as a prostitute at the time.

K What can the subconscious tell us about Jesus?

SC His purpose in his life was here for us to come to this place now and to embrace healing, love energies in the ways we now do. As people step into that more and find the peace in their hearts, not following religion … just following peace and love … the world will begin to change more and more. It is already changing and we will see many things coming even more so.

K Are there more beautiful things coming?

SC Yes.

K Karen believes there is a Great Awakening, is this true?

SC That is true. There are more and more souls awakening.

K There are some differences in perceptions and interpretations of Yeshua, but the essence of Yeshua is always the same. Is that true?

SC Yes. There are differences in perceptions and interpretations.

K Was the client able to channel Yeshua in her session. Was that correct?

SC That is correct.

Harmony Channeling Yeshua

K Can we channel Yeshua?

SC We may try. (*The voice now changed as Yeshua came through.*) Dear one know this … do not doubt what you get. Do not doubt what comes from love. Ask yourself what would love do? Am I being kind? Those are the questions that need to be brought forward into the consciousness of all. You can help this with your book. We bless you for this work. And as a group consciousness, collective, there will be more to come. They will present themselves to you one by one.

The message was addressed to (me) Karen. As predicted, there were
many more clients that would come to me. It has been stated that they
were drawn to me because of my experience with Yeshua.

K   Thank you. Did Harmony and Karen know each other in that lifetime?

SC Yes. They were both healers. They were both part of the group.

I had never asked if a client and I had known each other before in a
lifetime. At the time I don't know why I had asked this question, other
than I was guided to ask it.

K   What was your life like later in that lifetime? Did you still teach about
Yeshua?

SC She lived a happy full life. She taught them about love, about the
understanding of who God was, and what Yeshua was there to do.

K   What did you teach her about God?

SC That was where everything came from and that those energies came in with
lives with lessons, parables, I believe he called them.

K   Thank you.

SC You are so welcome.

Harmony's Impressions after Her Session

In coming out of the session Harmony's first response was, "Wow ... Wow!
That was cool!" She also indicated that the session was better than she thought it
would be. She was surprised that the session lasted three hours, as it seemed more
like twenty minutes. This happens quite often, clients tend to be surprised at how
long the session transpired, compared to their perception of time. Harmony also
indicated that she had channeled before.

Chapter Sixteen

"...these were then called Essenes. This school taught "the mysteries of man and his relationship to those forces which might manifest from within and without."
EDGAR CAYCE, READING 993-L-5

JACOB

A friend recommended Jacob to come for the Quantum Healing Hypnosis session. Jacob spoke of a need to come for a session. I have found that people are drawn to this work when they are ready to gain greater understanding. In his current life he has a successful practice as a physical therapist.

In Jacob's first past life experience, he spoke of being from another planet and was sent down to bring light to the planet. I included this part of the session, as it was a confirmation of Ellie's channeled session. In his second past life experience, he indicated that he was a teacher to Yeshua when he was young. I decided to include some information related to the information hidden by the Essenes in the scrolls at Qumran. This was the third client who spoke of the Essenes as a small group of wise, spiritual teachers of Yeshua at an early age.

The Past Life Session

After coming off the cloud to the surface, Jacob described himself as glancing the planet Earth from the outside on a spaceship which looked like a big glass canopy. Jacob described his clothing as being a basic cloth like a robe. He spoke of the dwellings made of clay using the energy of Atlantis.

K Do you have a mission?

C I seem apprehensive in coming.

K Why are you apprehensive? Did they prepare you for this? What did they say?

C (*Becoming very emotional*) They said, "You're going to do great no matter what!"

K Who are the "they" you speak of?

C (*Crying*) The Pleiadians. I'm not from that planet. It is a name you wouldn't understand.

K Does this planet have a sound for their name?

C Shemakasheaka! (*Sounded like*)

> *I will ask for sounds when clients have difficulties with pronunciation of a name or place.*

K Did they tell you that you were going to have a body on Earth?

C Yes.

K What else did they tell you about Earth?

C It's a very loving planet, if you give it a chance. I just know it's not where I should be ... it going to be a lot of work.

K Did you volunteer to come to Earth?

C Yes. (*He also said there were some who also volunteered.*)

K Who told you to come to Earth?

C The Pleiadians. They came to me through thought.

K How did you know what Earth was going to be like?

C They showed me everything. I saw the volcanic beginnings, and I saw when they seeded the planet.

K Did they explain why they seeded the planet?

C It was all an experiment.

> *This was a confirmation of Ellie's session when she channeled Yeshua and he explained that Earth was an experiment.*

K What was the experiment?

C They wanted to create. They check all the time.

K Did they speak of the energy being heavy, more difficult?

C Yes ... that's why I'm scared. It's not easy.

K So how did they prepare you?

C I've been here before?

K So how did they prepare you each time?

C Each time it gets harder.

>   *He spoke of having fifty lifetimes on Earth.*

K Why does it get harder each time?

C (*Becoming very emotional and crying*) Because no one is getting it! It makes me want to give up sometimes.

K I understand, but you coming brings so much light.

C That's why they want me to be there. (*Crying*)

K So what was the most important lifetime that you experienced on Earth?

>   *After asking the question, there was a very unusual loud sound coming from him. This was a sound like I have never heard before. I felt that his energy was changing in order to access the lifetime with Yeshua.*

C I was an Essene named Mustafa.

>   *I was not sure of the spelling, I used the name as it sounded like to me. I also discovered later that the name Mustafa was an actual name and is a common name in Turkey today.*

K As the Essene Mustafa, were you considered a leader?

C Yes ... teaching.

K What did you teach?

C Healing.

K What type of healing? Healing of the body or spirit?

C Healing of the mind, body and spirit as they are not separate.

K So they did not separate the mind, body, spirit connection?

C No. Everything is One.

K Were you a large group?

C We were small at the time.

K So how many of there were you?

C Sixteen.

K Did you speak about others being from another planet?

C That was not known at that time. We did not converse of such things ... it was not important.

I asked this question because he had experienced a lifetime on another planet.

K What was important?

C Being present. (*Breathing very heavily*).

K Did you go into other communities to heal?

C We healed from afar.

K How was that accomplished?

C Thought.

K Were you able to read minds at that time?

C No. You don't read minds to heal! There is nothing you need to do or say ... you just need to heal.

K Do you need to have intention to heal?

C You could say that. That's even more complicated than we make it.

K Yes. Thank you, I understand. Do you live together in a community?

C Yes.

K What does your community look like?

C Made of what you call clay. But we really use energy much like you would see in Atlantis to bring light, and the basic necessities ... it's easy.

K And did you live in Atlantis?

C I spent time there.

K So you brought some of that knowledge with you?

C Yes.

K Were you a healer in Atlantis as well?

C Yes.

K You said you healed from afar. Who did you heal?

C Everyone.

K Do you have any other psychic gifts? (*I had to explain what psychic gifts entailed*). Can you predict future events?

C No. That is not my area of expertise … just healing.

K Can everyone in the group also do healings?

C No. We all do different things. There are some that do future readings.

K Is that helpful?

C I don't think so, because you are not being present.

K So being present is important?

C It is important to me.

K Why is it important to you?

C We only exist [in the] here and now.

K Do you ever leave your group?

C I like to spend time alone.

K What do you like to do when alone?

C I wander the sands.

K So were you live is it warm?

C Very warm.

K How do you get water?

C It is created as you call it. It comes from what you call evaporation. You have much of the technology today. It was much simpler.

K Now move to an important day, a day that you consider important in that lifetime. What is happening?

C I'm in a large crowd and I just entered the city.

K So there were times when you traveled away from your community?

C My village is very close to Jerusalem.

K Is there a name for your village?

C Qumran.

> *Archaeologists say that the Essenes lived in the area call Qumran. Most archaeologists speak of them being a small mystical community of men and many of whom were great scribes.*

K What do you notice as you enter the city?

C There is a lot of commotion. They are talking about a healer named Yeshua.

K What are they saying?

C That he is a miracle.

K Do they say anything else about Yeshua?

C Well, you know, there are two sides to the coin. Some people view miracles as you know ... things they don't understand.

K Do you believe in the devil?

C No! But many of the people do.

K So are you saying some say Yeshua is the devil?

C Incarnate, you could say that.

K But some say he is a miracle?

C Absolutely!

K So did you get to meet Yeshua?

C I got to teach him healing.

K How old was he when you taught him?

C Yes. He was about six or seven years old.

K Was he gifted then?

C He was always gifted. He could do pretty much anything he put his mind to. It was a matter of controlling.

K So did you help him learn control?

C Yes, balancing the ego.

K So he had an ego.

C Much more subdued than most. He was always conscious of his ego. He knew that it was not in his best interest to let his ego run his True Being.

K Could Yeshua levitate?

C When he was older he could. He was about seventeen years old when he levitated.

> *I asked this question because in Ruth's session, Yeshua as a young child, spoke of his mother asking him not to levitate, as others wouldn't be able to understand this. He may not have been aware of this during these times, since Mary told Yeshua to keep it a secret.*

K How did you teach him healing?

C Through thought. Being One together as one can transmit a short amount of data this way.

K Did Yeshua have any questions?

C I think we taught each other. He taught me compassion. That was something I didn't understand.

K Why didn't you understand?

C In the places I lived compassion is not needed.

K Where did you live where there was no need of compassion?

C Societies where there is Oneness. What you would call Unity Consciousness. One does not need compassion if you can feel everyone else's thoughts.

K What about suffering. There was no suffering?

C No suffering.

K Do you see suffering around you?

C There was much suffering on Earth.

K So did Yeshua teach you compassion on Earth?

C He taught me compassion on Earth.

K Did he teach you anything else?

C Not really. That was my biggest gift from him however.

K That's wonderful, thank you.

K Did Yeshua come to your community to be taught?

C Yes, he came to be with the various Elders.

K Did Yeshua stay for a periods of time or did he come and go?

C He would go back and forth. He would stay for short periods of time, no longer than a couple of weeks. He would travel.

K Where would he travel?

C I never considered myself of such things.

K Moving to an important day, a day that you consider to be important in that lifetime. What is happening now?

C There is a lot of commotion again.

K What is causing the commotion?

C I believe Pontius Pilate just committed Yeshua to crucifixion.

K Does Yeshua see you in the crowd?

C I'm in the crowd. He does not see me. I am just an observer.

K Do you have compassion for him?

C Absolutely! But I know he's simply doing what he is meant to do.

K Did he ever tell you this?

C No. I just know!

K Did you ever see him when he was older?

C No. He didn't need me anymore. He already had everything he needed to know.

K Did you hear of things that he did?

C Yes, I did many great things.

K Can you explain?

C Many great healings ... teaching the way being the center. What you would call in esoteric realms, as the way between.

K Can you explain the way between?

C All about being present, being loving ... and much love.

K Did he speak of God, Source, or Creator?

C He did discuss things at times.

K What did he say?

C I heard most through the grapevine, as you would call it that we are all sourced from One God, Creator. Many people do not understand this concept.

K Did you discuss this when you were teaching him?

C I have transmitted much information to him in this fashion, of Oneness. Oneness meaning we are also one with God.

K That must have been difficult for people to understand at that time.

C As we know, it is difficult to conceptualize the world we live in due to its density.

K So what did people call him? Did they have other names for him?

C Yeshua.

> *Once again, when asked the question did he have another name, Jacob said it was Yeshua.*

K Did some call him the Savior or Master or other names?

C Some people called him that but I thought they were silly. He was just another person.

K So he was just a man?

C Indeed!

    This is another confirmation that others felt he was just a man.

K So was there anything else that you heard about Yeshua?

C He traveled much of the world apparently. He traveled as far away as India to learn from their Masters.

    India seems to come up quite often when clients speak of his travels to other lands.

K When you were in his presence, did you feel anything different?

C Just love! Yeshua loved all things!

K Was that new to you?

C No. It was very familiar. One thing I wished everyone understood.

K Me too!

K Did you hear about healers that were with him?

C Yes. He had a group of disciples.

K Did you hear anything about them?

C Yes. They all wanted to live up to his expectations. Well maybe expectations is not the right word ... his view of life basically.

K Now moving to another important day, a day that you consider to be important in that lifetime. What is happening?

C I'm looking at the sky and there is a meteor shower. They always are beautiful. I'm looking back at my life, and being happy with what I accomplished.

K What do you feel you accomplished?

C I feel like I accomplished what I came here to do ... to heal.

K Was there a time when healing was close to the person, and not remotely to a person?

C I did it remotely. I spent most of my time healing the collective.

K How did you do heal the collective?

C Through thought. (*Again confirming earlier statements*).

K When you were in the crowd when Pontius Pilate was condemning Yeshua, what was happening in the crowd?

C It was mixed. Some were delighted to hear of his crucifixion, and others were extremely saddened.

K Could you see Yeshua?

C He seemed perfectly happy.

> *In my session I spoke of feeling Yeshua was at peace when he was in front of the crowd.*

K What did they say was the purpose of dying on the cross?

C That is what you call resurrection. And that suffering is not needed even in the worst of time. Suffering is created in the mind.

> *This was also addressed in Ellie's channeled session, where Yeshua said suffering is an illusion we created.*

K Where you there when he carried the cross or died on the cross?

C No, it wasn't my place.

K Why wasn't it your place?

C I feel somehow I would have interfered. I bring too much light to this world.

K Wouldn't they need that light during this dark time?

C It was not as dark as you think.

K Can you explain?

C That one single event brought much light to this world.

K Did you feel he died on the cross?

C No. He did not die ... he resurrected.

K Did he live another life?

C Yes.

K Did he carry on?

C He did.

K Some say he lived on, and lived another life in another country.

C France is a popular one. I do not know much about this though.

K Did you feel he was a special soul?

C Absolutely! He is what you would call an Ascended Master.

K Did you understand what an Ascended Master was in that lifetime?

C Oh yes!

K Who else would you call an Ascended Master in that lifetime?

C Mother Mary, mother of Yeshua. I am old now about 90 years old.

K Isn't that a very old age for that time?

C Some say this. Carrying this much light makes you young.

K Are the others in your community getting older as well? And are there new ones coming in?

C Our group is dying out.

K Why is your group dying out?

C We are no longer needed. We buried much of our information.

K Where did you bury the information?

C In a cave. Hoping someone someday when needed, the information will be brought forward again.

> *Another client mentioning about burying information in the cave which could be the Dead Sea scrolls found in the caves in Egypt.*

K Was the information about Yeshua?

C Some, but most about life being One … Oneness.

K So when speaking of Oneness are you saying everyone is a part of the whole?

C Exactly. We all have Divine Source.

K That must have been difficult for many to understand.

C Unfortunately.

K So how did you understand that concept?

C I just knew.

K You called yourself an Essene. Were there any others in your community?

C No just us.

> *This is quite an interesting statement as historian speak of the Essenes as a larger community of people. There were also clients who said there were many different Essene groups in different locations, which could explain many of their recollections. So perhaps there were others that called themselves Essenes in other places that he was not aware of at that time.*

K Were there people who knew about you outside of your community?

C Some knew about us. They viewed us as religious kooks.

K Were those of the Jewish faith those who viewed you as "kooks?"

C Probably more the Romans. We had monotheistic tendencies. We did adhere fairly strictly to Jewish law. I never really considered myself Jewish ... some used the term Gnostic.

K What does Gnostic mean to you?

C Gnostic means Oneness.

> *This is a different interpretation of the word Gnostic. The Greek interpretation means "having knowledge." The concept of Oneness is considered to be related to the ancient knowledge. There were many ancient scrolls that were found in the caves in Qumran. The Gnostic Gospels were found in the caves in Egypt. Perhaps the scrolls found in Egypt could have been taken to Egypt for safekeeping from Qumran.*

K So were your parents Gnostic?

C I always was Gnostic. I do not remember much of my parents. I believe they died when I was very young and I was adopted by the community.

K Did they recognize your abilities?

C They always held me in close regard.

K Is it because not everyone could do what you do?

C I feel everyone can do what I did. They just need to believe it.

K How old were you when you went into the community?

C I was very young, about three or four years old.

K So did you start learning from your teachers at that age?

C One would suppose, but my memory was not good.

K Were there other children?

C A few.

K Were they healers as well?

C Not all were healers. Some were mystics, scientists. Not the way you would think but scientists of the natural world, [and the] study of the stars.

K Did you have libraries?

C Oh Yes! There was anything you possibly could imagine.

K Where did you get this information?

C Much of it was passed down from generation to generation.

K What did you learn from this information?

C Much knowledge that is very ancient. Yes, you had Atlantians ... you had Lemurians. There was somewhat an erasing of Atlantis.

K Can you explain what you mean about the erasing of Atlantis?

C Like you would take an eraser.

K Who erased them?

C Pleiadians.

K Why did they erase Atlantis?

C There is too much corruption and misuse of power. They could not be let to be, or else they would have destroyed the whole planet.

K Were some Atlantians saved?

C Oh yes. They try not to interfere. There is free will.

K What other information was there in the library?

C What would you like to know about?

K When did life begin as we know it on Earth?

C We are seeded from the stars. Much was an experiment.

In Ellie's session she said that life on Earth was an experiment. Yeshua also spoke of Earth being seeded by other planets in that session.

K How is the experiment going?

C So, so ... not quite being what was planned.

K What was planned for Earth?

C In plain terms, to bring about love.

K Are there other planets of love?

C This planet is one in a billion you would say. There is much interest in this planet. I'm having a hard time putting into words. Many species have a vested interest in it.

I have also heard from another client that the Earth was created to be a planet of love and that other planets are interested in what is happening on Earth. In Yeshua's channeled session with Ellie, he said, "Earth is the hope for the galaxy." Another client, who is not included in the book, said Earth was meant to be the planet of love and felt that there were many species interested in Earth.

K Is this in the scrolls in your library?

C There is this information in the scrolls.

K Is there information on God, Source in the scrolls?

C I think that is a loaded question. That is something you are not to understand.

I always think it interesting that I am told that we are not to know everything at this time.

K So there are some things we are not supposed to understand? Is that correct?

C Correct. It's part of being human. (*Interesting statement.*)

K Is there anything else that we need to know about the scrolls?

C They do need to be brought forth one day.

K Some of scrolls have been found. Are there more to be found?

C We buried about fourteen dozen.

> *Today many of the Dead Sea scrolls are difficult to transcribe and many are only tiny fragments. He did mention some were buried, so there may be many more yet to be discovered that are under the ground.*

K Moving to an important day, a day that you consider important in that lifetime. What is happening?

C I'm swimming with my friends and having a good day. It's a good day to be alive.

K Moving to the circumstances of your death. How did you die in that lifetime?

C Died of old age. My time was over. I died about 95 years old.

K As the soul is releasing from the body, what is happening?

C I'm entering a beautiful rainbow.

K Is there anyone to greet you?

C My parents. I'm very happy indeed.

After the death experience, Jacob is guided to a place to review that lifetime with greater wisdom and knowledge from a higher spiritual level of awareness. Each soul has a life review after each lifetime. This is a place of self-reflection.

Review of that Lifetime from a Higher Level Awareness

K Now let's move to that peaceful place to review that lifetime where you have more wisdom and knowledge available to you than while you were in that lifetime.

K What gave you the greatest happiness in that lifetime?

C Teaching Yeshua. It was the primary reason I was there.

K So you knew about this ahead of time?

C I knew in retrospect.

K Was there a difficult time in that lifetime?

C Being in that city sensing the suffering.

K Was there lessons learned?

C To create light.

K What did you learn or accomplish that can help you in your current life?

C To have no fear and to be present.

K As we can release anything from the past, we can also bring forward gifts, talents or knowledge from the past. Would like to bring forward the knowledge of healing from the past?

C Yes.

> *At this point in the session, Jacob was breathing heavily and had various body movements while healing information was downloaded and brought forth. This is not uncommon when clients are downloading information.*

K Let me know when it is complete.

C It's complete.

Jacob's Impressions after His Session

Jacob explained that he saw a hexagon while coming out of hypnosis. He was also surprised that the entire session was a little more than three hours which felt more like thirty minutes. This is very common when in hypnosis; as there is no time. He felt that it was a pretty amazing journey. There were some things he already knew but there was other information that he had no knowledge of and some of the details were knew to him. Overall he felt the session was very helpful.

After some time, Jacob spoke about how the session had helped him in his healing work with clients. Also for him physically he stated, "I've been able to release stuff that I haven't been able to before, which is great. My hands are feeling quite a bit better than usual and overall less tightness as well."

Jacob's Impressions after a Few Months

Jacob emailed me his impressions after a few months of having his session. He stated, "I'm still baffled that the session lasted as long as it did, because it only seemed like fifteen to twenty minutes. My healing abilities are definitely changing, improving, intensifying. Our session definitely proved quite helpful."

Chapter Seventeen

"There is no fear in love, but perfect love casts out fear."
JOHN 4:18

"Lead with love, and always put love in front of you.
When you look at people, look with love. When you
speak with people ... speak with love."
ANGELA

ANGELA

Angela came for a session for greater understanding concerning various personal isssues and connection with her guides. I met Angela at my past life journeys class at a local college. In the group regression at the college she experienced a lifetime with Jesus. Angela was working as a realtor at that time.

Angela stated that she felt a deep connection with Jesus, but wasn't sure if it was real or imagined. She came into my office with a mask over her mouth. She explained she had severe allergies. This was one of questions she wanted addressed; why these severe allergic reactions. I explained that she needed to remove the face mask for the session, as I needed to hear her speak throughout the session. *(This was many years before the coronavirus.)* She was able to release her allergic reactions by releasing a past life issue of fear. After the past life session she was able to move into her subconscious in order to receive answers to her prepared questions.

Angela in the Subconscious

K Do I have permission to speak with Angela's subconscious?

SC Yes. Jesus is here. It's just Jesus and I and he is showing me all the glory. He brought me up in the air around Earth to the heavens to God. He presented the Earth to me. I am surrounded by the glowing Light of God.

K Angela wanted to know if she had a lifetime with Jesus? Did she have a past life with Jesus?

SC Yes ... they were very close.

K She briefly mentioned that she had a lifetime with Jesus before in her past life session. Can she receive more information?

In her first session, Angela briefly went into a past life with Jesus, but then went into another life to release certain issues that needed to be addressed. Clients will be directed to the lifetime that they need for greater healing and understandings.

SC She was young and felt these energies. She was believed and guided through those energies. And then fear came and she released her connection with Jesus and built her life around this fear. And now that she [has gotten] around this fear ... clear channels will be open and the connections will happen.

K What caused that fear in that lifetime to lose the connection with Jesus?

SC She was confused about the energies. She chose the fear.

K Why did she choose the fear?

SC The fear was strong.

K What was she fearful of in that lifetime? What created that fear?

SC Just a bit of doubt ... doubtful of herself.

K So did she doubt Jesus?

SC She pushed him away. And allowed fear in everything ... every single thing. And you can only do that for so much and then your body gets sick.

K Did Jesus try to help her with her fear?

SC She slept on one side of her bed ... so Jesus could share her bed. He would come to her and try to tell her, but she had so much clutter. She held onto the clutter ... everybody else's clutter.

K So she took on others' issues?

SC Yes ... like today.

K Then she needs to let it go. Can the subconscious clear the clutter?

SC Yes ... removing the clutter. I will be breathe easier. Love yourself. Do only what shows love for you. By giving permission, I am able to clear all! (*Long pause*) It's done!

K   It is my belief that Jesus was understanding. Is that correct?

SC Yes ... patient.

K   Did he give her any advice?

SC It was her path.

K   So he let her go on her path?

SC Yes.

> *This is an important spiritual statement by Jesus that we should not interfere with another's path. Sometimes we may feel we are helping another or judging another, but it is their lessons, their experience that needs to be addressed. This is similar to Andy Tomlinson's observation that if we interfere in another's path, it will do harm to another's journey which is similar to a weapon wounding that person.*

K   Did he give her any advice or anything she needs to hold on to?

SC She is precious!

K   In the beginning of the session, you said they had the same mother, is that correct?

SC Yes.

K   So was she a sister or half-sister?

SC Godmother ... she was chosen to participate in the baptism of Jesus.

K   So she was much older?

SC Yes ... she was from Joseph's side.

K   So Mary was not her mother?

SC Jesus said Mary is her mother ... that was her stepmother.

> *This is new information, not provided in the* Bible *that Joseph was married before and had a daughter.*

K Did she know Jesus was special?

SC Yes.

K From the beginning?

SC It was just a known feeling.

K So everyone knew it?

SC A lot of people doubted it ... a lot of people and those people would pull more and more people to doubt. That was the fear and the confusion that people were against Jesus.

K Did she bring that feeling that people were against her?

SC Yes. (*Crying*)

K So now it is time to release that feeling.

SC It's been carried on. It's a lot of fear. Fear is the opposite of love ... so now she needs to bring the love.

> *Angela was able to understand that there was still some fear left that needed to be addressed and released. At this point in the session, all the fear was released with the help of her subconscious. The fear first manifested in her body with her severe asthma. Sometimes, issues need more attention in order to heal. This usually comes forth when there needs to be greater healing. It is important to make sure any difficulties, both physically and emotionally, are addressed more than once in order for a complete and total healing.*

K What was the most powerful thing Jesus said to her? What were the words that meant so much to her?

SC You have brought more healing to others.

K So she was a healer then?

SC Right now she is being healed. (*The subconscious was healing.*) Jesus said we all have the same amount of God in each of us and to lead our lives with that!

This statement was very similar to Ellie's channeled session with Yeshua.

K   Now she can see that the others have the same amount of God in them? The light is always there, is that correct?

SC We all have the choice to see it and be with it. Some people struggle and choose it and push it away. It's not entirely their fault ... there's too many influences. It's still there is choice!

K   Did she travel with Jesus?

SC Yes.

K   Was she a healer in that life?

SC Yes.

K   Did Jesus teach her to heal? If so, how did he teach her healing?

SC It is through God.

K   Does it matter how each person heals? Did he show her any techniques or didn't it matter, the form of healing?

SC It's complicated in that there needs to be faith and beliefs, and there are openings and channels. Individuals ... all are able to heal.

K   It is my understanding, that if it is needed for their growth or another's growth, healing will not occur? Is that correct?

SC That is correct.

K   What else is needed for her to understand about her life with Jesus?

SC It was a time of pure ... a time of the birth of faith, the true meaning of faith.

K   Did Jesus ever tell her why he came on the Earth plane?

SC It's just the path. It's not complicated. It's just the path.

K   What was his mission? Did he mention why he chose this path?

SC It's his path. Unable to communicate. ... I am unable to communicate.

At various times in a session, the information is not available to us and the subconscious will not answer.

K   Why are you unable to communicate?

SC It's not understandable.

K   OK, Thank you. I understand, but could you put into more simple terms for us humans?

> *Sometimes when I persist in asking questions of the subconscious they will answer and sometimes they are very forceful refusing to answer the question, so I respect its wishes at that point.*

SC Jesus was a gift. Allowed God to work through Jesus, and Jesus multiplied God's powers to others, and that multiplied. To this day, it multiplies.

K   Were there many followers of Jesus? It was my understanding that many people came and went. Is that correct?

SC Yes.

K   Did he send out other people to heal as well?

SC What happens is, once you come in contact with Jesus, and you believe, you're connected to the other person that believes.

K   What else do we need to know about Jesus that would be helpful for others to know in the book?

SC That it continues and grows and it strengthens. The connections grow. You will have many more to come. It will all be given to you. It will be constant. You will gather the information. There's many perspectives.

> *It was interesting that she spoke of people having different perspectives of Jesus, which was something I have expressed in this book. This makes perfect sense as we can have different perspectives about the same event, even in our own lifetime. But what remains constant is their feelings of total love in Jesus' presence.*

K   Just like in this life.

SC Yes. Some who were close and some who observed.

K   It sounds like she was very close. What were her impressions?

SC Sisterly ... is very protective and fearful of his fate but now it is released.

K   So now she understands that was his path as others have chosen their path.

SC Yes.

K   Is everything complete from that lifetime?

SC Yes.

Angela's Impression after Her Session

Angela said she didn't remember everything. Her first impressions was, "I was able to forgive myself." "It was a way to survive." She also felt her asthma was also cleared. What surprised her the most was how much fear she held that began at the time of Jesus, because of worry about his fate. Once she released all fear, her asthma was released at that time.

Impressions a Few Days Later

A few day after our session, Angela called me crying stating that she had "ruined" the healing of her asthma. She said she went to her allergist and he said she still had the allergies. Upon hearing this, she then doubted her own healing. I calmly encouraged her to listen to her CD of healing with her subconscious as many times as healing was needed. I also said if she needed more healing she was to come back, we would work on the healing once again. A day later, she called with great excitement with the news that her asthma was gone completely. To this day, many years later, her asthma has not returned. This demonstrates how powerful our faith can be to heal. It also demonstrated that we need not listen to others opinions about the healing that occurs, as our thoughts and belief can influence whether we heal or not.

Angela's Second Session

"This is my commandment, that you love one another as I have loved you. This I command you, to love one another."
JOHN 16:12; 17

Angela decided to return for another session. This time she came for a Life between Life session as she wanted more information about her life with Jesus. She first went into a past life with Jesus in the session. Her asthma was not present, and had not been an issue for a period of time. She described herself as a female and was barefoot with white clothing.

The Past Life Session

C There is much to be done for our savior.

K What do you have to do?

C We're getting ready for all the people

K Can you explain in more detail?

C People are coming to hear our Savior

K Why do you call him your Savior?

C He is saving people.

K What is he saving people from?

C Their sins.

K And how does he do that?

C God's word to everyone. He prays first that all that gather will be open to God's words. Come with me and I will show you.

K Who is speaking about coming with me?

C I am saying come with me.

K Why do you want me to come with you?

C I want to show you where Jesus is. To prepare ... it's a lot of work. We must organize. A lot of people come and bring their children. Jesus loves the children the most.

K Does he have certain group of people that organize?

C Everybody organizes, [but] not Jesus. Jesus spends his time in prayer and preparing mentally.

K And who is there to help prepare?

C People in the village. Faithful people, who have already heard the message ... accept and believe the message. We all work together and we gather what we need ... we build fires. We make bread with the wheat. We get fish ... whatever we need so we can feed the people. We never know how many people will come. You never know when Jesus is ready.

K Can you explain that statement?

C He is given permission from God, and when he is allowed, he presents himself to us.

K So you are saying he is not always allowed to speak?

C It's so beautiful .... his choice of words and he's so wise. It's on God's time ... it's not on Jesus's time. ... It's not on our time ... God decides, Jesus follows through.

K So God speaks through Jesus?

C Yes, to all of us. Jesus speaks his message through his message from God. We work so hard to prepare, so that we can sit with him and so we can also reap the benefit of Jesus. You don't want to miss a single word or a minute. We just want to be there, so you work really fast and hard. You get the twigs to prepare the fire ....you get the pots ... you get the water ... you get the wheat ... you make the bread and you get the fish. It is such a wonderful, happy feeling. It is a gift.

K How did you first meet Jesus?

C It's all I know. We were born in the same family.

K How were you related?

C My father is his father. Joseph is my father. ... I remember his birth when Mary brought him to us, and Mary presented him to us. We all know how special and different he was from the moment we saw him.

   This is a confirmation with her previous the session.

K How did you know he was special?

C He had a uniqueness like no other. It's a feeling you receive when you meet Jesus. It's a feeling of peace. It's a feeling of forgiveness. It's a feeling of love and acceptance, and unconditional love. You think you know it from your mother and your father, but it is more than that. It is a feeling of Home! It's a feeling of trust. It's all the goodness that you know. You just want to share that with everybody. You want them to experience it as well. I was around six when he was born. We were all changed. We chose to fulfill God's will and serve and take care of the people, and take care of Jesus. We were not concerned about ourselves any longer.

K Where was Jesus born?

C He was born somewhere and brought back with Mary and Joseph.

K Why did they leave?

C We were all separated. There was taxing and military ... causing us to separate.

K So was Jesus in danger?

C Mary was in danger, as she was about to give birth and did not feel safe. She did the right thing.

K So did God tell her to leave?

C Yes. Mary is brave and good. I was so young when Jesus was presented to us.
   She indicated she was around six years old when he was born.

K Did you know he was special?

C Yes, we all did! We all changed! We all became serving. We all chose God's will and to serve, to take care of people … and take care of Jesus. We were not concerned with ourselves any longer.

K So what changed?

C We had a knowing.

K If you would hear your name called, what was your name?

C Rebekah with a "k." I am so proud of Jesus.

K You said Jesus can release your sins, how was this done?

C I don't know. He is a Savior and he knows. It's a reward … your faith your belief.

K Going back to the time when you were planning for the large group of people coming to hear him. How many people came?

C Two hundred … they're everywhere … sitting on rocks and trees. I am just mesmerized by the beauty of it all! I turn around and there is not enough food for everyone. I see their faces.

K So when he speaks, what is happening?

C It's so quiet. Sometimes people agree and they shout out.

K What words does he say that means so much to you and the crowd?

C So much about love. We need to love one another, and to focus on your similarities … always.

K Does he speak of God?

C He has such respect for God that he does not mention him in that way.

K What is happening now?

C His words are to the point. He quiets everyone at first.

K How does he greet them?

C As brethren. He says he is grateful that so many have come. He says that today we all have made the right choice for coming, and that those who have chosen not to come ... will live in regret.

K What most resonates to you that Jesus says?

C He wants us to not be persuaded, that we are always on the right path, and that things pull us away and lead us down the wrong path. [They are] external things ... outside things.

K And they pull us away from what?

C Stay true to your path ... goodness and love. If you have the want to, share your words, or what you do something out of love. Do not have anyone or anything to prevent it ... that is God whispering to you. And all these words that Jesus is so wise to announce ... it's constant!

K Is Jesus alone a lot of the time?

C People don't know that he's alone a lot in his thoughts and meditations, and his connection with God.

Other clients have also expressed that he was alone many times in meditation.

K Moving to an important day, a day that you feel that is important in that lifetime. What is happening? What are you experiencing?

C Jesus is walking in towns and villages with his disciples with him. So people are coming to the side of the road and the disciples gather there. People are injured and they're strewn about.

K So did they come to see Jesus?

C They were hoping that this will be their answer. It's almost like ... some are ignored.

K Can you explain this?

C It's almost like, they are not ready. I want to say not worthy, but I know, in Jesus all are worthy. Some are not ready ... you must prepare. You cannot ask for something or demand something and not be confident in your request. You must prepare. You must SHOW your belief in your faith! Can you imagine meeting Jesus and not having the faith and then asking him to heal you? It is not right! (*She seemed to be very upset with this statement.*)

K Does Jesus perform the healings or do others assist him with the healing?

C It's funny, because he knows everybody, he knows everything. He knows the ailment and the cause of your ailment, so when you go to him, you have changed your belief and faith ... so that your love of God is expanding and growing. He knows that ... and then you are healed!

   This is a common theme among clients about Jesus knowing everything when healing.

K So they are doing the healing?

C Exactly!

K Does he say anything while healing others?

C He always is preaching. He's always reading peoples. He spots and is answering them, but in the perfect way, like the wisest perfect choice of words that allows that person to hear and absorb. It's almost like being fed to the Light of God within you and that allows that light to expand in you and grows. Can you imagine a flame and God speaking to you and that flame gets bigger and bigger!

K Does he have a group of people he teaches to heal?

C Yes.

K But does he have people that he shares his method or knowledge of healing?

C The process can be shared. Each individual person is made up of a different part of God. Just because two people have the same ailment, their healing process is different. We all carry the same Flame of God, yet every flame is different.

K Are some brighter than others?

C Oh Yes! Yes! It's true that the flame is real!

K I have had others speak of Jesus having a group of healers, is that correct?

C Jesus shared everything. He knows he is limited with time and amount of information he wants to share is limitless. He constantly shared information. And I cannot say that there is a group, but if anyone who is ready in their life to accept in that ability to do that ... [they] will gain that. I cannot say that he will say there will be healers. And yes there were many that could heal.

She acknowledged that there were others that were healers and that Jesus spoke many could heal. Many other clients including myself, spoke of this groups of healers.

K So everyone in the group understood him?

C Yes. There were doubters and sometimes it gets the best of them, and you know that their light shrinks when that happens. And it's like a circulation ... constantly moving. It's like it moves in one direction ... clockwise and then if you have a doubt or negativity or disbelief you send it back, and turns counter clockwise. And just as the flame is given in each of us, and it is there ... and should be nourished and protected and fed ... when you are distracted, it shrinks ... it shrinks.

What she is describing sounds similar to the chakras and energy flow.

K Is this what Jesus taught you?

C This is what I know! And I believe all that I know is from Jesus!

K Moving to another significant event in that lifetime. What is happening? What are sensing, experiencing?

C (*Long pause*) I do not wish to go there.

When clients express that they do not want to go somewhere in their lifetime, I try to ease it in latter in their session, and any times it becomes an important part of their healing process.

K What was the most significant thing that he taught you?

C (*A pause and then crying.*) It's so beautiful. Lead with love, and always put love in front of you. When you look at people, look with love. When you speak with people ... speak with love. Whenever you feel separation or isolation and you meet or see something your first reaction is to tear apart. You must end that. You must first look at love and find the similarities. This is your focus. So much greatness will be achieved with each step we walk towards love. We give love, we receive love. Focus on similarities. If you don't, you will have regret. Spend time finding similarities. Find what is common in each other. That is how you bond!

She was speaking of Oneness in this statement through love.

K And those who doubt, what do they say?

C Not a lot of time is spent on those people. Jesus focuses on those who know and they need to be there, and know they need to listen. And they are so close to understanding the Light of God that's in them. All his energy is focused on those people because time is short.

K You spoke of time is so short. Does Jesus speak to you about this?

C We don't understand at the time that he will be leaving for good and he never leaves us and we know that. However, it is such a beautiful time to be near him and to hear him, and to anticipate his next meeting ... his next gathering. And for those of us, for him to be taken away so violently is just shocking. Such a terrible, terrible gift that is taken away from us all. And we know that it is God's will [but it's] very hard. It makes us even stronger believers.

K You spoke of the disciples, were there others with him as well?

C There are people who wanted to be so near to him and they travel with him, and it gives the family comfort to know that there is comfort companions.

K So you don't travel with him all the time?

C No. There is my mother and father and I have to take care of them. It's not our journey, its Jesus' journey!

K But do you hear him speak at any time?

C Yes … mother and father go, and we are in the front. We are still with everyone.

K Does Jesus allow questions to be asked?

C Yes. You just have to shout it out.

K What are some of the questions people ask?

C Why should we listen to you? And Jesus says, "Well, why did you come?" He says, "I want to know." (*Jesus says*) "And that's right because you need to know." They answer their own questions mostly.

> *This is similar in my session when a man answered his own question when asked a question of Jesus.*

K Does Jesus speak of what we call Heaven?

C He speaks constantly of eternal life.

K What does he say about eternal life?

C Eternal life is what you perceive it to be.

K Was that confusing to others?

C Maybe … also precious information. Our lives were hard and rustic and rough, and to know that there is a place at the end where you have eternal peace and eternal life, was so rewarding. Just knowing that and focusing on that will get you through your current life, and rewards you with eternal life. He knows to obtain eternal life is to follow on this path. Acknowledge God's Light in you and feel it and feed it!

K Is there a sense that there is a light around him? Can you see a light around him?

C Not to see but to feel. So we each have this light within us. So if you could imagine this light multiplying, that is what Jesus is carrying within him. But not only that, he was implanted with so much wisdom and knowledge.

K Who implanted this wisdom?

C God chose him. He had such knowing!

K Why was he chosen by God?

C You know we think he was good and we were not, but that's not it. This plan … this is the creation from God. God's creation planned Mary to be his mother. Mary was tested … she passed the test.

K What was the test?

C I do not know the exact details but she was presented with obstacles, and she passed. This is a child who knew and understood that God was in her, respected it, protected it, and cherished it. That was her determination, her focus, and that's what God knew and that's what God saw. She was chosen and there are times in our lives when have known that it is there and we were distracted. Distraction is everywhere.

> *It has been said by many that Mary was chosen by God, and this is a beautiful message of why she was chosen. Also there was another interesting statement concerning Mary passing the test. I have had other clients speak of passing or failing the test with regard to fulfilling their purpose on Earth.*

K Were there others that were in the plan, other than Mary, who were considered to be Jesus' mother?

C It was more that the plan was formulated and that (*Long pause*) this person is needed in this plan or scenario, and so Mary stood out.

K Did Jesus come from a large family? Did he have brothers and sisters?

C We are all brothers and sisters. We are all family, and that's how he treated all of us. I am his sister but through my father. But if you would ask Jesus, he would say I'm his sister.

K Was there someone special in his life? Someone that he felt connected with. I am speaking of Mary, not his mother?

C I never saw intimacy. She was in awe of him and he acknowledging. I don't know ... that all I've seen. It never occurred to me then ... [that it was] more like student and teacher.

> *She only spoke of what she knew at the time. Even if clients are unaware of something in a lifetime, they will be honest that they unaware of a situation.*

K When Jesus went to different locations, did people in the village take care of him?

C Yes, exactly!

K What was the most important day in the life with Jesus?

C The time of his death. It was so tragic. Turmoil surrounding the village ... the crying, the confusion ... no understanding as to the reason.

K Was Jesus crucified?

C Yes.

K Did he die on the cross?

C Yes.

K Did he come forth later after his death? Did you see him or did you hear from others?

C He presented himself to a chosen few. His mother is the one I know of.

K Did you hear what he said to his mother?

C She came to me and asked me to prepare because he has arrived, and I was in disbelief. And then I was asleep. I didn't believe it. She aroused me and said "Wake up! It's time." "We need to prepare." So when I had my senses, I was able to hear and understand what she was saying. And you cannot imagine the glorious feeling that overcame me! We prepared! It's as if he was speaking again! (*Spoken with great emotion.*)

K So he spoke to people after his death?

C Yes.

K What did Jesus tell them?

C He announced that this was God's will. This was all according to God's plan, not that we should understand it, but according to the plan. That gave us a lot of relief, as you could imagine.

K Did he speak of ascension?

C Yes. You know people talk about him coming again and this will be. He is coming to each soul individually. So be prepared!

K How did he say this would come about?

C It's a process.

K Could you expand upon that?

C It's not something I'm permitted to say, and any thoughts I have right now will be erased.

> *Rebekah would not divulge anything about the process. In many cases, if we are not to know certain information, it will not be given. She also stated that her memory of it will be erased, which indicated, that this was something again we need not understand.*

K What is the most important thing you took away from that lifetime?

C I could tell you being with Jesus is having your body stand upright completely. You have no weight on you. You have no regrets. You have no doubts. You have no hatred. You have no guilt ... no fear. It is the most complete essence of who you are!

K After his death, did more people come to believe him?

C I thought about that and I determined that … it is all according to God's will.

K How does free will play into this?

C But that is God's will. This free will you speak of, is the biggest part of free will in his plan. I believe it was so important to introduce Jesus to the world because it was this root, his seed for this free will. The free will is in combination of the Light of God in each of us. If you lead with love, your free will … will be perfect. Your free will … your choices that you make will be simple. It will be laid out.

This is a wonderful explanation of what we call "free will."

K So when you are on purpose or plan, then everything will fall into place?

C Exactly. If you are on the right course it is simple. If you are not following God, you're challenged and it is stressful.

K As you are so eloquent, did you speak to others about Jesus?

C If I was to repeat what Jesus said, it would not be the same. I have copied him, but I have always said these are Jesus' words.

K What did Jesus say about Rebekah?

C He never said. The love is in his eyes and I for him. As you can see by all the people, you can tell by their eyes. You can feel the love. When you see Jesus and look into his eyes … the love is like none other to compare to. You compare everyone else's love by Jesus eyes!

K Yes I understand. (*I also had this same feeling while in my session, when looking in his eyes.*) What happened after his death?

C We tried to remember. Some words are written down in a book. We are trying to never forget and pass it on.

K And were you successful?

C Now look ... all years gone by, Jesus words remain and that's good.

K If you were to give a speech about Jesus, what would you say his most important message was?

C I believe I said to you, it is to seek out the commonality in each other and to give freely your love. Share it. When you do that ... you feed the light of the other person ... you feed God's Light. And so when you give love you are spreading that light, and that light grows inside of that person, as well as your light grows. And how simple is that!

K Thank you! Moving to the circumstances of your death in that lifetime.

C A flood. We were all trying. We remember Jesus and we succumbed. It was immediate.

K What is happening after the soul is released from the body?

C The gates open for me!

Angela explained that she drowned in a large flood. She indicated there is no need to release any fears of water.

Angela's Impressions after Her Session

Angela continues her spiritual search on many levels. She is presently a Reiki practitioner. She also has attended many spiritual workshops to gain greater knowledge and understandings. Her severe asthma has not returned after many years and she continues to be following her spiritual journey. To this day she remains committed to expanding her spiritual knowledge.

Chapter Eighteen

"Truth is all within ourselves. We don't need to find it
from outside ourselves. We don't have to go to someone
else ... we have the power ourselves."
CRYSTAL

"Peace comes from within. Do not seek it without."
"Three things you cannot hide for long, the moon;
the sun and the Truth" "
GAUTAMA BUDDHA

CRYSTAL

I met Crystal in one of my classes when I taught Past Life Journeys at the local college. She is a mother and works as a professional in her field. She said she had always felt a closeness to Jesus and wanted find out if there was a reason for that connection. Crystal is very joyful, and loving person, with a positive outlook on life.

The Past Life Session

When Crystal came off of the cloud to the surface, she described herself as wearing a burlap robe with a rope around the middle and wearing sandals on her feet. She described herself as a male in her teens with brown hair and tan colored skin in a dry and dusty area with large stones.

K What is the reason why you are standing there?
C I think I'm waiting for something.
K What or who are you waiting for?
C Some kind of group that is supposed to come.
K Who is this group that is supposed to come?
C I think it is Jesus and his followers.
K Have you heard him speak before or is this the first time?
C I think I know him. (*Her voice was spoken firmly*)
K How do you know him?
C I think I have heard him before.

K When was the first time you heard him speak?

C I think that I'm going to follow with him as they come by.

K You said you were in your teens, how did your parents feel about you following Jesus?

C They were fine with it.

K Now move to the first time you heard Jesus speak. Moving to that time when you first heard him speak.

C A lot busier there. It's close to the market, but people are selling things.

K So does Jesus speak in that area?

C He spoke and then I talked with him afterwards.

K What were you speaking about? What did he say that resonated to you?

C (*Pause*) Not sure … it's the way he made me feel.

K How did he make you feel?

C You could feel the love. He was very gentle.

K When you looked into his eyes what did you feel?

C I felt the Love and peace. And he has these piercing blue eyes that seem to look into your soul.

> *This feeling of total love and his piercing eyes looking into one's soul seems to be the experience of the clients when in his presence. You could hear a sense of awe in their voice when they were explaining how they felt.*

K Was it a large or small group that came to hear him speak?

C It was small.

K How did the people receive him?

C I think they felt like I did.

K You indicatcd that you spokc to him, what did he say to you? What were the words spoken to you?

C He said to show them the Way.

K Can you explain what he meant by the Way?

C The Way of God!

K Did he speak of God?

C He said God is within all of us.

K What did you call him?

C Yeshua!

K Were there other names he was called by?

C Not sure.

> *Again this indicates that clients will not give information they are not aware of at the time.*

K Moving to an important day, a day that you consider important in the lifetime. Moving to that important day, what is happening?

C There is a lot of people. I think Jesus is coming. (*Long pause*) It's like a celebration. A lot of noise, cheers … waving things.

K Why is there a celebration? What are they celebrating?

C Jesus is riding a donkey. We're waving palms. I think people believe he is the Messiah now.

> *Crystal indicated after the session that she always loved the time of the Easter when Jesus rode the donkey with the palms. I believe we are drawn to events, times and places that we have had experiences in our past lives. This is the reason why we resonate to certain times and experiences in our current life.*

K What does he say about that?

C He looks content.

K Does he tell you who he is?

C I KNOW WHO HE IS! (*Crystal responds to this very loudly with conviction.*)

He is the one who I was following!

K Why did you follow him?

C Because he was different. He spoke the truth. He was loving.

K Did you stay with him always or did you come and go?

C I stayed with him for a while, maybe five or more years.

K At that time did he travel to other places? Did you go with him?

C Someplace that was by the sea. It had cliffs and there were houses built on the side of the cliffs. That was above the town.

> *In the area of Mount Arbel in Israel beside the Sea of Galilee, there are caves that were the cliffs used as hideouts for Jews who fought the Greeks and Romans. These cliffs may be the same cliffs that she was speaking of, as there seems to be a history of these caves used as hideouts. It is interesting that his area is called "The Jesus Trail".*

K Did it look different from the town above?

C Yes. I think it was sort of a hiding place.

> *Crystal had no previous knowledge of a hiding place or of that location in her current life.*

K Why was Jesus hiding?

C There were some people who didn't want to hear what he had to say.

K So he went into hiding?

C We would meet there to plan what we would do.

K What were you planning?

C The way to tell more people his message.

K What was his message?

C That God was in everyone, and love is the answer.

K What were the words that resonated to you the most?

C Show them the Way. We need to tell others, to let them know God is in each of us.

K Did he speak of being the Son of God?

C He said he was a man. He had just learned more.

> *Once again, a client speaks of Jesus explaining that he was a man.*

K How did he learn?

C He had teachers.

K Who were these teachers? Did he go to other places to learn?

C He learned through Buddhism. I think Tibet.

> *Many of Jesus' teachings are similar to the teachings of Buddha. Other clients spoke of Jesus' travels to Tibet as well. In 1887 Nicholas Notivich, was one of the first of several people to document the life of Issa when in the Tibetan area which is known to them as Jesus. The monks had given him an ancient document describing the man called Issa who came from Israel who was a great teacher and healer in Nepal area. It described Issa's teachings, healing abilities and many similarities to his teachings in the Bible. It was also noted that there are documents in the Vatican concerning Issa's travels to that area which have not been available to the public.*

K Did he tell you about his travels?

C That was before we met.

K Did he say he went to any other places?

C Egypt and the Mediterranean.

K What did he say he learned from Buddhism?

C We're all the same. Everyone is the same. We're all from the same source.

> *In 1932 Edgar Cayce stated in his reading that Jesus traveled to India, Persia and Egypt between the age of 13 and 30 years old.*

K Did Jesus speak of the Source or speak of energies?

C He talked about the Source and the light.

K What did he say about the light?

C The light is love, and we all come from the Source. And we need to get back to the Source.

K Did he give you some advice as to how we get back to the Source?

C Love is the answer! We don't love each other like we should. We need to love each other!

K And how do we need to love each other?

C We need to end war and poverty.

K Were there followers that came and went?

C Yes. There were many. We wanted to be like Jesus.

K How did you want to be like Jesus?

C He knew so much ... we wanted to have that knowledge.

K Did he ever speak of having different lifetimes?

C Not sure ... he said it like that. He said that this is not all that is ... that you have many experiences.

K And did you understand that he was speaking of other lifetimes?

C Not sure I understood that then.

K Did he have what we call the disciples around him?

C There were always a group with him, and others like me that came and went.

K Did you witness any healings with Jesus?

C He would put his hands on people.

K What happened when he put his hands on people?

C It seemed to give them a sense of relief. I think they felt the love through him.

K Did you see or hear about any physical healings?

C Not that I ever saw that, but I think I heard about it.

K Did he speak of having a group of healers?

C There were people that helped the lepers. And some were healed.

K Did Jesus speak of healing others?

C I think he spoke of it in different way. It was about positive energy.

K Can you explain further?

C He talked about positive energy, and how the energy can do all kinds of things. You just have to believe it!

K Did he explain energy to you?

C Like positive thoughts and thinking about things.

> *Jesus was speaking about intention with positive thoughts and the power of manifestation.*

K Did he have women with him?

C Yes, a couple of women.

K Did he have any women that he was particularly close to?

C Mary.

K What was Mary called by?

C Mary Magdalene. She had dark hair.

K Did you ever meet her, and what were your impressions of her?

C I liked her. We all liked each other.

K Do you feel they were married?

C They acted like that. She did always seem to be with Jesus and he trusted her.

K Did Jesus tell you how they met?

C I'm not sure I knew that.

> *Clients will always be truthful in hypnosis if they had no knowledge of the situation when asked. They are always very honest with not saying something that they have no knowledge of at the time.*

K Now let's move to an important day, a day that you consider important in that lifetime. Moving to that important day, what is happening?

C The sky is very dark, stormy, but not a storm.

K How are you feeling?

C I'm angry!

K Why are your angry?

C They've taken Jesus calling him a criminal. I really don't understand what he did wrong. I think they are afraid of his power.

K What was the power that they feared?

C People are beginning to listen to Jesus. They're realizing they could get to God themselves and that it's in each of us.

K Is that what Jesus taught?

C Yes! He showed them the Way when he said it is within self ... salvation.

> *Like Jesus, Edgar Cayce and many spiritual teachers speak of the Kingdom is within many times in their readings. Ellie and many other clients spoke of the kingdom is within, as well.*

K What does salvation mean to Jesus?

C Salvation ... is right and wrong, and truth is all within ourselves. We don't need to find it from outside ourselves. We don't have to go to someone else ... we have the power ourselves.

> *I have found the current interpretations of various words such as salvation had a very different meaning during the time of Yeshua. Many times a word might have a different meaning in another language. And since the Bible has been written in different languages, the interpretation of a word could be quite different from the English word. This is the reason for asking clients their meaning of a word and their interpretation of the words during the time of Yeshua.*

K So did the priests like this statement?

C They are CORRUPT! (*Very forcefully stated*)

K Who was involved in taking Jesus away?

C Roman swords and they had a shield.

K What did Jesus say as they took him away?

C He just told them to continue what they were doing.

K What happens to Jesus as they took him away?

C We were there! (*Crying*) He's on the cross.

> *She became extremely emotional and crying while speaking.*

C We kept telling them they were wrong.

> *Crystal continues to become extremely emotional and crying. I also felt this same intense emotion during this time of the crucifixion.*

C Not everyone loved him.

K Why?

C They didn't understand.

K What happens after he died?

C We went to the hiding place.

K Did all of you go?

C No! Just a couple of us.

K Why did you go there?

C We had to figure things out. We need to continue his work.

> *Many of the clients including myself, felt this deep commitment to continue his teachings by sharing their experiences with Jesus. Perhaps that is why I was guided to write this book to continue reminding others of his teachings in the present life.*

K Did you continue his work?

C I'm not sure.

K If you were sure, what happened after his death?

C I feel like I was able to continue for a while … just in small groups.

K What did you say about Jesus?

C I called him the Master.

K Why did you call him the Master?

C He knew so much and he taught us. I told many people what the Master told me.

K What did you tell others what he taught you?

C I told them that we're all the same. We can find God within ourselves ... that we don't need someone else to do that, and that we have the power. I think I helped a lot of people. I tried to use my thoughts, and positive energies.

K Did Jesus tell you how to do that?

C He said to concentrate and imagine it, and to clear your mind.

> *In this statement she speaks of Jesus talking about the power of the mind, manifestation and how we need to clear the mind.*

K Did you hear what happened to Jesus after he died?

C I heard some people saw him after he died.

K How did you feel about hearing this?

C I thought it was possible. I think he wanted to show people do live again.

K Did his followers speak about Jesus work?

C I think some, but some were afraid.

K What name would they call you by?

C John.

K Move to a significant event in that lifetime, a day that you felt was important in that lifetime. What is happening? What are feeling, experiencing?

C I'm at a cave that overlooks water. [There's] water below. I'm by myself.

K So you are by yourself, what happens next?

C Guards are coming for me, the same guards.

K Are they Roman guards?

C Yes, two of them. I have nowhere to go! (*Crying*) They grab me! I say this is wrong. (*Extremely emotional*) They say I was breaking the law.

K How were you breaking the law?

C By continually talking about Jesus. They wanted the power. They are dragging me. I'm trying to get away.

> *I could hear the anguish in her voice as she is extremely emotional.*

C THEY THROW ME OFF THE EDGE!

> *At this time she became extremely emotional, crying hysterically, so I quickly had her remove herself from any discomfort. I explained that it was time for her soul to be released from the body. I feel there is no need for anyone to stay in the experience of their death scene if it ends up in such anguish. It will then be addressed later if the death affects the current life.*

K What does it feel like as your soul has released from the body?

C I feel light!

K And there is no discomfort in the body now?

C No.

K Is there anyone to greet you there?

C Jesus is there.

K Wonderful! Does he say anything to you?

C He says I've done well. (*Crying*) It makes me happy that I pleased him.

K I'm sure. You've done well and you should be proud.

C My mother ... she hugs me.

> *She is speaking of her mother from that lifetime.*

K How are you feeling?

C I feel peaceful.

After the death experience, Crystal is guided to a place to review that lifetime with greater wisdom and knowledge from a higher spiritual level of awareness. Each soul has a life review after each lifetime. This is a place of self-reflection.

Review of that Lifetime from a Higher Level of Awareness

K Now that you have more wisdom and knowledge available to you than while you were in that lifetime, what gave you the greatest happiness in that lifetime?

C Teaching.

   She stated she recognized this type of happiness in her current life.

K What was the most difficult aspect of that lifetime?

C The time when the guards had such control and power over everyone. Everyone felt hopeless and Jesus gave them hope.

K After Jesus died did that hope continue?

C Not with all ... some.

K What did he say was the reason he came?

C It was part of his learning.

   In Ruth's session she also speaks about it being part of Jesus' learning as his reason for coming to that lifetime.

K How does that affect your life when you feel people are taking power over everyone?

C I don't like when things are unjust. I need to stand up more. I think I will now be speaking out more.

K You also spoke of feeling that you should have done more to help Jesus, can you explain?

C I think we felt we should have done more to help Jesus.

K Do you think you could have?

C Jesus acted like it was inevitable. I think he knew it would end eventually. He said not to fight it anymore.

K Is there a need to forgive self or others in that lifetime?

C Yes.

> *At this time in the session, I asked Crystal to imagine a corral and look inside and see who was in there that needed to be forgiven. She expressed that the guards and herself were in the corral. I explained that event was in the past and needs to be released and let go. All of the weights of the past should be lifted off the body. After a session clients say they can feel a lifting of the weights of the past. Forgiveness of self or others is probably the heaviest weight we carry, so it is important to forgive others in this life so we will no longer carry that heavy weight into our next lifetime. Forgiveness is freedom from the past, where we can finally be free. We need to forgive and release the soul of that person or persons as well as ourselves. We no longer need to be attached to that event or person. Forgiveness was complete.*

K What did you learn or accomplish in that life that can help you in the current life?

C To be more understanding of people. To understand we are all the same. Love is more important than power and control.

K What was the lesson?

C I could be a leader. The ones when we showing the way. Where I was considered a leader of many followers.

K Is there a fear of falling off the cliff and did you bring that in the current? What part of the body did that fear manifest in the body?

Crystal told me in the pre-talk, she had a fear of flying and could not get on a plane. Many times, people hold on to their fears and phobias from past lives. These fears and phobias can be released in their past lives. From my own personal experience, I was able to release my fear of water, as I had drowned three times in my past lives.

C In my heart.

I found it helpful to ask the client where in the body the issue manifested. I believe most of our illness, discomfort, and disease comes from some emotional issue that is unresolved whether in this life or the past. Louise Hays and numerous other sources, also believe that many of our physical difficulties are related to our emotions. I ask the client to visualize that fear, take it out of the heart and put it into a box. Then let it just fade away never to return and if you need help you may ask your guides or angels to take it away. At that point she said, "I can't let go of the box." As she was unable to let it go, I then asked her to ask Jesus to help her and take it away. And like my experience, she was able to release it to him. It was a very moving moment for her as well as myself. Crystal was able to release her fear of flying which was related to that lifetime.

K Is there anything else that needs to be released from that lifetime that is affecting the current lifetime?

C I don't know if I did enough! Jesus did so much. I don't know if I did enough to continue his work.

K I would now like you to look at all the people you did help. Can you see them? Can you feel what they were feeling? And it is time for you to believe you did enough.

C Yes. I feel their love.

K And if Jesus was standing there, what would he say to you?

C I think he would say I did enough?

K Yes, I know Jesus would say that you did enough. Now, I want you to say out loud, "I did enough." Can you believe it now?

C Yes!

After experiencing another lifetime, I asked Crystal's subconscious to come through for even a higher level of understanding.

Crystal in the Subconscious

K   Do I have permission to speak with Crystal's subconscious?

SC Yes.

K   Why was the lifetime with Jesus shown to Crystal?

SC Because that was the most significant lifetime.

K   Why was that the most significant lifetime?

SC She learned what it's all about.

K   What did she learn what it's all about?

SC She did as Jesus instructed her to share with others about the Source.

K   What does she need to tell others about the Source that they didn't understand?

SC Everything is based on love. Once you've learned that ... it's so much easier to learn about everything else.

At this point, I asked the subconscious to move to a higher level of awareness, to the highest level she can reach that is appropriate for her at this time. When I feel that a client needs to go to a higher level, I will give them the suggestion to move to that level.

SC She is quite advanced.

In her current life Crystal is very humble, and this is something she would never say about herself. The subconscious will tell us things about ourselves that we would normally not say in the conscious state.

K Is she aware of this?

SC She is beginning to be awakened.

K Was she awakened in the time of Jesus?

SC Yes.

K What was the most important thing she should remember about that time?

SC She knew the answers then … she knows the answers now.

K So it is a remembrance?

SC Yes.

K Is there something the subconscious would like to speak to her about that hasn't been addressed?

SC She was quite a significant leader.

K So she downplayed that role?

SC Yes. She changed many people's lives.

K She had some difficulty understanding she did enough. So can she now realize she did do a lot?

SC She did a lot.

K Can the subconscious help her to realize that she did a lot?

SC Yes.

K What was the most significant thing Jesus said?

SC "Share the Way!"

K Was everything she said about that lifetime with Jesus or correct. Is there anything that needs to be changed?

SC No … all is correct.

K   Can the subconscious explain the levels of awareness?

SC It is a knowing. Her knowing is very high.

K   Can the subconscious give Crystal a message?

SC She has learned a great deal already … just don't doubt!

K   Are you speaking about her lifetime with Jesus?

SC She doubted she was worthy of such greatness!

I find that most people have difficulty saying they have greatness. We are taught not to be think that there is greatness within us. However, our subconscious always has this knowing of our greatness. We just have to believe it.

K   Can the subconscious work with her on her doubt and worthiness?

At this point the subconscious began to assist in the healing. The subconscious went to the areas of her body where these feelings were located. Crystal then indicated that all was released.

K   Is there any physical issues that need to be addressed from the lifetime with Jesus?

SC My back. When I fell off the cliff.

K   I know the subconscious is very powerful and can heal anything in the body, so I ask the subconscious to work on Crystal's back to be healed. Can the subconscious heal her back now, so she will not have any other problems in that area of the body?

SC Yes.

K   How will the subconscious heal the back?

SC It's sending light. … It is complete.

Crystal's Impressions after Her Session

Crystal's first impression was that she already knew some of the information, however there was a great deal of new information provided in the session. This was a confirmation for her. She said she always felt different in this life, and this was another confirmation. Many times we already know the information, but we do not always listen to what is provided. When we hear our voice in the subconscious speaking us of the truth, there can be no denial. Crystal said the lifetime with Jesus was very powerful and she has never felt that kind of love on Earth before.

Sometime later, Crystal indicated that she has felt great since the session. She had a greater understanding of the information brought forth from the session. Crystal understood that it was not her time to be doing healing work, but that she would eventually pursue this path in the future.

Chapter Nineteen

"The greatest gift is love. Love can heal. Love can harmonize.
Love can break down all barriers."
AMANDA

AMANDA

Amanda had two previous past life sessions with another therapist. She was drawn to my work with the subconscious. She came for the session to become more connected to her subconscious and release various issues in her life. She felt separated from herself, and had many lifetimes of feeling unworthy, and undeserving. At the time of the session she worked in the business world. Amanda began her session with a past life as a slave.

Before she went into the lifetime with Jesus, the subconscious told her to, "Stand in your power. Be powerful, be loving, peaceful and joy. You are a magnet for your own good. You are not a victim. You can choose love or choose fear." And the subconscious said she would now be able to take her power back. After releasing issues from her two past lives, her subconscious came through and indicated that she had a lifetime with Jesus. She began by stating she was a male and was an Essene. Her subconscious said, "Jesus has always been your teacher."

Amanda in the Subconscious

K Is there a need to review other lifetimes for healing?

SC Yes. (*At this time, she indicated that she knew Jesus*).

K Has she had lifetimes with Jesus? Can we go to that lifetime?

SC Yes.

K Moving into the lifetime when you were with Jesus. How did she first meet Jesus? What was their relationship?

SC She was part of the Essenes. They studied and practiced together.

K   Were they good friends?

C   Yes.

K   What did they learn with the Essenes?

SC Some very powerful teachings.

K   What were those powerful teachings?

SC You have the power to heal ... to heal your own life and to teach people to heal their own lives ... reside in peace and power. You forgot these lessons along the way.

K   Was she with Jesus when they were older or just as children?

SC No. They were practicing and learning as children and went their own separate paths. They met up when he was teaching the masses and then they separated again. He taught others. They learned a lot together as Essenes.

K   Who were their teachers?

SC Leaders in the Essene community.

K   What were the names of the Essene teachers?

SC Their names are not important.

K   Did he also perform physical healings?

SC Yes.

K   How many years did you teach and do healing work?

SC After Jesus died we had to go underground, because of chaos and turmoil. We continued to teach and heal and guide.

> *This is similar to my experience when his follows went into hiding after Jesus' death.*

K   How many years did you teach and guide?

SC Until I became old.

K   Did you hear about Jesus after he died?

SC I heard of his death and my heart was broken. I became sad and disappointed.

K   What happened with that disappointment? Did you continue to teach and heal?

SC Yes, but I was not sure if the teachings were effective.

K   Why not?

SC Because they did not listen to Jesus, why would they listen to me.

K   What was Jesus's main message that they didn't listen to?

SC Love! They did not want to hear about love.

K   Why not?

SC They preferred power over love.

K   Some of the people he spoke with were powerless. What other kind of power were they seeking?

SC They were seeking external power.

K   What was the most important thing that you learned from Jesus in that lifetime?

SC The greatest gift is love. Love can heal. Love can harmonize. Love can break down all barriers.

K   Did you feel Jesus was special?

SC Yes ... very special.

K   What made him so special?

SC He was unafraid to speak the truth and have others disapprove.

K   There have been many interpretations of Jesus's life. Was he married to Mary?

SC Yes.

K   Did he have any children?

SC It is believed.

K   What was his physical appearance?

SC Auburn brown curly hair ... his skin is tanned.

K Can the subconscious explain if there was a crucifixion?

SC There was a crucifixion.

K Did the man we knew as Jesus die on the cross?

SC There was an appearance of death.

> *Rose also indicated that there was an "appearance of death" in her session.*

K Did Jesus go to other locations after his death?

SC He regained consciousness at a different level. He appeared for a brief period of time and into the world and then receded.

> *This was an interesting statement about Jesus regaining consciousness at a different level, which is most likely a higher level of consciousness.*

K Did people recognize him?

SC Some did and some did not.

K Did he look different?

SC Yes. He was a Light Being ... he became filled with the light.

> *This may be what he called a different level of consciousness.*

K So you recognized his essence?

SC Yes.

K Was he at the crucifixion?

SC He just heard about it.

K Did Jesus appear to him after the crucifixion?

SC Jesus came to him in dreams.

> *Her subconscious also said that Jesus came to Amanda in her dreams as well.*

K Does he want to give her any information?

SC To wake up ... to be awakened. And she will awaken.

K How did she learn to heal?

SC They both learned, [from the] Essence practices. There was healing in the hands ... through the hands.

K How did Jesus heal?

SC He healed with his hands. His healing energy was more powerful through his hands. He was able to channel light energy very powerfully through the hands.

The subconscious told Amanda, "You can do this as well."

K It is my understanding that healing is about intention? Is that correct?

SC Yes. The heart must be purified.

K Does it matter the way in which one heals?

SC Healing is healing!

K Thank you. She spoke of her fear. Where does fear come from?

SC Fear comes when one believes in lack of and separation from the Source.

K Does she feel separation in her current life?

SC She seeks healing.

K How will healing be accomplished?

SC Let's do light energy.

K Let me know when healing is complete.

There was several minutes where she was breathing heavily as healing was accomplished. This is quite common for client's breathing to become more pronounced when healing is occurring in the body.

SC It's complete.

K What level of the subconscious am I speaking to?

SC Superconscious.

K Is it possible to access a higher level at this time?

SC We are now in the Astral plane.

K Where was the subconscious before?

SC In human terminology, there are levels. In the spiritual realm it is just an EXPANDED AWARENESS! (*Loudly spoken*)

K Is information more correct on that level of awareness?

SC There IS GREATER CLARITY! (*Loudly spoken*) We will bring in the expanded awareness into alignment with the human awareness.

K Is it similar to downloading?

SC It is an alignment.

K Are there any messages for her?

SC Embody and practice divine love. Let your words be filled with compassion, love completely. Forgive everyone. Hold on to nothing, no one, and embrace everything. This is it!

Many times, the subconscious will tell me to stop the session by statements like; "this is it," or "the body is tired." This will indicate to me that we need to close the session. As I always say, the subconscious always takes care of the client and understands what is for their highest good.

K Thank you. Will she believe this completely?

SC If she chooses.

K Then it is all about free will, her choice?

SC Yes.

K How can she heal?

SC Step forth and use then ... what you already have. Let the road unfold in front of you. As you move, you will be directed in the right path. Stay connected to [your] Higher Self.

K Is there anything she needs to remember that she may have forgotten?

SC You are a radiant, divine, loving being. You have everything you need. There is nothing you need that you don't already have. Give up the belief you are alone in this world. I will never leave you or forsake you. You are always loved. You know this fully and completely.

K   Beautiful! Thank you.

While in the subconscious, Amanda spoke about the different levels of the subconscious, as being an expanded awareness. I have found this to be true with my work in the subconscious. Clients receive the information based on their own level of awareness. This is why some clients receive information on a higher level of awareness than someone else. They receive the information that they are ready to understand at that time. You cannot expect someone to have an understanding at a level they really can't understand or benefit from. Again and again the message was that of love when speaking of Jesus' teachings.

Amanda's Impressions after Her Session

Amanda felt the session was helpful, and indicated that she was feeling good. She explained that much of it made sense to her, which related to her current life. She was able to release a great deal of physical issues from her past lives that had manifested in her current life. Her body reacted to her healings with various bodily movement while healing occurred. Amanda also exhibited periods of heavy breathing while healing was occurring. Many times clients will exhibit movement in their bodies when healing occurs. She also felt the physical sensation of energy around her and a light glowing underneath her eyelids. It was similar to a tingling sensation and the heaviness in her chest was released. After the healings, the subconscious said, "All energies are being brought into alignment."

With regards to her lifetime with Jesus, Amanda was surprised that she had a lifetime with Jesus. Amanda spoke of her early years in the Catholic Church which was based on judgment and fear, where she almost felt a resentment of Jesus. But as she began her search for the truth, she realized those teachings were not what Jesus taught, and were far from who he was. She said Jesus felt more like a friend and a comforter to her now.

Chapter Twenty

"...he answered them, "The Kingdom of God is not coming with signs to be observed; nor will they say, Lo, here it is! Or There! For behold, the Kingdom of God is in the midst of you!"
LUKE 17:20

OLIVIA

Olivia previously had a past life regression with another therapist which did not include the lifetime with Jesus. She came for a session to gain greater spiritual knowledge, and to heal some issues that affected her current life. In her current life she worked as an accounting clerk. She was very surprised to learn she had a lifetime with Jesus.

The Past Life Session

K Coming off the cloud down to the surface, very gently coming back down on the surface. Tell me the first thing you become aware of as you come back to the surface. What are your first impressions?

C I don't know if this is right ... I feel the Christ. I feel enveloped. I feel his arms around me. Oh my ... oh my! It's dark I don't see anything.

K Why can't you see anything?

C I don't know.

K If you could see something what would you see?

C I see him smiling. (*She is becoming very emotional.*) I'm just standing there and his arms ... Oh my! [His arms are] around me!

K Is this the first time you met him?

C No.

K Moving to the first time you met Jesus in that lifetime?

C I must be with men and Jesus is sitting on stones. They're talking among themselves. I don't know who I am.

K (*Given the suggestion*) Your memory is greatly enhance. You are now able to remember everything.

C I want to say, "Mary." But I'm going over and I am sitting on a rock. Jesus is talking ... I just hear ... "Be at peace." (*Mary was a very common name in time when Jesus lived.*)

K How did you first meet Jesus?

C I see him walking down the street and people are following him.

K How many people?

C Maybe fifty people.

K What do you do?

C I am curious as to what is going on. I put on my scarf and I follow them down ... going down, sloping. We are right down there, gathering to listen to what he is saying.

K And what is he saying?

C "I am like you ... I am part of you, I am part of All That Is. You are a part of All That Is ... we are not separate. (*Very emotional*) Listen to your heart!" Then he's stretching his arms like he is a human cross. And he is saying, "You don't be afraid ... you don't have to go to a church to know me!"

K Did they have a church then?

Sometimes clients will use words which they understand in their current life in order to relate to a symbolic meaning related to the lifetime that they are experiencing in a session. You will note later in her session that she refers to the word temple and not church.

C I don't know ... that's just what I hear.

K What is happening in the crowd?

C Everyone is listening.

K Did they understand what he is saying?

C I think so, because not one of them is arguing.

K How did you know he was coming to speak?

C I don't think I knew he was coming. I just heard the commotion and I came out.

K After you hear him speaking what happens next?

C He's getting down and leaving. We are all getting up and I ask him if I can come with him. (*Laughing*) And he looks down and smiles and says, "If you want to" ... so I am walking with him.

K Do you have a family?

C I see a house with a place with animals.

K Does anyone else follow him?

C They seem to be dispersing, and I think there is someone waiting up at the top, because they are looking at him. (*Becoming emotional*) I tell him I want to know the secrets. He just smiles.

K How did you know there were secrets?

C Good question. I felt there was more to life than what I experienced.

K Does he ever respond to that, to give you the secrets?

C He's pointing to my heart ..."All will be revealed for you to know and you will know. Don't ever doubt."

K Did you ever doubt?

C Oh yes!

K What did you doubt?

C Just doubt the existence of everything ... anything.

K Did you see any women following him?

C I don't sense them right now.

K So were there others following him?

C I don't sense other men following him. Yes, I want to say ten.

One has to realize this is from her perspective at the time.

K Where do you stay when you were with him?

C I just see trees and I lean against trees, [and I am] resting. He's walking around and looking at everything. He extends his hand to me and I am getting up. He's pointing out ... the sky, and the landscape and smiling.

K How are you feeling?

C Very happy.

K Moving to an important day, a day that you consider important in that life. What is happening? What are sensing, feeling?

C I see soldiers.

At this point she became very uncomfortable with a moaning sound.

K What are the soldiers doing?

C They are killing him! (*Crying*)

K Can you tell me more?

C He's on something.

K Going back in the time before the soldiers came. What is happening? What are sensing, feeling?

C I seem to be talking the other people. They are saying that he said too much.

K What kind of things did he say so much?

C He's angered the people in power. They fear him.

Once again, there was talk of people angered and feared by Jesus.

K Why do they fear him?

C Because people are listening to him.

K What are you feeling?

C We wonder what's going to happen. I think he knows.

K Why do you think he knows?

C I just feel it.

K Does he say that he knew or understands in any way?

C He's not saying. There's no smile ... but looks of acceptance. I just feel.

K Did he have other groups that followed him?

C I'm seeing lots of people. I'm seeing turbans.

K So are there are other people from other places?

C Yes.

K Did everyone have different jobs, or things they would do to help Jesus?

C They came from different places. They come from places to listen and then they don't stay.

K Do some come and some leave?

C I think that would be appropriate.

K Did he teach his method of healing?

C When you say that, I see him taking my hand. But, I can't say for sure.

K If you could say for sure, what would he show you?

C He's turning my hands over, so my palms are up. He is taking his thumb and circling inside my palm. (*Once again there is the mentioning of using the circle.*) I am feeling happy. I see his forehead next to mine. He is giving me something.

K What is he giving you?

C It's like a light.

K That is wonderful, isn't it?

C Yes!

K As he gives you that light, what happens?

C I just look into his eyes. Oh dear this is really weird ... I am kissing him gently and then pulling apart. He puts his hands together.

K So is this a kiss of kindness or passion?

C Kindness!

K Did you feel you were receiving anything?

C Yes something ... to be able to heal. I get the feeling that no one is supposed to leave and do whatever they are supposed to do. I am walking away.

K So he wants you to go away and heal?

C I think so.

K Did you ever witness him healing?

C I recall a person kneeling in front of him. His hand are on his shoulders. He must be doing some type of healing.

K What was it that Jesus was healing in this person?

C I want to say cancer.

K Is this person healed?

C Maybe, I wasn't aware of it.

> *Sometimes clients tell me things that are not a part of their experience, but still may have actually occurred.*

K Are there any other times when you experienced Jesus healing someone?

C I'm seeing water. The shoreline seems to be muddy, and I think a group of his followers, and Jesus is walking along the muddy shore.

K What happens next?

C We're walking on this shore, and in the distance there is land and the sky was kind of grayish, bluish. And I'm thinking I would like to see it colorful. (*Laughing*) And then I see Jesus lifting his hands and changing it.

K And what does he say?

C Something like, "It is for you."

K Have you seen anything else he's done to be miraculous and different?

C He has his hand someone's head and he is offering him healing. I think the hcaling is for their thoughts.

K And what needs to be healed?

C I want to say they are jumbled. After he puts his hands on him. They are crying, and he lifts the face toward him and smiles at them. They're okay now!

By saying they were jumbled, it indicates that she believed it was some type of confusion that needed healing. This could have been the reference in the Bible in Luke 9:42, "...the demon tore him and convulses him. But Jesus rebuked the unclean spirit and healed the boy." At that time, they may have not understood epilepsy or mental illness and assumed it was the demon.

K Does he say anything to you or others about this?

C I'm getting the impression, "This man is healed."

K When he talks to you about healing, does he talk about that not everyone can be healed? Or can everyone be healed?

C Seems like it always comes back to the heart ... what's in the heart. I have the feeling that everyone can be healed, but it's in the heart.

K Does he train other groups to heal? Does he send them out to different places?

C I see the men who are with him. He's giving them something. He seems to be walking to them. It's different, and I am sure it involves healing. I'm trying to picture it. Maybe ... it's like when he took my palms and rotated his thumbs, but not the forehead thing. I'm getting the impression, "This is everything ... this is all ... this is all of us."

K What is the most important thing that he spoke to you about?

C There is no death. There is only perception. (Long pause) Oh!

This statement tells me Jesus may have explained more spiritual truths to his followers than have been written in the Bible. She mentions perception of how we view life from our point of view which may be quite different from what is real.

K What is happening?

C He just ... he says, "I love you!" I just don't feel worthy of that!

K Why don't you feel worthy?

C I just don't.

K Isn't it time to let that go? Doesn't Jesus make everyone feel worthy?

> *She indicated that she had many lifetimes where she didn't feel worthy.*

C Yes.

> *She was able to let it go of feeling unworthy later in the session.*

K Did he speak about this?

C He awfully very kind. He says, "You are my daughter and you are worthy of the Kingdom of Heaven. You were with me."

> *Jesus refers to everyone as sons and daughters even though they are not his direct relatives.*

K So, now it is time to feel that worthiness and take in those words. Did he talk to you about the Kingdom of Heaven?

C It seems to be a knowing on my part rather than an explanation what he says. The Kingdom of Heaven is everywhere. And no matter where you are ... it is.

K What does he look like?

C Color of his eyes are blue green. He seems to be taller than normal. His hair is reddish brown ... wavy hair, with olive skin.

> *Many clients have stated that Jesus had blue eyes and some said blue green eyes.*

K What is he wearing?

C Some kind of white tunic. Sometimes I see a bands of braid ... and it goes to the ground. I wear a brownish, loosely woven scarf.

K Moving to another important day, a day that you feel is important. What is happening as Mary?

C I keep seeing these soldiers. I see the tops of their heads, that's all I see.

K What is happening with the soldiers?

C They are standing around ... I am sad.

K Why are you feeling sad?

C I don't like them. I don't want to be near them.

K What is happening with Jesus?

C I think he's dead.

K How did he die?

C On a pole ...Looks like a tall pole and his arm are outstretched and his head is lowered.

> *It is interesting to note that her description of the cross was a pole, which appear to be her perception at that time. Today it is known as a cross. It would make sense at that time someone might call it as they see it literally.*

K Were you there?

C Yes, but I am standing away. Not real far away.

K Did you hear him saying anything?

C No he is dead.

K Who takes him down?

C I see a ladder. Somebody is up there. Somehow they are loosening. I don't know how they're doing it.

K Were these people his friends or family?

C There are people there. His body is coming down. Someone is taking it. His mother is there taking it. There must be men who had the body. They lay him on the ground.

K Is anyone else there?

C Yes, there is another Mary. I want to say sister ... They are covering him. They are taking him somewhere. We are all going down a road. I'm looking at his face. He said, "That there is no death, but he is dead! So how can this be! My heart is heavy.

She became very sad and crying when she was talking about looking in his face.

K Where do they take him?

C They are taking him inside. A tomb, I think. I'm looking in. It's like he is lying on a shelf or something like that. There're putting something under his head ... like a pillow or something. (*At this point she became upset.*) They are saying goodbye.

She is very descriptive of what was happening with the body of Jesus in her statements.

K Are they preparing the body?

C I don't know what they are doing ... they are doing something. I see people around the body. I see his mother.

K How is his mother doing?

C With a very calm continence. She's calm in the sense she knew it was coming.

K Did he tell her or did she know?

C I think she just knew.

K Did everyone know?

C She did.

K What happens as everyone comes out?

C They are closing it and then putting it back together. This is a big rock or something in front of it. I see people.

K And who moves the rock?

C I just see people moving it. I see a doorway shaped like a dome. I see people coming out of it and then it's closed. I don't see a rock. [There is a] door made of stone.

K What happens after that? Where did you go after his death?

C Some kind of wooden structure. Other people are there ... and they are eating something.

K Is this a gathering? What is the gathering about?

C Fear comes to mind.

K What are they fearful of?

C Soldiers ... I am fearful that they might come because they might kill us too.

K When did this happen?

C I want to say days after his death. (*Heavy breathing*) ... someone was at the door. There's light at the door. There's light, it's all light and it is coming through the door! I think it is Jesus! It is all light! [There is a] form inside this bright form ... it's white, it's gold, but it's ... Oh! ... Oh! ... And he is smiling again. (*Spoken with great emotion.*)

K What happens next?

C He tells us to sit down.

K What did you hear?

C "Why are you here?" He said," I come to show you. I've come to be with you. I've come to love you as I have always loved you." And he is talking to all of us, "I'm going to return in a little while."

K So is he going to manifest in body?

C I don't know what he means.

K Does he stay for a while?

C He's going out the door.

K What happens after he leaves?

C No one can talk! (*Laughing*) We say, "What was that? You saw it! ... I saw it! He has risen and there is no death. If this is the Way, then this is our Way too." Some just run to the door to see where he is. I don't think he's there anymore!

K Moving ahead to an important day in that life, a day that you consider to be important in that lifetime. What is happening?

C I'm dying.

K Moving to the time before you died. What happened between his death and when you saw him?

C I want to glow too. There is something about the soldiers.

K What happens with the soldiers?

C They took me away. I'm hollering ...they seem to be carrying me away. I'm hollering. (*She is extremely emotional at this time.*)

K What are you hollering?

C I want to be free! They're taking me away.

K Eventually where do they take you?

C To a fortress ... They are dragging me and I'm kicking ... dragging me ... "Let me go!" (*She became very emotional.*)

K What happens next? Where did they take you?

C It's dark. I think it is a dungeon. There are others there too. I sense there are other people there, I don't know who they are.

> *In my session, I also saw myself in a type of dungeon or prison with other people around me. Although I am not certain if we were there at the same time, we could have been together in the prison.*

K Did you discuss Jesus with them?

C I see myself sitting down with people. It just seems like ... something like that. I think they knew him. I don't want to be there.

K What were the circumstances of your death in that life?

C I think there is a sword. Somehow a sword is thrust into me.

K Where does sword enter the body?

C I want to say the heart. I say to myself …"I'm going to be golden."

K Now it time to leave that body and soul is releasing. What is happening?

C I'm going toward a type of balcony … And on this balcony there many people waving to me. I am going toward them. I must know these people and they are all around me. They are all welcoming me. Ah! Jesus is waving to me! (*Laughing*)

> *She is describing what happened after she died, and is now meeting others in the interlife. It was so beautiful to hear her words about being golden. It is a very common occurrence when clients speak of being greeted by loved ones, and sometimes Jesus comes forth.*

After the death experience, Olivia is guided to a place to review that lifetime with greater wisdom and knowledge from a higher spiritual level of awareness. Each soul has a life review after each lifetime. This is a place of self-reflection.

Review of that Lifetime from a Higher Level of Awareness

K Now that you have more wisdom and knowledge available to you than while you were in that lifetime. What gave you the greatest happiness in that lifetime?

C Being with Jesus, of course!

K What was the most difficult time in that lifetime?

C His death!

K What insight can you gain from that difficult time?

C That there is no death like he said.

K Is there a need to forgive yourself or others?

C There are the soldiers.

K So it is time to forgive the soldiers.

> *She was able to release and set free the soldiers and herself with the act of forgiveness. And she was able to complete forgiveness and be free from the past.*

C I am flying out of the corral. It's done.

K Were their lessons learned in that lifetime?

C To believe and not to doubt. And to accept and not to judge.

K Did you gain spiritually?

C Yes I think I did. I learned it is not just all material. That there is a deeper and higher meaning to "All That Is." And miracles are just another reality.

K What did you learn or accomplish?

C Most obvious thing is healing.

K Would Olivia like to bring forth the healing abilities from the lifetime with Jesus into your current lifetime?

C Yes.

> *At this time she was able to bring forth her knowledge and understanding of her healing abilities from that lifetime. As we can release difficulties from our past, we can also bring forth various gifts and talents from our previous lives.*

K Is there a need to release the feeling of unworthiness from that lifetime?

C I think that would be nice.

K What would Jesus say about unworthiness?

C There is no need to feel unworthy.

K Take those words and bring them to your heart. It is time to release those feelings of unworthiness. You are always worthy, and you are always loved. And now feel it, believe it. If you would like, you can put it in a box and let your Angels take it from you. So you can choose however you wish to release it from your body, your soul. (*She indicated that it was released*).

K Is there any need to release any physical issues from that lifetime that has manifested in the current life?

C Migraines. They were caused by being in that dungeon.

K It is time to release the migraines as that was in the past and it is no longer needed. You can heal the body. That is what Jesus taught you, and he can come to assist you in the healing. That was in the past. There is no need to carry this with you any longer. It's time to be free of these migraines.

C I feel his hands on my head.

K Wonderful! Miracles can happen.

C Yes. No more migraines.

K Is there a need to heal the heart from that lifetime when you killed by the sword?

C I do have pain but was told it was my esophagus in my heart area.

K Once you understand when and how that manifested in the body, you can release it. It is now time to remove the difficulty in your heart from that lifetime.

> *When the healing was occurring, she began to breathe heavily. Many times client's breathing will become more pronounced when healing is occurring.*

K Is everything complete?

C Yes.

K Please relay a past life message to the current life self. What would that past life self wish to say to the current self Olivia?

C Don't be afraid. Accept what has been given to you and use it wisely.

K Now what would Olivia wish to say to her past life self?

C I would just like to say how lucky you were. And I would like to say thank you.

Olivia's Impressions after Her Session

Olivia said she was surprised at the "whole thing." Her feelings of unworthiness were released and she felt lighter after the session. Along with any physical difficulties, many of our beliefs and feelings can be traced to past life issues. Once understood, our issues can be released and healed. Since Olivia had an understanding of when and where her issues first manifested in the body, she was able to release and heal those difficulties. We are also able to bring forth any gifts and abilities that we had in previous lives into our current life. Olivia was able to utilize her understanding of healing with the memory of her life with Jesus.

Chapter Twenty One

"All things are possible to him who believes."
MARK 9:23

"To recognize the light of truth in us is to recognize ourselves
as we are. Truth cannot be learned, but only recognized. There
is a light in you which cannot die, whose presence is so holy
that the world is sanctified because of you. The light in you is
what the universe longs to behold."
A COURSE IN MIRACLE

AMY

I first met Amy at a Mind, Body, Spirit event where I was conducting a group regression that she attended. After the group regression she explained that she felt she had a lifetime with Jesus and wanted to explore that lifetime in more detail. After speaking with her, she decided to have a Quantum Healing session to access her subconscious and work on some of her physical issues, as well as understanding her life path. At the time, she was not employed due to various physical issues.

This is only the part of the session when she spoke of her life with Jesus when in the subconscious, as there were other personal issues that needed to be released and healed. Her voice changed dramatically with a very robotic and very deep sound in her voice. She was also breathing very deeply as she was nearing the end of the session.

Amy in the Subconscious

K   Do I have permission to speak to Amy's subconscious?

SC Yes.

K   One of her questions was did Amy have a life with Jesus?

SC She walked with Jesus ... yes.

K   Was she one of his followers?

SC Yes.

K   Which one of the followers?

SC She was Peter.

Peter was a very common name in Biblical times.

K   And was she a healer?

SC   Her hands.

K   Did Jesus show her how or did she already have that knowledge?

SC   He showed her how. He touched her hands and gave her the gift.

At this point in the session Amy began to hit the arm of the chair with her hand over and over again.

K   Why is she banging her hand on her chair?

SC   Because they haven't been used. They have so much power. We tried so hard. We tried.

The subconscious was somewhat dismayed that she was not using her healing abilities. I have sometimes felt the disappointment of the subconscious while speaking to clients at that level. Occasionally the subconscious will seem to feel somewhat frustrated with us, and will tell us the truth if we are not on our path. There is no judgment, more like a disappointment that we are not using our abilities, talents or knowledge in order to fulfill our purpose.

K   I know the subconscious has tried. But as you stated, she has to believe it. Would the subconscious wish to continue. We ask the subconscious if we need to review the lifetime with Jesus at another time. (*She began breathing very heavily.*)

SC   Yes.

The subconscious knows when a session should end, so I always ask if the session should continue or should end.

Amy's Impression after her Session

During Amy's session, her breathing became extremely heavy and she said that the body was tired. She was in the session for almost four hours and I felt the subconscious wanted the session to end. So I listen to the subconscious' cues to end the session. The subconscious will indicate when the body is tired. I understand this indicates the session needs to be wrapped up. Our subconscious will always take care of the client and let me know when to conclude a session. All of my sessions continue as long as needed. I never end a session due to a time restraint, unless given that instruction by their subconscious. A session should not last longer than five hours.

When she came out of the session, her breathing continued to be heavy and it was difficult for her to talk. She indicated that she had remembered some of her past lives, but didn't remember what her subconscious had spoken of in the session. Amy remembered seeing Jesus and two angels.

Amy's Second Session with Jesus

"And he said to him, (a leper) "Rise and go your way; your faith has made you well."
LUKE 17:19

Amy decided to come back for a second session to learn more about her lifetime with Jesus. She described herself as a male in his late 20's, wearing sandals and a white burlap type of robe.

The Past Life Session

K How did you meet Jesus?

C We were by the water. [There were] a lot of people. It was really sunny and really hot.

K What is happening?

C He's coming down over this hill and all are there waiting for him. We're all here to listen.

K How did you know about Jesus?

C There was someone who came to tell us and he is coming.

K And what did they call him?

C He was the Messiah.

K What does Messiah mean to you?

C He was sent by the Heavenly Father.

K Why was he sent?

C To teach us.

K What is happening now?

C He's coming down now and he is talking and everybody is listening.

K What is he speaking about?

C (*Long pause*) He's telling us we must pray ... be good and that we are all loved. And he is going to take care of us and to show us the Way.

K What is the Way you speak of?

C If we trust in him, believe in him then everything will work out.

K What is it that you need to believe in him?

C He was sent here as a messenger to teach us to believe in eternal life and to love one another. We don't need to fight. We need to love!

K What was the most important thing that resonated to you about Jesus?

C He can't do it all himself. He wanted me to help him.

K What kind of help can you provide?

C He's got his hands around me. He says he sees and feels a light around me.

K What did you feel about what he was saying to you?

C Oh! I just had that feeling in my heart. It was just overpowering. It was just like what I needed to do. I had heard of this great person, and for him to do that and ask me to come.

You can tell from her response that she felt like it was a great privilege.

K Do you see the light around him?

C Uh ... huh. (*Indicating a yes.*)

K Why do you feel you had this connection?

C Because he told me that we had this connection. I was sitting by the water and he told me. He saw the Light around me and I saw the Light around him. I guess I knew when I saw him. I needed to go with him.

In this statement it indicates that she and Jesus could see auras.

K So were there others that walked with him?

C Many ... maybe ten. They weren't as close to him. They were people that would go and tell people he was coming. They were like messengers.

K So were they what we called his disciples?

C No. They came later.

K So this was earlier?

C Yes.

K Did Jesus have other people with him?

C They didn't stay. [They went] back and forth. He didn't get his disciples till later ... to stand beside him. He had people come to the villages before he came. They were messengers. It was a long way between villages.

This is a confirmation that people would come and prepare villages for his arrival. In Paul's session he spoke of announcing Jesus' arrival in his statement, "And so I would run to get there and tell them that they were coming."

K Did he have women in his group of followers?

C Yes.

K Did he have any of the women that he was close to?

C He called her Mary.

K Did they have a close relationship? Do you feel they were they married?

C They were real close. Not married as a union ... but they were close.

K What was your role with Jesus?

C I started to look around ... who needed to heal ... so we could help people.

K Did he show you how to heal?

C He took these rocks. One night we were sitting out and he took these rocks and put them in his hands and he lit them up ... like glowing. (Long pause) And he told me to open my hands, and with his hands in my hands, he just whispered in my ear... to help heal the world.

K Did he help others how to heal?

C Not with their hands. The others could see and hear and their senses would be amplified.

K So there were different methods of healing which depended upon the person?

C Right.

This was another indication that there are different methods of healing depending on the healer. Some heal with their hands, some just have the knowledge and belief that healing has occurred. This also includes healing of the mind as well. It is my opinion that there is no wrong or right way to heal if it for the highest good.

K What did Jesus say about healing?

C That we can heal.

K Did everyone believe this?

C No, that's why everybody left. That's why we were just a few because not everybody believed what he did.

K Did he teach the disciples to heal?

C He gave them other things to do. He trusted me. We communicated with our minds.

K Did he have anyone else have that communication with the mind?

C Mary Magdalene. We call her Mary.

K How did they meet?

C She was down by the water washing. That's when he saw her.

K Moving to a significant event. An important day when something is happening in that lifetime. What is happening?

C We're in a crowd with a lot of people ... there are sick children there.

K What is happening?

C We're in a cave. We have them laying out.

K Why are they there?

C They have a disease. They are really thin ... malnourished.

> *From my experiences with other clients, I felt this to be a place where the village of lepers had lived. There were several other clients that spoke of Jesus healing the lepers. In Matthew 8;1-3 it also speaks of Jesus healing leprosy, "... a man with leprosy came and knelt before him and said, "Lord, if you are willing, you can make me clean."*

C Jesus stretched out his hand and touched the man. "I will, be clean!" And immediately his leprosy was cleansed."

K Were they considered lepers?

C They are separated … yes.

K Is everyone healed?

C No, we're trying. We can't save them all. There are too many of them … it's like they drain us. The ones that are not as far gone. We can't help and he doesn't like that.

K Why?

C Well, he knows they will be with the angels … all glowing … all light. And you just hear angels singing. It's just beautiful!

K Beautiful! So do you go with him many times to heal and do you go in groups?

C I go with him and have a few that are outside … they watch. I can get through the body. I can touch here.

Amy indicated what she was experiencing with her hands.

K Do you see illness, disease?

C I just feel it. The others can heal, but not medically … maybe emotional. I'm trying to describe it. They can't take something out of the body. They prayed over them and listened to them.

Other clients have said that they were also taught to heal and spoke of healing the emotional body as well as the physical body.

K Moving to an important day, a day that you consider important in that lifetime. What is happening?

C (*Long Pause*) A lot of people around … a lot of turmoil.

K Why is there turmoil?

C It's like they're non-believers …and they're yelling.

K What are they yelling about?

C They are saying he's not real. He's not real, that he is not the Messiah.

K What does Jesus say about this? What does he tell you and the others?

C He's just normal. He doesn't feel he's special. He was sent here to do a duty …

a given thing. He doesn't see himself that way.

> *Again another client speaking about Jesus' not wanting others to feel he was special. According to Josephus, the early Jewish historian, he spoke of Jesus being a wise man and a teacher in his writings, "About this time there lived Jesus, a wise man, if indeed one ought to call him a man. For he was one who performed surprising deeds and was a teacher of such people as accept the truth gladly."*

K But others see him that way?

C Yes.

K Does he speak of God?

C That he is everywhere.

K What does he speak of often?

C The Truth ... happiness ... eternal life.

K What does Jesus say about eternal life?

C That we are in the now and we will be back!

> *This is another reference to reincarnation when she stated that we come back.*

K What do the people think about this? Is it accepted?

C They don't accept it ... not in those times.

K Did the disciples accept this belief?

C They're more open than the public.

K Were the disciples told secrets?

C We all need to love. That man will destroy itself one day.

K Did he explain how man would destroy itself?

C Because of ego. Well, they would be destroying their soul.

K What was the most important thing that resonated to you?

C How he put his hands up on me and he showed me the light around me, and showed me … what I felt inside.

K What did you feel inside?

C It's like I knew it was inside, but he made it happen.

K What is happening?

> *I sensed that something was happening. She indicated it was a hot day and she was able to physically feel the effects of a hot day. Clients will have the ability to feel the experience physically as well as emotionally.*

C I'm hot. (*Long pause*) He's talking to these people. He's sad that they don't believe him. They don't trust him.

K Was he sad often?

C It's not that he's not happy. He just got hurt (*She begins to breathe heavily*). He was trying to tell them of what he could do and how he could help them believe. If you believe in me … I will make it better. Pray with me.

K What does he mean by making them believe in him?

C They did not want to see him. They were afraid of him. He was so different. All he wanted to do is to show them Love and get rid of the fight, [get] rid of the anger. I believe in him. Each person has a different way of teaching, of looking. That's why we had different people. He didn't have to teach everybody to heal with their hands. People could heal with just talking. He showed them different ways. He would help them. Everything would be amplified.

> *I also believe that there are different ways of healing. One could heal with their words as well.*

K Were you with Jesus for most of the time?

C Yes. But there was one time when I had to stay back with the children. It took a lot of energy. I was there for a few weeks. I was drawn to children. I would travel to villages and help mostly with children.

K Was Jesus crucified?

C Yes ... that was bad.

K Were you there?

C I didn't go with him because they wouldn't let us ... the soldiers.

This was also my experience when the soldiers were holding people back from going to the actual crucifixion as it was so chaotic.

K What happened after Jesus died?

C He came back to show us that there is eternal life.

K Did he say anything?

C That he would be with you and for us to keep doing his work. All we had to do was to call him.

K What did you teach others about Jesus?

C He was Holy. He was love. [He is] in all of us. All you have to do is call on him.

K How many years did you teach?

C Long time.

After the death experience, Amy is guided to a place to review that lifetime with greater wisdom and knowledge from a higher spiritual level of awareness. Each soul has a life review after each lifetime. This is a place of self-reflection.

Review of that Lifetime from a Higher Level of Awareness

K Now moving to the place to review that lifetime, now that you have more knowledge and wisdom available to you than while in that lifetime. What gave you the greatest happiness in that lifetime?

C Working with Jesus and the children.

K What was the most difficult aspect of that lifetime?

C Having him go and not being there with him.

K What was the lesson learned in that lifetime?

C I have the power within. I had the power. I didn't have to wait for him to show me.

Amy in the Subconscious

K Do I have permission to speak to Amy's subconscious?

SC Yes.

K I know the subconscious could have brought forth many lifetimes for Amy to experience. Why was this lifetime with Jesus shown to her?

SC To teach her. (*Her voice changed drastically and her tone became very deep*).

K What did he teach her?

SC He taught her to take care of the children. To look within. She had it all along.

K What was the reason why Jesus came at that time?

SC To teach. He wanted to show love. I have the power within. I had the power. I didn't have to wait for him to show me.

Amy's Impressions after a Few Months

After her first session, Amy said she was happy that she came. She felt that she was still trying to put some of the pieces of the puzzle together. She now feels that she is really here to help others. She is aware that she is receiving guidance from her guides.

Impressions after a Few Years

A few years later, Amy sent me an email stating that she felt the experience was amazing. She spoke of having a psychic reading where she was told of her abilities to heal many people. She wrote, "I can close my eyes and go back to the first visit with you. I also tell people that it's an experience that everyone should experience once in life. Since our last visit my abilities have really grown." It is always so rewarding to hear from clients how their sessions have helped them and given them greater guidance and knowledge. After a few years Amy said, "I'm living much happier than ever before. What a true Blessing!"

Chapter Twenty Two

"Jesus said, "Whenever you enter a town and they receive you,
eat what is set before you; heal the sick in it and say to them,
The Kingdom of God has come near to you."
LUKE 10:8-9

SOPHIA

I have known Sophia for many years and we often spoke on various spiritual topics. Many years later, she decided to come for a session as she wanted to know more. It had been a few years since we had spoken. Sophia at that time was a retired teacher. She is a kind and giving Soul with many talents and gifts.

When Sophia came off the cloud onto the surface, she described herself as male wearing light clothing and then became extremely emotional as she said, "I feel like I am Jesus." She seemed very conflicted with that statement. I asked her to remain calm and start her breathing and relax. She became extremely emotional, so I asked her to go to an important day as a child in that lifetime. Sophia went on and described the home as having a thatched roof made of clay. In the session she said Jesus was a teacher, a rabbi who had the gift of healing. She spoke of him healing those who had leprosy. She also spoke of the followers being seekers who were trying to find the truth within themselves.

In her subconscious, she explained why she took on the personality of Jesus. Her subconscious explained that she was a strong empath taking on the feelings of Jesus in order to heal. The word empath comes from the term empathy. There are different degrees that an empath can experience. Sophia was on the stronger side of her empathic feeling. An empath is a highly sensitive person who takes on the feelings, emotions and thoughts of others. While in the subconscious, she came to understand that she was really a man called Simon. It is important to be open to whatever a client is experiencing in a session, and it will eventually reveal the truth of what the client needs to understand.

I have included the parts of this session which confirmed other clients' statements about Jesus. Even though she was not actually Jesus, she was able to express much of what he was feeling.

The Past Life Session

K These friends, did you have a name you called them?

C Students...followers.

K Did they stay with you or did they come and go?

C Some came and went and there were groups that stayed. After a while a group that stayed.

K Were you close to them?

C Yes...They were all different from each other...they were seekers.

K Seeking what?

C Trying to find the truth...find themselves.

K Did you teach in the synagogue since they called you Rabbi?

C No! I didn't agree with what they were saying.

K What didn't you agree with what they saying?

C Didn't agree with interpretation and when I questioned it...they got angry.

K Why did they get angry?

C I felt I should because I didn't agree with their interpretation.

K What were they missing?

C They were full of themselves. They were missing the human part.

K What was the human part?

C Compassion. It was all about money, power, position, wealth.

K Did you have teachers when you were younger and were those teachers helpful?

C Yes...I think they had different beliefs and I try to question, but they said it was word of God. ... But it did help me develop my mind to learn.

K What was the main message you want others to know?

C Love yourself and love others. Fight against injustice ... don't follow what is evil.

K What does evil mean to you?

C Hurting others ... taking advantage of others and being full of yourself.

This is a similar definition of evil expressed by other clients, and a different interpretation of the Western ideal of "evil." According to various sources, the Hebrew meaning has a broader meaning having a much wider range of translations such as causing hurt, pain, affliction, doing harm, dishonesty, including ethical and immoral issues.

K Did you teach that to others to forgive?

C Yes ... they thought it was impossible. They didn't understand.

K So where do you think you received all this knowledge?

C I feel like it was put in my head.

K From a child?

C Yes. I didn't let a lot of people know. I think my mother knew. Joseph ... I think he knew too. He tried to protect me.

Sophia in Her Subconscious

K   It is my understanding that the subconscious could bring forth many lifetimes for her to experience? Why was that lifetime shown to her?

SC We keep coming.

K   Who keeps coming?

SC Jesus. She thinks about him a lot.

K   So why did he choose to come to her in that lifetime?

SC Because she always wanted to be a teacher.

K Why did Jesus come in that lifetime?

SC God felt it was needed at that time.

K So was he sent?

SC Yes.

K Are there others sent by God?

SC Yes.

K What was the most interesting thing about Jesus?

SC His love and compassion.

K What is the most interesting thing about Yeshua that needs to be understood in the current life?

SC Some people say he was just a teacher.

K So he was more than a teacher?

SC Yes … the Holy Spirit.

K Can the subconscious explain the Holy Spirit?

SC God sends the Holy Spirit down and you can see the Holy Spirit in him. People could see that in him.

> *When speaking of the Holy Spirit, I also feel it can be called the Christ Spirit. Ellie says, "It is a mirror that is being held up to see the face of God, the part of us that connects us to God." At this point I asked her to go to an even higher level of the subconscious.*

K How was Sophia connected to Jesus? Was she with Jesus or was she him? Can the subconscious please explain the connection?

SC Yes. She was with him and in him.

> *This was an interesting statement which could explain her first feeling of being with Jesus.*

K Can the subconscious explain? Was she a follower?

SC Yes.

K Did she take on everything he felt in that lifetime?

SC Yes. (*At this time she began breathing heavily.*)

K As a follower what was her name in that lifetime?

SC Simon.

K Was he a disciple?

SC Yes.

K Did Yeshua have other lifetimes?

SC Yes.

K What were they?

SC He can be exploded into many places ... aspects of him in many.

K Is that unusual?

SC No.

K What was important that was not revealed?

SC That you can survive pain ... hatred. The light survives.

K Why did she come through as Jesus?

SC She felt it stronger.

K In that lifetime, was she an empath?

SC Yes.

> *An empath is a person who will take on the feelings and emotions of another, as if it's a part of their own experience. They will actually feel and experience what that person is going through. This seems to be the case with Sophia, where she took on some of the feelings and emotions of Jesus in that lifetime. It is very rare that an empath will take on a personality of a person, but she seemed to be more empathic than most with regard to that lifetime. She is also a strong empath in her current life. Being a strong empath can cause one to become stressed and anxious if not grounded.*

K What were Simon's feelings about Jesus?

SC He was very taken by him ... his Spirit, and his light. His love just emanated.

K Why did her subconscious choose to come that way, as it was extremely emotional for her?

SC So she could finally let it go.

K What does she need to let go?

SC She always felt it emotionally.

K About his death?

SC Yes.

K Did that emotion manifest in the body of Sophia? And if so where in the body?

SC Down the spine into the hips ... legs ... walking.

K So she needs to move forward?

SC Yes.

K So I understand that the subconscious can heal anything in the body as it is very powerful. She doesn't need this anymore. It's time to release it from her body, and return to the original blueprint of her body. Can the subconscious direct it out of her body?

SC Yes. (*She began breathing very deeply now, as it was released.*) It's done!

K Never to return. How did the subconscious heal the body?

SC Breathe in the positive ... sent out negative. (*In a very deep voice.*)

K Thank you. When she said Jesus didn't feel he completed everything in that lifetime was that Simon's feelings?

Sometimes the conscious mind can slip in, and the information presented could be from the client's perspective.

SC Yes.

K So what did Simon feel he didn't complete in that lifetime?

SC Passing wisdom.

K Did he teach others about Jesus?

SC Yes.

K But he reached many people in that life didn't he?

SC He helped many with his teachings.

K He needs to bring that understanding forward now to be at peace.

SC Yes. (*Breathing heavy as she is healing and her body began to vibrate.*) ... Complete.

K Why did Simon take on the emotional feeling of Jesus?

SC He just loved him and wanted to be like him.

K What is the most important thing he taught Simon?

SC Forgiveness.

K What did Jesus tell him about forgiveness?

SC You need to let go or else it will eat you up. You just have to forgive and move on and take the light with you.

K Did Jesus speak of the light?

SC Yes.

Sophia spoke of the need to connect with her spirituality. She said there is a need to remember Jesus and bring him forth, as he was a great teacher for her.

K What does she need to remember from that lifetime with Yeshua?

SC To let the good things in.

K Is she speaking of manifesting.

SC Yes.

K Did Jesus speak about manifesting?

SC Yes.

K Did you understand manifesting at that time?

SC Some.

K Why does she cry at church and at home?

SC She needs to find her way back to the light. She's remembering it, but not always following.

K What would be helpful for her?

SC Meditation, books ... the Bible, but parts of it.

It is interesting that the subconscious recommends only parts of the Bible to be helpful for her to find her way back to the light.

Sophia's Impressions after Her Session

Sophia first reaction was to say, "Wow." She said she felt the session was very helpful, and that she felt energized afterwards. She also felt that it was a very different experience while in the subconscious. In the beginning of the session she said, "I felt like Jesus but then I wasn't, I was Simon." We talked about her being a strong empath. Sophia spoke of an earlier incident when a spiritual teacher picked up that she was a strong empath. I believe that since she is such a powerful empath, she began taking on the energy of Jesus. She was able to tap into his feelings, but also tapping into her feelings as well. Sophia indicated that she felt the healing as her body was vibrating as the healing process was happening. She even felt it in her feet. Vibrations in the body during the healing process occurs quite often in sessions.

Chapter Twenty Three

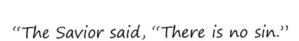

"The Savior said, "There is no sin."
GOSPEL OF MARY

"There is no sin! There are only burdened souls who have
for some reason come into a situation where they are not as
aware of the light and the love, and the peace."
NAOMI

MIA

I met Mia when I was teaching a past life class at a local college. She had previously read an article about my work in a local magazine. At that time she was working as a nurse. When participating in the class group regression, she briefly touched on having a lifetime with Jesus. She came for a past life session to explore that lifetime to gain additional information, as well as a confirmation. Mia also wanted to release her repeated patterns and understand her purpose in this life.

The Past Life Session

When Mia came off the cloud onto the surface, she described herself in that lifetime wearing sandals and wearing a long gown. She was a young adult male with light brown hair.

K What is happening around you?

C There is a field of sheep

K Move to the type of dwelling that you lived in. In that life, what type of house or dwelling did you live in?

C It's a small house.

K How is it constructed?

C Some type of clay ... it looks like a straw roof.

K What is it like inside?

C One room, it's small with a little type kitchen, a table made of wood and only two chairs.

K What types of food would you be eating if you see yourself eating a meal?

C Some kind of meat, potatoes or something like that.

K Do feel you have a family?

C I feel like there is a family.

K Now, moving to a time when you were with your family.

C My wife and a son.

K Are you close to your wife in that life?

C Yes!

K Move to an important day, a day that you consider to be important in that lifetime? Moving to that day now. What is happening?

C Today is the day they are crucifying him.

> *She became extremely emotional with tears of the pain when describing what she was experiencing.*

K Who are they crucifying?

C Jesus!

K Did you know Jesus?

C Yes.

K Let's go back to the time when you first met Jesus. How did you first meet him?

C I met when we were like in a town, at school.

K Did you feel close to him then?

C He was very kind.

K What kind of things did he do that were kind?

C He talked to me

K What did he talk about?

C He was just nice to me. I was very quiet and he just came up to me.

K Where there other children that he became friends with too?

C Yes, but we became friends very quickly.

K If you were to hear your name called, what would he call you by?

C Samuel.

K Did you ever go over Jesus' house?

C Yes. We spent a lot of time together.

K Did you ever meet his parents?

C Yes.

K What did you think about his parents?

C They were always nice to me.

K Did you notice anything different about Jesus?

C He was taller than me and he was smart.

K You said that he was smart, what gave you that impression?

C Common sense wise.

K You also said you went to the same school, how was the school conducted?

C It was outside.

K Did you have a teacher?

C Yes. (*He indicated that his teacher was a male.*)

K What did he teach you?

C He taught us about life.

K Did he teach any religious teaching?

C I believe so.

K Did he speak of God and if so what did he say about God?

C Yes. He is the giver of life.

K Did Jesus talk of God?

C He said he is Divine.

K What else did he say that resonated to you?

C God was the source of all good and that we are on God's side. And we would need to battle against evil.

K Move to an important day, a day that you consider important in that life as Samuel. What is happening?

C We're together and we're older now. We were in a base of a mountain ... talking.

K What are you talking about?

C Something he needs to do.

K What does he need to do?

C (*Long pause*) God's asking him to do something. He needs to go somewhere by himself and I just don't understand why?

K Does he explain why?

C He says he needs to be alone, but he'll be back. He needs to talk to God.

K Where does he go to talk with God?

C He wants him to go up the mountain.

K So do you follow him?

C No ... I wait for him.

K How long do you wait for him?

C A long time.

K What about your family, your wife and son?

C I don't have them yet.

K So this is when you were still rather young?

C Yes.

K So what happens when he returns from the mountain?

C There's a bright light around him.

K He didn't have that before?

C No!

K Does he tell you what that is about?

C He tells me he has been given information and he needs to tell everyone. He seems much wiser than before and he needs to spread the word.

K What is word that he needs to spread to the world?

C Word of God.

K And does he tell you what the word of God is?

C (*Long Pause*) Peace!

> *The Bible speaks of Jesus going into the wilderness where he was tempted by the "devil," however she speaks of him receiving spiritual information given to him by God. It appears that Jesus was being downloaded important information while at the mountain. Throughout the years, many of my clients have indicated that important spiritual information was being downloaded to them by higher spiritual beings.*

K After he has come off the mountain, where does he go?

C Everywhere.

K Does he go to any other countries?

C Yes, neighboring countries like Egypt, India.

K Why does he go to other countries?

C To tell everyone about God.

K And was he given the message by God to do this?

C Yes.

K Does he go by land and sea, or just by land?

C Land ... but there are seas.

K Does he have anyone to take him there?

C Yes.

K Do you go with him?

C Yes.

K Who else goes with him?

C There are many other people who go with him .... but mostly men.

K Are there any others from his childhood that are with him?

C Yes.

K So he was close to a lot of friends from his childhood?

C Yes.

> *This was confirmation in Joy's and Ruth's session when they said he was close to his childhood friends.*

K As a child, did you know there was something special about him? And how did you know?

C Yes. I just knew.

> *There were other sessions indicating that his childhood friends knew he was special.*

K So when Jesus goes to these other places, countries, what is he learning?

C He is learning that there is a lot of evil people in the world.

K Does he tell you this?

C Yes.

K What does he tell you about this situation?

C That we have to teach them and have to make them see differently.

> *This statement suggests that Jesus doesn't see others as "evil," but that they are unable to see things from a spiritual perspective. I began to address client's concept of evil and its meaning to them at the time. It is important to remember that most people at that time only understood the concept of good and evil. This is my reasoning behind asking questions concerning what the word "evil" meant to the client in that lifetime. I have also found that humans need words to describe everything in our world, therefore words can be interpreted differently depending on our experiences, beliefs and conditioning.*

K Was he successful?

C Eventually.

K When he was going to other countries, was he learning about other cultures and their religions?

C He said it was okay to believe differently, but there is only one God.

> *Once again, this is a very different interpretation from the* Bible *concerning his acceptance of other beliefs. Additionally, this was another confirmation that Jesus was learning from other religions and cultures.*

K Were you there many years with him?

C Yes.

K Did he ever explain to you what happened on that mountain with God?

C (*Long pause*) No.

K When did your wife and child come into your life? Did you leave him at that time?

C Yes, I must have.

K Were there others with families that had to leave as well?

C Yes ... as we grew older.

K How many years were you with him?

C A number of years.

K So were you older when you got married?

C Yes.

K Did you invite Jesus to your wedding celebration?

C Yes.

K That must have been wonderful. What was that like, what happened?

C Wonderful!

K I'm sure it was beautiful! Did Jesus have many close friends?

C Yes.

K Did he have any women that were his friends?

C Yes.

K Who was his best friend that was a woman?

C Mary.

K Did Jesus and Mary ever get married?

C I don't know.

> *Like many clients, Samuel did not give information that was not known to him at that time.*

K But were they very close?

C Yes.

K Were there other women that were with him?

C A few others.

K How did you meet your wife? Was she with Jesus as well?

C She must have been because I was with Jesus all the time.

K Was she close to Jesus too?

C Yes.

K Did she have the same beliefs?

C Yes.

K Did Jesus ever tell you who he was? You said he was special.

C Yes.

K What did people call him? Who did they say Jesus was?

C Son of God.

K What did that mean to you?

C It means that he was special, he was great. He was sent to us for a purpose.

K When you asked Jesus what did he say?

C He said, "Yes he was."

K What was the most important thing he said to you?

C He said to love everyone and to teach everyone about God's love.

K Did you ever ask him questions that you wanted to understand?

C I asked him how he knew God. How he knew he was the Son of God.

K What did he say?

C He said, "Because he speaks to me."

K Does he say God can speak to you?

C Yes. I speak to God all the time.

K What does God say to you?

C He says you have a purpose here.

K What is your purpose?

C To take care of everyone ... to heal people.

K And how did you learn to heal people? Did Jesus show you?

C Yes.

K How did Jesus show you how to heal?

C With his hands.

K So were there a group of healers he taught to heal?

C Yes.

> *There were many clients that spoke of a group of healers that were taught by Jesus.*

K And when he showed you how to heal, what happened?

C People got better.

K So how did he instruct you to heal?

C He said we have energy in us.

K Did that make sense to you at that time?

C No. Our energy comes from God. We can use it in good ways to help people. And that we need to concentrate and pray in order to strengthen the power to heal.

K Did he give you a prayer to say or did you have your own prayer?

C Intention to do well and help others.

Once again, intention is mentioned when healing others.

K Who was the person that he healed, that had the greatest impression on you in that lifetime?

C Young boy who couldn't walk. His mother brought him into the street. He had something wrong with his legs.

K So what did Jesus do to heal this boy?

C He held his hands up high first and asked God to give him the power to heal this boy. He knelt down and touched his leg and prayed to God and the little body was able to get up and walk.

K Were there many healings?

C Yes.

K Did people come all the time to be healed?

C Yes.

K And what did Jesus say about this?

C He told us that we could help him by doing the same thing.

K I'm sure there were many?

C Yes.

K So you helped take some of burden off of him?

C Yes.

K Did you help with the healing when Jesus wasn't able?

C I continued to help.

K Was your wife a healer as well?

C Yes.

K Was there a group that followed him everywhere? Who were they?

C The disciples.

K Did they stay with Jesus most of the time?

C Yes.

K What was the most important day that you were with him?

C (*Long pause*) When they took him off the cross and wrapped him up.

K Who took him off the cross?

C The men took him down ... three men. I guess they were followers. And they wrapped him up. And took him to the cave and put him in there.

K Did you help?

C I was just watching.

K Was it a big cave that they took him to?

C It had a tall opening ... not too deep.

K Did his mother and Mary come?

C Yes.

K Did they go in with the body?

C Yes.

K What did they do?

C They wrapped him up.

K Did they prepare the body in any way?

C I don't know.

K Did they close the opening in cave?

C Yes.

K Then where did you go?

C I stayed there.

K Why did you stay there?

C Because I didn't want to leave. I was sad.

K Were there a lot of people that stayed as well?

C Yes ... there was a lot.

K So what happened next?

C When I woke up, the cave was open!

K So what was your first reaction?

C What happened?

K Did you hear what happened?

C He was gone!

K How did you feel about that?

C Scared .... worried. ...The angels took him to heaven.

K Did he say anything to you?

C No.

K Did he come back in spirit?

C Yes.

K What did he look like? Did he look the same, or did he look different to you?

C He looked like an angel.

K Did he have wings?

C Yes!

> *I feel Jesus would appear to those in the way they could believe and understand at the time.*

K Did he say anything to you?

C Thank you.

K Did he talk before he died about the fact that he would come back?

C Yes.

K So when you saw him, how did that make you feel?

C Happy ... relieved.

K Did he show himself to any others?

C Yes.

K So did many people see him?

C Yes ... everyone who believed in him.

K Did he give any messages?

C He said, "Live your life as I taught you to. And always believe in me and I will be here for you."

K Did he ever speak to you that he would be crucified?

C He said they would come and get me, and they would kill me.

K Did he say that was necessary for him to die?

C He needed to save us.

K What did he need to save us from?

C From evil in the world. From our ways of evil that make us sin. If we pray to God he will always take care of us and always fight the evil. It never ends.

K What does he call sin?

C Things that hurt people .... bad emotions .... bad feelings ... hurtful things we do to others.

K So things that affect others in a negative way?

C Yes!

> *What he was describing as sin, was actually those things that are harmful that affect ourselves and others in a negative way. This is very different interpretation of sin than what is taught by many religions. In Hebrew the word sin means, "missing the mark" or "to go astray."*

K Did he say what the most important lesson to be learned was?

C Always love everyone.

K Even the ones you call evil?

C Yes. Spread the word.

K So did you spread the word?

C Yes.

K Where did you speak?

C Outside. (*Taken literally while in hypnosis.*)

K Did your wife speak as well?

C Yes.

K Was it dangerous to speak about Jesus?

C Yes.

K But you spoke about him anyway?

C Yes.

K Did you see any of the other followers?

C Yes.

K Did you write anything down about what Jesus spoke of to you?

C Yes. It's like a type of journal. So I could remember.

K So you wrote down your memories of Jesus?

C Yes.

K Even when you were a child with Jesus?

C Yes.

K Did anyone else read your journal?

C Yes.

K Did the others write journals too?

C Yes.

K Did they have similar things to say?

C Yes.

K So each wrote about their different experiences?

C Wrote about the good that he did.

K Was his mother with him when he was traveling?

C She was there from time to time.

K Was he close to his mother?

C Yes.

K And to the other Mary?

C Yes ... she was there a lot.

K How did they meet, did he ever tell you?

C No. She was just always there.

K What was she like?

C She was very nice.

K Was she kind, like Jesus?

C Yes. She was a good friend.

K Did Jesus ever talk to you about people who wanted to do him harm and why?

C Yes, because they didn't like him.

K Why didn't they like him?

C They were jealous of him because he was a King.

> *Again there was a feeling that others were jealous of Jesus.*

K Why was he a King?

C Because he was sent from God. They said they didn't believe, but I think they were just jealous. People say they don't believe, when they are really jealous.

K Earlier you spoke of a light around him. Did he continue to have that light around him?

C Yes.

K Did people see that light around him?

C People that believed him, did.

> *I found this to be an interesting observation speaking of the light around Jesus with those who believed in him. I also saw a beautiful light around him in my session.*

K What color was that light?

C Whitish gold.

K Did he ever tell you what the light was?

C It was the Light of God.

K Now let's move to an important day, a day that you consider to be important, when something important is happening. What is happening?

C I'm old. I think she is sick.

K Who is sick?

C My wife ... she is dying

K What happens after her death?

C I think I stayed there.

K Now let's move to the circumstances of your death. Moving to the last day for your life in that lifetime, feeling no discomfort.

C I died of old age.

K Did you give anyone your journal before you died?

C My son.

K Were there any last words to your son?

C I told him to keep teaching.

K What was your son's name? What did you call him?

C Ezekiel.

K As your soul lifted off his body, what is happening?

C I have a lot left to do.

K What do you have left to do?

C To teach everyone about Jesus.

After the death experience, Mia is guided to a place to review that lifetime with greater wisdom and knowledge from a higher spiritual level of awareness. Each soul has a life review after each lifetime. This is a place of self-reflection.

Review of that Lifetime from a Higher Level of Awareness

K Now move to that peaceful place to review that lifetime where you have more wisdom and knowledge available to you than while you were in that lifetime. What gave you the greatest happiness in that lifetime?

C Knowing Jesus.

K What was the most difficult time of that life?

C Watching him die.

K So you were there?

C Yes.

K What insight can you gain from that lifetime?

C There is life after death.

K What else did Jesus tell you?

C He said you will have the opportunity to help others in many lifetimes.

K Did he say that to the others that were healers?

C Yes.

K Did Jesus speak of having other lives?

C Just his life with God.

K Did he believe in people having other lives?

C Yes.

K Is there a need to forgive yourself or any others from that lifetime?

C Yes ... those for killing him!

> *At that point Mia was able to forgive herself and others. She began feeling a release from the body and feeling lighter. Whenever clients are ready to release the feelings of unforgiveness, they always feel a lifting of*

the weights of the past. They literally have the feeling of a heavy weight lifting off their body and they are finally free.

K What did you learn or accomplish in that life that can help you in your current life?

C I learned ... I have amazing powers to heal others.

K Does everyone have this power?

C Yes.

K What did Jesus say about healing?

C You have the ability to help others ... and heal others, and teach others about me.

Mia was able to bring forth her powers of healing from that lifetime with Jesus. Even though we are able to release difficulties from our past lives, we are also able to bring forth abilities and talents from other lifetimes. That knowledge is always stored in our subconscious.

K What was the lesson learned in that lifetime?

C We all come from God, and will go back to him. It's our job to go forth and do good.

Mia's Impression after Her Session

After the session Mia said she felt different when she was around Jesus. We spoke of some of the differences of others and their perspective of what Jesus said to them. When asked how she felt about the session, she said she felt lighter.

A Few Months after Her Session

After a few months Mia wrote me about her session. I was happy to hear that the session had helped her move forward with more confidence and understandings. Sharing her impressions, Mia said, "He spoke to individuals at their level of understanding which could have been different for each person. I'm feeling more confident in my decision to work towards becoming the person I want to be, even if it's not traditionally acceptable. If I was really a friend of Jesus, I must realize that I was not accepted by everyone then. So, I need to accept that I am still different from the norm, and I must devote myself to my purpose regardless of how odd that may be. I'm looking into some training in the energy healing field as well as energy helping treatments for myself. Thank you for the session we had together. It has made a great impact on my life."

Chapter Twenty Four

"This is the first lesson ye should learn: There is so much good in the worst of us, and so much bad in the best of us, it doesn't behoove any of us to speak evil of the rest of us. This is a universal law, and until one begins to make application of same, one may not go very far in spiritual or soul development."
EDGAR CAYCE, READING 3063-1

"I am not what happened to me, I am what I choose to become."
CARL GUSTAV JUNG

LILY

I firmly believe there are no accidents. I remember telling my friends long before Lily came for her session, that wouldn't it be interesting to have the perspective of a Roman soldier. Just before the book was to be completed, I was surprised when a client stated he was a Roman soldier in the time of Jesus. He was not only a Roman soldier, but a Roman advisor to the Emperor! Hopefully, this session will give a different perspective that not all Romans were cold and heartless. I firmly believe she was sent to help us understand forgiveness in the truest sense. Even though this lifetime did not have direct association with Jesus, I felt that it was important to include the session because of its effect on Jesus' life and his death.

After given many details, it was made clear that she was in that lifetime when Jesus was crucified. She had a great deal of difficulty getting to the real truth of her involvement. Sometimes clients who have difficulty getting to the truth of what happened will not always access significant events quickly. I then have to gently revisit the event later in the session, in order to uncover what actually had transpired. This is important to address what needs to be brought forth for greater understanding and healing. She explained that she was very analytical, which can sometimes interfere with accessing needed information. I explained that she needed to let that go and just go with what she is sensing and feeling. As Lily was not a visual learner, I addressed her questions using her first impressions with what was she feeling and sensing. Nonvisual clients have to rely on their other senses to experience the events in their past lives. By not visualizing past life events, her ability to tap into her emotions in the session was greatly enhanced.

Lily began by describing herself wearing Roman type sandals with male legs and wearing a dark red robe. She explained she felt very strong. His dwelling was a large building with columns.

The Past Life Session

K Do you feel that you are wealthy in that lifetime?

C I'm part of a court, like a decision, an advisor... of importance.

K Are you well respected?

C I think so. I feel like there is a lot of power. I don't think I'm an Emperor. I am an advisor.

K Who are you an advisor to?

C The Emperor.

K What kind of advice do you give the Emperor?

C It's like war strategy.

K Are there other advisors to the Emperor?

C Yes, there are others.

K Are you getting ready for war?

C Whew! ... Oh ... whew ... Oh! (*She became very disturbed at this time.*)

K Can you explain what is wrong? Why are you so upset?

C Whew ... oh! I'm just getting ... I don't know why .... I just had a rush of emotion come over me. I am worried that it has something to do with ... whew! I'm worried it has something to do with Jesus! (*It was extremely difficult for her to get the words out.*)

K What is it that you feel so worried about it having to do with Jesus?

C Something. (*Crying, unable to speak*).

K It's okay. Everything is okay. (*Trying to comfort her.*)

C I don't know why I am crying.

K Can you tell me what is happening?

C I don't get anything.

> *At this point it was very emotional for her, I decided to move to another event, knowing that I would revisit this event later in the session.*

K Moving to an important day in that lifetime, a day that you consider to be i important in that lifetime. What is happening?

C It's like a beheading or something. There's a lot of people ... like an execution is happening. It's like I'm there but just watching it. Yet I feel like I should be stopping it ... like I can't stop it. I should be stopping it.

K Why do you feel that you should stop it?

C I don't have the power to stop it. It's like I can't stop it ... it's already happening.

K Do you know who is beheaded?

C It's like an execution. I don't know if it's a beheading ... it's an execution.

K Why is this person being executed? What was the crime?

C It's many people ... lots of people watching the execution. It's old. [There are] lots of stone buildings. (*He indicated no one was stoned.*)

K What was their crime since there were so many people watching?

C I think they are being crucified! It's not a beheading!

> *Many times clients initially have difficulty understanding what really was happening, and have to sort it out to get to the real issue. Even though it may take some time to get to the truth of what really is happening, eventually the truth will always come to the surface.*

C A lot of sadness ... there is so much sadness, and I have to be stoic. But I have deep regret. It's what it is but I had a hand in it.

> *By him feeling what he described as "stoic," he was unable to become emotionally involved in what was happening because of his regret.*

K Do you know why they are being crucified?

C No.

K How many people are being executed?

C Maybe three.

K You mentioned Jesus before, was he one of them?

C I can't see it.

> *Most clients visualize their session like a movie or with pictures, however some clients do not process their lifetimes visually. Everyone has their own way to process information, and sometimes clients will have to use their other senses. Occasionally, clients have difficulty accepting they are not visual learners. However, they can access as much information as a visual person, they just need to let go.*

K It's okay. What are you feeling? What is your first impression?

C My impression is, yes.

K Do you hear Jesus saying anything?

C No ... No! (*Having difficulty explaining.*) It feels like me watching the people and the sadness. Like I have to just stand there! The overwhelming sadness!

K Did you ever know Jesus?

C I had to make a decision and I had to advise on something and when I did ... I just know by standing there, I regret it. I have deep regret because I was a part of it, and I KNOW IT'S WRONG! (*Spoken loudly*).

K How do you know it is wrong?

C I just know it's wrong. I just know.

K You said you had something to do with the decision, can you explain?

C I can't put that part together.

K It's okay. What else are you feeling about that day?

C It's just a part of my job, and I have to continue what I am doing.

K Moving to an important day in that lifetime? What is happening, what are you sensing, feeling, experiencing?

C I'm being married to the woman that has long dark black hair. She seems very exotic for some reason. I am very attracted to her for some reason. She's alluring.

K How did you meet her?

C I'm sailing. It's a part of my position. ... It's another part of my position, just another thing I have to do. It's like manning a fleet, and I have men I lead. Had to get on a boat to go. It's like a peace offering, some sort of peace like to meet ... like an alliance.

K Is this before or after the event with Jesus?

C Before.

K Are you making peace with a country or a person?

C An important person.

K Is this where you met your wife?

C It's like it was in secret. There is something like it could be forbidden in a way.

K Why was it forbidden?

C I don't know.

K Moving to an important day in that lifetime. What is happening?

C I think she is dying. I think it was brief. I don't think we were together very long. (*Very sad*)

K Moving to the time with Jesus. What is happening?

C There is a disconnect. Sometimes I am him and sometimes I am not.

Sometimes there is a disconnect when facing a difficult event in the client's past life. It appear that he had great difficulty not being able to face what was actually happening.

K You said you were a part of the decision, do we need to go back to look at how you were a part of it?

C I know it's just guilt. I know I was in a position that I couldn't do anything, and I knew it was wrong. But I have forgiven myself.

K Were you there at the trial or questioning of Jesus?

C I don't think so.

K You said you worked for the Emperor. Was it the Emperor's decision that you had to follow?

C Yes ... I knew something. I was a part of it.

K How do you feel about being part of the decision?

C It feels impersonal. It's like I'm his advisor and I advise. I had something to do with it, but I didn't make the decision. But see myself watching it and feeling very guilty. That is all I know.

K What was the day like when Jesus was crucified?

C It was a beautiful day ... other than the sadness.

K Can you hear what people are saying?

C No.

K Did you hear any stories about Jesus?

C No. It is like he was considered a trouble maker in some way. Sort of something that had to be taken care of.

K Why was he called a trouble maker?

C He was going against the Emperor ... making the Emperor look bad.

K How could he make the Emperor look bad?

C It was something he was saying.

K What was he saying?

C It's not coming to me.

K Now move to the time when you were talking with the Emperor.

C I think I am saying if you don't take care of it, it could get out of hand.

K Are you speaking about Jesus at that time?

C Yes.

K So are you saying Jesus was creating some sort of trouble or chaos at that time?

C He was causing problems for the Emperor.

K Why did you think he would cause trouble at that time?

C Something about ... he would undermine his [the Emperor] beliefs, but that it would put him out of his position, or something like that.

K So did the Emperor order his execution?

C I think I ordered it.

K Did you ever come in contact with Jesus?

C It's nothing personal. It's like I seized him.

K What do you mean that you seized him?

C It's like I ordered to get him.

K Did you personally go to get him?

C I think I was there.

K Where did you "seize" Jesus?

C It's like a small hut and a stone wall and wooden benches. I can't see it, it is my impression.

K What happens after Jesus' death?

C I think that's when I got the recognition.

K For that event?

C I think it was. Like I was a good commander. I didn't feel that way.

K After his death, did you understand who Jesus was?

C I knew then when it was happening. I didn't know who he was. I just knew it was very wrong.

K How did you know it was wrong?

C It's just a feeling I had.

> *It is very interesting that he was feeling something was wrong, but unable to express it. I was feeling that his inner knowing was speaking to him. Our subconscious speaks through us, but we don't always listen. At the time, he felt he had no choice. This is dilemma for many people throughout history and even today. When we know something is wrong; do we act upon it, or just go with what is accepted at the time.*

C Moving to another important day in that lifetime, a day that you feel is important. What are sensing, feeling?

C I am very peaceful. I'm feeling wheat fields. My wife has passed ... there is no one there. I have my own stone building.

K So you are no longer a soldier or advisor?

C No.

K What were the circumstances of your death?

C I died alone in the hut. I'm very old.

K As your soul is releasing from the body, what are you feeling?

C Just relief from a long lifetime.

After the death experience, Lily is guided to a place to review that lifetime with greater wisdom and knowledge from a higher spiritual level. This is a place of self-reflection. Every soul has a life review after each lifetime.

Review of that Lifetime from a Higher Level of Awareness

K It is time to review that lifetime now that you have more wisdom and knowledge then while you were in that lifetime. What gave you the greatest happiness in that lifetime?

C I don't think there was a lot of happiness. A brief happiness with my wife.

K What was the most difficult aspect of that lifetime?

C Just sadness, and the loss of the execution and loss of my wife.

K Is there a need to forgive yourself or any others in that lifetime?

C Everyone needs forgiveness, everyone needs to forgive. I saw I need to be forgiven from all those people.

> *When working on forgiveness of self, Lily was able to release and forgive herself in that lifetime, enabling her to be free. I used the image of Jesus standing before her, and asked her what he would say to her. She said, "Of course he forgives me." Lily spoke of her feelings of guilt manifesting in her heart as the color red. I asked her to release the red from the heart to be healed and transformed. She was able to send in the white light to heal and release the red from her heart. She indicated that the healing was complete.*

K What did you learn or accomplish in that lifetime that can help Lily in the current life?

C To always do what you feel is right even if you can't feel it can be done. Always speak up.

> *In this life Lily feels she has learned to speak her truth.*

Lily's Impressions after Her Session

Lily's first response about the session was that it "was very interesting." When speaking about her lifetime as the Roman advisor, she understood there was nothing he could do, but when it was happening he felt it was wrong. At the time he said it felt more like it was his job to protect the Emperor. She also felt he remained very stoic in his mind, but his heart was telling him what was happening was awful and heart wrenching. In my session, I said "They don't know who he is," and he didn't really know who Jesus was in that lifetime. Lily stated, "What was astonishing was the emotion that hit me when I knew I was a part of it."

After I contacted her to see how she has been after her session she emailed me this response, "I've been continuing on my spiritual journey slowly but surely. I am keeping a positive attitude towards all of my experiences and I include the experience with you as one of them."

Similarities in the Clients' Statements and Feelings in their Lifetimes with Yeshua/Jesus

There were many more similarities than differences in the client's past life experiences with Yeshua/Jesus. Some of the similarities are not included, but are addressed in their individual sessions. The following are quotes from clients speaking about the same topic.

Clients' Feelings when in Jesus' Presence

He had a uniqueness. It's a feeling you receive when you meet Jesus.

It's a feeling of peace, a feeling of forgiveness. It's a feeling of love and acceptance and unconditional love. You think you know it from your mother and your father, but it is more than that, it is a feeling of Home! It's a feeling of trust. It's all the goodness that you know. You just want to share that with everybody, you want them to experience it as well. We were all changed!

You could feel the love. When you meet him it's a feeling of peace, of forgiveness, acceptance and unconditional love, a feeling of trust.

It gave me a light I never had. It's like we always knew, but it's indescribable. He was wonderful!

We all feel our light shining brighter because of him.

You could not be in his presence and not feel light energy. It was of Him and you felt and you knew you were close to God.

Once in contact with Jesus, you believe.

What happens is, once you come in contact with Jesus, you believe, and you're connected to the other person that believes.

Peace fell upon everyone. Peace came over everyone like a spell. It made everyone love each other.

Just being in his presence, I'm like several hundred feet away and I can literally feel the warmth of his heart. I can't even see him, but I can feel him, but I know exactly where he is in the crowd because I can feel his heart coming through everybody.

You know, sometimes just to be near him changed them. You can't help it. It feels so good to be near him. You want more of it. You want to be it!

It was such a longing and so deep inside me to hear these words. I didn't even know I had that longing before!

Not so much as to what he says, but the feeling you get, there is something beyond. All of this is around us.

I felt lighter around him. I felt safe with him, he gave me hope.

I felt lighter ... hopeful.

He was simple, when he smiled you knew you were safe, and when he touched you, you knew you were safe. He didn't need anything. He just carried his message and his healing powers. And then he was cared for by the people who followed him.

His realness, when he smiled at me, it was real, there was no agenda. It was pure, divine love of the greatest kind. I've never seen it since and I don't know if I will see it again.

He knew who I was. He made me hungry to know more. It was a beginning of a new direction.

He knew who we were, and what we were.

Well, he knew me! I knew him and he knew me.

He touches our hearts. He touches our truth, who we truly are. He knew who I was. He looked right through me.

It's funny because he knows everybody, he knows everything.

He saw things differently, he talked differently than everyone else. He was present. He really was noticing me and my essence.

Some people in life, not very many, but there are people whose hearts and minds meet and resonate at center point and reflect that lightened vibration. You could not be in presence and not feel white energy. It was of Him and you felt you knew you were close to God.

He is wise.

He is genuine. He touched my soul, very kind.

Jesus is very kind. It's beautiful, his choice of words and so wise. You don't want to miss a single word or a minute.

He was very kind.

He still was there, patient and loving, serene.

(Felt) Passionate, passionate kindness.

We feel blessed. He made us feel special.

He offered hope and I never had hope. All full of despair, but the hope thought was always in my heart, it never left me. I put too much into the physical. He was showing me how to see with other eyes, to open my eyes and see the truth.

I could tell you, being with Jesus is having your body stand upright completely, you have no weight on you, you have no regrets, you have no doubts, you have no hatred, you have no guilt, fear. It is the most complete essence of who you are!

You can feel the love is warm and white.

I felt loved.

Jesus, the love for no reason, just the love.

You could feel the love. He was very gentle.

You could feel that light and love from Jesus. There was this different love. It just teaches and engulfs you!

He had so much knowledge. He did things that people didn't know how to do, the healing. It was to share, not just for one, for all!

He was implanted with so much wisdom and knowledge. He had such knowing!

He knows more, he knows all. Jesus does give the best hugs. When he holds you, it's like love is just all around you. You don't feel where he begins and you end.

There is no beginning and no ending.

It's like he sees and knows everything. He doesn't have to say anything.

I told others he was a great man. He taught us all about the greater things, important things, the love we have for each other. That we are children of the Father that we were given the responsibility to help each other whenever possible. That we were never alone, he would always be there for us.

His answers were so profound and beautiful, and sometimes made me think a different way.

Sometimes the way he looked at things was slightly different than the way I saw them, and it allowed me to open up to a different perspective.

A love connection. It's as if we are men of few words, but much knowing that needs not be explained.

He was charismatic. Then that just brought your heart open and wide and flowing, and life was easy and beautiful.

He is charismatic, so you want to listen to him.

His hands would be warm, his voice was soft. There was a resonance to his voice that when he spoke, you were pulled to listen as though you were pulled away.

How he put his hands up on me and he showed the light around me and showed me what I felt inside. I need to go with him.

He was unafraid to speak the truth and have others disapprove.

He understood how to put God's message to the man, to all men at all levels, through the vibration of his voice they would hear God. It was something with the vibration. He didn't teach it, he was it!

Of course, he was the greatest that ever lived.

Jesus the Teacher, Master Teacher, Healer

He is a teacher, the Master, Teacher of Truth

We called him the Master, he knew so much and taught us.

James says he is a teacher. He knows more. He knows all.

He is a great teacher.

They call him the Master.

Yes, I call him Master

I'm with the Teacher.

He says I'm a teacher, a man.

Called him Teacher, Rabbi

Some just called him "Rabbi." We thought of him as a teacher.

I'm a teacher, I am here to teach for those who will listen.

As he is the Master Teacher.

(*He was called*) Master Teacher.

A great teacher.

He is a teacher of the truth. He is a true teacher.

He considered himself as a teacher and a healer.

He is a teacher, he is a master. He is a teacher of the truth. Jesus was a teacher.

He truly was the most gifted teacher on Earth so far. That is because he understood how to put God's message to the man, to all men at all levels, through the vibration of his voice, they would hear God.

He became my teacher. So he gave me all this knowledge on how to educate people and lead them.

The Way, the Truth and the Light

He was the Way, he was forgiveness. He was love.

(He taught us).the Way, the only Way, the Way of the Father, the Way of truth.

The Way, only the Way, Way of the Father, the truth.

He says, I am the light, and the Way, I am the path, I am doing the work of the Father.

(Jesus said) I am the Way, I am the light, I am All.

He is showing us his Way, but we accept his Way.

He said, "I was sent to you to show the Way, the truth and the light".

You must walk in truth and light.

(He said) The truth will set you free.

He is the Way, the love and the light.

Jesus is the embodiment. He is the Way.

The Light Within

Where ever darkness, send the light.

Everyone has the light.

He radiates light.

He was emanating such light.

That is how you know he is of the light. We are all of the light.

(Jesus said) The power has always been inside me, now it is time to know who you are. It's like a light inside of you that has been there since the beginning of time.

So we each have this light within us. So if you could imagine this light multiplying, that is what Jesus is carrying within him.

The light is always there. We have a choice to see and be with it.

The light survives.

He talked about the light that never dies. It might get so tinny, a flicker, and it's my job to see that in others and in myself.

Let your light shine. We feel our light shining brighter because of him.

He's giving me a light.

We have a light inside us, and that light reached up to the highest power that there could be.

(Jesus said) I come to bring light so what all may see their way, the Way of the truth, Way of the light.

Jesus' Teachings of Forgiveness

He spoke of forgiveness, love, oneness and healing.

He talked of forgiveness, forgive our enemies.

We need to learn to forgive. It may be difficult, but necessary for that person, but also for us, also for our enemies. Everyone matters.

We have to forgive ourselves. As we forgive another we forgive ourselves.

Taught love, peace, loving one another.

He speaks of forgiveness. We must forgive, as it affects the body as well.

You need to let go or else it will eat you. You have to forgive and move on and take light with you.

He told us to not be angry at the Romans and to forgive them.

Jesus' Teachings

He truly was the most gifted teacher on Earth so far. That is because he understood how to put God's message to the man, to all men at all levels ... through the vibration of his voice they would hear God. It was something with the vibration. He didn't teach it. He was it! It's not that he tells me things, it's that he shows me things. He lives it!

Of course, he was the greatest that ever lived.

He's always reading peoples. He spots and is answering them, but in the perfect way, like the wisest perfect choice of words that allows that person to hear and absorb. It's almost like being fed to the light of God within you and that allows that light to expand in you and grows. Can you imagine a flame and God speaking to you and that flame gets bigger and bigger!

His answers were so profound and beautiful and sometimes made me think a different way. But sometimes the way he looked at things was slightly different than the way I saw them, and it allowed me to open up to a different perspectives.

We have the power within. I had the power. I didn't have to wait for him to show me.

It was about love, God and understanding. [And] trying to make people powerful.

Right and wrong, and the truth is all within ourselves. We don't need to find it from outside ourselves. We don't have to go to someone else. We have the power ourselves.

We all believe what we create.

He says we are all here to fulfill a purpose.

He was the Master, but he would say we are all with God.

Jesus always says you need to trust in yourself.

(Jesus said) I am like you. I am part of you. I am a part of All That Is. You are a part of All That Is. We are not separate. Listen to your heart.

He taught us all about the greater things, important things, the love we have for each other. That we are children of the Father, that we were given the responsibility to help each other whenever possible. That we were never alone.

He would always be there for us.

He could have changed what he said. He could have changed what he did, but he had to be who he was. He had to remain true to the light and to God, and to that which he is. And by doing so, he gives hope to others, and shows others how to hold onto their faith.

There is no death, there is only perception. He is drawing a circle, teaches us about the circle of life. We all have circles to complete, and his circle is almost complete.

(Jesus said) I never died. This is what I was showing, there is no death.

(Spoke of the Truth) that it is very deep within us.

A lot of what he was teaching was what religion was not. It was God's message. He was trying to correct the damage done in the outer community, letting people to know God was in each of our hearts, and that if we went inward through prayer and if we did not fill us up us with ourselves there would be room for God. And money complicates things and not unless it's given back.

And how do we treat others and many of what we call enemies.

He taught of understanding God.

There needed to be a new way, a new way of thinking about things, a new way of relating to the Father, a new way of treating people.

He would say, "It's that simple, give appreciation and gratitude and the gifts you have and more will be brought to you."

He said to give to the poor, take care of your brother.

That we are all One. Loving your neighbor and sharing.

He spoke of love. When he spoke of loving everybody and God's love and loving the lowliest of the lowest and loving the ugliest, but not condoning their behavior and yet still being able to love.

He said that everyone has the light and should be treated just like that.

Jesus said we all have the same amount of God in each of us and to lead our lives with that.

He tells them that they are special, that they do not sin. He says they are misled.

To be kind to one another and help each other.

Message of love, non-judgment and acceptance.

He spoke of forgiveness, love, Oneness and healing.

There are many messages and all important, Forgiveness.

By watching him, I learned a lot by his example.
He tells stories ... not just to us. But look at those stories closely, there are so

many levels of understanding. So if you are in one place in your journey, you get what you need. Someone else is in a different place. They have evolved in a deeper understanding and they can hear the same story and still come away with something they need.

[Did He speak in parables or stories?] Stories. He told us about a sheep that was lost and how if he is a good shepherd, he will leave the other sheep even if there are 99. Isn't that a funny number 99 to find the lost sheep? But he said he really wasn't talking about sheep, it was about us!

He spoke of rooms in Heaven. There must be a lot of room up there! He said they're mansions ... big rooms.

It was such a longing and so deep inside me to hear these words. He said my Father has many mansions.

Jesus' Teachings of Love

He taught loving one another.

He talks with everyone. He loves all people.

He loves all people.

Jesus loved you unconditionally.

Love is the answer. Always love everyone.

To love and to always put love first ... to be loved ... to show love and to see love in everyone.

Love is the Answer! We don't love each other like we should. We need to love each other!

To love yourself and to love one another.

Love your brother as yourself.

To never forget to love and to be kind and to see God in everyone she met.

Always love and to do everything out of love. And where ever there is darkness, send the light because no matter how dark things are, there is always light in the darkness, even if it's just a flicker.

He said they do it because they experience lack of love, or at least they think they experience lack of love, but they are always given love by God. They don't remember or recognize it. And he says that the only way to show them the light, is for us to send more love.

Always love and do everything out of love. Through unconditional love they are able to access everything. Love is unconditional.

Best prayer to invite love and ask others to invite love. Inviting them to tap into the love that already is there. Inviting them to tap into the river of love

His main message is love. The greatest gift is love. Love can heal. Love can harmonize. Love can break down all barriers.

His message of love, non-judgment and acceptance. That we all make mistakes, but what is important is what we learn from them.

His message was love and to always put love first ... to be loved ... to show Love, and to see love in everyone.

Have mercy, grace, above all love. There is nothing above love. There is nothing that love cannot cure, or heal, or brokenness. Love will never fail you. It's the light within you!

He says to not treat him as a God, "What I can do you can also do!" Love is the ultimate. We are all one, love all ... forgive all".

Greatest message is love yourself and others.

He said to love everyone and to teach everyone about God's love.

Well God's most important message. Love one another as I have loved you.

Lead with love. Always put love in front of you. When you look at people, look with love. When you speak with people, speak with love. Whenever you feel separation or isolation, and you meet or see something [your] first reaction is to tear apart, you must end that. You must look first look at love and find the similarities. This is your focus. So much greatness will be achieved with each step we walk towards love. We give Love ... we receive love.

He spoke of love. When he spoke of loving everybody and God's Love and loving the lowliest of the lowest and loving the ugliest, but not condoning their behavior and yet still being able to love.

But he spoke of love. And that was new, and that they could not understand. Yeah, there should be no hatred ... no hatred.

"The Kingdom is Within"

The truth is within ourselves. We don't need to find it from outside ourselves. We don't need to go to anyone else. We have the power within.

The Kingdom of Heaven is within!

Don't forget the Kingdom of God is within.

The Kingdom is within. Kingdom is not a place. It's here!

He told me about the power I have in me.

The Kingdom is within. The truth will set you free!

He said the Kingdom is within!

I have the power within.

He teaches them the Kingdom is within. It is not a place, but we have all the answers within us. Learn to pray.

We have the power within. I had the power. I didn't have to wait for him to show me.

Right and wrong and truth is all within ourselves, we don't need to find it from outside ourselves. We don't have to go to someone else. We have the power ourselves.

He said God is within all of us. Teaches them the Kingdom is within. It is not a place, but we have all the answers within us. Learn to pray.

That the Kingdom of Heaven is everywhere, and no matter where you are, it is.

Yes, it is true the Kingdom is within. Heaven is within. All realms are within.

He talks about God and universe … and that the Kingdom of Heaven is within. Don't forget the Kingdom of God is within.

He says, that the Kingdom of Heaven is everywhere. And no matter where you are … it is!

Teachings of God

He's talking about God. That's the light and that's the way to get to God through love.

It's all about God and connection to the Spirit within us and to follow the truth.

God was the source of all good.

Misunderstanding about God above rather than God within. God is in everyone.

Connection with God is within us and that's where it comes from.

We are one with God and through the route to God is from within, through quiet and counsel.

We all come from God.

He was the Master. But he would say we are all with God.

He said God is within all of us.

God is all love.

The misunderstanding of the God above, rather than the God within. God is all love ... everything!

God is all loving. Man judges ... God doesn't.

Father loves us unconditionally.

God is a presence and has pieces of Him in all of us. God is a brilliant presence, bright light that makes you feel warm.

That is where everything comes from that those energies come in each of our lives with lessons. Parables, I believe he called them.

He said "He *(God)* is Divine. He is the giver of Life."

He always says that you are the Divine Love of the Father and that there is only one Father. He says that there is only One.

He says your Father loves you and blesses you, and all are a part of the Father.

The Father, He is Father to us all.

He is a wise counsel, unconditional Love, guidance. We are all sons of the Father generosity.

We are all sons of the Father.

The God Source ... God Intelligence ... God Light is in everyone when they choose to listen to it. Those that listen to it and hear its Voice can be the hands of God ... the Voice of God. God is omnipresent, everywhere, everywhere with everyone and not an isolated entity.

"We are All One" Teachings

We are all One.

We're all One. There is no division, no separation ... all One.

You are a part of All That Is ... we are not separate.

Taught there is no separation.

We are all one family.

We are all Sons of God, Child of God as it is misinterpreted. God is a presence ...
   pieces of Him in all of us.

We're all the same. Everyone is the same. We're all from the same Source.

And when they see themselves as One, the person would see their Oneness with
   the Father.

(Jesus says) That we are all One.

Everything is One.

(Jesus taught) That we are all One.

We are One with God and through the route to God is from within.

The Oneness, beyond the Father is beyond this world of illusion. It's beyond this
   appearance of the separation.

We are One with God. We are One with him. So, if he can do it so can we.

Best thing anyone can do is remember Oneness! Take the focus off the virus.

Take the focus of what is not wanted entirely and focus on the Unity and the Oneness with the Creator, and with the joy and harmony of that and that will change. Change everything around it. It's like a ripple in a pond.

He spoke of forgiveness, love, Oneness and healing.

I am like you. I am part of you. I am a part of All That Is. You are a part of All That Is. We are not separate.

Jesus' Purpose

He knew he was serving mankind for many different reasons.

He was sent to us for a purpose.

Why he came, it's just the path ... it's his path. He allowed God to work through Jesus, and Jesus multiplied God's power to others, and that multiplied.

Of course, this was his path. We all knew it, he knew it.

Because the message had to be carried forward in the world. It was all about his message.

It was all about his message. He came to carry the message.

He was sent here as a messenger to teach us to believe in eternal life and to love one another. We don't need to fight. We need to love!

You see the entire thing was a lesson to show people that you are beyond your physical body. That was the greatest lesson of the entire crucifixion and later the resurrection. This was his mission to show people consciousness and that you're beyond your body.

He came in human form to show there is no death. But the form dissolved. It was a collection of matter, and then it dissolved into spirit form.

He could have changed what he said. He could have changed what he did but he had to be who he was. He had to remain true to the Light and to God and to that which he is. And by doing so he gives hope to others and shows others how to hold onto their faith. He shows us. But had he done anything differently, he would not have helped the millions and billions of people that he has the potential to help.

He came to people, as they needed a reminder of love.

To bring more light to the Earth. To bring more light, so that others could see the light within themselves.

(Jesus said) I came, with the explicit purpose of bringing more light to a higher vibration than had been on the Earth before to help illuminate, to help wisdom and enlightening awareness for the evolution of the planet.

To help the evolution of man. He knew that deep down to help the evolution of man. He knew that deep down.

He needed to do this mission to get humanity on a different tract. A tract that was God oriented ... not all this my ego ... selfish ... power trip.

Because the world was dark and people needed a reminder.

(Jesus said) I'm here for those who want to listen.

He was here to teach people lessons that God wanted them to know.

To teach. He wanted to show love.

All he wanted to do is to show them love and get rid of the fight, get rid of the anger.

The information is the understanding of how to raise the minds of common man as to as well to raise our own vibration, as you call it vibration, so it can be better understood, and then to be aware of how it's landing to be able to read that.

His purpose in his life was here for us to come to this place now. To embrace healing love energies in the ways we now do. As people step into these energies more and find peace in their hearts, not following religion.

He knew he was to come to create the story and that's what he did.

To take care of everyone. To heal people

To open the hearts of woman and man that is the heart. He was there for the heart.

The Healings

He healed the blind. He healed the blind, lame and leprosy. He healed a blind man, and the leapers.

He made the blind man see. A blind man comes and he is healed. More come to be healed. One man with legs that couldn't walk and Yeshua healed him. Yeshua put his hand on his head and said "You are healed."

The blind man was there once. We were on the road talking and he puts his hand on top of the boy's head, just in passing. And the man says, "I can see, I can see."

He healed children that couldn't see. He touched them. I couldn't hear him. It was like the transference of light. He healed many people.

Yes, she saw him heal the lepers.

I think he was a leaper who had like sores oozing. It was even painful to look at him. His sores were crusty like yellow seeping, bleeding. So I felt so sad for him. He smelled, but Jesus didn't care. Jesus hugged him. Jesus smiled at him and placed his hands on his face. He just said greatest of these is love and it was as if everything came off the man. Like he was clean. He went from unclean to clean. There were no sores and he washed away his sins, although he said there was no sinner. That is not of God's love. God can heal you. He loves you and then it was gone. It was like magic! He fell to his knees and he was clutching Jesus's feet, he was crying so much and thanking him so much. He was so grateful, it doesn't even explain it. Not even the physical pain, it was the pain inside. He healed him of that burden. Jesus hugged him.

(The lepers) We can't save them all there are too many of them. It's like they drain us. The ones that are not as far gone, we can help. He talked about "standing up boy" to the boy that can't walk, "Stand up, you are healed. Walk on," and he walks.

All I can see, recall a person kneeling in front of him. His hands are on his shoulders and he must be doing some type of healing. I'm getting cancer. After that, he puts his hands on them. They are crying and he lifts the face toward him and smiles at them. They are okay now.

A young boy who couldn't walk. His mother brought him into the street as he had something wrong with his legs. He held his hands up high first. And asked God to give him the power to heal this boy. He knelt down and touched his legs and prayed to God and the little boy was able to get up and walk.

A woman brought her child. He was ravaged with fever. He had sores. He looked to be dying. Jesus touched her on the head and whispered some things to her and she wept, she felt unworthy. I laid his hand on the boy. It was a miracle! It was a miracle! It was not like he jumped up and down and all was fine, but suddenly you could tell that a transformation had occurred and you could tell a burden had been lifted from this child. And I wonder if it was not only Jesus' love and belief, but also that of the mother.

He ignited the healing within the child himself. He connected people to their inner abilities, that's all he did but they didn't know it. They thought it was him and that what he taught.

Laying on of hands for healing.

Healing, it was a sharing.

He has his hand someone's head and he is offering him healing. I think the healing is for their thoughts. He put his hands on people to heal. I want to say they are jumbled. After he puts his hands on them. They are crying, and he lifts the face toward him and smiles at them. They're okay now. I'm getting the impression, "This man is healed."

There was a man there, he couldn't walk. Jesus put his hands on him and he walked.

He healed many people. He touched them.

Jesus healed all the time just by him being Jesus. Yes, he definitely healed.

He would put his hands on people and, yes, they would follow him. And it seemed they learned how to heal by seeing him. Intention to do well and help others.

He says we all have the power.

We all have that ability, but his belief and his understanding and his connectedness to the divine is so great that it heals physically. And that it heals not just physically but emotionally.

That we all heal each other.

It's complicated in that there needs to be belief.

He told us we could do the same thing *(when healing a boy)*.

If you believe, you have the power to change the environment.

He states that all are not ready to be healed. People are able to heal because they had the belief.

Some are not ready. You must prepare. You cannot ask for something or demand something and not be confident in your request. You must prepare. You must SHOW your belief in your faith! Can you imagine meeting Jesus and not having the faith and then asking him to heal you?

Because they weren't ready, it wasn't their time. They weren't ready to receive. *(Healing)*

Seems it always comes back to the heart, what's in the heart. I have the feeling that everyone can be healed, but it's in the heart.

The heart must be purified *(To heal)*.

He healed with his hands. His healing energy was more powerful through his hands. He was able to channel light energy through his hands.

He said we have energy in us and our energy comes from God. We can use it in good ways to help people. That we need to concentrate and pray in order to strengthen the power to heal.

(Healing is) Connection with God is within us and that's where it comes from.

(Healing) It comes from God. It's from God, not about me. It's love.

Jesus would heal the mind, it was mind energy. That is what people made decisions about themselves and then Jesus would clarify and release. And that was through their electrical body.

He knows everything. He knows the ailment and the cause of your ailment. So when you go to him, you have changed your belief and faith, so that your love of God is expanding and growing. He knows that, then you are healed!

I saw some healings. It was the manifestation of the sins the person felt they committed in a raw unfiltered form.

He raised someone from a great illness, but they weren't dead. There was one that looked dead.

He touched people with his hands and he asked God, "May their affliction be healed and their pain be eased and erased." It's about love.

I saw some healings. I saw it being healed. It was a bone coming through the flesh, it was very bad. And then it was perfect after the bone was not going through the flesh. There was no blood. The bone was perfect and it scared people.

The Healers

Probably twenty of us followers *(Healers)*.

Absolutely! They were taught to heal, as he healed. He taught them to use their hands to send their energies to Divine Source to open their hearts to help them with all their physical ailments as well as their fears.

People helped the lepers.

There were a group of healers.

Actually there was a group. We would lay hands on people. Sometimes is was physical affliction, sometimes it was mental. Sometimes it was just pain, grief or mourning or hurt or loss.

Others became healers.

I was a healer in that life and traveled with Jesus.

(Mary Magdalene) She also was an incredible healer. He didn't understand healing as she did. She could heal the bones, that wasn't what Jesus did. Jesus would heal the mind. She would heal the bones and the heart, so they worked together beautifully.

Mary *(Magdalene)* knew about healing.

(Mary Magdalene) I was a healer. I healed. Healing took its own form, but I used crystals and sometimes I used my body as a healing vehicle ... light touch and sound.

(Did Mary and Mary Magdalene have the gifts of healing as well?) Yes.

He didn't have to teach everybody to heal with their hands. People could heal with just talking. He showed them different ways. He would help them, everything would be amplified.

He teaches us about healing. He's showing us his hands, both hands. This is how he heals. It is about intention. He's indicating that by raising his hands. He's raising the vibration, connecting with the intention of healing. He states all are not ready to be healed [and that] makes him sad sometimes, but he understands.

He would put his hands on people and yes they would follow him...And it seemed they learned how to heal by seeing him. Intention to do well and help others

He teaches us about healing. He's raising the vibration, connecting with intention of healing. You have to have the intention, pure in thought. You have to have the knowing.

And it seemed they learned how to heal by seeing him.

He said we have energy in us and our energy comes from God.

We can use it in good ways to help people. That we need to concentrate and pray in order to strengthen the power to heal.

They were taught to heal as he healed. He taught them to use their hands to send their energies to Divine Source to open their hearts to help them with all their physical ailments as well as their fears.

The Light around Him

Light around Jesus.

He radiates light.

He was a light being. He became filled with the light.

He had a bright light around him, I don't know if everyone can see it.

He radiates light. I don't know if everyone can see. Bright, white golden sparkles.

He was emanating such light!

He is the embodiment of light and love, and all that is pure.

He saw the light around me and I saw the light around him. *(What was the color of the light?)* Whitish gold. It was the Light of God.

(Is there a Light around him?) You would feel it. You could feel it. It's a resonance.

Jesus as a Child with his Friends

We played. We jumped in puddles, trees, and ran, and laughed and rode donkeys, played with chickens, and got into trouble. Always laughing. We're laughing.

Someone said a joke and it's funny and just making fun of each other. They were friends.

Oh, yes! And Jesus plays. They play together. *(Indicates Jesus is 9 years old now.)* My daughter Sarah is 6 and they play [and] they get dirty together and play. They get very dirty ... very dirty. Just [having] fun with sticks and balls. We call them and they're late. Where are they?

I see a stick. I can't see well. My friends ... we play, talk. We just tell stories. We're rough. Mostly my friends. They don't mean any harm. They just say, I can't follow them as fast.

"There is No Sin"

There is no evil, no sin. Again, it is the state of discomfort from being out of alignment, which is the natural state of being. It is going against the natural flow of life that is all. It takes on all manner of form, all the gruesome form it takes on, but remember it is an idea that is not permanent in the mind of the Creator.

There is no sin. There is no evil. Sin is man made in that the church needed something it could control people with.

Sin, as it was spoken of by others and by those in the church. Those of other understandings. They're more concrete in their understandings and so as they look at sin and they look at as a flaw. The minute you call it as sin you are judging! There are only burdened souls who have for some reason come into a situation where they are not as aware of the light and the love and the Peace.

They get caught up. Those filled with rage ... those filled with anger are the most closed to their divine aspect. There is no sin!

*(When asked what is sin.)*Transgression about your fellow brother ... against God ... not being pure of heart ... not loving your fellow man as you love yourself, stealing, coveting, adultery. "Not a big deal"... he (Jesus) said.

And that they do not sin. He says they are misled.

Traveling to Other Lands and References to Joseph of Arimathea

(Joseph) He took him to many places, China, France, Greece and other areas.

There was a man. He was Joseph, a holy man that was of our community. They were on Joseph's boats. They were under Joseph's protection.

(Joseph of Arimathea) I am the protection! I am the Uncle.

(Did he travel by sea with anyone?) Yes, his Uncle...Joseph.

He went with his Uncle Joe. His Uncle Joe had lots of money, more than Jesus's family. *(Traveled on his boat)*

(Joseph says) He travels with me. I take him to different parts. Everywhere ... China area, Greece, France, Spain, England and snowy areas where it is cold.

Yes, neighboring countries ... in Egypt, India.

He traveled extensively.

He traveled much of the world apparently. He traveled as far away as India to learn from their Masters.

He studied in India.

He studies other religions.

He had teachers who taught Buddhism. And in Tibet, Egypt.

He learned through Buddhism, I think in Tibet, Egypt and the Mediterranean.

He had to learn from the Masters at the Himalayas.

Yes, [he went to] Turkey, Tunisia, Egypt, Iraq, Europe

He was in Egypt.

Connection with the Essenes

(Essences taught) Some very powerful teachings.

Was she *(Mary)* with the Essenes? Yes.

Mary was not an Essene. Joseph was an Essene.

(Was Jesus an Essene?) He has been with us. He learns from us. We did not have women in our group.

We're a reverend group and a peaceful group, if you live from your heart. You do call us Essenists *(Essenes)* today. We have old wisdom. We all have deep wisdom and understanding. We love to sit and share and talk and figure things out, the mysteries.

We need to be in nature and be in peace. We are a peaceful people.

It was the Essene, I feel I shouldn't say. We knew it was important to be quiet, to live quietly, to walk quietly and be peaceful. We are very self-sufficient and very communal. Nobody was poor, we shared everything with everyone. No one was left alone when they got older. We took care of everyone.

We do not speak of its name. You are familiar with it? They were called the Essenes.

The Essenes were master record keepers. They chronicled history meticulously. I learned from them and shared with the Essenes. It wasn't all learning, it was also sharing what I knew as well.

Jesus' Gift of Speaking with People

But he found a different way to talk to people about it. Where there has been so many masters on the planet, more than anyone has ever realized, but not every master knows how to share the information with the public. Some masters could have been more masterful by being able to connect with another heart, and it would be more amplified in that moment and so Jesus understood that.

He truly was the most gifted teacher on Earth so far. That is because he understood how to put God's message to the man, to all men at all levels, through the vibration of his voice they would hear God. It was something with the vibration. He didn't teach it. He was it!

Peace came over everyone like a spell. It made everyone love each other.

Jesus' Eyes

His eyes are so blue, like the ocean.

His eyes are blue. Really blue, like the ocean.

He had piercing blue eyes. He seemed to look into your soul.

He had just radiant blue eyes, like full of diamonds.

When you make eye contact, it's like he sees and knows everything.

Light green, blue sparkly and they changed colors of his eyes are blue green.

He had purplish blue eyes and his eyes dance.

(When you look into his eyes.) They were captivating, full of life, light and joy.

His eyes were mesmerizing. They were different than anything I've ever seen.

They pierced you. Looking with love and kindness and that's what emanated
through them.

His eyes, however were mesmerizing.

They were always captivating! Full of energy, life and light and joy.

(When you looked into his eyes.) Light, I felt warm, unconditional loved, happy.

(When looking at his eyes). I felt love.

When you see Jesus and look into his eyes, the love is like none other to compare
to. You compare everyone else's love by Jesus eyes!

Jesus Was a Man

Jesus was a person. He had a life.

(So he was just a man?) Indeed. He was just another person.

He did not see himself as the Messiah. He saw himself as just another human being, but one that was enlightened, to know the love of God and what that brought into your lives.

Jesus told them and it's the truth that he was not alone of God. We are all of God. He never made himself different, only us, we did.

He's just normal. He doesn't feel he's special. He was sent here to do a duty, given thing. He doesn't see himself that way.

[*Jesus said*] I am like you.

He said he was a man. He had just learned more.

He felt human. Sometimes humans, having human needs of food. I think he judged himself for being human sometimes. He forgot he was so connected to God that indeed he was a human when he was here. He was a spiritual being in a human life.

He is uncomfortable with people calling him God. Oh, they give him a lot of titles that are very ... well those that admire him. They give him many titles, The Savior, The Christ, The King. He never accepts that, but he gently and humbly says okay and gives it to God what is God that belongs to God.

No. He was never greater than anyone. It never was about him. It was about God.

(Jesus said) The *Bible* was not interested in showing I was a man just like you, that had remembered my Oneness with God ... my relationship with God.

His Name is Yeshua

I prefer Yeshua.

Yeshua.

His mother called him Yeshua.

He would be called Yeshua. Because to him that was his name! That is what his mother called him.

(What was he called?) Yeshua.

Yeshua, that's it!

(What was he called?) Yeshua!

The Followers

I wanted to follow him. I must spread the word.

I wanted to follow him. My time with him was short, but I wanted to follow him and be in his presence all of the time because it felt so good.

I needed to go with him.

I'm getting in a cave like place, we are meeting together. It's how we can spread truth.

I think that I'm going to follow with him as they come by.

Those who loved him were followers.

Oh yes! Many people chose to be followers.

Mary Magdalene

He was close to Mary. He acted like they were married. They were always together.

[*Were they married?*] They acted like that. She did always seem to be with Jesus. And he trusted her.

Don't know, but they were very close.

They were married.

Yes, he was with Mary Magdalene.

(Was Jesus married?) Yes, Mary Magdalene.

They were real close. Not married as a union, but they were close.

I'm feeling there was a love between Mary Magdalene and him.

You know, marriage in today's world is different from marriage back then. They were together and so, actually he needed her for part of ... there is a part of the heart ... an energy transfer.

They were very close and Jesus loved her very much. He was married to her in love, but not in formality.

His wife, Mary Magdalene.

Jesus had a relationship with Mary. They were married because they came to me. They brought their Spirits to me.

(Jesus said) I was committed to her. What makes a marriage, it was a commitment.

(Was he married to Mary?) Yes.

Speaking in Gatherings

He is speaking to a large group on the seashore. There are so many of them it's hard to find a spot. He just holds his hands up to the crowd.

I feel joy and love. And people feel love and joy. And the babies are still. And sometimes he is quiet. And he just holds his hands over the crowd and doesn't say anything.

We gather around him and he blesses us by holding his hands up in the air. We feel his energy.

People were all just gathering because they wanted to hear what he said, but there were soldiers there and they didn't like it and people were kind of nervous and jumpy until Jesus started to speak.

He speaks on top of the hills. They are quiet, they listen.

People just wanted to listen and it was quiet.

Peace fell upon everyone. Peace came over everyone like a spell. It made everyone love each other.

Then we came to a gathering and people started gathering and people started gathering. People just wanted to listen and it was quiet.

They are noisy. Then start to be quiet, and the babies are still.

They were quiet.

There is a gathering, he is traveling through.

He is holding out his hands and we feel his love, everyone feels his love. There are many people. He says take this love and express it. Wherever he went he would speak to them. So there were big crowds and small. There were many.

I follow them down a sloping. We are right down there, gathering to listen to what he is saying

Many, many others sitting all around gathering. People are coming to hear Yeshua talk.

And crowds of people down here at the water and the place is filled with love and joy.

Fear and Jealousy of Jesus with those in Power

The feared the power he had. People were listening.

They were jealous of Jesus.

They were jealous. Didn't like the following he had that undermined his authority. His teachings opposed too many of their teachings.

They were jealous of him. He was just different. He was like a rock star and there was a lot of jealousy.

They said they didn't believe but I think they were just jealous…People say they don't believe things when they are jealous.

It was the Elders, the Romans had interest in it also. Jealous, each person has their own agenda.

They were jealous. People have their own agenda when he spoke. Romans didn't like what we were doing.

He's angered people in power. They fear him, because people are listening to him.

Priests are here. They were here to watch him. They don't like him.

Didn't agree with interpretation and when I questioned they got angry. It was all about money, power, position and wealth.

People in power didn't like him talking about equality. They felt threatened when people got stronger.

He threatens the church. He speaks the truth and they are political. They want power and they want money for their church. He was turning people away from the established church and the government because government want the power, the money. They want the statutes. They want to build their beautiful things.

That time period was all about control of information and history. It was driven by those afraid of the following that he was getting. Many working class were following him and any kind of coordination for the workers worked against the political direction. Oppression wouldn't work well.

(Jesus said) Some didn't listen. They thought I was preaching against their gospel, their faith, and their beliefs.

(Jesus said) Thought I was leading them on wrong path, that I was leading them to mutiny.

The rulers of the town, they don't like people to think different. It's against the grain.

Conclusion

"As a society...as each of us knows the truth and knows who we are, it all comes together like pieces of a puzzle, like droplets of rain coming back to form the pond."
NAOMI

"He truly was the most gifted teacher on Earth so far. That is because he understood how to put God's message to the man, to all men at all levels through the vibration of his voice they would hear God. It was something with the vibration. He didn't teach it. He was it!"
GRACE

There is an acknowledgement in John 21:25 that not everything has been included in the *Bible*, "But there are also many other things he did; were every one of them to be written, I suppose that the world itself could not contain the books that would be written." There is so much more to the life and work of Jesus that is not included in the *Bible* as we know it today. This is quite evident in the accumulation of the stories presented in this book, of those who had past lives with Yeshua/Jesus. One can come to the realization that there is much more to the story than what is presented in the *Bible*. Like many clients, Grace spoke of the *Bible* as not always being correct. She explained, "Man's way is to be exclusionary. So all of the exclusionary parts of any of God's story, is human! And in Ellie's channeled session, Jesus speaks of things not included in the *Bible* with the following, "The emphasis on those gifts being available to others is there, but what seems to be missing are the examples of those who walked as I walked ... who were able to do feats as I was able to do feats. They were not expressed there and this is a phenomenon that occurred. The *Bible* makes it appear as though I was the only one able to express Spirit through the physical and give what you would call illusion or miracle ... its day in the sun. But there were others that were able to do so. Not just my disciples, that were there and whose books are written about in the *Bible*. There were other disciples, my students, those who followed me, who did miracles even beyond what I did in that time. They are not written about."

This is a unique offering of looking at the lifetime of Jesus richly presented by many of the people previously not mentioned in the *Bible*. And of those individuals that were mentioned in the *Bible*, there are additional interesting insights into the life and times of Jesus and those around him. This is a more personal depiction of those who came in contact with Jesus and his teachings. When you read all of the client's experiences with Jesus/Yeshua, there are so many similarities that can't be denied.

This book embodies Jesus speaking his truth, even though he was faced with many challenges and adversities. He recognized everyone's light even when there was darkness. In Ruth's channeled session, Jesus says, "When a choice is made to back away from light, in essence one is choosing darkness. In essence there is no darkness to choose. It's just a stepping away from light. There is a new energy. All energy has a frequency and these frequencies are attracted to similar frequencies." He called on us to bring that light to others, so they may shine their light even brighter. Jesus explains his reason for coming, "I come to bring light so that all may see their way, the Way of the Truth, the Way of the Light." Other clients expressed this teaching using the similar words. In *John 12:36*, Jesus says, "While you have the light, believe in the light, so that you may become Sons of Light."

The *Bible* portrayed "the Way" as being the only way to salvation is through Jesus. However, this book speaks of Yeshua's life as a demonstration of the Way to remembering the truth. In Crystal's session she said, "He showed them the Way when he said it is within self." The Way was explained in Ruth channeling Jesus, "The Way of experiencing back into truth, by remembering."

There was also a consensus among clients that Jesus felt there is no sin. In Naomi's session she said, "The minute you call it as sin you are judging! There is no sin! There are only burdened souls who have for some reason come into a situation where they are not as aware of the light and the love and the peace. They get caught up. They try so hard to do the right thing, even the murderers. Those filled with rage, those filled with anger are the most closed to their Divine aspect." When asked the question about sin, Ruth says, "The choice … the free will you've been given allows you to make the decision to step into love or turn your back on it."

Jesus said the Kingdom is not in a place, but it is within. In Ellie's channeled session, Jesus said, "God is within. God is within the Higher Self realizing the Source is within and not outside of you is a great step toward empowerment." And in Crystal's session, Jesus explained, "Truth is all within ourselves. We don't need to find it from outside ourselves. We don't have to go to someone else. We have the power ourselves."

In the sessions, Jesus was consistently speaking about Oneness. It is ultimately the understanding that each one of us is a part of the Whole, a part of the Source; all are One. In Ruth's channeled session, Jesus explains, "There is no separation. There are no separate experiences. You can step into my experience any time you want to." Whenever there is division, ego is trying to explain it with sense of judgment rather than looking at the illusion of separateness. And in Ellie's session Jesus said, "The best thing anyone can do is remember Oneness!" ..."Remember your Oneness with the Father. The origin from which you came, for all who came it is essential for the healing process. Knowing the Oneness, knowing that there is no separation is essential to a perfect state of healing, because in that state of Oneness, anxiety, fear, and worry are dropped and gladness takes hold. Joy and peace take over. The harmony is restored and everything can mend."

Many clients witnessed and spoke of Jesus' healings. They also indicated that there were other healers, including his mother Mary and Mary Magdalene. In Grace's session she said, "Mary also had her miracles, but they are not spoken of," and "She (Mary) was an incredible healer." And in Ellie's session, Jesus confirms this by saying, "There were other disciples, my students, those who followed me, who did miracles even beyond what I did in that time. They are not written about." There was also mention of Jesus' form of healing the mind, body, spirit of a person rather than just the physical manifestation. In Naomi's session she speaks of this, "His belief and his understanding and his connectedness to the divine is so great that it heals physically and that it heals not just physically but emotionally."

Clients spoke of Jesus learning from various cultures and spiritual beliefs. In both channeled sessions Jesus confirmed that he had learned from many different cultures. It seems rather suspicious that the *Bible* does not include the many years between the age of twelve and thirty years old. There is only one mention of Jesus in *Luke 2:36-52*, of his time in Jerusalem where he was learning and asking questions of the teachers as a young twelve year old boy. There are many sources stating that he indeed was learning and teaching in other places, such as India and Tibet. Clients also spoke of Jesus traveling with his Uncle Joseph to many different parts of the world. In Emma's session as Joseph she says, "He travels with me. I take him to different parts." When asked if Jesus studied all religions, Emma responded, "Yes, of course! It is as it should be."

Clients spoke of Jesus feeling that he was misrepresented as being greater than others. He stated many times in my client's sessions, that he was just a man. In Emma's session she said, "Jesus told them, and it's the truth, that he was not alone of God. We are all of God. He never made himself different, only us. We did." In Tiffany's session she said, "It never was about him. It was about God." And in Ruth's channeled session, Yeshua said, "I tried to dissuade others from putting me above them. We were all each other's beloved." He was a demonstration of how we should live our lives.

As many clients have stated, it was not Jesus' intention to create a religion, but a movement of teaching unconditional love, Oneness and our connection to God. Jesus did not create Christianity; man created the dogma and the rules associated with Christianity. He was not a Christian, but spoke of universal truths and unconditional love of all people. He did not distinguish between persons based on class, religion, ethnicity or even spiritual beliefs. He looked into the very essence and the soul of every person he encountered on his journey with unconditional love and compassion, for the soul's true essence has no religion, race or nationality.

Many people ask how they can become a more spiritual person. Spiritual awareness is more about looking within, and in looking within, it is how we choose to live our most meaningful life. Many times we come to doubt or do not listen to that inner knowing, our inner truth. The truth will always resonate as beautiful music to ones ears. It will be like a song you have remembered from long ago. The truth does not have a complicated melody, but flows easily, touching the soul. This is the true "Soul Music!" I believe the truth will come to those who are ready to hear and remember.

Everyone has the right to think differently. Everyone has the right to question the beliefs of others that no longer resonates with them. Wasn't Jesus labeled as being different, and the messages he spoke weren't they words people hadn't heard before? What if his fear of being different prevented him from completing his work? How would that have changed the world? The ancient knowledge is calling out to us, for that wisdom to once again return. It was never lost, and once found, then you can truly be free.

This time in history is very much like the time of Jesus. He spoke of Heaven on Earth and he was trying to show us that we individually, and collectively, can literally change the world from a place of fear to a place of love. It is a call for all to awaken, it is a call to let go of separateness, it is a call to let go of feeling that others are less than. It is a call to be the awakened souls that you were destined to be. It is a call to say yes to forgiveness, joy, compassion, understanding and unconditional love. Take his words of love and use them daily, not with words, but in actions with your fellow man. Take another in your heart and show them compassion and unconditional love.

Perhaps one of the most significant messages in the book was spoken in Ellie's channeled session with Jesus' years before the coronavirus. Jesus gave this prophetic statement when asked about the chaos in the world that is eerily relevant at this moment in time, "It is one thought, an erroneous thought that gets picked up like a virus by the thoughts of others, which is really One. It is held onto for a while until it is let go. The best thing anyone can do is remember Oneness! Take the focus off the virus. Take the focus of what is not wanted entirely, and focus on the unity and the Oneness with the Creator, and with the joy and harmony of that and that will change, change everything around it. It's like a ripple in a pond."

In Harmony's session she sums up Jesus' message by saying, "His message was love and to always put love first. To be loved, to show love and to see love in everyone." As Emma explained in her session, "His love was so great, and his love of Yahweh, and his love for all of us. How could he change his destiny? His love would not allow him." He possessed the Christ Spirit, as well all can attain it."

This book is another way to explore and empower others to begin asking questions about their beliefs and discover their truth. There are many paths to spiritual knowledge, and this has been my personal journey. One must find their truth, and that truth cannot be taught, coerced, or dictated by another's perspective of the truth. As Jesus spoke through Ellie, "The seeker has the answers. It's just finding a way to bring it to itself. It could get the answer directly. It needs not the other form to get the answer. As the seeker begins to remember its Oneness with all Creation, as it begins to remember it's the answers as well as the question, it will no longer need form to support itself." We are all seekers of the truth. In Naomi's session she describes the truth as, "The truth is our awareness, complete unadulterated awareness of the divine that we are. And when you are in the complete understanding that is the goal, you are enlightened and there you will feel peace, wisdom, understanding, appreciation, gratitude and connectivity."

This book also is a demonstration of the true Jesus. As Naomi said, "Jesus is the embodiment ... he is the Way." The Jesus who spoke of love for all, who said the Kingdom is not a place, but is always within us. He was the great Master Teacher who showed us how to live our lives with compassion, forgiveness and love. This awakening is a new way of looking at each other with Oneness. I feel this is just the beginning of the Great Awakening, and this book is hopefully one step assisting in the awakening to the truth, through the words of the One who was truly awakened to the Way, the Truth and the Light!

"We're all One. There is no division, no separation ... all are One. What I can do, you can do. What I have, you have. It lets you hear the Voice of God. Go to that peaceful place that is your central being and peace. You're One with your brother... you truly are. ... Love is the glue. It's what you are!"
YESHUA CHANNELED BY ELLIE

They will all know some day that they all are Sons of God ... a Child of God.
YESHUA CHANNELED BY RUTH

"The keys to a spiritual life are not to be found in institutions, religions, governments, or the media. True and honest answers are alive in the compassionate heart and the enlightened mind of each individual – In You! In the quietness of spirit resides All Light, All love and All that is called God."
HENRY LEO BOLDUC

"Jesus is the man, the activity, the mind, the relationship that he bore to others. Yea, he was mindful of friends. He was sociable, he was loving, he was kind, he was gentle. The pattern is in Jesus."
EDGAR CAYCE READING 533-7

BIBLIOGRAPHY

A Course in Miracles, Published by the Foundation for Inner Peace, Mill Valley, California, 1992, Lesson 188, #4, p.357, Chapter 6;16:4, p.95, Lesson 140 #8, p.272.

Bolduc, Henry Leo, *The Journey Within, Past Life Regression and Channeling*, Adventures into Time Publishers, Independence, Virginia, 1988, p. 129.

Bolduc, Henry Leo, *The Journey Within*, Adventures in Time Publishers, Independence, Virginia, 1988, p. 291, p.130.

Cannon, Dolores, *Jesus and the Essenes*, Ozark Mountain Publishing, Huntsville, Arkansas, 1992.

Cannon, Dolores, *They Walked with Jesus*, Ozark Mountain Publishing, Huntsville, Arkansas, 1994.

Cerminara, Gina, *Many Mansions*, New American Library Division of Penguin Books, New York, 1978.

Dunn, Christopher, *The Giza Power Plant*, Simon & Schuster Publisher, Bear and Company, August 1, 1998.

Edgar Cayce Readings, Association for Research and Enlightenment, Virginia Beach, Virginia.

Head, Joseph and S.L. Cranston, *Reincarnation: The Phoenix Fire Mystery*, Julian Press, New York, 1977, p.153, p. 145

Holy Bible, Revises Standard Version, Thomas Nelson & Sons, 1946, 1952.

Josephus, Flavius, Testimonium *Flavianum, The Antiquities of the Jews*, translated by William Whiston, Book 18, Chapter 3:63

Kardec, Allan, *The Spirits' Book*, Spiritist Educational Society, Thousand Oaks, CA, 2020, Part 2, Chapter VIII, #166, p. 107, Part 2, Chapter VIII, #168, p.107.

Notovitch, Nicolas, *The Unknown Life of Jesus*, Translated by J.H. Connelly and L. Landsberg, Sanger, California, Original Published 1890, Chapters VI paragraph 5, 13, X, paragraph 21.

Prophet, Elizabeth Clare, *Reincarnation; The Missing Link in Christianity*, Summit University Press, 1977, p.57, pp. 276-277.

Prophet, Elizabeth Clare, *The Lost Years of Jesus*, Summit University Press, 1984, p. 60.

Roerich, Nicolas, Altai-The Himalayas - *A Travel Diary, Frederick A Stokes Company, New York, 1929*

Scott, Cyril, *With an Introduction, Afterword and Notes, The Boy who Saw True*, Rider, Random House Publishing, London, 1953, 1988, p. 224.

The Gospel According to Mary Magdalene, Gnostic Society Library, Chapter 4:26, CHAPTER 9:4,

The Gospel of Mary, Karen L. King translation, Chapter 9, 3-4.

The Gospel of Truth, The Nag Hammadi Library, Codex I, translated by Robert M. Grant, p. 24.

The Secret Teachings of Jesus, Four Gnostic Gospels, the Book of Thomas, Translated by Marvin W. Meyer, 1984, Random House and The Gospel of Thomas, Inc., New York, 1984 , Chapter 4, Paragraph 13, p.45, Codex II, Saying 3, p.19.

Tolstoy, Leo, Moscow: Magazine, *The Voice of Universal Love*, 1908, No. 40 p. 634. (Concerning a letter Tolstoy wrote before his death in 1904.)

Tomlinson, Andy, *Insights from the Life between Lives; Exploring the Eternal Soul*, John Hunt Publishing, Deershot Lodge, The Ropley, Park Lane, Ropley, Hants, UK, 2007, pp.69-70

Weiss, Brian, *Many Lives, Many Masters*, Fireside, Simon and Schuster, Inc., New York, 1988.

William Shakespeare, *Romeo and Juliet, As You Like It.*

Winston, David, *Logos and the Mystical Theology of Philo of Alexandria, Cincinnati: Hebrew Union College Press*, 1985, p.42.